Metropolitan Commuter Belt Tourism

T0270899

With the current rise of metropolitan regions as a present location and driver of the development of rural tourism, agritourism, food tourism and nature tourism, there is a need to analyse the major economic, social, political and managerial aspects of these types of tourism that occur within the rural-urban fringe.

This book establishes a current inventory and appropriate future selection of commuter belt tourism products for metropolitan areas. It also explains how public and private resources can be combined to achieve synergistic effects in tourism promotion and provides a structural analysis for the proper management of tourism organisations in metropolitan areas. Additionally, there is insight into how the development of metropolitan areas affects rural tourism and agritourism within broader social, economic and environmental relations. The issue of the growth of metropolitan areas, which is a complex and multifaceted challenge, is elaborated on with diverse examples in Poland and further afield.

This is valuable reading for students, researchers and academics of tourism, as well as rural and urban studies, business management, farm management, and leisure studies.

Michał Jacenty Sznajder is Professor, rural economist, former Dean of the Faculty of Economics and Social Sciences, and Head of the Department of Market and Marketing at Poznań University of Life Sciences, Poland.

New Directions in Tourism Analysis
Series Editor: Dimitri Ioannides
E-TOUR, Mid Sweden University, Sweden

Although tourism is becoming increasingly popular both as a taught subject and an area for empirical investigation, the theoretical underpinnings of many approaches have tended to be eclectic and somewhat underdeveloped. However, recent developments indicate that the field of tourism studies is beginning to develop in a more theoretically informed manner, but this has not yet been matched by current publications.

The aim of this series is to fill this gap with high quality monographs or edited collections that seek to develop tourism analysis at both theoretical and substantive levels using approaches which are broadly derived from allied social science disciplines such as Sociology, Social Anthropology, Human and Social Geography, and Cultural Studies. As tourism studies covers a wide range of activities and sub fields, certain areas such as Hospitality Management and Business, which are already well provided for, would be excluded. The series will therefore fill a gap in the current overall pattern of publication.

Suggested themes to be covered by the series, either singly or in combination, include: consumption; cultural change; development; gender; globalisation; political economy; social theory; and sustainability.

For a full list of titles in this series, please visit www.routledge.com/ New-Directions-in-Tourism-Analysis/book-series/ASHSER1207

Metropolitan Commuter Belt Tourism

Edited by Michał Jacenty Sznajder

Routledge
Taylor & Francis Group

LONDON AND NEW YORK

First published 2017 by Routledge

2 Park Square, Milton Park, Abingdon, Oxon OX14 4RN
605 Third Avenue, New York, NY 10017

Routledge is an imprint of the Taylor & Francis Group, an informa business

First issued in paperback 2022

British Library Cataloguing in Publication Data
A catalogue record for this book is available from the British Library

Library of Congress Cataloging in Publication Data
A catalog record for this book has been requested

ISBN: 978-1-472-46486-6 (hbk)
ISBN: 978-1-03-233963-4 (pbk)
DOI: 10.4324/9781315607221

Typeset in Times New Roman
by Deanta Global Publishing Services, Chennai, India

Contents

Figures

Tables

Contributors

Michał Jacenty Sznajder is the main author and editor of this volume. He is Professor of Economics at the Poznań University of Life Sciences, former Dean of the Faculty of Economics and Social Sciences, Head of the Department of Market and Marketing and a traveller using agritourism facilities all over the world (Poland, Slovenia, Canada, New Zealand, Italy, Germany, Russia). The author of an internationally relevant book *Agritourism, Ekonomia mleczarstwa (The Economics of Dairy Production)* and a travel book *Gwinea w ukrywanej kamerze (Guinea in Hidden Camera)*, he is also the producer of video travel reports and an agritourism video in English: *Green Tourism,* (available at https://www.youtube.com/watch?v=e2BPorZF71g) as well as the organiser of and participant in agritourism seminars and conferences, and coordinator of the research subject *Green tourism in metropolitan areas.*

Agata Balińska is a lecturer at the Department of Tourism and Rural Development, Faculty of Economics, Warsaw University of Life Sciences. She was conferred with a PhD in Economics in 2001 for her doctoral dissertation, *The Determinants of Rural Tourism Development: A Case Study of the Bug River Valley.* She is the author of more than 90 publications in the field of tourism, and a researcher and co-researcher in the area of tourism. Her main area of research interest is rural tourism.

Małgorzata Bogusz is an assistant at the Rural Development and Counselling Unit, Hugo Kołłątaj University of Agriculture in Krakow. She is an expert and lecturer cooperating with the institutions supporting the development of agritourism in Poland and worldwide. She is author or co-author of more than 40 scientific and popular science publications, reports, training materials and brochures concerning the problems of rural tourism, agritourism and the EU Common Agricultural and Structural Policy.

Adriano Ciani is a full Professor of Agricultural Economics and Rural Appraisal at Perugia University. Fluent in six languages, he has written several books and 235 other publications. Director of the International Summer School in Sustainable Management and Promotion of Territory, he has taken part in collaborative activities in more than 50 countries. He was awarded the 'Laurea

Honoris Causa' in Economic Engineering for Agriculture by the University of Agricultural Sciences and Veterinary Medicine Iaşi (Romania).

Damian Dudziak holds an MSc in Economics and completed studies at the Faculty of Economics and Social Sciences in Poznań University of Life Sciences, and postgraduate pedagogic studies at State School of Higher Vocational Education in Leszno. Currently a law student at the Poznań School of Social Sciences, he works as a recoveries and receivables coordinator in the accounts department of an international production and trading company from the road construction industry.

Katarzyna Dzioban holds a PhD in Physical Culture Sciences, and is Assistant Professor at the Department of Recreation, Warsaw University of Physical Education, having graduated from two fields of study: Tourism and Recreation and Physical Education. The Faculty Coordinator of the Erasmus Programme, her scope of interest is the problems of tourism and recreation in protected areas. She is the author of numerous publications on this subject and a participant of numerous national and international scientific conferences.

Klaus Ehrlich holds an MBA in Economics (Diplom-Kaufmann), having studied Economics Business Administration at the Universities of Siegen (Germany) and Seville (Spain) from 1976 to 1983. He co-founded the regional rural tourism associations RAAR and AHRA in Andalusia. He was president of EuroGites – the European Federation of Rural Tourism – from 2002 to 2010. Since then he has been the secretary general. He is a member of working groups and consultative bodies related to tourism and rural development at the European Commission, and undertakes independent work in consultancy and training in private industry and at academic institutions.

Michał Gazdecki holds a PhD and is employed at Poznań University of Life Sciences, Department of Market Analysis and Marketing. His main fields of scientific interest are internal trade, distribution and consumers' behavior. Additionally, he runs research focused on tourism and tourists' activity and preferences.

Józef Kania is Associate Professor at the Department of Rural Development and Extension at the University of Agriculture, Kraków. His research interest is the problem of agricultural consultancy, including analytical and concept studies concerning the role and tasks of consultancy in the implementation of the Common Agricultural Policy instruments, systems, types and trends in the development of agricultural consultancy all over the world; models of links between science, consultancy and agricultural practice; and the development of enterprise (especially agritourism) in rural areas.

Elżbieta Kmita-Dziasek is chief expert of the National Agricultural Advisory Centre, Branch Office in Krakow, an experienced worker in public agricultural counselling and a university lecturer, as well as coordinator of national and international rural development projects. She propagates and supports the cooperation of groups of scientists, counsellors and practitioners involved in rural tourism by organising Polish agritourism symposiums regularly, which she started in 1994. Since 2011 she has been implementing and coordinating the Polish Educational Farm Network.

Joanna Kosmaczewska is Associate Professor and Head of Department of Tourism Management at the University of Economy in Bydgoszcz. She holds a post-doctoral degree in economy (Warsaw University of Life Sciences). She is the Editor-in-Chief and member of the Advisory Board for the *European Journal of Tourism, Hospitality and Recreation* (www.ejthr.com) and member of the GITUR (International Tourism Research Group), Peniche, Portugal. She was the chairperson of the International Conference of Tourism, Hospitality and Recreation 2014 (EJTHR 2014), which took place in Poznań, Poland from 19 to 21 May 2014. Her main research interests in tourism encompass tourism economics, regional development and rural development.

Andrzej Kusztelak is Professor at Poznań University of Life Sciences, physics teacher at Teachers' College, and holds a postdoctoral degree in pedagogy (Adam Mickiewicz University, Poznań, Poland). His career spans teaching and administration in primary schools to Vice-Dean for Education, College of Humanities and Journalism; Professor at Agricultural University/Poznań University of Life Sciences; and Head of Department of Pedagogy and Postgraduate Department of Pedagogical Training. His scholarship includes 11 books, 110 articles and 151 methodological elaborations.

Janusz Majewski is a senior lecturer at the Department of Rural Tourism, Poznań University of Life Sciences. He specialises in building rural tourism products and branding, and is an expert in projects in Poland, Belarus, Ukraine, Moldova and Georgia (UNDP, USAID, EU funds). He has prepared many tourism development strategies and is the author of several dozen scientific papers and a few popular books on rural tourism.

Milena Malinowska is a biologist and is involved in research focused on rural tourism and agritourism at the Department of Market and Marketing, Poznań University of Life Sciences. Currently she is the staff administrator responsible for projects development at Poznań University of Life Sciences.

Sylwia Marek is an economist and completed postgraduate studies in European funds management and in pedagogy at the Poznań University of Economics. She is about to complete her doctoral dissertation on normative modelling at the Poznań University of Life Sciences. She is head of the department of promotion at a local government unit, responsible for the organisation of events, publishing, and contacts with the media and councillors.

Katarzyna Mikrut graduated from Environmental Protection studies at the Catholic University of Lublin, where she worked at the Department of Ecology for two-and-a-half years. Since 2006 she has been employed at Kampinos National Park, where she is responsible for granting access to the park and international cooperation. She has participated in many national and international conferences and seminars on tourism in national parks.

Arkadiusz Niedziółka received a PhD in 2008 for his doctoral dissertation 'Agritourist Services as Factor of Local Development in Lesser Poland Voivodeship'. He is the author or co-author of 102 scientific articles on conditions of the development of agritourism, the role of agritourism services in rural development, forms of management in agritourism and determinants of the development of tourism and recreational services in rural areas.

Piotr Senkus is a Professor, formerly of Poznań University of Life Sciences, Department of Market Analysis and Marketing. His main fields of scientific interest are e-business, structural analyses of organisations and non-profit organisations. Additionally he runs research projects focused on the application of the internet to tourism.

Jan Sikora works in Poznań University of Economics, and his areas of scientific research interest include socioeconomic conditions of tourism and agritourism and development of enterprise in rural areas; management and marketing in tourism; sociology of rural areas; and the Polish community. He is the author or co-author of several dozen books including *Managing a Tourist Enterprise* (2008), *Agritourism: Enterprise in Rural Areas* (2012) and *Selected Conditions of Rural Tourism* (2013) and of more than 400 scientific articles.

Irma Potočnik Slavič is an Associate Professor at the Department of Geography, Faculty of Arts, University of Ljubljana, Slovenia. Her contemporary research focus comprises rural ageing, agritourism and farm income diversification, business zones in rural areas, short food supply chains and the impact of globalisation on rural areas. She has been involved in several projects at local and national levels and in the 7th Framework Programme research project of the European Union.

Ewa Tyran is a PhD graduate and a university teacher. She graduated from Kraków University of Agriculture, and for five years worked as a farmers' advisor before returning to University. The main part of her career involves agribusiness and her research topics include all aspects of tourism, especially rural tourism, agritourism, insurances systems in agriculture, rural development and diversification of farms' activities.

Jarosław Uglis is a PhD graduate, a teacher and a researcher at the Department of Rural Tourism, Poznań University of Life Sciences. His studies concern the determinants of the development of agritourism, rural tourism and culture tourism in rural areas. He is the author of more than 40 publications on tourism and rural development and his research interests include investigating the motives for the choice of agritourism as a tourist destination of urban agglomeration inhabitants.

Andrzej Piotr Wiatrak is a full Professor at the Faculty of Management, University of Warsaw. His main research interests are management of public, social and private organisations and quality of management; organisation, functioning and development of agribusiness; local and regional development; the structural transformation of rural areas and agriculture; tourism and agritourism. He has written around 500 publications, including 7 books individually and 29 as co-author. He is currently the president of the Association of Agricultural and Agribusiness Economists.

Jolanta Wojciechowska is a geographer, researcher and university lecturer, and Associate Professor at the University of Łódź in Poland, Faculty of Geographical Sciences, The Institute of Urban Geography and Tourism. Her areas of interest are tourism geography with particular focus on agritourism and tourism policy. She is the author of the books *Activating the Countryside Through Tourist Activity*, which is addressed to tourism practitioners in rural areas, and *The Processes and Conditions of the Development of Agritourism in Poland*. She has participated in several research projects, for example, Phare Tourin, Sapard, and has lectured at universities in Giessen and St Petersburg. She teaches agritourism in Russian to students from Eastern Europe.

Monika Wojcieszak is a PhD graduate and lecturer at the Department of Market and Marketing, Poznań University of Life Sciences. Her areas of scientific interest are the problems of agritourism, rural tourism, ecotourism, and nature tourism.

Acknowledgments

I would like to thank the National Science Centre in Krakow. Chapters 1, 2, 7, 9, 24 and 25 were written as part of the research project 1908/B/H03/2011/40 (application number N N114 190840). 'The Conditions and Perspectives of the Development of Agritourism, Rural Tourism, Ecotourism and Culinary Tourism in Selected Metropolitan Areas in Poland and Their Social and Economic Significance', which was financed by the National Science Centre in Krakow. The National Science Centre also financed the authors' meeting during which they planned coordination of this book.

I would like to thank my colleagues Julita Jurga, Agnieszka Kurasz and Milena Malinowska for their hard work on this book, especially for correspondence with the authors, editorial work on the manuscript, figures, index, numerical data and other laborious work which improved the quality of the book.

I would like to thank Jacek Żywiczka for the enormous work he put into translating this book from Polish into English.

I would like to thank:

- Centrum Doradztwa Rolniczego in Krakow, Krakow Branch for permission to publish Figure 18.6.
- EUROSTAT (Luxembourg) for sharing the map 'Metro regions in the UE' (Figure 1.1).
- Fotolia.com for allowing us to publish the following images: 11.3, 20.1, 20.2, figure in chapter Introduction, Conclusion, Part I, Part III, Part IV, Part V, Final matter.
- Grzegorz Okołów from Poland for image 'A view of Warsaw from Kampinos National Park' (Figure 13.2).
- Jacek Kozłowski from Kampinos National Park, Poland for sharing the photograph 'The route of the first excursion in the Polish lowland' (Figure 13.1).
- Jhon Ruzz Merca from Dubai for sharing the photograph 'Burj Khalifa Fog' (figure in front matter) free of charge.
- Koželj T. from Slovenia for extra preparation for this book of the following maps and figures: 10.1, 10.2, 10.3.
- Manfred Zentgraf, Volkach, from Germany for sharing the map of 'Ways of St. James in Europe' (Figure 9.1).

- Paweł Boczar from Poznań University of Life Sciences, Poland, for sharing the photograph 'Shanghai downtown' (figure on title page in Part II).
- Piotr Kiszka from Poland for permission to quote excerpts from his website (amigowka.pl) in Chapter 20.
- PWN Polskie Wydawnictwo Naukowe for sharing the graphics 'The efficiency and effectiveness of promotion' (Figure 8.1).
- Sayed-Mahdi-Almodarresi from Karbala, Iraq for permitting us to quote in Chapter 19 excerpts of his article 'World's Biggest Pilgrimage Now Underway, and Why You've Never Heard of it!'
- Solis B., Jesse T. for allowing us to quote 'The Conversation Prism' (Figure 11.2) under cc Creative Commons conditions.
- Szymon Sznajder from Poland for sharing the map of Conakry (Figure 4.1).

Burj Khalifa: the tallest building in the world – covered in fog in October 2012. Jruzz Merca told the following story on the shooting of the photo. 'My previous office was located opposite Burj Khalifa and I was based on the 40th floor. I had a fantastic view. This picture was taken on a foggy morning shortly after I arrived at work. The view was surreal, I couldn't help but reach for my camera and take the shot.'

Source: Photo by Jhon Ruzz Merca.

Introduction

In contemporary times people, especially those living in metropolises with populations of a few million, need to be in constant contact with nature. However, it is very difficult in big cities. Many inhabitants of metropolises are no longer satisfied with one long holiday a year and some people cannot afford it. Submetropolitan areas have enormous natural resources, which are perfect for people's systematic contact with nature. Regardless of their financial status, metropolitan dwellers are willing to use nearby natural resources for tourism purposes. This monograph, titled *Metropolitan Commuter Belt Tourism*, discusses the problem of people's systematic contact with nature as part of tourism.

The title of this monograph is seemingly provocative, but if we analyse it in more detail, we will see its innovative value. What is special about tourism in the metropolitan commuter belt? It is every type of nature-based tourism practised in the area marked as the metropolitan commuter belt. There are justified substantive reasons to distinguish the area of tourism discussed in this book with a catchy name. The most important reason to use the name 'commuter belt tourism' is the tight time budget of a metropolitan inhabitant who wants to be in systematic contact with nature. From results of the studies by Dzioban (Chapter 14) and Wiatrak (Chapter 17), which are cited in this monograph, we see that the main participants of metropolitan commuter belt tourism are metropolitan inhabitants who want to spend their free time – weekends, holidays or even free time during the day – in contact with nature. In view of this fact, the travel time which is necessary for a short tourist stay should not be longer than the time of an everyday commute to work so as not to tighten the metropolitan dweller's time budget even more. Therefore, the commuter belt is the right area for a metropolitan inhabitant to be in frequent contact with nature.

Metropolisation and the development of nature-based tourism in suburban areas are considered to be absolutely conflicting tendencies, where one can only develop at the expense of the other. Metropolisation is considered to be the dominant and developmental factor, whereas tourism is thought to be the recessive factor. Not negating the inherent, deductive conflict between these terms, in practice not only can we observe the dynamic development of tourism on the outskirts of large urban agglomerations but we also see that metropolisation strengthens this development. We can find constructive examples of this co-existence in metropolitan areas all over the world, and we cannot fail to consider the development of nature-based tourism in metropolitan studies.

Among different forms of nature-based tourism practised in the metropolitan commuter belt area we can distinguish nature-based tourism, ecotourism, forest tourism, rural tourism, agritourism and many others. Originally the editor of this monograph intended to present only the issue of rural tourism and agritourism in metropolitan areas. However, this concept turned out to be too detailed and poorly balanced as the development of tourism in metropolitan areas requires a holistic approach. From a supply standpoint, the holistic approach required inclusion in this monograph of all types of nature-based tourism and corresponding agritourism products, whereas, from a demand standpoint, the holistic approach required description of tourism segmentation.

Rural tourism and agritourism are particularly important and they are characterised by their special position in this book. Rural tourism and agritourism are very important components of the global tourism industry. There are several related branches of tourism, e.g. culinary tourism, wine tourism, etc., which should be considered together. The socioeconomic role of these types of tourism is growing constantly and dynamically all over the world. They are undergoing constant development and diversification, which can mostly be seen in their enormous product diversity. This revolution offers great opportunities for this territorially dispersed activity. The appearance of these types of tourism in metropolitan areas is a new phenomenon and a trend that can be observed all over the world. However, so far there have been few publications about it. The aim of this book is to bridge this gap and to highlight these phenomena, especially in metropolitan areas.

Rural tourism, agritourism and related types of tourism have evolved from economic activities of little significance to essential elements of the tourism industry in almost all countries all over the world. Statistical and economic information about farms is systematically gathered by statistical offices in different countries. As a result, we have a relatively exhaustive characterisation of farms. By contrast, information about agritourism farms and rural tourism is only beginning to develop, so the database is still relatively limited. Marzejon-Frycz (2012) gathered available statistics on Austria, France, Poland and Italy and revealed that there were 5,704 agritourism farms in Austria, 73,973 in France (members of Gites de France, the biggest of several French agritourism organisations), 8,696 in Poland and 14,822 in Italy. The actual number of agritourism farms in these countries could be much greater, because some of them operate informally or belong to smaller agritourism organisations, which are not monitored. When we extrapolate these data to other European countries, we can assume that there could be even as many as 444,000 agritourism farms in Europe. This research shows that agritourism has grown to become an important social and economic sector of the national economy. Despite the lack of statistical data on the turnover of rural tourism and agritourism, estimates indicate that their share in the global tourism market amounts to about 10 to 15 per cent and it is still increasing (see Ehrlich, Chapter 7).

Additionally, rural tourism, agritourism and related types of tourism have a huge impact on the quality of life of metropolitan residents who are involved in these activities. Due to the growing economic and social importance of rural tourism, agritourism, culinary tourism, ecotourism and nature tourism, these activities are a major focus of the economic and social policies of many governments and international organisations. The governments of countries such as the USA, Canada, New Zealand, India and, above all, the European Union created or continue to create favourable conditions for their development by funding several programmes, in spite of the fact that enterprises in the traditional tourism sector are dissatisfied that agritourism businesses in many countries are favoured by tax deductions.

Owing to the increasing role of rural tourism and agritourism in metropolitan areas the National Science Centre in Krakow (Poland) financed research on the subject between 2010 and 2014.[1] Scientific essays based on the research are included in this publication.

Metropolitan commuter belt tourism is on the verge of dynamic changes that have altered it radically or will change its characteristics soon. The railway was the first engine of its development but today there are many other engines, especially motorisation, urbanisation, the growth of metropolitan areas, global communication, and the information and communication technology (ICT) revolution. The popularity of modern lifestyles based on health and quality of life is an important factor. Tourism includes elements of modern lifestyles such as the desire to explore the world, adventure and relaxation. Weekend, public holiday and even afternoon tourism are elements of contemporary lifestyle. The increasing wealth of many people around the world is an important driving force underlying the development of these types of tourism. The aforementioned types of nature-based tourism perfectly satisfy these needs. For many years rural tourism, agritourism and related types of tourism were regarded as segments targeted at poorer tourists but modern findings do not support this view.

The book, *Metropolitan Commuter Belt Tourism*, focuses on the most important contemporary engines of the development of rural tourism, agritourism and related types of tourism, that is: urbanisation and the development of metropolitan areas. It indicates trends in their development and redefines their paradigms for the twenty-first century. The process of urbanisation has been comprehensively documented in the literature as a current, global phenomenon. During the whole twentieth century the percentage of the world's rural population was continuously decreasing and, in consequence, the number of urban dwellers increased. This process will accelerate in the twenty-first century. We should expect that, soon, perhaps in 2050, 80 per cent of the world population will live in cities and 20 per cent will live in rural areas. There are several consequences of metropolitan development. The first is that cities become bigger and bigger. At present the population of more than 509 cities in the world exceeds 1 million people; indeed the population of more than 12 metropolitan areas is greater than 20 million people. The process of urbanisation is accompanied by the development of metropolitan areas. Some people live in city houses or blocks of flats in the central part of cities, whereas wealthier people often prefer dwelling outside cities, in rural areas that surround them. In consequence, the number of satellite cities is rising and metropolitan areas are growing. Metropolitan areas have become an important area of rural tourism and agritourism.

Metropolitan areas have been expanding into newer and very attractive land in the countryside. However, economic ratios indicate that newly created metropolitan areas do not lose their rural nature and still retain a significant amount of agricultural, horticultural and animal production. At present it is possible to see very attractive forms of nature in metropolitan areas. For example, Kampinos National Park (the venue of a panel meeting of the authors of the book), which is situated within the limits of the Warsaw metropolitan area, has outstanding and attractive forms of nature: forests. Similarly there is Borivali National Park in the Mumbai metropolitan area, and Greater London National Park. Natural resources refer to the land topography, flora and fauna. What is more, metropolitan tourism resources include numerous major historic buildings and monuments.

Agritourism farms are unequally distributed in space. There are regions characterised by particularly intensive agritourism activity, as shown by the data concerning the four countries under analysis. There are more agritourism farms in the areas which are more attractive to tourists. In Austria the most agritourism farms can be found in the Alps, in France in the Rhone-Alpes region, in Poland in the Tatras and Podhale and in Italy, in Tuscany and Alto Adige. Agritourism is usually offered by small farms. Metropolitan areas are important and developing centres of rural tourism and agritourism.

It is natural human need is to be in constant contact with nature. Unfortunately, metropolisation and the urban lifestyle constantly loosen this contact. Tourism in metropolitan areas reverses this unfavourable trend and helps to nurture people by enabling them to have contact with nature throughout their lifetime.

Metropolitan areas have vast and very attractive resources, which make them very important and attractive to the development of rural tourism, agritourism, culinary tourism, ecotourism and nature tourism. The main cognitive goal of the book is to highlight present and forthcoming trends in the development of rural tourism, agritourism, ecotourism, food tourism and nature tourism in metropolitan areas.

The key aims of the book are to:

- provide definitions and theoretical knowledge concerning the development of different types of tourism in the metropolitan commuter belt;
- investigate metropolitan areas as they are currently used and will in the future drive the development of nature-based tourism comprising rural tourism, agritourism, food tourism, ecotourism and nature tourism, etc.;
- investigate nature-related human needs as basic human needs;
- make an inventory of existing tourism resources in metropolitan areas which support and enable the development of rural tourism, agritourism, food tourism and nature tourism;
- establish an appropriate selection of rural tourism, agritourism, food tourism and nature tourism products and services for metropolitan areas;
- explain how public and private resources can be combined to achieve synergy in tourism promotion;

- make a structural analysis for the proper management of tourism operators in metropolitan areas;
- gain insight into how the development of metropolitan areas affects rural tourism and agritourism within broader social, economic and environmental relations.

A brief description of the monograph contents

This book examines and determines key phenomena and challenges for rural tourism, agritourism, food tourism and nature tourism products arising from urbanisation and the development of metropolitan areas. It analyses major economic, social, market and managerial aspects. The issue of the growth of metropolitan areas, which is a complex and multifaceted challenge, is elaborated on with diverse examples of metropolises in Poland and worldwide. In general, as the book uses various findings, case studies and literature, it provides a rich source of material from which we can develop greater comprehension of key urbanisation processes, which are relevant to present metropolitan regions, and importantly, we can understand the capacity of regional development and/or ability to anticipate and respond to these challenges.

Part I Metropolisation and suburban tourism

This part is theoretical and explains the reasons for using the term *commuter belt tourism* and the title of the monograph: *Metropolitan commute belt tourism*. It has a dual character; on the one hand, it describes the process of urbanisation and its dynamic acceleration in the last two centuries; on the other hand, it describes the possibilities provided by submetropolitan tourism to satisfy the essential human need for contact with nature. This part gives definitions concerning urbanisation, including the classification of metropolises and the consequences of urban sprawl. It also considers the philosophy of nature in the context of urbanisation, especially questions about the position of humans in nature. The theoretical considerations are supported with examples of people's ambivalent attitude to the devastation of the natural environment and an example of internal development of the Afrometropolis of Conakry. This part also provides an explanation of how submetropolitan areas satisfy the human need to be in contact with nature.

Part II New paradigms and opportunities for Metropolitan Commuter Belt Tourism

Each human activity should be theoretically and practically organised within a specific framework so that it can be developed successfully. This assumption is the basis for the presentation of trends in the development of this activity. The beginning of this part shows how different theories of economics can be used to explain the mechanisms of development of rural tourism and agritourism. The twenty-first century poses new challenges and opportunities, which have not been known in tourism so far. In particular, these challenges and opportunities are related to the sustainable development of tourism and to goals of sustainable development. This part also presents normative modelling as a method of coordinating social actions in the promotion of rural tourism and agritourism, financed from both public and private funds. The idea is that the combined funds should result in synergy. Paradigms of the development of rural tourism and agritourism, which are the most important forms of tourism available in submetropolitan areas, are presented. This part formulates new paradigms for tourism in the metropolitan commuter belt area and new opportunities for development.

Part III Natural resources in metropolitan and submetropolitan areas

Metropolisation, which is developing dynamically all over the world, increasingly causes metropolitan areas to spread into rural areas with unique natural resources. This part defines natural values, which are divided into exhaustible and inexhaustible resources. It contains an inventory of the most important natural resources in all 12 Polish metropolitan areas, which must be retained for future generations. This part presents a method of space valorisation according to its natural values and verifies this method with examples of three Polish metropolitan areas. It includes an elaborate description of natural resources in Kampinos National Park, which is situated in the Warsaw commuter belt, as well as legal regulations concerning the use of the park by tourists. This part also describes the history of tourists gaining access to the park. It characterises contemporary tourists and the way they use Kampinos National Park. There is a case study of Otulina agritourism farm, which is situated in the park.

Part IV Types of tourism and tourism segments in metropolitan commuter belts

Tourism in metropolitan commuter belt areas has its specific character, which results both from the type of natural and anthropogenic resources the area possesses and from market forces, which influence the type of products that consumers expect to be offered. When both of these factors are taken into consideration, both the demand and supply will be favourable to the future development of tourism in these areas. A vast majority of submetropolitan areas meet the conditions of rurality and they have large potential for the development of different types of rural tourism, namely culinary, shopping, educational, recreational, business and health tourisms as well as agritourism. Weekend and holiday tourism are becoming increasingly important in these areas. This part describes the making of a network of educational agritourism farms. Social farming is a form of leisure that was developed to mitigate the consequences of ageing populations. Tourism pedagogy plays a significant role in education and achievement of the goals of sustainable tourism. This part also presents a case study of 'Amigówka' agritourism farm near Krakow. The final section describes the fascinating phenomenon of pilgrimages in metropolitan areas with examples of pilgrimages crossing metropolitan areas to reach Allahabad, Karbala and Santiago del Compostela.

Part V Portfolio offer for tourism in submetropolitan areas

Tourism traffic in submetropolitan areas is chiefly individual, but its future also depends on the development of a network of tour operators and the products they offer: this part presents legal forms of this activity. A polarisation model was used to show that the tourism offer in submetropolitan areas was changing, with the change depending on natural resources and the distance of a particular service offer from the city proper. The tourism market is strongly diversified and can be divided into a large number of specific markets, including nature-based tourism, rural tourism, agritourism, and such. This part presents a new classification of tourism products and services which can be offered by agritourism farms both in metropolitan areas and outside of them. This part systematises products and services and uses research to specify the selection of goods and services in five European countries and in four metropolitan areas in Poland. It analyses the number of products offered by agritourism farms. As it turns out, the basket of services in metropolitan areas is different from those offered away from metropolises due to the specific demand in metropolitan areas. The final section presents the rules of tourism segmentation in these areas.

Although the editor imposed a specific form on the book, because it has been written independently by several authors representing different fields of knowledge, it was necessary to make a formal summary of its structure. Apart from that, the final part of the book (Conclusion) is an independent essay that synthesises innovative theoretical and practical achievements of nature-based tourism in the metropolitan commuter belt.

The book also provides a glossary with over 40 key definitions and an index with 200 entries.

Michał Jacenty Sznajder
Poznań University of Life Sciences, Poland

Note

1   The publications included in this book were written as part of programme No. 1908/B/H03/2011/40, *The Conditions and Perspectives of the Development of Agritourism, Rural Tourism, Ecotourism and Culinary Tourism in Selected Metropolitan Areas in Poland and Their Social and Economic Significance*, financed by the National Science Centre in Krakow.

References

Marzejon-Frycz, I. (2012). Specyfika agroturystyki Polski na tle wybranych krajów Unii Europejskiej (Specifics of Polish agritourism in the context of chosen EU countries). *Ekonomia*, Uniwersytet Warszawski No. 29, pp. 66–85, Warszawa.

Part I

Metropolisation and suburban tourism

Satellite map of European cities, night.

1   Ecumenopolis commuter belt tourism

Michał Jacenty Sznajder

Toward Ecumenopolis

In 1967 Constantinos Doxiadis made a forecast based on demographic prognoses and the rate of urbanisation (Sassen 1991). He said that one day nothing more would exist except the city – Ecumenopolis (Caves 2005, p. 143). At the time nobody knew that the concept of the urban footprint could be used to monitor human activity on Earth. Nowadays, if we look from space at the Earth illuminated by billions of electric lamps, inevitably we need to ask the question whether Doxiadis was right in his opinion that urban areas and metropolises all over the world would merge one day and form one global city. The world population is constantly increasing and there are more and more people moving to cities, especially mega-metropolises. Nearly 25 per cent of the world's population lives in 509 cities that have more than one million inhabitants. There are as many as 36 cities with more than 10 million inhabitants and this number is still growing (Demographia 2016).

If we look at world metropolises from space, we can say that these areas consist not only of the industry, business, housing and free space, but also green space, such as forests, farmland and waters. Green space, forests and waters occupy considerable areas of metropolises, for example, more than 37 per cent of the area of Berlin (Pacholsky 2000, p. 3). These are natural resources which the inhabitants of this metropolis can use for tourism. The greater the distance of these areas from the city proper, the more fascinating natural resources for tourism can be found.

One of people's numerous needs is for systematic tourism, especially in the areas closest to their place of residence. Weekends and holidays are the right time for systematic tourism as long as the destination is at a reasonable distance, for example, within the metropolitan commuter belt. On the one hand, metropolitan areas create an enormous demand for tourism; on the other, they have considerable natural, infrastructural and human resources which can help to satisfy this demand. There is a problem of what to call systematic or spontaneous tourism in metropolitan areas where the inhabitants of a particular city use the natural tourism resources of their area. There are a few possibilities: nature-based tourism in metropolitan areas, submetropolitan nature tourism, suburban tourism, or metropolitan commuter belt tourism.

Paradoxical hypothesis

Peoples' attitudes to nature and human development are still rather divided and these attitudes have been changing over the years due to the development of the philosophy of nature and the role of humans in it. This role varies widely from, at one extreme, the Biblical recommendation: 'Be fruitful, and multiply, and replenish the earth and subdue it, and have dominion over the fish of the sea and over the birds of the heavens and over every living thing that moves on the earth' (Genesis 1:28) to the exceptionally ecological questioning of the role of humans in the ecosystem. Many people, especially those who lived in the late nineteenth century and in the first half of the twentieth century, retained aspects of the attitude that treated nature as something to be fought and overcome. This approach generated several environmental disasters. The doctrine of struggle with nature (борьба с природой) was applied in the former Soviet empire during the entire period of its existence. The Soviets created conspicuous geo-engineering projects which caused gigantic ecological disasters, such as the drying up of Lake Aral and the Bay of Kara-Bogaz-Gol in the Caspian Sea and the enormous erosion caused by ploughing the soil in the Tselina Virgin Lands Campaign (Tselinograd, currently Astana, Kazakhstan). Even those countries that seem to exploit their natural resources rationally sometimes made mistakes and caused the 'anger and revenge' of nature. The almost everlasting lightning storm on Lake Maracaibo, which earned the top spot as the place with the most lightning strikes, receiving an average rate of about 233 flashes per square kilometre per year (Connelly 2016), could be considered by some to be a symbol of angry nature.

Alternatively, there are radical ecological ideas which consider humans to be not only harmful but also an unnecessary element of nature. In spite of environmentally friendly declarations, these movements also lead to extreme situations, causing both the anger of people and nature. When Białowieża Forest in Poland was attacked by woodworms in 2015, immediately it became a political arena for the two aforementioned opposing concepts of the philosophy of nature. Białowieża Forest is not the only place on earth where we can see a conflict between radical supporters of nature conservation and local inhabitants who demand due development in their place of residence. Therefore, we need a rational compromise between protection of the natural environment and human development. In view of this fact, humanity is taking increasingly balanced steps to achieve this goal. For example, the EU climate package, also known as the climate and energy package, is a set of legally binding acts which are supposed to prevent climatic changes. Nature-based tourism in metropolitan areas is consistent with the philosophy of sustainable human development due to rational use of renewable natural resources.

There is a subtle difference between the terms *urban agglomeration* and *urban sprawl*, although they are sometimes used interchangeably to refer to the process of increasing urbanisation and the growth of cities. Urban sprawl is a centrifugal tendency, where colonisation spreads from the central city to new areas, whereas urban agglomeration is a centripetal tendency, where settlements are concentrated around the central city. Metropolisation comprises both urban sprawl and urban agglomeration and it is an increasing global phenomenon caused by continuously and comprehensively growing significance of big cities in the development of humanity. It is chiefly manifested by rapid urban sprawl to new rural and agricultural areas as well as forests, lakes, seas, deserts, and even the lower layer of the atmosphere. Radical ecologists find it regrettable that metropolisation is an inevitable and unstoppable process, because it is commonly thought that a big city provides humans with better opportunities of comprehensive development and a greater sense of broadly interpreted personal security. There are different forms of urban sprawl, ranging from building luxurious residences in shallow seas to uncontrolled, illegal colonisation of suburban agricultural areas, forests or even marshlands by poor people. The colonisation of the artificial Palm Islands on the coast of Dubai or the Pearl-Qatar in Doha are extreme examples of rich metropolitan dwellers' households sprawling into new areas. Extreme expansion of cities can also be observed in lower layers of the atmosphere, for example, Burj Khalifa in Dubai, a nearly 830-metre tall skyscraper. Conversely, poor people tend to colonise new areas, such as the Afropolis of Conakry, which is the most populated and constantly growing place in Guinea, aspiring to be called a city or metropolis (see Chapter 4).

In 2007 the urban population of the world exceeded 50 per cent of the total world population (54.5 per cent in 2016) and it is still growing rapidly. The spontaneous process of settling in metropolises and metropolitan areas indicates that humanity can see better prospects for the future in these areas. The inhabitants of the most urbanised country in the world, the Belgians, say that there is no place in Belgium from which one could not see any buildings. As much as 98 per cent of the population live in cities. Some people welcome metropolisation with hope and enthusiasm, whereas others are reserved and apprehensive. The enthusiasm or apprehension results from one's personal answer to the key question concerning the philosophy of nature, namely the position and role of humanity in nature. Regardless of one's personal answer to this question, usually people stress the fact that the term *metropolisation* by itself stands in opposition to nature and metropolitan sprawl inevitably causes the disappearance of the natural environment. However, metropolitan inhabitants more and more often tend to exhibit their need to have contact with nature. The situation causes a paradox, because increasing metropolisation is accompanied by growing demand for contact with nature. The main thesis of this book included in the phrase 'nature-based tourism in metropolitan areas' sounds paradoxical. However, the main paradoxical thesis emphasises the complementary character of nature and tourism in metropolitan areas rather than the antagonism between the two. The paradoxical thesis is manifested by the statements that metropolisation favours the development of nature-based tourism and that nature-based tourism lets metropolitan inhabitants better understand and protect nature to save it for future generations.

Thus, the first part of the book is not a synthesis of the metropolisation theory but it is a necessary description of one of significant phenomena of the process, that is, the relationship between metropolitan sprawl into new suburban areas and perspectives of the development of nature-based tourism in these areas. The explanation of this phenomenon requires a broader conceptual context, which comprises classification and functions of the metropolis and metropolitan areas. It is important to know the current distribution of metropolises and metropolitan areas around the world as well as the natural, social and economic consequences of metropolisation. The inevitability of the development of nature-based tourism in metropolitan areas is the vital main thesis of this book, which is also the basis for both further theoretical and practical developments of nature-based tourism.

The city and the country

It is commonly believed that the city is an area where the natural environment is degraded, not to say devastated, whereas the country is an area of natural idyll. More and more often it is quite the opposite – a modern and well organised city protects people from a degraded agricultural environment. We could give endless arguments supporting or contradicting either thesis. However, it is doubtless that urban areas create the demand, whereas rural areas offer a supply of goods presented by nature-based tourism. Therefore, we are going to start our considerations of nature-based tourism with a definition of the city and the country and the factors which make the city the place that creates the demand for this form of tourism and the factors which make the country the place where this demand can be satisfied.

Every day the words 'city' and 'country' are commonly used in every language. The range of their meanings seems to be evident and easy to understand both for the speaker and listener in the process of communication. However, in fact, the variability of the terms 'city' and 'country' is so big that every person has their own unique image of what they are. Initially these images were created through people's direct contact with the city and country throughout their lives, influenced also by information from other people. Scientific progress, the development of knowledge, technology, culture and growth of welfare create a need for people to constantly update their image of the city and country.

I spent my young years on the border of a small town and village in Lower Silesia in Poland. It was not an administrative boundary demarcated on a map, but it was the actual border between the city and country, which was noticeable even to a child. Whatever was east of my house was densely populated and was unquestionably a town, with a municipal charter granted in 1290. It had administrative, communal, educational, health care, judicial and public safety functions as well as many others. The east was also the place of the electronic, textile and machine industries as well as trade and rail and road transport. My town was characterised by urban development with an infrastructure of roads, sewers, water supply and power supply systems. There was a theatre, local newspapers, different organisations, unions and societies. The town was also characterised by many other traditional and modern buildings and structures: the market with the town hall, historic churches, the synagogue with a Jewish cemetery, defence walls, fair, stadium and swimming pool. The town was too small for a cathedral, university, airport, opera house or many other places and institutions which are characteristic of a metropolitan city.

The *city* is a historically developed settlement, which has been granted a municipal charter (at least in some countries). It is characterised by a high density of buildings and population and little farmland. It has many urban functions, the inhabitants are employed outside agriculture and they have an urban lifestyle.

The areas stretching from my house in the other directions were villages with low population. They lacked the urban infrastructure. The buildings and households were oriented to agricultural production. Villagers dealt with crop and animal production, horticulture, pomiculture and forestry. The excess of labour was absorbed by the nearby town. The inhabitants of surrounding villages used all services offered by the town. The countryside was also characterised by the rural lifestyle, religiousness, folk tradition and culture and it developed comprehensive mutual neighbourly help.

The *village* is a developed settlement characterised by a low density of buildings and population, and the area is mostly farmlands. The inhabitants are employed in agriculture and have a rural lifestyle.

There are different criteria of urbanity in different countries. In Poland the possession of a municipal charter is the requirement a place needs to meet to become a town. It is granted or repealed by the Council of Ministers. It is not only the population itself but also the percentage of urban population in a particular community and population density that are important elements of urbanity. In a traditional sense of the city it is either completely void of agriculture or there are very few elements of it. Not more than 25 per cent of the urban population can be employed in agriculture. In the Polish tradition, on the one hand, there are towns which are very small settlements with a population of 2,000 to 3,000 but with a municipal charter. On the other hand, there are also large towns in Poland with a population of a few million.

Urban and rural areas

The world has always been divided into urban and rural areas. The city and the urban area are not synonyms, nor are the village and the rural area. It is common for rural areas to be included into the administrative area of the city. The village is an area with low population density and characterised by various rural functions. Sometimes there are typical urban developments in rural areas. As we know from history, cities have always been the pride of countries and the visible display of their strength. Therefore, leaders have always placed great importance on their development. In ancient times and the Middle Ages there was a sharp border in the form of city walls separating the city from rural areas. As time passed, settlements developed beyond the city walls and the border between urban and rural areas became less visible. Nowadays, there are scientific, statistical, economic and demographic reasons why it is necessary to distinguish between cities and villages and urban and rural areas. In the past the city walls or turnpikes marked the border; at present the border between urban and rural areas is marked by conventional demographic indicators. There are no standardised global definitions of urban and rural areas, because this division depends not only on quantifiable indicators but also on the historical and cultural heritage of nations. There are different interpretations of urban and rural areas: Until recently it was generally acceptable that whatever was not considered to be an urban area was defined as a rural area. However, contemporary statistics needs specific indicators to identify urban and rural areas. The literature lists different determinants of urban and rural areas, such as:

- population density per 1 km^2
- minimum population in an administrative unit
- percentage of population making their living from agriculture
- distance between neighbouring buildings.

Threshold values assumed for the aforementioned determinants differ not only between countries but also between different spatial planning concepts. For example, due to utilitarian demographic and economic analysis, Eurostat (the Statistical Office of the European Union) abandoned traditionally and legally recognised terms 'town' and 'village'. Instead it uses the terms 'urban and rural areas' and uses demographic grid cell geocoding standards to identify statistic territorial units, known as Nomenclature of Territorial Units for Statistics (NUTS). The EU statistics uses two of the four aforementioned determinants as thresholds to distinguish between urban and rural areas, namely the population density and the minimum population in an administrative unit. The minimum population density for urban areas is 300 inhabitants per km^2 and the minimum total population of 5,000. The areas which do not meet either criterion are classified as rural by Eurostat. As we can see, according to the concept of Eurostat, the rural area does not totally cover the definition of a village, whereas the urban area does not cover the definition of a city. As far as Poland is concerned, a large number of the 332 towns with a population under 5,000 are situated in rural areas.

The terms 'urban area', 'urban agglomeration' and 'built-up urban area' are in a way synonymous. According to Demographia (2016), 'A built-up urban area is the new urban area term now used by National Statistics in the United Kingdom and it may be the most descriptive short term for urban areas', and 'an urban area contains no rural land, all land in the world is either urban or rural. A built-up urban area is a continuously built-up land mass of urban development that is within a labour market'. The largest built-up urban area is New York,[1] it is 11,642 km^2. Its area is larger than the area of some countries, such as Cyprus, Lebanon, Kosovo, Gambia, Jamaica and Qatar. The second largest built-up urban area is Tokyo–Yokohama at 8,547 km^2. Many countries have laws protecting the use of land for housing development and it is necessary to have an administrative permission to start construction.

According to Demographia (2016), the population density in urban areas ranges very widely from 400 to as many as 44,000 inhabitants per 1 km^2. As was mentioned before, in many countries there are even lower population density thresholds used to classify a particular place as an urban area, for example, in Canada it is only 150 inhabitants per 1 km^2. The most populated built-up urban

Typology of metrolitan regions (at the level of NUTS 3) (¹)

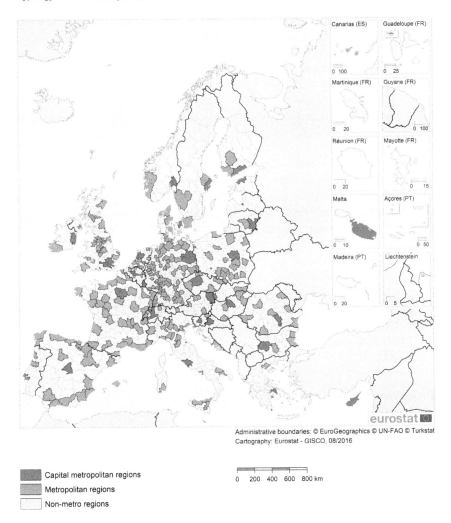

Administrative boundaries: © EuroGeographics © UN-FAO © Turkstat
Cartography: Eurostat - GISCO, 08/2016

Capital metropolitan regions
Metropolitan regions
Non-metro regions

0   200   400   600   800 km

Figure 1.1 Metro regions in the UE.

Source: Eurostat, JRC and European Commission Directorate-General for Regional Policy.

(¹) Based on population grid from 2011 and NUTS 2013.

areas are in Bangladesh, Pakistan, India and China, that is, Dhaka, Bangladesh – 44,100 inhabitants per 1 km²; Hyderabad, India – 41,200; Vijayawada, India – 31,200; Chittagong, Bangladesh – 29,200 and Mumbai, India – 26,000.

Another important indicator of urbanity is the percentage of inhabitants employed outside agriculture, which should not be lower than 75 per cent in urban areas. The density of buildings causes a lot of problems as a criterion of classifying a place as an urban or rural area. The maximum distance between buildings in urban areas is 200 metres (Kasper *et al.* 2015).

Contemporary scanning and mapping of the Earth by means of satellite transmitters or sensors enables precise identification of urban and rural areas according to human activity, which can be seen from space. It is easiest to understand the concept of urban footprint by looking at spectacular night views of the Earth illuminated with millions of electric lights photographed from space. They show the spatial distribution of the population of the Earth, the population density and even the scale of economic activity. This simple visual analysis lets one understand that the footprint is not only a mark left by a foot on a surface but also the impact that mankind has on the Earth and the environment. There are computer programs which can be used for urban-footprint mapping to identify levels of spatial density in a built-up area. For example, the Urban Footprint software (Urban Footprint 2012) includes a library of more than 35 place types and 50 building types for California. Another software, the Urban Landscape Analysis Tool (ULAT), distinguishes the following footprint classes on an urban footprint map:

- urban built-up area
- suburban built-up area
- rural built-up area
- fringe open land
- captured open land
- rural open land
- water.

Urban sprawl

Since the beginning of the establishment of cities it has been evident that they could not provide accommodation to all the people who wanted to live in them. Ancient and medieval cities satisfied different demands, of which the need for personal security was the most important. In the early Middle Ages there were settlements beyond the city walls which provided services for the city. Whenever it was necessary, the inhabitants could hide in the city. The prices of houses and land in cities, especially in the city centre, have always been higher than on the outskirts or places situated away from the city. The process of urban sprawl into rural areas, sometimes in a completely uncontrollable manner, has always existed. However, it became more dynamic in the second half of the nineteenth century and boomed in the second half of the twentieth century. The phenomenon of uncontrollable expansion of cities is called *urban sprawl* or *exurbanisation*. It consists of building new settlements in suburban areas and migration of city inhabitants to these areas. Both city inhabitants and migrants coming from non-urban areas settle there.

Uncontrollable migration of poor rural inhabitants to urban and suburban areas of big cities is a special case of urban sprawl into rural areas. These people settle on the outskirts of big cities in an unplanned manner, thus extending urban areas and creating urban slums. Nowadays there are districts of extreme poverty in big agglomerations all over the world, especially in Asia, South America and Africa. Poor districts are a shameful problem in developed countries. Some highly populated places can hardly be regarded as real cities, because they have not developed urban functions yet or they are still in their infancy.

The proper process of urban sprawl into suburban areas began in Europe in the late nineteenth century together with the development of railways, tramways and underground rail lines. These means of public transport enabled city inhabitants to move rapidly to suburban areas. The costs of living and building in suburban areas have always been lower than in the city, so people moved from city centres to suburban areas. In this way satellite settlements were established around public transport routes leading to the city centre. The automotive industry has accelerated and revolutionised the process of urban sprawl because it separated the process of people's migration from public transport. There have been new settlements built away from traditional road routes.. The exurbanisation caused by the automotive industry began in the US in the 1920s. In Europe it developed particularly strongly in the 1950s and 1960s. It came to Poland only in the 1990s and at present it is at its prime. This process caused a decrease in urban population and increase in the number of suburban inhabitants. Szukalski (2014) researched the process of depopulation of big cities in Poland and found that the main factor causing a decrease in the population is migration, especially to suburban areas – it marks the process of suburbanisation. Between 1995 and 2013 Poznań was the city that lost the most inhabitants, 27,600 (4.7%) in the process of exurbanisation. According to forecasts, even more Poznań inhabitants will move from the city to suburban areas. Neither Warsaw nor Kraków have experienced depopulation yet. Sim and Mesev (2011) employed metrics to describe land development. Urban sprawl was measured with the following dimensions: size (spatial extent of urban area), density (the amount of developed land per capita), continuity, scattering, shape and loss of green space.

Metropolises

A previous paragraph titled 'The city and the country' discusses villages and small towns of fewer than 50,000 inhabitants. This paragraph discusses bigger towns, especially metropolises and metropolitan areas. The word *city* is used to refer to a relatively large and extensive settlement; sometimes it is used to refer to the centre of a big town. However, there is no clear semantic division between the town and city in terms of the number of inhabitants. In the past in England a city was a higher form of settlement than a town. For example, it needed to have a diocesan cathedral. In modern English the word 'city' has more than one meaning, so it can be interpreted in different ways. According to the Functional Urban Areas (FUA) of the Organisation for Economic Co-operation and Development (OECD 2015), a city is defined as a local administrative unit (LAU) where the majority of the population lives in an urban centre of at least 50,000 inhabitants.

According to the definition of Eurostat, cities with more than 250,000 inhabitants are classified as metropolises.

According to Duché (2010), a *metropolis* is a city proper, which dominates a certain area. It is distinguished by high population; economic, political, social and cultural significance;' high attractiveness index and long range of spatial influence. It combines diversified functions, particularly specialised services. It influences the regional, national and international environment, functioning in a network with other big cities and surrounding medium-sized and small towns. Cities proper with adjacent communes make metropolitan areas. We also distinguish megacities and megalopolises, depending on the size of the urban agglomeration: A megacity is usually defined as a metropolitan area with a high population exceeding 10 million, of which there are.at present 36 around the world. A megalopolis is a clustered network of cities with a population exceeding 25 million, of which there are four.

At present the meaning of the word 'metropolis' is much different from the ancient Greek meaning of 'mother city' or the Latin meaning of 'chief city'. At present it refers both to a big city and a complex of many cities, known as a conurbation. According to Ładysz (2009), the first metropolises were established by the Sumerians, who founded them around a place of worship. City-states were surrounded by defensive walls. Their borders ran along irrigation networks, rivers or strips of uncultivated land. The best-known city-states were the Sumerian cities of Uruk and Lagash. A metropolitan city develops by annexation of satellite settlements into the structure of the city proper or by urbanisation of communes without annexation into the structure of the metropolitan city, where the communes remain independent administrative units.

Contemporary development of metropolises is a common multi-aspect, and global phenomenon, which is monitored, analysed and described by experts from different scientific disciplines. The attention of contemporary politicians, sociologists, economists and other scientific experts is focused on serious challenges presented by the global metropolisation processes, especially on the need to identify, create, name and define them clearly. The process involves numerous stakeholders, that is, individual researchers and scientific teams, managements of metropolises, state governments and international organisations. Each group of stakeholders analyses this process from its own specific point of view. Therefore, it is not surprising to see a multitude and diversity of terms, definitions and theories concerning metropolises and metropolisation. Theoretical elaborations and comparisons of data prepared by the UN Statistics Division, Eurostat, OECD, Demographia (Wendell Cox Consultancy) and statistical offices in different countries, especially the US, deserve particular attention among this diversity of information.

Considerable funds are allocated to metropolitan studies in order to improve inhabitants' quality of life. Each metropolis is a special case. Managements of metropolises prepare and implement strategies of their development not only to eliminate countless problems but also to constantly plan and prepare programmes to improve quality of life. For example, there are concepts of a garden city, park city or other programmes promoting better quality of life for inhabitants. The enormous scientific and developmental work of these metropolitan studies resulted in the cataloguing of specific theoretical accomplishments, a system of definitions, and methods of analyses, planning and theory of spatial development related to the development of metropolises and metropolitan areas.

It is reasonable to make a distinction between urban areas and metropolitan areas. A metropolitan area is a coherent space occupied by a large number of highly urbanised settlement units. These units comprise the city or cities proper (metropolis) and small administrative units, villages, settlements and satellite towns which function as a compact organism. A metropolitan area is a sum of first, the urban area of the city proper; second, the area of satellite towns; and third, rural areas related with the main city, usually because the inhabitants of suburban areas are employed in this city and commute there. It is necessary to remember the definition of conurbation, which is a region comprising many cities, large towns and adjacent urban areas. A conurbation is usually polycentric. Urban footprint methodology enables precise determination of the boundaries of a metropolitan area. They may not be identical with the outer limits of components of a metropolitan area. A metropolitan area combines an urban agglomeration with zones that do not necessarily have urban character, but are closely bound to the centre by employment or other commerce. These outlying zones are sometimes known as a commuter belt, and may extend well beyond the urban zone to other political entities.

The world's greatest urban agglomerations

According to Demographia (2016), approximately one quarter (23.9%) of the world population lives in urban areas of 1,000,000 or more inhabitants. Less than 30 per cent (28.6%) lives in urban areas with 500,000 or more but less than 1,000,000 inhabitants. More than 70 per cent of the world's population lives outside urban areas with 500,000 or more inhabitants. In the last 50 years we have seen outstanding development of urban agglomerations. The populations of these agglomerations are usually estimated on the basis of censuses, which in many countries are usually conducted every ten years. The census procedure is very expensive and requires an effective administrative system, but there are poor and not well-organised countries which are unable to conduct a census. Nonetheless, it is necessary to estimate the population and the concept of the urban footprint perfectly facilitates the population estimating procedure. A Demographic Yearbook published by the United Nations Statistics Division every year contains the latest results of demographic studies conducted all over the world.

It is usually very difficult to compare the development of the population of one city over the period of its history. It is even more difficult to compare it with other cities and the conclusions drawn from these comparisons are rather uncertain. The comparison does not meet the condition of all other things being equal, because demographic indexes are acquired with different methods and with extraordinary variability of determinants. Therefore, making a list of the world's biggest cities is extremely difficult and subjective. Data concerning population are not stable and hardly comparable over a period of time. There are different reasons for population growth in the world's major metropolises, the main reason being the administrative annexure of new urbanised areas to the structure of the city proper. For example, the population and area of Mumbai increased rapidly as new satellite towns were incorporated into its structure. In 1951 the population of Mumbai was 3 million; in 1961, 4.2 million; in 1971, 6.0 million; in 1980, 8.2 million; in 1991, 9.9 million; in 2001, 16.4 million and in 2014, 22.9 million. At the time, the Mumbai built-up urban area expanded and incorporated several 'small' towns, for example, Thane (2.2 million inhabitants), Bhiwandi (0.6 million), Kalyan (1.24 million) and Vasai-Virar (1.34 million). The territorial expansion of Mumbai and the resulting drastic increase in its population as well as all dynamic migrations make it impossible to compare the demographic indexes referring to the city of Mumbai or to other cities. In spite of this problem, Table 1.1 shows a list of the world's 34 biggest urban agglomerations and their approximate populations in 1960, 1980, 2000 and 2014. The data were acquired from two independent sources, namely the United Nations and Demographia. The United Nations Demographic Yearbooks consequently publish official data based on censuses, where the data refer either to the city proper, (the city within its administrative limits), or the urban agglomeration (built-up area), or both indexes are provided. The UN Demographic Yearbook has defined *city proper* as a locality with legally fixed boundaries and an administratively recognised urban status, usually characterised by some form of local government. It has defined *urban agglomeration* as comprising the city or town proper and also the suburban fringe or densely settled territory lying outside of, but adjacent to, the city boundaries. There are differences between cities in population proportions in the categories 'city proper' and 'urban agglomeration' over a period of time. For example, in Paris the population of the city proper has been stable over decades and amounted to about 2.2 million, whereas the population of the urban agglomeration increased from 4.8 million in 1960 to 10.4 million in 2014. It means that Paris has not been annexing the surrounding built-up areas. The situation looks similar in many other traditional metropolises around the world. Other cities have adopted the policy of expansion and constantly annex new built-up areas into their structures. Shenzhen is the world's most expansive city annexing new areas. Until 1980 it was a small, unknown Chinese town with a population of 30,000. In less than 40 years it expanded into a metropolis with a population exceeding 12 million. Jakarta was another metropolis that developed expansively, from 2.81 million inhabitants in 1960 to 31.32 million in 2014. According to Demographia (2016), there are two gigantic urban agglomerations in the world: Tokyo (37.75 million) and Jakarta (31.32 million). There are ten other agglomerations with more than 20 million inhabitants. It is noteworthy that over the period of 40 years the rate of development of some cities decreased considerably. It is particularly noticeable in St. Petersburg. In 1960 it was a metropolis with 3.3 million inhabitants, whereas in 2014 the population increased only to 5.2 million, which was a much lower rate of growth than in many other cities around the world.

Table 1.1 The approximate population of the world's 34 biggest metropolises within the administrative limits of the city proper and within the limits of the urban agglomeration, in 1960, 1980, 2000 and 2014

| Urban agglomerations | Exact year for UN data[1] | United Nations (approximate data) | | | | | | | | Demographia 2014 | | Wikipedia 2016 | |
| | | 1960 | | 1980 | | 2000 | | 2014 | | | | | |
		City proper	Metro	City proper	Metro	City proper	Metro	City proper	Metro	City proper	Metro	City proper	Metro
Tokyo	(1960), (1980), (2000), (2010)	8.30		8.35	9.50	8.13	11.69	8.95	12.06	–	37.75	13.51	37.80
Jakarta	(1960), (1980), (2000), (2010)	2.81		6.50	–	8.39	–	9.61	–	–	31.32	9.61	30.21
Delhi	(1960), (1971), (1991), (2001)	1.67		2.41	3.29	3.65	7.21	8.42	9.88	12.88	25.74	16.31	21.75
Seoul	(1960), (1980), (1991), (2001)	1.65		8.37	–	0.99	–	10.01	–	–	23.58	10.12	25.62
Manila	(1960), (1980), (2000), (2014)	1.18		1.63	1.87	0.16	–	1.65	–	–	22.93	1.65	22.71
Mumbai (Bombay)	(1960), (1971), (1991), (2001)	4.94		5.97	–	9.93	–	11.98	12.60	16.43	22.89	12.44	18.41
Karachi	(R-1961), (R-1981), (R-1998), (R-2015)	–		–	6.91	–	15.21	20.27	24.00	–	22.83	–	24.30
Shanghai	(1960), (1970), (2000), (2014)	6.90		–	–	10.82	14.35	–	–	–	22.69	5.67	24.15
New York	(1960), (1980), (2000), (2012)	7.78		7.07	10.69	8.01	16.12	8.34	21.20	–	20.69	8.55	23.72
Sao Paulo	(1960), (1980), (2000), (2010)	3.67		–	–	7.03	–	10.43	–	11.15	20.61	11.90	20.94

(continued)

Table 1.1 Continued

Urban agglomerations	Exact year for UN data[1]	United Nations (approximate data)								Demographia 2014	Wikipedia 2016	
		1960		1980		2000		2014			2016	
		City proper	Metro	City proper	Metro	City proper	Metro	City proper	Metro	Metro	City proper	Metro
Mexico City	(1960), (1979), (2000 & 1990), (2014)	2.70	—	9.19	14.75	0.86	15.05	8.87	—	20.23	8.92	20.40
Guangzhou (Canton)-Foshan	(1957), (1982), (2000), (2014)	1.84	—	3.18	5.67	8.52	—	—	—	18.76	11.26	23.90
Osaka	(1960), (1980), (2000), (2010)	2.89	—	2.65	—	2.60	—	2.67	—	16.99	2.67	19.34
Moscow	(1960), (1980), (1999), (2012)	5.03	—	8.10	8.01	8.30	8.54	11.92	—	16.57	12.20	16.80
Dhaka	(1960), (1974), (1991), (2001)	0.41	—	1.62	2.06	—	3.40	—	5.33	16.24	6.97	17.15
Cairo	(1960), (1976), (1996), (2010)	2.85	2.99	5.07	—	6.80	—	7.25	—	15.91	10.23	20.44
Bangkok	(1960), (1980), (2000), (2010)	—	1.33	3.08	—	—	6.32	—	8.31	15.32	8.28	14.57
Los Angeles	(1960), (1980), (2000), (2012)	2.48	6.74	2.97	11.50	3.69	16.37	3.86	—	15.14	3.93	18.35
Kolkata (Calcutta)	(1960), (1971), (1991), (2001)	3.04	5.91	3.15	7.03	4.40	11.02	4.57	13.21	14.81	4.50	14.11
Buenos Aires	(1960), (1980), (1991), (2013)	3.77	4.60	2.99	10.07	2.97	11.30	—	13.34	14.28	2.89	12.74
Tehran	(1960), (1982), (1996), (2011)	1.57	1.66	5.73	—	6.76	—	8.15	—	13.67	8.85	15.23
Istanbul	(1960), (1980), (1997), (2013)	1.46	1.92	2.77	2.91	8.26	8.51	—	14.16	13.52	14.03	14.66

Lagos	(1960), (1975), (1991)	0.36	–	1.06	1.48	5.20	–	–	–	12.83	13.12	21.00
Shenzhen	(R–1960, (1980), (2000)	0.03	–	–	0.24	7.01	–	–	–	12.24	–	10.63
Rio de Janeiro	(1960), (1980), (2000), (2010)	3.12	–	5.09	–	5.86	6.32	–	–	11.82	6.45	12.09
Tianjin	(1960), (1970), (1991), (2014)	3.22	–	–	4.28	7.50	–	–	–	11.26	12.78	15.47
Lima	(1960), (1981), (1993), (2014)	1.26	–	3.97	4.60	5.68	6.32	–	9.74	10.95	8.85	9.75
Paris	(1960), (1982), (1999), (2010)	2.85	4.82	2.19	8.51	2.13	9.64	2.24	10.46	10.87	2.24	12.34
London	(1960), (1980), (1996), (2001)	3.23	8.22	6.85	–	7.07	–	8.28	–	10.35	8.54	13.88
Bogotá D.C.	(1960), (1973), (2000), (2014)	1.12	–	2.84	2.86	–	6.42	–	7.78	9.52	7.88	9.80
Chicago	(1960), (1980), (2000), (2012)	3.55	6.22	3.01	7.87	2.90	9.16	2.71	–	9.19	2.70	9.55
Hong Kong	(1961), (1980), (2010), (2014)	0.63	0.67	–	–	6.71	–	7.24	–	7.28	7.23	–
St. Petersburg	(1960), (1981), (1999), (2012)	2.89	3.30	4.68	4.59	4.68	–	4.99	–	5.14	5.19	–

Sources: United Nations Demographic Yearbooks; Demographia 2016; and Wikipedia, R - data in references for Karachi and for Shenzhen.

[1] Data for the years 1960, 1980, 2000 and 2014 are not available for all metropolises, so the data from years close to these dates has been included. The actual year of data collection is included in this column.

Classifications of urban agglomerations

The development of metropolitan areas is accompanied by the development of theoretical concepts. Table 1.2 lists some of them in chronological order.

Like all phenomena, urban agglomerations are subject to description, measurements and classification. Earlier we described the world's 34 biggest urban agglomerations according to three demographic categories, i.e. the population of the agglomeration, the population of the proper city and the population density. The analysis showed the development of the population over a period of nearly 60 years. Further characterisation of urban agglomerations comprises structural models, their functions and the range of their spatial influence.

As far as the structure is concerned, we can distinguish a *monocentric agglomeration,* where one major centre or city proper dominates the entire metropolitan area. For example, London, Paris, New York, and Buenos Aires are monocentric agglomerations. On the other hand, there are *polycentric agglomerations* or *conurbations,* which are complexes of cities of similar sizes without a clearly identifiable complex of the city proper. The following complexes are examples: Rhine–Ruhr–Wupper in Germany, the Upper Silesian conurbation in Poland, Guangzhou–Foshan in China and Osaka–Kobe–Kyoto in Japan.

As far as the territorial range of the influence of metropolises is concerned, Markowski and Marszał (2006) distinguish the following types:

- *Global metropolises*: characterised by very strong concentration of decisions and international functions of worldwide range, e.g. London, Moscow, New York, Paris, Beijing, Tokyo; smaller metropolises, e.g. Berlin, Rome and Brussels. It is noteworthy that Doxiadis made a futuristic concept of a global

Table 1.2 Selected concepts concerning metropolises

Author	Description of concept
Pred (1975)	Formation of metropolises as centres controlling the international flow of capital and information.
Friedman (1986)	A metropolis as a global city that is a banking and trade centre.
Sass (1991)	A metropolis as a global city based on Friedman's hypothesis and its strategic role in the concentration of capital, trade, banking and industry.
Gras (1992)	Metropolises involve the type of economy characterised by intensive spatial links, characterised by high employment in wholesale and low employment in industry; they are trade centres and transport hubs that dominate vast regions.
Castells (1998)	Metropolises are dynamic centres of development, technology, culture and economy.
Smętkowski *et al.* (2008)	Metropolises can generate an innovative environment in consequence of coinciding economic, technical, technological, institutional and social relations.

Source: The author's compilation.

metropolis, which he named Ecumenopolis. According to the concept, the current trends of urbanisation and population growth will cause all urban areas, metropolises and megalopolises around the world to merge into one system and make one global city: Ecumenopolis.

- *Continental metropolises*: characterised by a strong concentration of international enterprises and institutions with international influence, e.g. Buenos Aires, Cairo, Chicago, Mexico City.
- *Regional metropolises*: characterised by poorly developed metropolitan services and international functions, e.g. capital cities such as Budapest, Lima, Montreal, Warsaw.
- *Local metropolises*: smaller than regional metropolises and also characterised by poorly developed metropolitan services and international functions, e.g. Hanover, Manaus, Novosibirsk, Perth, Wellington.

Metropolises have many functions affecting their inhabitants, metropolitan areas and more distant areas. They are important for the socioeconomic development of humankind. Ładysz (2009) distinguished the following functions of metropolises:

- administrative: there are agencies of the state government and the local government, which guarantee public security;
- economic: international and national cooperation, including the economic-industrial function, economic-commercial functions and economic-services function;
- financial: the banking and insurance sector, stock exchanges and many financial institutions are located there;
- tourist-related with the tourist values of the city proper and resources of the natural environment in the whole agglomeration (this book analyses this function in detail);
- political: there are diplomatic missions, public authorities and international institutions located there;
- educational: there is a network of universities, secondary schools and scientific research institutions developing the intellectual potential of the region,
- cultural: there is a concentration of publishing houses, radio and television stations, theatres, museums, film studios and artistic environment;
- informative: this function is strongly related with the political, cultural and scientific functions;
- transport: usually there is a well-developed transport hub and a system of railways, roads, airlines and sea lines.

Each metropolis usually combines many functions, whose financial value is estimated by adequate agencies. Each of them may have a dominant or supplementary character in a metropolis. This means that a particular metropolis is specialised and may have, for example, a tourist, industrial or financial character. Metro Industrial Specialisation, which was developed by Parilla *et al.* (2015), is a detailed classification of city specialisation based on the North American Industry

Classification System (NAICS). It distinguishes specialisations of metropolises, which are referred to as industries, where each industry is divided into categories – see Table 1.3.

Each metropolis develops. The study by Parilla *et al.* (2015, p. 23) proved that metropolises with industrial specialisations are characterised by the highest rate of development. The following specialisations are critical to the rate of development of metropolises (in descending order): commodities, utilities, trade and tourism, manufacturing, construction, transportation, business, financial and professional services. Smętkowski *et al.* (2008) distinguish between concentrated and deconcentrated development. The former refers to the situation when the dynamics of development of cities proper is greater than the dynamics of development of outer

Table 1.3 A ranking of the development of the world's largest metropolises by Global Monitor

Metro	Rank Economic performance 2013–2014	GDP per capita change 2013–2014	Employment change 2013–2014	GDP per capita $US
Istanbul	3	2.0	6.5	24867
Delhi	18	4.4	3.3	12747
London	26	2.5	3.6	57157
Kolkata (Calcutta)	32	4.7	2.5	4036
Jakarta	34	4.3	2.6	9984
Lima	48	2.9	2.9	16530
Mumbai (Bombay)	52	4.6	2.1	7005
Shenzhen	64	5.1	1.6	33731
Beijing (Peking)	67	4.7	1.6	23390
Guangzhou (Canton)-Foshan	77	4.9	1.4	24870
Cairo	82	0.7	3.0	7843
Bogotá, D.C.	88	3.2	1.8	17497
Shanghai	92	5.2	0.9	24065
Seoul-Incheon	105	2.7	1.7	34355
Manila	139	4.1	0.5	14222
Mexico City	147	1.6	1.4	19239
Los Angeles	148	0.1	2.0	65082
Tianjin	152	3.3	0.5	24224
Rio de Janeiro	162	−0.2	1.8	14176
New York	177	0.1	1.4	69915
Tokyo	201	0.7	0.9	43664
Chicago	203	0.7	0.8	58861
Moscow	218	0	0.9	45803
Hong Kong	242	1.2	0	57244
Osaka-Kobe	247	0.6	0.2	35902
Paris	260	0.3	0.2	57241
St Petersburg	261	−0.2	0.4	23361
Sao Paulo	284	−1.5	0	20650
Buenos Aires	286	−2.8	0	23606
Bangkok	300	−0.5	−1.7	19705

Source: Berube *et al.* (2015).

Table 1.4 Top ten largest Larger Urban Zones (LUZ) in Europe

No.	Metropolitan area	Population
1	London	11,917,000
2	Istanbul	11,154,928
3	Paris	11,089,124
4	Madrid	5,804,829
5	Ruhr Area	5,302,179
6	Berlin	4,971,331
7	Barcelona	4,233,638
8	Athens	4,013,368
9	Rome	3,457,690
10	Hamburg	3,134,620

Source: Eurostat 2014.

zones. The latter refers to the situation when the dynamics of development of outer zones exceeds the dynamics of development of cities proper.

The rate of development of a metropolis indicates the competitiveness of a particular area. The Brookings Institution monitors and compares growth patterns in 300 of the world's largest metropolises with two key economic indicators: annualised growth rate of real GDP per capita and annualised growth rate of employment (Parilla *et al.* 2015).

Table 1.4 shows a ranking of the development of the world's largest metropolises by Global Monitor; however, Dhaka, Karachi, Lagos and Teheran were not classified. It is noteworthy that, apart from London, the rate of development of richer metropolises, measured with the GDP per capita, is much slower than in poorer cities.

Metro regions

The European Union uses the term Larger Urban Zones (LUZ) for statistical purposes. The aim of Eurostat was to guarantee good data availability and therefore it adjusts the LUZ boundaries to administrative boundaries that approximate the functional urban region. Larger Urban Zones (LUZ) have populations of at least 500,000. The current list of LUZ contains 127 European locations, ranging from the London LUZ with a population of 11.9 million to the Malatya LUZ (Turkey). Table 1.5 shows a list of the top ten largest metropolitan areas in Europe.

The OECD in collaboration with Eurostat and Directorate-General for Regional and Urban Policy (DG Regio) has developed a harmonised definition of urban areas. It is useful for the identification of metropolitan areas that are overcoming limitations linked to administrative boundaries. Three metro regions were identified in the European Union (EU) according to the NUTS-3-based typology. The EU metro regions cover all metro regions with at least 250,000 inhabitants. The typology distinguishes three types of metro regions: capital city regions;

second-tier metro regions and smaller metro regions. The map below shows the location of all EU metro regions.

Likewise, in 2013 the United States defined 1,098 statistical areas comprising 169 Combined Statistical Areas (CSA), 388 Metropolitan Statistical Areas (MSA) and 541 Micropolitan Statistical Areas.

The consequences of exurbanisation

Urban sprawl and urban agglomeration are common phenomena in the world undergoing urbanisation. There are numerous causes accelerating this process, especially:

- growing population of cities; in consequence, richer people search for locations with better quality of life;
- growing family income; richer people are characterised by strong consumer preferences, they want to have bigger houses with more rooms, bedrooms, bathrooms, larger balconies and a larger area of the plot for lawns and gardens;
- lower prices of land and buildings in rural areas;
- better infrastructure of new estates in suburban areas;
- lower public fees.

The consequences of urban sprawl are widely discussed by politicians, scientists and mostly by ordinary residents of suburban estates. Exurbanisation is held responsible for a wide range of positive and negative effects. It is difficult to determine the profits and losses because one effect is sometimes considered positive and sometimes negative. The following advantages of urban sprawl are emphasised:

- improved living standard and quality of life of inhabitants moving to suburban areas;
- short-term economic and employment boom resulting from the construction of new buildings;
- comprehensive development of communal infrastructure (roads, public transport, water, gas, electricity, sewage system, Internet, etc.);
- creation of new jobs to manage new homes and surrounding areas, e.g. the establishment and management of lawns and home gardens and a greater demand for communal services.

Urban sprawl also involves many negative consequences, which influence individuals, local communities and the natural environment:

- Suburban inhabitants' longer and more frequent car trips have many negative consequences, e.g.;
- increased air pollution, which may cause smog and health problems;
- higher risk of overweight in metropolitan inhabitants. It has been observed

that suburban inhabitants are less physically active, preferring to drive rather than walk or cycle over short distances. Metropolitan areas eliminate walking distances so that it is necessary to drive to the shop, school, commune council, church and other places, because they are too far to walk to. This decreased level of physical activity inevitably leads to overweight and health problems, such as heart diseases, hypertension and diabetes.

- Overconsumption of water. More water is consumed in metropolitan than in urban areas due to watering of gardens and green spaces. Some commune councils forbid watering during dry periods of the year when there is shortage of water.
- Utilisation of greater amounts of organic matter. Intensive fertilisation and watering causes a high increase in organic matter, but there is no space to utilise this organic matter in gardens and lawns. Metropolitan inhabitants do not breed ruminants so organic matter needs to be systematically removed from settlements. The problem of utilisation is handled by special enterprises.
- Unique wildlife habitats, which are common in rural areas, are endangered (see Sznajder, Chapter 3).
- Urban sprawl causes serious or even disastrous socioeconomic consequences for city centres and urban areas because people moving out of the city pay taxes in their new places of residence while usually the poorest and oldest people stay in cities. In consequence, city centres become depopulated, geriatric, pauperised and racially segregated. The consequences of urban sprawl in European cities are different and less drastic than in American cities. In both cases city centres definitely become depopulated. However, in Europe there are city centre revitalisation programmes and old towns become lively again. Tourist traffic favours revitalisation. Apart from a few exceptions, the centres of cities in the New World are not tourist centres. Additionally, in the US urban sprawl causes economic disparity resulting in racial segregation.

The influence of urban sprawl on increasing wealth of suburban farmers

Since time immemorial rural inhabitants have been poorer than the urban population because they have been employed almost exclusively in agriculture and many agricultural products had no market value. Different economic concepts have been implemented to eliminate the glaring disparity in the income of rural and urban inhabitants. The concept of multifunctional rural development, which consists in diversification of employment (especially outside agriculture), is an effective method reducing this disparity.

The neighbourhood of big cities, which grew into metropolises, and urban sprawl have significantly influenced the economic development of farms situated in suburban areas. The economic development of these farms is the result of market mechanisms caused by urban drift rather than the concept of multifunctional rural development, promoted by politicians. As railways began to develop in the second half of the nineteenth century, many men from suburban areas started commuting to work in cities, leaving their households to women, children and elderly people. In this way agricultural households in metropolitan areas became economically stronger, because they gained additional income from employment in the city. Additional funds could be invested in non-agricultural activities. Women also searched for employment outside agriculture. As the automotive industry developed, more households were characterised by dual employment and now former farmers commute to work from increasingly distant places.

Farmers from suburban areas noticed that by dividing farmland into building plots and selling them they can gain more economic profit than by cultivating this land. There is an increasing offer of new building plots in former agricultural areas. In many countries the sales of plots is regulated by law and controlled by government institutions to prevent the devastation of farmland and natural landscape. The sales of farmland by farmers releases labour resources and creates the need for new employment opportunities in the metropolis and metropolitan areas. Former farmers are employed in transport, trade and complex services provided to new residents of suburban estates.

Rural tourism, agritourism, culinary tourism, ecotourism and nature tourism provide chances for employment.

The population density in suburban areas is lower than in typically urban areas. There are more people employed in agriculture and there are longer distances between buildings. There are also different economic, demographic and social phenomena than in typically rural areas.

Metropolitan commuter belt tourism

Inhabitants of metropolitan areas differ in their financial status. Contemporary lifestyles include tourism, regardless of one's financial status. Wealthy inhabitants of urban agglomerations show their demand not only for long-term holiday tourism lasting several weeks but also for short-term tourism during weekends, public holidays or even for one day. This tourism has recreational and educational character, depends on the weather and season of the year. It uses rich resources of animate and inanimate nature in metropolitan areas, such as mountains, lakes, rivers and forests, as well as anthropogenic attractions, which can be seen not far from one's place of residence. Likewise, less wealthy and even completely poor inhabitants hope for tourism close to their homes. Managements of urban agglomerations support the concepts of school trips to the countryside and social farms for disabled and elderly people in submetropolitan areas. The travelling time to the tourist destination is very important. As far as the demand for this type of tourism is concerned, the metropolitan commuter belt is a reasonable area of penetration. This type of tourism can be called *suburban tourism* for short, or with a full name – *nature-based tourism in metropolitan areas*, or with another stylish and marketing name – *(Metropolitan) Commuter Belt Tourism*. There are considerable differences between urban tourism and metropolitan commuter belt tourism, at least in three aspects: segments of tourists, purposes and lengths of visits. Urban tourism refers to the most important historical, religious, sports and business sites, which are usually located in the centres of cities. Metropolitan commuter belt tourism usually refers to natural resources located beyond the city centre. Urban tourism is usually typical of tourists arriving from other cities and regions of the same country or from abroad. Metropolitan commuter belt tourism is practised by tourists from a particular metropolis. Urban tourism treats the city centre as an element of a longer tourist trip, whereas metropolitan commuter belt tourism usually refers to a short weekend trip (see Królik 2015). Commuter belt tourism covers everything that comprises rural tourism, agritourism, forestry tourism, nature tourism and even ecotourism.

The development of rural tourism, agritourism and the related branches of ecotourism, nature tourism and culinary tourism are chances both for traditional city proper inhabitants and for new populations migrating to metropolitan areas. On the one hand, they can use the natural resources of metropolitan areas, which have not been exploited by the tourist industry so far. On the other hand, there are residential buildings and farm outbuildings. Managements of submetroplitan communes and towns attract tourists to a particular area by promoting tourism in their own metropolitan areas. Urban sprawl facilitates the activation of dormant local markets not only for rural tourism and agritourism. The development of these types of tourism is a chance for farmers and other inhabitants of submetropolitan areas to develop economically because they create new, better-paid jobs.

The development of rural tourism and agritourism in the metropolitan commuter belt is financed from different sources. First, it is financed from 'native' farmers' own funds, which they retained as a result of increase in wealth caused by urban sprawl, for example, Amigówka farm in the Kraków metropolitan area (described by Kania and Bogusz in Chapter 20). Second, the development is financed from external sources, where foreign capital, which has not been related with agriculture, is invested in rural tourism or agritourism, for example, Otulina farm (see Tyran, Chapter 15).

The description and analysis of the causes and effects of the sprawl of cities and urban agglomerations into submetropolitan areas give grounds to question the hypothesis concerning the conflict between the need for nature conservation and the inevitable human activity. There is widespread recognition of the antianthropogenic hypothesis that questions the extreme ecological thesis saying that all human activity is by nature harmful to the natural environment. Moreover, scepticism is intensified due to the spreading view that urban sprawl degrades submetropolitan inhabitants' traditional lifestyles. Not negating the challenges faced by tourism in submetropolitan areas due to urban sprawl, it is relatively easy to prove the limited significance of this hypothesis. It is contradicted by the fact that tourist traffic constantly attracts millions of visitors who want to admire masterpieces of art created by humans, such as old towns, museums and temples; and archaic, ancient and medieval buildings, despite the fact that, in the past, they caused disorder to the natural environment. The Błędów Desert situated in the Silesian agglomeration in Poland is an interesting case of people's illogical approach to the natural habitat (see Chapter 3). What used to be regarded as an ecologically degraded area (covered with post-mining sands), is now, after spontaneous afforestation, considered to be loss of natural habitat. However, it is true that at present human activity is very aggressive towards the natural environment.

Hundreds of satellite estates built around metropolitan centres all over the world are such uninteresting architectural clichés that they will never attract tourist traffic. What is more, by entering naturally attractive places these estates reduce areas with tourist potential.

The real-life examples of the development of tourism in metropolitan areas given in this book by Dzioban (Chapter 14), Wiatrak (Chapter 17), Mikrut (Chapter 13), Tyran (Chapter 15) and other authors show metropolitan areas as places of significant and increasing tourist activity, because they are abundant in natural values which have not been used, or have been poorly used, for tourism purposes. All over the world there are enormous unused tourism resources, which can be triggered only by urban sprawl.

For example, in the last 60 years the Ślęża Massif (711 m above mean sea level), situated about 20 km south of the metropolitan city of Wrocław, has become not only an area of intensive settlement but also a destination of mass weekend tourism as a result of the development of car transport. The case of Ślęża is not an exception and it shows that metropolitan areas have considerable tourist resources, which are becoming places of intensive investments in tourism and recreation. Hiking, cycling, horse riding and canoeing routes are being designed and created. New, styled structures are being built to be used as watchtowers, restaurants and shelters.

Metropolitan areas are well suited for some forms of short-term tourism, such as weekend tourism, public holiday tourism, hiking and cycling tourism. The idea of this type of tourism is well defined with a colloquial term: *excursion tourism*.

There are different segments of tourists who are interested in metropolitan tourism. The main segment consists of people who live in the areas surrounding an interesting natural area, which has become a destination of excursions made by new settlers. Another segment consists of the inhabitants of more distant places but within the same metropolitan area. There is also a small segment of other tourists living further away in the particular country and a smaller segment of foreign tourists. This fact shows that urban sprawl activates tourism among the inhabitants of a particular metropolis. This dependence is confirmed by the results of the study by Dzioban, described in Chapter 14.

To sum up, there are no grounds to accept the thesis that urban sprawl does not favour the development of tourism in metropolitan areas, but there are premises that could persuade us to accept the opposite hypothesis. The dual tourist segmentation of metropolitan inhabitants is also justified. On the one hand are the inhabitants who are not active tourists and whose lifestyle is dangerous to their health, while on the other are the inhabitants who have migrated to new areas and use nearby tourist attractions.

Note

1 According to Demographia 2016. However, in Wikipedia, the Metropolitan Statistical Area is shown as 17,405 km², while the Combined Statistical Area area is 34,493 km² and New York itself is 748 km².

References

Caves, R. W. (2005). Entry: Ecumenopolis. In *Encyclopaedia of the City*. Routledge, London: p. 143.

Connelly, R. (2016). *Earth's New Lightning Capital Revealed*. https://www.nasa.gov/centers/marshall/news/news/releases/2016/earths-new-lightning-capital-revealed.html [Retrieved 3 May 2016]

Cox, W. (2016). *The Evolving Urban Form: Shenzhen*. New Geography. http://www.newgeography.com/content/004904-chinas-shifting-population-growth-patterns [Retrieved 30 April 2016]

Demographia. (2016). *Demographia World Urban Areas: Built-Up Urban Areas or World Agglomerations. 12th annual edition*. http://www.demographia.com/db-worldua.pdf [Retrieved 1 May 2016]

Demographics of Karachi. (n.d.). https://en.wikipedia.org/wiki/Demographics_of_Karachi [Retrieved 26 April 2016]

Duché, G. (2010). Metropolizacja, niezrównoważony wzrost a model globalnej akumulacji. Korzyści i koszty [w:] Brzeziński C. (ed.): Metropolia i jej region. *Acta Univeritatis Lodziensis, Folia Oeconomia*, Wydawnictwo Uniwersytetu Łódzkiego, Łódź.

ESPON. (European Observation Network for Territorial Development and Cohesion). (2014). *Western Europe: Hidden Potential of Small and Medium Sized Towns*. http://www.rtpi.org.uk/media/1093623/Western%20Europe%20briefing_TOWN.pdf [Retrieved 27 December 2014]

Eurostat. (2016). *Regions and Cities Glossary*. http://ec.europa.eu/eurostat/statistics-explained/index.php/Category:Regions_and_cities_glossary [Retrieved 14 April 2016]

Eurostat. (2014). European Cities: Spatial Dimension. http://ec.europa.eu/eurostat/statistics-explained/index.php/European_cities_-_spatial_dimension [Retrieved 15 May 2016]

Growth of Mumbai. (n.d.). https://en.wikipedia.org/wiki/Growth_of_Mumbai [Retrieved 22 April 2016]

Kasper, C., Helten, F., Crozet, N., Moustanjidi, Y., Giseke, U., Bock, G., Mdafi, M., Brandt, J. & Mansour, M. (2015). Urban-rural linkages and interacting spheres. In Giseke U. *Urban Agriculture for Growing City Regions*. Routledge, London.

Królik M. (2015). *Legal, Economic and Social Aspects of Urban Tourism in Poznań*. Manuscript of MSA thesis. Poznań University of Life Sciences, Department of Law and Management, Poznań.

Ładysz, I. (2009). *Konkurencyjność obszarów metropolitalnych w Polsce na przykładzie wrocławskiego obszaru metropolitalnego*. Publisher: Wydawnictwo CeDeWu, Warszawa.

Markowski, T. & Marszał, T. (2006). *Metropolie. Obszary metropolitalne. Metropolizacja,. Problemy i pojęcia podstawowe*. Publisher: Polska Akademia Nauk Komitet Przestrzennego Zagospodarowania Kraju, Warszawa.

New York metropolitan area. (n.d.). https://en.wikipedia.org/wiki/New_York_metropolitan_area [Retrieved 2 May 2016]

OECD. (2013). Definition of Functional Urban Areas (FUA) for OECD Functional Database. https://www.oecd.org/gov/regional-policy/Definition-of-Functional-Urban-Areas-for-the-OECD-metropolitan-database.pdf [Retrieved 18 January 2016]

Pacholsky, J. (2000). The Ecological Footprint of Berlin (Germany) for the Year 2000. Masters thesis, Environmental Management, Stirling University, Scotland. https://www.gdrc.org/uem/footprints/berlin-eco_footprint.doc [Retrieved 7 February 2016]

Parilla J., Trujillo J. L., Berube, A. & Ran T. (2015). *Global Metro Monitor 2014. An Uncertain Recovery*. The Brookings Institution, Washington, DC.

Sassen, S. (1991). *The Global City*. Princeton University Press, New York.

Sim, S., & Mesev, V. (2011). Measuring Urban Sprawl and Compactness: Case Study Orlando, USA. *Proceedings of the 25th International Cartographic Conference of International Cartographic Association* CO-437.

Smętkowski, M., Jałowiecki, B. & Gorzelak, G. (2008). *Obszary metropolitarne w Polsce: problemy rozwojowe i delimitacja*. Publisher EUROREG: Centrum Europejskich Studiów Regionalnych i Lokalnych Uniwersytet Warszawski Raporty i Analizy EUROREG 1/2009, Warszawa. http://www.euroreg.uw.edu.pl/dane/web_euroreg_publications_files/602/obszary_metropolitalne_w_polsce_problemy_rozwojowe_i_delimitacja.pdf

Szukalski, P. (2014). Depopulacja dużych miast w Polsce, *Demografia i Gerontologia Społeczna – Biuletyn Informacyjny*, No. 7. Publisher: Uniwersytet Łódzki, Łódź, pp. 1–5.

United Nations. (1960). *Demographic Yearbook 1960*. http://unstats.un.org/unsd/demographic/products/dyb/dybsets/1960%20DYB.pdf [Retrieved 15 February 2016]

United Nations. (1982). *Demographic Yearbook 1980*. http://unstats.un.org/unsd/demographic/products/dyb/dybsets/1980%20DYB.pdf [Retrieved 15 February 2016]

United Nations. (2002). *Demographic Yearbook 2000*. http://unstats.un.org/unsd/demographic/products/dyb/dybsets/2000%20DYB.pdf [Retrieved 15 February 2016]

United Nations. (2015). *Demographic Yearbook 2014*. http://unstats.un.org/unsd/demographic/products/dyb/dybsets/2014.pdf [Retrieved 15 February 2016]

Urban Footprint. (2012). Technical Summary. Model Version 1.0. Calthorpe Associates, Berkeley CA. http://www.scag.ca.gov/Documents/UrbanFootprintTechnicalSummary.pdf [Retrieved 30 April 2016]

2 Trends and conditions of the development of submetropolitan tourism

Michał Gazdecki and Michał Jacenty Sznajder

Metropolitan Commuter Belt Tourism: a new concept and old practice

The view of submetropolitan areas as perfect places for tourism is as much a new concept as the process of metropolisation is a new phenomenon. However, it is possible to prove that this concept is a mere continuation of the tradition of excursions beyond the city limits. It started due to the development of railways and dates back to the late nineteenth century. However, it is a new concept as it indicates the potential natural and anthropogenic resources for the development of tourism in submetropolitan areas, and shows socioeconomic conditions and perspectives for the development of this market. Showing the possibilities to use metropolitan and submetropolitan areas to develop rural tourism and agritourism is a new concept (Sznajder *et al.* 2009, p. 279).

We encounter a fundamental semantic problem – what to call tourism around metropolises. There are a few equivalent options, e.g. suburban tourism, submetropolitan tourism or metropolitan commuter belt tourism. Finally there is a funny and provocative name, at least in Polish, *wattle fence tourism*. The first original proposal which appeared during work on this monograph was *Rural tourism and agritourism in metropolitan areas*, but it was too limited to render the rich offer of natural tourism resources in submetropolitan areas. The second proposal extended the scope of the term, *Nature-based tourism in metropolitan areas*. As the work on the monograph progressed and there were more contributions, the concept was rethought and the term *Metropolitan commuter belt tourism* was found to best reflect the contents of the book. Probably it is also better for marketing purposes.

The global importance of the metropolis was increasing along with the development of humanity. Over the years, cities were developing and they became important economic, educational, cultural and political centres. They had various functions, such as educational, natural and health care functions as well as political, industrial, production and service centres. This multifunctional character of urban centres made them more and more attractive places to live, work or run a business. It caused the inflow of new inhabitants and stimulated further development of urban centres. Thus, we can talk of a self-propelling mechanism – the multitude of functions of urban centres increases their attractiveness to new inhabitants and, in consequence, stimulates their further development. All over the world we can observe the processes of development of powerful urban centres, which are economic, political and cultural centres. Urban sprawl has increasing influence on the neighbouring territories and it gradually transforms them into metropolitan areas. The development of metropolitan areas takes place as a result of increasing territorial range and population. The multidirectional development of metropolitan areas means that, in practice, an inhabitant may spend all their life in the metropolis. Therefore, it is important for the big city to fulfil its tourism functions and provide tourism products.

Premises for the development of tourism in metropolitan areas

The analysis of the premises for the development of tourism in metropolitan areas points to two groups of factors. The first includes the factors which concern potential tourists, the inhabitants of a metropolitan area, and the other includes the factors placed within a metropolitan area (see Figure 2.1).

Need of contact with nature

First, it is necessary to discuss needs so as to characterise the aforementioned premises. The needs theory is well described in economic, psychological and social sciences. Abraham Maslow's needs theory, which is generally accepted, divides all human-specific needs into two groups: basic needs and higher-order needs. Basic needs are related to survival, whereas higher-order needs influence an individual's achievement of quality of life. According to Maslow, basic needs

Figure 2.1 Premises for the development of tourism in metropolitan areas.

Source: The authors' compilation.

include physiological and safety needs. Physiological needs are the simplest, most common and identical for everybody, in fact, for nearly all animal organisms because they guarantee biological survival. Safety needs may be associated with the possibility to find shelter. However, at present they are mostly manifested by the search for financial safety, employment, home, family, which provides support, or simply, the search for stability in life. The satisfaction of basic needs guarantees the possibility of full participation in social life and proper personal development.

It is necessary to remember that basic needs should not be identified only with biological survival. This interpretation would considerably narrow perception and would be inadequate in view of the current knowledge of the human. Basic needs also include those that developed as a result of human evolution and can be defined as natural needs. The development and evolution of humankind was based on nature so we can say that contact with nature is a natural and basic need and it is specific to all people. This is a key statement for these considerations. Consequently, the need for contact with nature is universal (it applies to all people, though it may have different intensity) and satisfying the need has considerable influence on the quality of one's life. The fact that inhabitants of metropolises strongly feel this need is proved by the increasing care of existing green areas, putting plants in the places which used to be undeveloped (e.g. on the roofs of buildings), using plants to develop space in newly constructed office buildings, and such like. There is an increasing popularity of city farms, where food is produced in an urban area (see, e.g. Hackney City Farm 2011, or City Farm [n.d.]), community gardens or projects like Jadalnia Warszawa, 'Warsaw Canteen', where people look for edible plants growing in the city.

Financial resources

It is necessary to have appropriate resources in the household budget for tourism activities. Two aspects need to be considered: income and expenses in the household. As metropolises are strong economic centres, they make possible higher income than in other areas. This is shown in Table 2.1, which compares the gross national income per capita in the world's 20 richest and 20 poorest metropolises. The income is compared with the mean gross income per capita in the country where the metropolis is located. In most of the metropolitan areas listed in Table 2.1 the gross income per capita is greater than the gross national income. The possibility of earning a higher income can be treated as a specific rent for the inhabitants of the metropolitan area, because of its multifunctional character, or it can be treated as a compensation for the inconvenience caused by living in the metropolis. Everyday reports reveal one more important issue – there are significant centres of poverty in metropolitan areas. It particularly applies to less economically developed regions of the world. However, poverty is not the exclusive domain of these regions. For example, according to data published by the Census Bureau in 2010, in 10 metropolises with the highest level of poverty the percentage of people living in poverty ranged from 21 per cent to 36 per cent

Table 2.1 Comparison of gross national income per capita in metropolitan areas and the country where they are located, of the world's 20 richest and 20 poorest metropolises

Position in ranking	Region	Country	Metro Area	National GDP per capita (USD)	Metro Area GDP per capita (USD)	Ratio between GDP of Metro area and GDP of Country
1	North America	United States	Hartford	49,854.52	75,086.00	1.51
2	Western Europe	Norway	Oslo	99,091.09	74,057.00	0.75
3	North America	United States	San Jose	49,854.52	68,141.00	1.37
4	Middle East and Africa	United Arab Emirates	Abu Dhabi	39,057.84	63,859.00	1.63
5	North America	United States	Bridgeport	49,854.52	63,555.00	1.27
6	Western Europe	Switzerland	Zurich	83,270.24	63,236.00	0.76
7	North America	United States	Washington	49,854.52	62,943.00	1.26
8	Western Europe	Sweden	Stockholm	56,724.36	61,458.00	1.08
9	North America	United States	Boston	49,854.52	60,074.00	1.20
10	North America	United States	San Francisco	49,854.52	58,783.00	1.18
190	Latin America	Peru	Lima	5,759.40	6,961.00	1.21
191	Latin America	Colombia	Bogota	7,124.55	6,950.00	0.98
192	Developing Asia-Pacific	China	Xi'an	5,447.31	4,232.00	0.78
193	Developing Asia-Pacific	Philippines	Manila	2,357.57	4,181.00	1.77
194	Developing Asia-Pacific	Indonesia	Jakarta	3,469.75	3,468.00	1.00
195	Middle East and Africa	Morocco	Casablanca	3,044.11	3,450.00	1.13
196	Developing Asia-Pacific	China	Chongqing	5,447.31	2,819.00	0.52
197	Developing Asia-Pacific	Sri Lanka	Colombo	2,835.69	2,697.00	0.95
198	Middle East and Africa	Egypt, Arab Rep.	Alexandria	2,972.58	2,248.00	0.76
199	Developing Asia-Pacific	India	Mumbai	1,539.61	1,990.00	1.29
200	Middle East and Africa	Egypt, Arab Rep.	Cairo	2,972.58	1,989.00	0.67

Source: Berube et al. 2012. World Bank national accounts data and OECD National Accounts data files.

(Kurtzleban & Writer 2011). On the other hand, the average poverty index for the inhabitants of metropolitan areas in the United States was 14.2 per cent (as of 2012: DeNavas-Walt *et al.* 2013).

It is not only the amount of income gained but also the structure of the budget that is important. It is particularly important to analyse the share of expenses set aside for necessities and the amount available for discretionary spending, that is, the portion of income spent on higher-order needs, including tourism activity. This amount increases relatively as the amount of income increases.

Time resources

Time is a very important resource in households. Its significance is emphasised by the new home economics proposed by Becker (1965). When making decisions about the use of time resources, each person has to specify how much time will be spent working and how much will be spent as free time. Consumers who try to achieve higher income will limit their free time resources by increasing their work hours. Thus, free time resources are related to income earned. However, it is necessary to remember that this assumption has a wide range of limitations. It is possible to increase income without increasing working hours, for example, by finding a better-paid job. However, there are also situations where there are limited possibilities to do extra work to increase income.

We can identify two groups of people in metropolitan areas. The first group includes the people for whom insufficient financial resources are the chief factor limiting their access to nature tourism. The other group includes the people with limited free time. Nature tourism within the metropolitan area may be an attractive proposal for both groups. For the first group nature tourism may generate lower costs for the consumer than in outbound tourism. This is due to lower travel costs (short distances to travel, the possible use of public transport) and lower prices for tourism products. For the other group it may be convenient that access to nature tourism does not require much time, due to the short travelling time and the composition of the tourism product which enables consumption in a relatively short time.

Natural resources in metropolitan areas

The discussion of factors affecting the development of nature tourism in metropolitan areas should start with the fact that natural resources are diversified. The resources can be divided into two groups: natural areas and areas that were developed as a result of human activity (anthropogenic areas). The first includes forests, natural lakes, rivers, meadows, marshlands, and such like. The resources of the other group make the city's so called natural system – a specified part of the city with specific natural functions, such as climatic (e.g. spas), hydrological and biological, and with functions which are not related to nature, for example, tourism, relaxation, leisure and health. All the elements of natural resources in cities may be a good reason for tourism and recreational activities. When the resources are appropriately managed, they can be used to create various tourism products.

Table 2.2 Elements of natural resources in metropolitan areas

Category	Subcategory	Examples
Green space	Arranged greenery	Parks, roadside greenery, greens
	Wild greenery	Forests, natural meadows
Water areas	Flowing waters	Rivers, streams, canals
	Stagnant waters	Seas, lakes, dam reservoirs, ponds
	Wetland	Swamps, peat lands

Source: The authors' compilation.

Progressing urbanisation

It is a fact that urbanisation is progressing on a global scale. The World Urbanization Prospects 2014, issued by the UN, lists the following items as global urbanisation aspects and trends:

- Urban dwellers outnumber the inhabitants of non-urbanised areas. The phenomenon has a growing tendency; according to forecasts, 66 per cent of the population will live in cities by 2050.
- The increase in the urban population is much faster than the increase in the rural population. According to UN forecasts, by 2050 the rural population will have decreased slowly.
- We can observe continuous urban development. Globally the development of cities is concentrated in less economically developed regions, but is very fast: African and Asian cities with a population up to one million are the most rapidly developing metropolises. (United Nations 2014)

It is inevitable that urbanisation will be grow in the next 50 years. This increasing metropolitan population will lead to an increase in the number of potential tourists who might be interested in nature tourism.

Agritourism approaching metropolitan areas

One of the subcategories of nature tourism is tourism combined with the observation of or participation in food production or processing. It may be treated as an extension of agritourism and in this sense agritourism is more and more often present in metropolitan areas. This situation is favoured by many people's interest in food production methods and the increasing activity leading to the creation of agritourism products. It is very easy to find examples of this type of tourism, such as demonstration farms, theme parks, processing plants offering sightseeing tours and education about the production process. In addition, in metropolitan areas there are numerous entities related to the food economy that have not developed their tourism activity yet, for example, food processing plants, fishing farms, horticultural farms, vineyards and distilleries. Each of these entities is a potential tourism attraction to people interested in traditional and modern methods of food production or processing.

Recipients of submetropolitan tourism

According to the marketing approach, the first step to preparing a product offer is to clearly identify the clients, their needs, wishes and demographic characteristics. Different types of segmentations are the most advanced form of client analysis. Depending on the assumed criteria, we can identify behavioural-demographic segmentations, which are based on the analysis of behaviours and easily registered demographic features, and segmentations based on the analysis of purchase motives and psychographic segmentations, which include consumers' needs and attitudes to specific objects such as brands, products and enterprises.

The preparation of client segmentation involves a quantitative survey conducted on large samples. Such surveys can be expensive and may be a limiting factor for many enterprises, especially smaller ones who will have smaller marketing budgets. For this reason, it is reasonable to seek alternative tourism classification systems, based on the knowledge gained. One such approach may be the classification of tourism clients of nature tourism, based on the theory of needs, specifically the classification of needs according to Maslow.

It is possible to allocate specific needs related to nature tourism to each category of needs proposed by Maslow (Figure 2.2). Contact with nature is a basic necessity. The need to escape from the city can be categorised as a safety need. Affiliation needs will be manifested by the willingness to participate in tourism traffic, to belong to a group of people practising tourism and to spending time with the family. On the basis of Maslow's theory of needs we can postulate the urgency

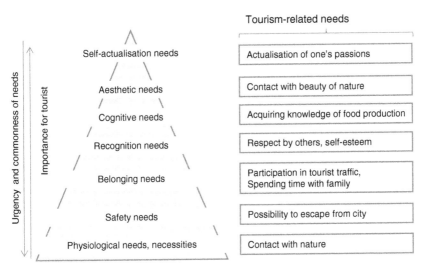

Figure 2.2 Maslow's pyramid of needs vs tourist need.

Source: The authors' compilation.

and commonness of these needs and their importance for tourists. The lower the needs are positioned in the pyramid, the more common and the more urgent they are for tourists. Alternatively, the higher a particular need is positioned in the pyramid, the more important it is in the tourist's subjective opinion. This means that among all the needs related to nature tourism there are the needs that are common to most tourists, but not very important to them. Conversely, there is a significant number of diverse, strongly individualised needs that tourists consider to be important.

We can propose the following classification of tourists on the basis of tourism-related needs (Figure 2.3). Starting at the bottom of the pyramid, we can talk about a mass tourist, who wants to satisfy their need of contact with nature. Another group of tourists consists of self-oriented people, who seek an opportunity to escape from the city. The next group includes people seeking contact with other people. They look not only for contact with nature but also for participation in a group, such as their family, peers or a group of people with similar interests. We can distinguish challenge-seeking tourists on the basis of the need for recognition and respect from other people. The people for whom tourism is mainly a way to acquire and broaden their knowledge of different issues (e.g. the tradition and culture in the region) can be classified as information-seeking tourists.

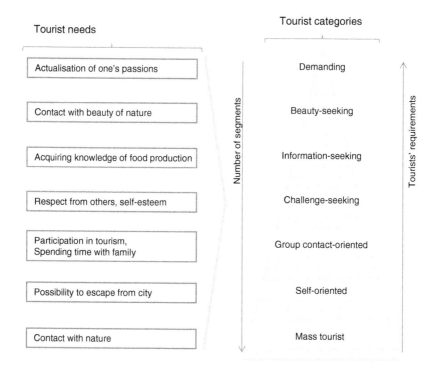

Figure 2.3   Tourist needs vs tourist categories.

Source: The authors' compilation.

The willingness to experience beauty and develop aesthetic needs are the main motives of tourism activity in the next category of tourists. On top of the pyramid are the most demanding tourists, people oriented towards self-actualisation, which may be manifested in various ways, such as the willingness to experience things that might be unavailable to most people.

The knowledge of the properties of the needs (especially their commonness, satisfaction urgency and importance for the tourist) enables initial characterisation of the identified groups of tourists. We can assume that the group seeking contact with nature is the largest among consumers of nature tourism. At the same time these are the least demanding tourists as the need for contact with nature is positioned among basic needs. Satisfying this need involves the consumption of relatively simple tourism products. We can reach more demanding groups of tourists by moving gradually to the top of the pyramid. These tourists are less numerous, but include people with higher demands who are looking for complex products.

These considerations may be enriched with the price aspect. Tourists' lower demands and less complex products result in lower product prices. As tourists' demands increase, we can expect their price sensitivity to decrease, which means they are ready to pay higher prices for more complex tourism products. This point has important implications for the marketing strategies of tourism enterprises, which have to make a decision whether to implement strategies to provide complex, expensive products. We should expect lower quantitative demand, which will provide the possibility for higher turnover due to higher prices. Another option is to concentrate on simpler products sold at lower prices, but these will generate considerable turnover due to the large number of tourists they attract.

Summary

Progressing urbanisation involves a wide range of consequences, both for the areas where it occurs and for the inhabitants of these areas. One of the consequences is the disturbed relationship between people and nature. Apart from the negative consequences of this situation, we consider it to be the key premise for the development of a new form of tourism in metropolitan areas, that is commuter belt tourism, with nature tourism being its integral part. The widespread character of the issue may result in a wide range of positive consequences for the inhabitants of metropolitan areas, entrepreneurs and local governments (see Table 2.3). These consequences include new employment opportunities, new sources of income for entrepreneurs, improved quality of life and the use of information about nature tourism for promotional purposes.

The development of metropolitan commuter belt tourism (both in the supply aspect – development of the offer, and in the demand aspect – tourists' activity) should be supported by the engagement of territorial governments. Facilitations for entrepreneurs and promotion of tourism activity among the inhabitants might be suggested as forms of support.

Table 2.3 Possible benefits from the development of commuter belt tourism in submetropolitan areas

Beneficiaries	Tangible benefits	Intangible benefits
Submetropolitan area inhabitants	Employment opportunity	Improved quality of life and satisfaction
		Improved health
		Cognitive benefits
Local authorities	Multiplier effect: increased income for local authorities	Possibility to use for promotional purposes
Enterprises	New sources of income	Possibility of cooperation with other entities

Source: The authors' compilation.

References

Becker, G. A. (1965). Theory of the allocation of time. *The Economic Journal*, 75(299), 493–517, pp. 493–517.

Berube, A., Nadeau, C. A., & Istrate, E. (2012). *Global MetroMonitor 2011: Volatility, Growth, and Recovery*. Brookings Institution, Washington, DC.

City Farm. (n.d.). http://www.cityfarmchicago.org/ [Retrieved 22 January 2016]

DeNavas-Walt, C., Proctor, B. D. & Smith J. C. (2013). Income, Poverty, and Health Insurance Coverage in the United States: 2012. US Department of Commerce & US Census Bureau. Income, Poverty, and Health Insurance Coverage in the United States [Retrieved 14 January 2016]

Global Metro Monitor Volatility, Growth, and Recovery 2011, The Brookings Institution, Metropolitan Policy Program 2012. World Bank national accounts data and OECD National Accounts data files.

Hackney City Farm. (2011). http://hackneycityfarm.co.uk [Retrieved 18 January 2016]

Jadalnia Warszawa (Warsaw Canteen). (2012). PIXXE: Projects Involving the Experimental Exploration of the Environment. http://pixxe.org/?page_id=79 [Retrieved 15 January 2016]

Kurtzleban, D. & Writer S. (2011, Oct. 7). 10 Metro Areas with the Highest Poverty Levels. *US News*. http://www.usnews.com/news/slideshows/10-metro-areas-with-the-highest-poverty-levels/1 [Retrieved 18 January 2016]

Sznajder, M., Przezbórska, L. & Scrimgeour, F. (2009). *Agritourism*. CAB International, Wallinford, UK.

United Nations (2014). *World Urbanization Prospects, the 2014 Revision*. Population Division, Department of Economic and Social Affairs, United Nation, pp. 1–27. [Retrieved 15 January 2016]

3 Case study

The Submetropolitan Błędów Desert, an ambivalent approach to devastation of the natural environment

Michał Jacenty Sznajder

The geographical area known as the Błędów Desert is situated about 40 km north-east of Katowice, the Silesian Metropolitan Area, which is the largest metropolitan complex in Poland. The desert is a particularly interesting example of geographical development and an ambivalent example of what is interpreted as ecological devastation. The landscape of this space was constantly changing. What used to be regarded as evident ecological devastation has, after several years, began to be recognised as an interesting and unique habitat. At present, a natural return of the environment to its original state is considered to be undesirable. It would be the same as if beautiful, grassy hills in Scotland were covered in forests again. This would do irreparable harm to the landscape. In the beginning this space was formed only by forces of nature, but since the Middle Ages humans has been rather unconsciously involved in this process. Only in recent years has a purposeful space development plan been written under the EU Natura 2000 programme (European Commission 2016). In coming decades we will witness purposeful development of this space, first to provide tourism functions and later agritourism functions. The programme will be chiefly financed from the EU budget.

Between the sources of the Centuria and Biała Przemsza Rivers in the north; the regions of Chechło, Błędów, Klucze, Bolesław, Olkusz, Bukowno; up to Siersza in the south and Maczki in the west stretches a vast area of quaternary sands, which were deposited by the most recent glacier. It buried deep valleys that had been formed in the previous geological epochs and the sand layers are up to 70 metres thick. From the early thirteenth century silver and lead mines and mills were developed in Olkusz, creating a high demand for wood and charcoal. Forests were cut continuously. 'Forest cutting in sandy areas and the use of clearcut areas as pastures intensified wind erosion processes, which destroyed the thin layer of soil and uncovered loose sands' (Bula & Wower 2012). The wind blew the sand from place to place and made typical desert forms. It is said that, at its peak, as much as 150 km^2 of land was uncovered. In those years the territory of uncovered sands was regarded as an ecological disaster area (although this term was not known at the time). As the time passed by, the sandy area was continuously decreasing because of overgrowing by self-sown trees and shrubs. This is proved by the current remnant of the Big Błędów Desert, which is almost completely overgrown. This area includes the Starczynów Desert, west of Olkusz, and

Dziadowskie Morze, near Bukowno. In the early twentieth century the sandy area was only 80 km². It was still regarded as a desolate place and a fascinating wilderness. Before World War II the area began to be referred to as 'desert', because all the phenomena typical of deserts could be observed there.

What is called the Błędów Desert today is 32 km² of wind-blown sand. It stretches from Błędów in the west (a district of Dąbrowa Górnicza) to the commune of Klucze in the east. In fact, the desert boundaries are not clearly defined. There are different parameters used, giving figures ranging from 6.5 to 10 km for length and from 3.5 to 4 km for width. The average sand thickness is 40 m. The Biała Przemsza River crosses the desert, flowing from west to east. The larger, southern part of the desert is almost entirely covered by vegetation, except for the eastern part. The northern part is still used as a range by the military, whereas the southern part of the desert is poorly used. Local communities see the future of this area in tourism and agritourism. The Polish Sahara Society was established and local communes are also involved in restitution of the desert. Their intention is to uncover sand again through systematic, long-term clear-cutting. The process of vegetation removal is planned to take many years: one, quick clear-cut might cause another serious ecological disaster. A concept of tourism and agritourism development of the desert was prepared. By 2016 nearly 200 hectares of the forest was felled and sand uncovered, making an impressive view from the surrounding hills. New funds are being allocated to renovate the Błędów Desert as a submetropolitan tourism attraction. The implementation of new ideas is favoured by the fact that there were some special historic events that took place in the desert. The novel *Pharaoh*[1] by Bolesław Prus was filmed there and armies used it to prepare for war, especially the German Africa Corps. The overgrown desert has particularly poor vegetation, with only 100 species counted. The desert has its natural curiosities, for example, an endemic perennial plant *Cochlearia polonica* and a walking and horse riding trail was marked. Nevertheless, it is still a place of uncontrolled, wild and sometimes dangerous tourism activity – it is a quad bike riders' favourite place. The next 20–30 years

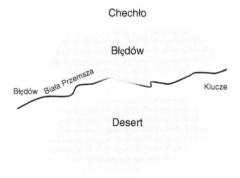

Figure 3.1 Desert Błędów.

Source: The author's compilation.

will be a period of intensified, planned development of tourism and agritourism spaces in the Błędów Desert.

This case of the Błędów Desert proves that people may have a very ambivalent approach to what is regarded as devastation of the natural environment.

Note

1 *Faraon* (*Pharaoh*): a 1966 Polish film adapted from the eponymous novel. It was nominated for an Academy Award for the Best Foreign Language Film and entered into the Cannes Film Festival in 1966.

References

Bula, R., & Wower, A. (2012): Pustynia Błędowska. http://przyroda.katowice.pl/pl/component/content/article/54-ochrona-przyrody/natura-2000/ostoje-siedliskowe/312-pustynia-bledowska-n2000?Itemid=294 [Retrieved 17 December 2016]

European Commission (2014). Natura 2000. http://ec.europa.eu/environment/nature/natura2000/index_en.htm [Retrieved 17 December 2007]

4   Case study

Vague hope for suburban tourism in Conakry Afrometropolis

Michał Jacenty Sznajder

Around the world there are so-called 'cities' with populations in the multimillions, but in fact these settlements emerged spontaneously and formed high-density clusters of people who left the interior of their homeland and headed for cities with the hope of a better life. It is difficult to call these places cities because they have not developed urban functions sufficiently nor have they built the technical infrastructure every city should have. In spite of their constantly increasing populations and sprawling growth into new territories, these centres cannot reasonably be referred to as metropolitan areas. The exploited or latent development potential of nature tourism has been illustrated with examples of many different metropolitan areas around the world, including as difficult an area as Mumbai, with a population exceeding 23 million. Doubtless there is enormous potential for the future development of nature tourism in the metropolitan areas of rich and well-functioning cities around the world. However, the question arises whether there is any potential for the development of nature-based, suburban tourism in spontaneously emerging, unintegrated settlements. The problem does not concern natural resources, because there is plethora of them in any place on earth. The point is whether the inhabitants are capable of using these resources. We can consider this problem by analysing the case of Conakry, the capital of Guinea, which is a poorly organised population centre and an urban organism which does not function very well. It still remains a place where a huge number of people are concentrated. This population is spreading into new areas and the people do not seem to be fully aware of the fact that they are creating something that might develop into a metropolitan centre with all the characteristic functions after many decades. The natural resources of the city and its surrounds indicate the potential for the development of nature tourism in the area. However, poor organisation in this population centre seems to contradict this expectation. In spite of this, there is a glimmering ray of hope for the development of nature tourism in the areas surrounding Conakry. In several decades it may develop a considerable demand for nature tourism.

One hundred and thirty years ago Conakry was a small village with not more than 500 inhabitants. It is situated on the coastal Atlantic island of Tumbo, which was later connected by a causeway with the promontory, the Kalum Peninsula. When the 'city' was expanding, it spread to the mainland and the population began to grow rapidly. In fact, it is difficult to estimate the population of Conakry precisely. According to different sources, the population ranges from 1.68 million (Demographia 2016) to more than 1.4 million (Guinea Population 2016). The city stretches from the east westwards along a strip almost 40 km long and six to seven km wide (see Figure 4.1), with a population density, according to Demographia, of 10,500 people per square km. The first 18 km of the strip, starting from the Atlantic coast, is the Kalum Peninsula, which emerges from the ocean as a nearly round promontory of the former island of Tumbo. This roundish plot of land is the central and most prestigious part of the city, the place of central state offices, military bases, fairs, the presidential palace, cathedral and many important institutions. Even though the peninsula ends after 18 km, the city stretches further into the mainland along a long, narrow strip because, on either side, its growth is limited by rivers and marshy mangrove forests. There is one big swamp on either side, so the city cannot extend across.

African metropolises are usually completely dissimilar from European ones. They differ from each another in all respects. The lack of organisation is the most important feature, which emphasises the fundamental difference between them. African cities are characterised by minimal architectural and organisational diversification. From the tourist's point of view, a long walk in Conakry does not make sense because what we can see in one place will recur in any other place, perhaps with a slightly different arrangement.

Conakry lacks all types of urban infrastructure: both the soft, the organisational structure, and hard, the infrastructure. To tourists' surprise, there is an asphalt dual carriageway running along the axis of the city, providing not only internal transport in the city but also a connection with the rest of the country. There are open sewers running along main roads and the roadside drainage system is open. It must be very efficient to drain the large amounts of water that occur during downpours in the rainy season. There are also two or three asphalt roads running parallel to the main thoroughfare and supporting urban traffic and numerous dirt roads with lots of bumps, which make driving either very unpleasant or completely impossible. The excess of vehicles in the city makes it difficult to get about and there are very few traffic lights. Real chaos starts after dusk when darkness

Figure 4.1 A map of Conakry.

Source: Szymon Sznajder

envelopes the roads: they are illuminated only by the lights of passing cars, which dazzle the drivers.

The lack of drinking water and sewage system is a significant problem in Conakry. The water supply system is poorly developed and there is usually a shortage of water in places with a water supply system. The water paradox in Conakry consists of the fact that, while there is excess of water from rainfall, there is no water in households. The paradox is illustrated with the following description.

> All night long raindrops were drumming heavily on metal roofs. It is raining cats and dogs. After all it is the peak of the rainy season. There are torrential rains almost non-stop. It was raining all night and it is raining in the morning. It might keep raining for a few days. There is so much water falling continuously from the sky but there is hardly any drinkable water running from taps in the capital city. During the dry season there is also shortage of water. It is a paradox or probably negligence. Although there is so much water falling in Guinea, it does not run from taps. The city must solve this problem somehow.
>
> (Sznajder 2013, p. 113)

The city is also grappling with the problem of an electricity shortage. There are round-the-clock power cuts in the city centre. The inhabitants have become accustomed to living without electricity. Some of them have never had electricity, because the supply is deficient. There are no real plans to solve this problem and every year the situation deteriorates. People are buying more electronic devices and the population is rising, but there is no more energy available. It is easy to predict that the energy deficit will increase.

There are enormous demands for city transport. In practice, getting around the city by means of public transport is impossible. Public bus transport is almost non-existent. We can say it is in its infancy. Yellow taxis seem to solve the problem. However, it is impossible to get into one during the rush hour. It is necessary to fight for a seat in a taxi. When one is about to pull up, passengers jump in before it has stopped. Immediately there are five, six or even more passengers sitting in it and ready to drive off.

Conakry is a new, poor city which is developing chaotically, without a noticeable plan. The city has not been able to afford expensive prestigious buildings and it is not likely that they will be built in the near future because it is a new, poor, colonial city. There is no city hall, market, opera house or other interesting buildings which the city could take pride in and which could attract tourists. There are some significant buildings, such as St Mary's Catholic Cathedral, the Grand Mosque, railway station (closed), presidential palace, parliament building, a dilapidated building of the Gamal Abdel Nasser University of Conakry and a hospital with an intimidating appearance. Apart from that, there is a stadium and a neglected seaport, which are more prominent places in the city. There are only a few statues on high pedestals that look very similar to socialist realistic monuments in Moscow. This is all the city offers in terms of architecture. Other structures include a 'sea' of local inhabitants' shabby houses and occasionally one can see nice-looking new apartment buildings, which seem to be like islands.

The city life is usually concentrated in the street. Fairs, repair shops, small-scale production, food outlets, barber shops, cooking and football – everything is done in the street. It is too hot and stuffy indoors so staying and working outdoors is practical. Asphalt roads are used not only for transport but also as football pitches. There are small goals placed in the streets and boys wearing sports clothes play matches – they are not bothered by car traffic. Drivers need to move their cars so as to disturb players as little as possible and road users try not to disturb one another.

There is a very poor outlook for the development of general tourism in Guinea, let alone nature-based tourism. Guidebooks confirm risks that are particularly dangerous for foreign tourists. The author of this story personally experienced them when he visited that country a few years ago. There is a long list of dangers:

- lawlessness and criminality are widespread
- most of the crime is committed by officials in military uniforms and usually targets foreigners
- taking photographs can be considered as espionage and can land you in jail
- corruption is extremely widespread
- there are no emergency rescue services
- water is unsafe for consumption as are fresh vegetables
- the most lethal type of malaria – *Plasmodium falciparum* – is prevalent
- anthrax is very common in the herds in some areas
- locally bought medicine is of dubious quality.

If humans fail, the question arises whether nature does not, and if this place is suitable for the development of general tourism, and nature-based tourism in particular. It is doubtless that at present it would be an extreme trip for a European traveller although there are so many natural attractions around. Let us start with the climate – it is warm temperate. Both the golden dry season and slightly blueish rainy season make two different and fascinating sceneries. During the dry season Guinea is more scorched and yellow but free from excessive heat. It looks different in the rainy season when water falling in torrents from the sky determines the dynamics of life. Naturally, tourists prefer the dry season, but rivers full of water, dynamic waterfalls and lush vegetation make the rainy season unusually charming. Moreover, the fauna and flora in Guinea are enormously diverse. There is a plethora of different species of trees, amphibians, birds and big mammals. Waters are full of fish and there are dangerous crocodiles living in rivers. Different species of crops and farm animals are interesting and they could be an attraction. Tropical rainforests are an outstanding asset of Guinea. Not only the fauna and flora but also inanimate nature is noteworthy: There are mountains and lowlands, magnificent rock formations, swift and slow-flowing rivers as well as numerous waterfalls, the ocean, islands and even pleasant sandy beaches. Other attractions for tourists would be visiting traditional villages with farmers and fishermen, watching folk rituals and religious ceremonies, or even eating meals in traditional households.

If there are so many attractions, why do tourists not come to Guinea? There are no foreign tourists due to health reasons, and the lack of political safety and adequate infrastructure. It is most important that tourists should not be afraid to come to Guinea. They must not be threatened either by the military or police, who extort protection money – this is unacceptable. Tourists must not be persecuted for taking photographs. The flow of domestic tourists is minimal and economically insignificant and the native inhabitants have too many primary existential concerns to bother about tourism. However, the following story shows that there is a ray of hope for the development of nature-based tourism in this 'metropolis'.

> There is a harbour and a marina on the pier. I was surprised to see yachts in such a poor country. I stood at the edge of the pier gazing at the massif of the archipelago of Iles de Los, which was about 10 km away. I wanted to go there. It was also the area of the Conakry Afrometropolis. I might get there. During the dry season one can reach the archipelago for €2 only. During the rainy season there are no boat cruises to that place. I thought of hiring a carrier, though Maria had warned me a lot of times not to do it. She forbade me to sail there because it was too dangerous. Perhaps she was right and I should give up this idea. A young man interrupted my considerations. He offered to take me for an all-day trip to the island for €100. I negotiated the price and suggested €20. The man did not agree and insisted on €100. He told me to come with the money on Friday so we could sail there. However, I did not take advantage of this uncertain opportunity to experience a ray of hope for nature tourism in this African metropolis.
>
> (Sznajder 2013, p. 117)

References

Demographia. (2016). *Demographia World Urban Areas (Built-Up Urban Areas or World Agglomerations). 12th annual edition.* http://www.demographia.com/db-worldua.pdf [Retrieved 1 May 2016]

Guinea Population. (2016). *World Population Review.* http://worldpopulationreview.com/countries/guinea-population/ [Retrieved 20 December 2016]

Sznajder, M. (2013). *Gwinea w ukrywanej kamerze* [Guinea with a Hidden Camera]. Publisher: Horyzont, Poznań.

Part II

New paradigms and opportunities for metropolitan commuter belt tourism

Looking for tourism opportunities: Shanghai downtown.

Source: Photo by Paweł Boczar.

5 Tourism in submetropolitan areas analysed by selected theories of economics and regional development

Agata Balińska

Introduction

Being a multidimensional and interdisciplinary phenomenon, tourism is the object of interest in various scientific disciplines, including economics, geography, sociology, management, law, natural science and physical culture. Each of the disciplines has slightly different research tools at its disposal and analyses a different aspect of tourism. Economics provides a wide range of possibilities in the analysis of tourism. The main areas of research interests are tourism economy, the position of tourism in the national economy, the market of tourism services, the economics of tourism, tourism in regional and local development and institutional conditions for the development of tourism. Economics focuses on the analysis of economic theories, which are used to explain the functioning of markets and tourism reception areas. This chapter attempts to refer selected economic theories and regional development theories to rural tourism.

Rural tourism according to regulation theory

Regulation theory attempts to find answers to two questions: Why does the state regulate particular sectors of the economy? and Is this regulation effective in a particular market? or, in other words: Which conditions must be met for the regulation to be effective? (Nagraj 2012, p. 149). Regulation theory distinguishes the concepts of public and private interest. According to the former, the market is characterised by certain unreliability, so state interventionism is necessary to reduce it. According to the latter, the state does not act in the public interest, but it acts in the interest of specific groups, for example, businessmen. The public interest is realised when it is convergent with the interests of private entrepreneurs or interest groups.

Regulation theory can be referred to the tourism branch of the economy in its broad sense. At the state level the theory is implemented as a tourism policy, which takes into account not only the interest of the state but also the interest of the tourism branch. Tourism entrepreneurs want to see the tourism policy being implemented for the following reasons:

- the development of tourism is significantly influenced by the development of overall infrastructure, especially transport infrastructure (a network of expressways, the number of airports, ports, etc.) and other elements of technical infrastructure (the electrical grid, water supply system, sewerage, sewage treatment plants) and social infrastructure (sports and cultural facilities, etc.);

- the interdisciplinary character of tourism – the changes which take place in different branches of the economy (e.g. industry, transport) and areas of human activity (e.g. education, health care) affect the intensity and structure of tourism traffic;

- the possibility to stimulate tourism traffic through the organisation of different cultural or sports events (e.g. the European Football Championship, Volleyball World Championship, bicycle races, etc.);

- the significance of legal regulations to the development of tourism, including the regulations concerning only tourism – for example, Directive 90/314/EEC (EEC (1990) – and a wide range of laws concerning both tourism and other branches of the economy (e.g. regulations concerning business activities, driver's working time, etc.);

- foreign policy, especially towards neighbouring countries (the number of border crossings, visa regulations, etc.);

- state support in the form of preferential credits, tax deductions, etc., because of the seasonal character of tourism, which generates a slower rate of return on investments than other sectors of the economy (Wodejko 1997, pp. 167–168; Balińska *et al.* 2014, pp. 21–22).

As briefly listed above, these measures taken by the state towards tourism can either significantly stimulate or limit the development of the tourism economy. For example, the development of transport infrastructure is crucial to the attractiveness of a particular area to tourists and it contributes to the development of the tourism infrastructure in a particular area. On the other hand, the deregulatory changes concerning the occupations of tourism guide and courier in Poland evoked anxiety and discussion about the influence of this solution on the quality of services provided by guides and couriers – the deregulation (Kancelaria Sejmu RP 2013b) consists of abolishing the licensing course and examination for candidates for tourism guides and couriers.

Rural tourism and agritourism are in accord with the concept of private interest. The main aspect of the regulatory role of the state is the establishment of legal regulations on agritourism, or in fact, the absence of such regulations. It is not in accommodation providers' best interest to change the legal basis for this business activity. At present, agritourism in Poland is usually an extra activity for farmers.(Kancelaria Sejmu RP 2013a) Therefore, they do not need to register this activity or to pay taxes if not more than five rooms are offered for rent.

Rural tourism according to equilibrium theory

A particular market remains in a state of equilibrium when it meets all the conditions of individual equilibriums (consumer, producer, market and branch equilibriums), which means that factors of production are optimally allocated and utility is maximised. An equilibrium which takes place in the entire economy, that is, it is simultaneous in all markets, is defined as overall equilibrium, whereas an equilibrium in an individual market is called an individual equilibrium (Bezat *et al.* 2009, p. 9). The concept of equilibrium was developed by L. Walras in the second half of the nineteenth century and in the following years it was consolidated by Arrow and Debreu (1954) and McKenzie (1955).

The concept of market equilibrium assumes an interactive balance between the forces of supply and demand. This means that increased demand causes higher prices and thus the point of equilibrium is shifted.

In spite of the fact that rural tourism is an element of tourism in its broad sense and products of rural tourism are offered and purchased in the tourism market, when analysing the market of rural tourism with reference to equilibrium theory, it is necessary to distinguish rural tourism from the broader tourism market, where hotel owners and organisers of tourism (some of whom are international corporations) operate. The demand for tourism is only one of many factors affecting the development of supply in rural tourism. For several years there has been a similar number of rural tourism facilities, especially agritourism farms. This can be interpreted as a state of equilibrium. We might pose the question how an increase in the demand will affect the supply. It is more likely that the amount of accommodation in existing facilities will increase and will be more specialised, rather than that there will be a greater number of facilities.

From the historical perspective we can see that there was a different intensity of demand for products of rural tourism as early as the nineteenth century, when city dwellers arrived at suburban summer resorts and mountaineers' white chambers (representative guestrooms with white walls were called white chambers). The development was more orderly after 1990, when agritourism began to be promoted as an additional form of non-agricultural activity in rural areas. In this way the supply was stimulated. The development of the supply of rural tourism combined with its promotion among potential clients (in Poland rural tourism was initially promoted at agritourism and tourism fairs in Warsaw, Poznań and Kielce) triggered the development of the demand.

Another question that should be asked is how lower prices affect the demand. In contrast to the market of travel agencies, where lower prices of trips to a particular destination increase the demand for these trips (where sometimes tourists may face danger, for example, in trips to Egypt), it is difficult to observe this dependence in the rural tourism market. A lower price will not encourage people to spend time in the country if they do not take rural tourism into consideration. There is a similar situation in other niche tourism markets (such as fishing, speleology, horse-riding, and canoeing).

The demand in tourism is affected by a wide range of non-economic factors. Therefore, higher prices for services in rural tourism do not have to cause a lower demand. Niche tourism, where rural tourism can be classified, gives an opportunity to satisfy both one's basic needs (rest, health recovery) and higher-order needs (respect, recognition, social belonging). As a result, most of the people to whom the offer is addressed are regular clients. Therefore, the demand for services in rural tourism is characterised by low flexibility in prices and income.

Rural tourism according to consumer rational behaviour theory

It is necessary to ask the question whether tourism, including rural tourism, can be considered in the context of consumer rational behaviour theory, which was developed Jevons, an English economist, in the second half of the nineteenth century. This theory introduced the term utility, which is defined as the consumer's total satisfaction with the possession of particular goods (Nasiłowski 2007, p. 98). There is a substitutability of goods, which is understood as the ratio between the increase in the consumption of one product and the decrease in the consumption of another product (Nasiłowski 2007, p. 101). Tourism products are usually categorised as luxurious or non-essential products. Although Wodejko (1997) emphasises that there is relatively high internal substitution of the demand for tourism, in Poland almost 50 per cent of people aged 15 years or older do not take part in tourism trips. However, we can assume that when active tourists choose an offer of a trip, they select the product which best meets their expectations and they move along the indifference curve. Consumers' behaviour is a complex effect of their economic, psychological and social situation (Senda 1998, p. 159). This is easily noticeable in tourism, where non-economic factors largely determine decisions about trips and the budget available for tourism. In the results from studies conducted by Balińska and Sikorska-Wolak (2009), and Zawadka (2010), although low price is one of the main reasons clients choose rural tourism, only three per cent of domestic short-term trips and four per cent of domestic long-term trips were made to agritourism farms in Poland in 2013. Thus, a typical tourist does not behave like a classic *homo oeconomicus*, who chooses the least expensive offer. If it was so, the demand for agritourism services would be much higher.

Tourism according to selected regional development theories

When analysing the development of the tourism economy in a particular space, we can refer to a regional development theory. Butowski (2010) proposes an interesting analysis of tourism as a factor of development with reference to selected regional development theories. The author makes references to the main factors of tourism attractiveness, that is, tourism values, tourism development and transport availability. In this case transport availability should be referred to as internal transport availability. According to the paradigm of tourism proposed by Kozak (2009), these values are of secondary significance to tourism attractions, especially those which are man-made (e.g. amusement parks, thematic villages, spa and wellness facilities, festivals, artistic events). This concept is reflected in practice. Human capital or, more broadly speaking, social capital, is the most important element of the internal potential of a particular area (Fiedor and Kociszewski 2010, p. 85). Culinary tourism is a good example: The preparation of culinary tourism destinations and routes requires profound knowledge and creativity at each stage of construction of a tourism product. The unique developmental potential of the region is appreciated in endogenous development theory, which assumes that each region has its own set of qualities, which make its specific developmental potential. According to endogenous development theory, the local government is also a significant stimulator (Korenik and Zakrzewska-Półtorak 2011). Due to the specific character of the tourism economy, or tourism more broadly interpreted as a multidimensional phenomenon, the significance of the local government is usually much greater than in other sectors of the economy. The local government stimulates tourism mostly by taking the following actions:

- including tourism and its specific character in documents concerning the strategic development of the administrative unit corresponding to the scope of competence of this local government;
- cooperating with other local government units, e.g. communes, cities, counties (e.g. in associations), in order to develop the infrastructure (e.g. tourism routes);
- promoting tourism;
- cooperating with tourism businesspeople, e.g. in local tourism organisations.

Tourism is an extremely dynamic phenomenon. Depending on ideas, consumer trends or fashions, different resources of a particular area are used. Therefore, it is difficult to determine the endogenous factors precisely. The factors are very diversified in individual places and regions.

Endogenous development theory only partly accounts for the phenomenon of the development of tourism, including rural tourism, mostly making references to selected elements of the supply aspect.

The role of tourism in the development of a particular area, such as a region or commune, can be referred to the economic base theory. This theory concerns the role of endogenous and exogenous factors participating in the process of development of settlement units and the fundamental assumption is to base regional development on exportation (Grosse 2002, p. 26). Thus, development takes place through the implementation of exogenous functions, that is, through the opening of a particular unit to its surroundings and its position in the geographical division of labour. The level of production and employment depend on exportation, which is influenced by external demand and by deductions, benefits and economic privileges granted by the central authorities: these are exogenous variables (Korenik and Zakrzewska-Półtorak 2011). Inbound tourism provides the possibility of exporting the goods and services produced and sold in a particular area. What is more, as far as inbound tourism is concerned, it is possible to sell the products that would be difficult to export. For analytical purposes there is a division between the base activity, defined as the economic base of the region (Grosse 2002, p. 26) and carried out for exportation purposes, and the non-base activity, directed to the internal market. It is not easy to divide activities into base and non-base, and in consequence it is difficult to divide the income from these activities accordingly (Korenik and Zakrzewska-Półtorak 2011, pp. 43–44). As far as tourism activity is concerned, this task is even more complicated not only at the level of communes or regions but also at the level of countries. This, the economic base theory, also includes the regional multiplier effect, which assumes that finances flowing to the region stimulate new types of activities within it. The base activity may be based on one branch of production, which usually involves high technology, or it may be diversified. The former solution entails the risk of decline of the predominant branch and withdrawal of the leading investor. The base activity may also become so considerably intensified that it will undermine the endogenous potential and cause breakdown of the local enterprise. Economic base theory puts the main emphasis on the exogenous factors of development, and appropriate development of the endogenous zone is the condition of appropriate functioning of the exogenous zone (Korenik and Zakrzewska-Półtorak 2011, pp. 47–48). In other words, the condition for local development is the presence of such a developmental base in a particular commune (town) that will significantly increase the spatial aspect of the influence of local business entities producing goods and providing services (Szewczuk *et al.* 2011, p. 38). Apart from the exogenous functions, the unit also fulfils endogenous functions, which involve satisfying the needs of the indigenous population and which express the self-sufficiency of a particular enterprise (Brodziński 2010, p. 15).

The essence of a tourism product is that it is always meant to be exported (Butowski 2010, p. 9). We can observe this phenomenon in business tourism, where the tourism traffic and tourism investments are concentrated in cities – business centres. It is rather unlikely that rural tourism could be regarded as a leading branch of the economy. It is usually perceived as an element of multifunctional rural development. Thus, it can be treated as one of the basic branches of the economy.

The group of economic theories describing spatial concentration of regional development also includes regional polarisation theory (Perroux 1955; Hirschman 1958; Myrdal 1958). It describes uneven development of regions, which is caused by political, economic, social and cultural factors within a historical spectrum. According to Myrdal, one of the main theses in the concept of regional polarisation is the rule of circuitous cumulative causation, which means that development processes are accompanied by feedbacks between the cause and effect (discussed in Paczoski 2010, p. 74). The regions that attract developmental factors from surrounding areas contribute to limited development of peripheral areas. According to the assumption, they may exert positive influence on the surroundings through the extension effect, that is, moving business directly or indirectly to underdeveloped areas.

Spatially uneven economic development was the subject of interest to G. Myrdal. In his opinion, it is a long historical process affected not only by economic factors but also by social and historical factors (discussed in Grosse 2002, p. 28). As time passes, the diversification in regional development is deepening. This means that rich regions are developing faster and faster, whereas stagnation is deepening in poor regions. Developmental tendencies spread from centres to peripheral areas. Apart from benefits, negative phenomena can also be observed as peripheral areas become dependent on centres.

Over time, differences in the development of regions increase. We can also observe this phenomenon in tourism, especially in rural tourism. New investments are usually located in places where tourism is developed.

Uneven development at the regional and local level is explained by growth poles theory, which is similar to regional polarisation theory. Originally it referred to the dominance of business entities in the market. Later it was applied to the analysis of the most developed regions. The poles dominate less developed peripheral areas and make them dependent on their own trends in development. According to the theory, economic development is polarised. Clusters of enterprises located in a particular space are usually growth centres (this concept is oriented to spatial development). The spatial system where we can distinguish a pole and its relationship with the nearest area is defined as a polarised system (Szewczuk *et al.* 2011, p. 41). There may be technical, income, psychological or geographical forms of polarisation. According to F. Perroux, a growth pole can be defined as a set of economic enterprises located at a particular point in space and interconnected in a network of dependences (discussed in Paczoski 2010, pp. 78–79). Usually it is a leading industrial sector based on new technologies. Thus, the development of a region depends on the activity of growth poles. The most developed regions win the economic contest over peripheral regions and make them dependent on their own industrial and trade policies (Grosse 2002, p. 28). Metropolises are the main growth poles. According to the author of this concept, it is necessary to strengthen the existing growth poles or create new ones. In view of the title of this publication, it is necessary to ask the question whether the tourism economy can be pivotal to the location of growth poles. Many towns that are regarded as tourism resorts, for example, Zakopane, are specific growth poles. We can observe a similar situation in spa resorts. As far as rural tourism is concerned, model tourism villages established in Poland in the 1990s were supposed to be specific growth poles. Unfortunately, the project was never fully implemented.

Individual theories describing the specificity of the development of tourism as a form of consumption and the spatial development of tourism are varied in terms of their usefulness. The regional development theories that were briefly described in this chapter provide interesting and useful interpretations of the phenomenon of development in tourism areas. The development of tourism in metropolitan areas is best described by economic base theory. Metropolises are attractive places visited by domestic and foreign tourists, especially by business tourists. They are also tourism traffic emission centres. Therefore, in the vicinity of metropolises we can find spa and wellness facilities and conference centres, on the one hand, and educational and agritourism farms, on the other hand.

References

Arrow, K. J. & Debreu, G. (1954). Existence of an equilibrium for a competitive economy. *Econometrica*, 22(3), pp. 265–290. https://web.stanford.edu/class/msande311/arrow-debreu.pdf [Retrieved 12 January 2017]

Balińska, A., Sieczko, A., & Zawadka, J. (2014). *Turystyka – wybrane zagadnienia.* Publisher: Difin Warszawa.

Balińska, A., & Sikorska-Wolak, I. (2009). *Turystyka wiejska szansą rozwoju wschodnich terenów przygranicznych na przykładzie wybranych gmin.* Publisher: Wydawnictwo SGGW, Warszawa.

Bezat, A., Figiel, Sz., Klimkowski, C. & Kufel J. (2009). *Zastosowania modeli równowagi w analizie sektora rolno-żywnościowego.* Publisher: IERiGŻ PAN, Warszawa.

Brodziński, M. (Ed.). (2010). *Gospodarka regionalna i lokalna.* Publisher: Wydawnictwo ALMAMER Wyższa Szkoła Ekonomiczna, Warszawa.

Butowski, L. (2010). Turystyka jako czynnik rozwoju w świetle wybranych teorii rozwoju regionalnego. *Turyzm*, 20/1. Publisher: Wydawnictwo Uniwersytetu Łódzkiego, Łódź.

Debreu, G. (1991). The mathematization of economic theory. The American Economic Review, 81(1), 1–7.

EEC. (1990). Council directive of 13 June 1990 on package travel, package holidays and package tours (90/314/EEC). *Official Journal of the European Communities.* http://eur-lex.europa.eu/legal-content/EN/TXT/HTML/?uri=CELEX:31990L0314&from=PL [Retrieved 8 January 2017]

Fiedor, B., & Kociszewski, K. (Eds). (2010). *Ekonomia rozwoju.* Publisher: Wydawnictwo Uniwersytetu Ekonomicznego we Wrocławiu, Wrocław.

Grosse, T. (2002). Przegląd koncepcji teoretycznych rozwoju regionalnego. *Studia Regionalne i Lokalne*, No. 1 (8). Publisher: Uniwersytet Warszawski Centrum Europejskich Studiów Regionalnych i Lokalnych (EUROREG), Warszawa.

Hirschman, A. (1958). *The Strategy of Economic Development.* Yale University Press.

Kancelaria Sejmu RP. (2013a). Article 3 of the Act on Free Business Activity of 2 July 2004. *Official Journal* 2013, Pos. 672. www.isap.sejm.gov.pl [Retrieved 20 May 2014]

Kancelaria Sejmu RP. (2013b). The Act of 13 June 2013 on change in the laws regulating licenses in selected professions. *Official Journal* 2013, Pos. 829. www.isap.sejm.gov.pl [Retrieved 20 May 2014]

Korenik, S. & Zakrzewska-Półtorak, A. (2011). *Teorie rozwoju regionalnego – ujęcie dynamiczne.* Publisher: Wydawnictwo Uniwersytetu Ekonomicznego we Wrocławiu, Wrocław.

Kozak, M. (2009). *Turystyka i polityka turystyczna a rozwój: między starym a nowym paradygmatem.* Publisher: Wydawnictwo Naukowe Scholar, Warszawa.

McKenzie, L. (1955). Equality of factor price in world trade. *Econometrica*, 23(3), pp. 239–257.

Misaki, K. (2017). Fundamental Economics: History, philosophy, and development of Walrasian economics. In: *Encyclopedia of Life Support Systems (EOLSS).* https://www.eolss.net/Sample-Chapters/C04/E6-28-38.pdf [Retrieved 12 January 2017]

Myrdal, G. (1958). *Teoria Ekonomii a Kraje Gospodarczo Niedorozwinięte.* Publisher PWE, Warszawa, pp. 61–69.

Nagraj, R. (2012). Przesłanki regulacji rynków w świetle teorii rozwoju publicznego. *Studia i Prace Wydziału Nauk Ekonomicznych i Zarzadzania* No. 27. Publisher: Uniwersytet Szczeciński, Szczecin, pp. 149–162.

Nasiłowski, M. (2007). *System rynkowy. Podstawy miko- i makroekonomii.* Publisher: Wydawnictwo Key Text, Warszawa.

Paczoski, A. (2010). *Kreowanie regionalnej i lokalnej polityki gospodarczej na podstawie teorii i koncepcji rozwoju terytorialnego.* Publisher: Wydawnictwo Uniwersytetu Gdańskiego, Gdańsk.

Parliament, Ustawa z dnia 5 sierpnia 2015 r. o zmianie ustaw regulujących warunki dostępu do wykonywania niektórych zawodów, Dz.U. 2015 poz. 1505.

Perroux F. (1955). Note on the concept of growth poles. *Economie Appliquee*, 7, pp. 307–320.

Senda, J. (1998). Podstawowe aspekty zachowań konsumenckich. *Ruch prawniczy, ekonomiczny i socjologiczny.* Year XL, Book 2. Publisher: Uniwersytet im. Adama Mickiewicza and Uniwersytet Ekonomiczny w Poznaniu, Poznań.

Szewczuk, A., Kogut-Jaworska, M. & Zioło, M. (2011). *Rozwój lokalny i regionalny. Teoria i praktyka.* Publisher: Wydawnictwo C. H. Beck, Warszawa.

Walras, L. (1896). Éléments d'économie politique pure, ou, Théorie de la richesse sociale. F. Rouge.

Wodejko, S. (1997). *Ekonomiczne zagadnienia turystyki.* Publisher: Wyższa Szkoła Handlowa, Warszawa.

Zawadka, J. (2010). *Ekonomiczno-społeczne determinanty rozwoju turystyki wiejskiej na Lubelszczyźnie.* Publisher: Wydawnictwo SGGW, Warszawa.

6 Strengthening the sustainability of rural tourism and agritourism in the twenty-first century

Adriano Ciani

Promote sustainable development strategy

Since the very beginning, the theory of welfare economics has promoted reflection on growth and development models (Solow 1956; Hirshman 1958). The quantitative importance of development has been predominant until the mid-twentieth century, which brought about lesser consideration of issues such as environmental equilibrium, intra- and intergenerational equity, and sustainability strategy. The principles of sustainable development have been discussed at several stages, and thanks to that, it is currently a widespread heritage among the most important international institutions. Some of them are worth mentioning: Albert Hirschman (1958); Rachel Carson (1962); the Club of Rome (Meadow *et al.* 1972); the United Nations (1972); the World Commission on Environment and Development (1987); the 1st World Summit on Sustainable Development in 1992 with the Agenda 21 proposal (UNSD 1992); the Millennium Goals in 2000 (UNGASS 2000); the WSSD of Johannesburg in 2002 (UN 2002); the promotion of the Decade of Education for Sustainable Development by United Nations Educational, Scientific and Cultural Organization (UNESCO 2005–2014); UNESCO World Conference on Sustainable Development in Bonn (UNESCO 2009); G8 University Summit in Turin, (2009); United Nations General Assembly Special Session Resolution for Rio+20 (UNGASS 2009); The Future We Want (UN 2012); and the Sustainable Development Goal 2015–2030 (SDSN 2014). Besides these general stages, including the Bonn Declaration, other deliberations, such as university conferences, also took place. The most important of them were: the Talloires Declaration (ULSF 1990), the Halifax Declaration (1991), the Earth Summit Agreements (1992), the Swansea Declaration (1993), the Kyoto Declaration (1993), the Copernicus Charter (1993), and the Student Declaration for a Sustainable Future (1995). Numerous scientists, researchers, and universities all over the world contributed to the evolution of the principles, issues, and methods for the evaluation of Sustainable Development. Consequently, the twenty-first century is commonly characterised as the era of sustainability (Sachs 2013).

The future of the world, as they say, is the basic theme of the forthcoming Rio +20 Summit, based on the affirmation of a programme firmly pointing to integrated and sustainable development (SDSN 2014). The aim of the abovementioned programme is to stress the need for integrated support to channel synergies, exceeding the monothematic approach that is often used in development processes and actions, because that innovative approach is more effective. In order to achieve integration we need to have a model which is capable of improving the economic growth in real sectors of each sensitive area of the world, while also emphasising the maximum opportunity to add value to these realities. Thanks to the typical specificity of each of these sensitive areas, if properly guided they may turn their elements of weakness into elements of strength, being providentially involved in the process of socioeconomic modernisation. This course of action should be characterised by more endogenous rather than exogenous development, bottom-up rather than top-down approach, and should receive support in the field of scientific and technological innovation. The means of sustainable development should not be considered only in relation to utopian matters, but also of preserving the environment; they should lead to a perspective of intra-and inter-generational fairness developed through at least the following five key aspects:

- economic (income adjustment)
- social (adaptation of the quality of life)
- environmental (productive conservation and sustainable use of natural resources)
- cultural (management of cultural diversity)
- management (sustainability management).

The formation of human capital, research development and technological innovation are essential (Ciani 2012; Tinbergen *et al.* 1976). However, there are two options to be taken into consideration to avoid the risk of introducing mechanisms that will lead to a break between past and present structures, and also with the hierarchy of social values, which are still significant. However, this involves criticism and harsh transition for many countries around the world. We must invent a technological 'sweet innovation', without impact on either the economic or social environment, because it is not possible to quickly achieve desirable alterations within the scale of values, and there should be a low level of risk management. Improved professional formation of human capital should facilitate the acquisition of social subjects (Romero 1995), particularly within the weakest areas, where it is necessary to use a special flexible skill, which is suitable for the creation of increasingly self-rooted new values. The type of communication changes when a company becomes engaged in the processes of modernisation with fairness and sustainability.

Sustainable development is the result of political strategy affecting the culture of all people and nations. It is necessary to develop the projects helping young people in particular to receive higher education (as much as possible), facilitate their entry into the world of work, with the added result of real acceleration. The projects should involve the process of overcoming the unavoidable deep crisis, including the current phase of development model, as a billion people live below the minimum level of nutrition, and 20 per cent of the world population have only 1.4 per cent of the global wealth.

In this context, all projects of international cooperation, including mutual consultation, will become operative through a coherent, comprehensive, frequent, clear and penetrating atmosphere, with a modern quantity of contact with new modes of media (ECA 2005; G8 2009). All the features mentioned above are supposed to enable gradual establishment and positioning of the elements that link science as instruments of peace and solidarity (Summers *et al.* 2005) through the use of technological innovations, increasing user-friendliness and general accessibility. All initiatives should follow the guidelines of the ambitious future programme, attempting the establishment of a 'common house' to supply scientific global scale research (Delors *et al.* 1996; Leal Filho 2011). Its wide planning involves the full potential which each socioeconomic wave brings: the areas of education, science and technology, and the 'spearhead' of necessary actions to achieve the affirmation of the sustainable development culture.

The action could and will be characterised by gradual development of a scientifically successful framework, which is based on the values pointing to more concrete awareness and knowledge of new generations. A scientific society within which the university may be once again the universitas (the whole world) is going to mark the beginning of new renaissance, in a process related to each country and to the whole world society.

Today the multitude of young people should be given concrete signs of hope and freedom, leading to more sustainable life and livelihood, to overcome the systematic way of working nowadays, which dominates our modern 'easy times' 'as a prison' in order to create a happier and sweeter society. In this sense science must facilitate removal of the barriers (Rychen and Salganik 2003) that have often overshadowed the ancestral values of ancient societies, which are not to be approached as if it belonged to a museum but with the spirit of revival and rediscovery. This should be a kind of science that rewards not only property but also humanity (Allen 2010).

The growth of university research centres will increasingly make them a window of consciousness (Ciani 2012) together with their spirit of analysis and skills brought by all people making autonomous decisions in a global society. As a preparation for the general assembly in Rio +20 it is very important to have a conference to discuss the guidelines and analyse what, how, and when has to be done to follow the International Sustainable Development Strategy requirement set by the university system.

This is a way to support the strategy of sustainable development. Even if it might be weak in terms of Cartesian analysis and predictive power, it has a concrete productive approach that is able to promote the culture of territorial sustainability (Allen 2010, Ciani 2012). At the time of deep global crisis and lack of generally available economic governance models we think that it is sufficient to start working on proper management and promotion of the territory as a great vital resource, and thus starting the mechanisms of real wealth and healthy production and to start acting against the damaging strength of globalised international financial speculation lobbies.

The 'Future We Want' and the Sustainable Development Goals 2015–2030

In this way we support the final document of Rio+20 'The Future We Want' (UN 2012) as the Sustainable Development Goals (SDG) 2014–2015. The Sustainable Development Solutions Network (SDSN) made the following proposals for the SDG 2015–2030 (SDSN 2014):

- Ending extreme poverty and hunger
- Development and prosperity for all without ruining the environment
- Education for all children and youth
- Gender equality and reduction of inequalities
- Health and wellbeing at all ages
- Increasing agricultural production in an environmentally sustainable manner to achieve food security and rural prosperity
- Making cities productive and environmentally sustainable
- Curbing human-induced climate change with sustainable energy
- Protecting ecosystems and ensuring sound management of natural resources
- Improving governance and business behaviour aligned with all the goals.

In this vision the 'increase in agricultural production made in an environmentally sustainable manner to achieve food security and rural prosperity' involves a special role of the territory, its potentiality and management. Exploring the best practice of territory management could support real sustainability for rural tourism and agritourism in the next century.

The new paradigm of tourism development from mass to niche

The tourism movement could be presented with official data. According to the United Nations World Tourism Organization (UNWTO), there has been a virtually uninterrupted growth of international tourism arrivals – from 25 million in 1950, to 278 million in 1980, 528 million in 1995, and 1,035 million in 2012 (WTTC 2013). This growth is very impressive and the socio-economic data are also impressive. Tourist activity makes up 9 per cent of the total GDP worldwide, provides employment to 1 of every 11 people, generates $US 1,300 billion in export, 6% of the total export and 6% of the total export in the least developed countries. (WTTC 2013).

The model of sustainable development that is taking shape – with the green economy, the Third Industrial Revolution linked with the evolution of information and communication technology (ICT), the bio-based economy, research into Gross National Happiness (GNH) in lieu of Gross Domestic Product (GDP) – is setting new paradigms for the processes of development.

From an inverse relationship with the environment (the natural resources of traditional development) tourism is switching to a possible direct relationship between development and environmental resources. It is transforming from a mono-criteria approach (only quantitative and monetary) to a multi-criteria approach (economic, environmental, social, cultural, managerial). This is a simple consideration of the problems of the present generations transformed into an intra- and inter-generational vision. The current approach, which is strongly characterised by the development of ICT, proposes a series of paradoxes (Naisbitt 1994; Naisbitt and Aburdene 1990). One of them is the unstoppable spread of ICT (e.g. there are 6 billion mobile phones in the world [BBC News 2012]). It has led to the spread of invasive images of places, landscapes, traditions and such like to an increasing amount of the population. In view of this situation, the traditional approach suggests that the need to have tourists experience these realities should gradually fade with the replacement of communication images. It is a complete paradox that, instead, there are more and more images and each person is encouraged to experience these places directly. Behavioural economic analysis made some time ago predicted a significant increase in tourism worldwide despite the prospect of instability in many parts of the world. Another paradox is the decrease in the phenomenon of mass tourism and the development of thematic tourism as a niche. Farm and rural tourism are significant areas in this field.

Why rural tourism and agritourism?

Market research (Ohe 2003) highlighted the following points made by consumers in their choice of services:

- contact with nature
- freedom
- sunbathing, being outdoors
- non-routine activities
- holiday equilibrium
- rest, quietness

The following characteristics refer to visitors and they can easily be extended to aspects of rural tourism:

- love of nature
- pleasure of genuine things
- desire for peace
- new experience
- ability to adapt.

In the current situation the tourism movement in rural areas depends on the role of the actors who play there, creating an attractive unpolluted environment, landscape biodiversity, tradition and culture, which together make a mesh of so-called ecosystem services. The SDG 2015–2030 (SDSN 2013) indicates that it is necessary for agricultural and rural areas to achieve prosperity. In this context, it becomes crucial to understand who creates and manages these ecosystem services, and that they provide the benefit at zero cost instead of for profit. These services have been provided and will be provided by agricultural operators, who guarantee good management practices and promotion of the area. Therefore, it is necessary to make a distinction between farm and rural tourism in order to highlight the reality and contribute to better understanding.

Agritourism is defined as a service of tourism, which is related and complementary to agricultural activity. This means that the farm is a service that can be offered only by farmers. It might be impossible to talk about the farm without the presence and activity of primary agriculture. In this context, in order to obtain the benefits of an innovative, integrated activity, which reinforces the multi-functionality of the farm, farmers need to provide most ecosystem services, which are the basis of attractiveness of rural areas for tourists. *Rural tourism* is any form of tourism services offered in rural areas by operators who are not farmers.

It is essential to make a distinction to offer the niche tourism movement rural sustainability due to the prospect of consolidation in the future. The operators of rural tourism come mainly from non-agricultural sectors and typically have greater financial and organisational capacity in making necessary investments to introduce a regime. These are operators who do not actively participate in the best practices of territory management, but benefit from its potential to the same or even greater extent than those who are the real actors – the farmers.

Therefore, the role of the farm must be strengthened to avoid the risk that the niche in tourism will gradually lose its niche character and will be transformed into a mass movement. At present, rural areas enjoy the richness and dynamism of the territory supported by farmers and this is a great opportunity for them (Tchetchik 2012). Some countries, for example, China, seem to follow this direction, where we can speak of more than 100 million tourists in the domestic market of rural areas in 2020. In this case, the paradigmatic character of rural tourism, sustainable tourism, the multi-criteria approach, and the intergenerational character of rural tourism will be totally lost to the progressive deterioration of land, which will no longer have the force of a local attraction but it will have the flat indistinct attractiveness of globalisation.

Territory: why, what, who

Why the territory?

The situation in the world and specifically in many countries shows a trend of continuous degradation of land and its use for purposes other than agriculture (Coldiretti 2014). This results from the inability of both local and national governments to cope with hydro-geological instability, which occurs more and more frequently even in view of the looming effects of a global change in the climate. According to estimates by the International Federation of Red Cross and Red Crescent Societies (IFRC), global damage calculated for 2011 amounted to over 311 billion dollars (IFRC 2011).

The territory is a physical substrate (including soil, arable land, water, forest, biodiversity, renewable energy, non-renewable resources, landscape, buildings and infrastructures), where economic, social, historical and cultural aspects are stratified (Romstad 2010). Being innovative activities, the actions of territorial programming and planning must be carried out and strongly supported by an appropriate and widespread use of advanced instrumentation of ICT. The technologies of GIS (Geographic Information System), GPS (Global Positioning System), DSS (Decision Support System) and broadband Internet should be the key elements of a 'user-friendly' store of knowledge in modern management of the process of sustainable development strategy. Taking the territory into consideration is an indispensable way to guarantee the sustainable future of any activity in rural areas and particularly in rural tourism and agritourism.

What is the territory?

The territory is an open book written in ink that we cannot normally read, but it is our duty to make it readable for everyone with an innovative, smart and skilled approach. This is because the territory has different roles and functions, as in the following open list:

* showing and representing
* telling stories
* speaking
* singing
* smelling
* tasting
* stimulating feelings
* catalysing creativity
* stimulating inventiveness
* attracting
* inspiring
* enthralling

The territory in its widest and most holistic form, together with humans with their capacity to analyse, choose and operate together with their fellows, which distinguishes them from all other living creatures, should be brought back to the centre of strategies used by any development model by using a concrete, operational parameter in order to create the basic conditions for an indefeasible New Renaissance.

Who is to be in the territory?

This will focus on the strategies of protection, conservation and enhancement of different areas around the world, the relationship between urban and rural areas, the challenge of renewable energy, the green economy and the eradication of poverty. Therefore, these objectives and issues need to be put into practice in a local, national and international context by professionals who, from the perspective of 'global thinking and local acting', have obvious modern know-how and an ability to act that matches the on-going revolution, known as the third industrial revolution.

New paradigms, approaches and opportunities for sustainability

New paradigms

In view of the evaluations made in the paragraphs above it is very likely that, in future years, the new paradigms and new approaches that the territory has to offer will be developed.

In addition to the three paradigms of sustainable development presented above we can include the following new paradigms:

- the territory is a living entity to be seen as a book to read;
- the territory is a reservoir of resources to be put into the cycle of a sustainable production system of goods and services;
- the territory is an intelligent cognitive system for education with a smart use of ICT;
- the territory is specific, unique and special but socially inclusive;
- the territory is TRADI-OVATION[1] (Ciani 2012). In this sense it is the key concept and the main theme around which any innovative process can be structured to give effective credibility and to erase the increasing disillusion that accompanies major international meetings in order to move from words to actions and create the foundations for the New Model of Management and Promotion of Rural Areas;
- the territory provides us with an option to overcome the systemic 'prison' of labour by offering free time and the opportunity to recover in environmental space.

New approaches

- Transformation of the paradox 'the more you see an image and the more you desire to experience it directly' into strict behaviour of the human in the twenty-first century;
- the role of new-generation ICT such as the broadband, wireless, GIS, drones, etc.,
- wellness and life in open air;
- guarantee of the origin and participatory style of production (e.g. of wine bought at a winery);

- colloquium with the territory and discovering the feeling approach;
- the didactic and social inclusion of farms.

New opportunities to exploit

Farm and rural tourism products can now be defined as a little 'ripe'. Some regional farms, as well as the Italian tradition, are at a moment of exhaustion, if not in decline, because tourists increasingly demand innovative services. Expanding the services provided by the farm by developing education, including licensed educational farms, is an opportunity that should definitely be seized. On the one hand, it will improve cash flow throughout the year with school visits distributed over the school year. On the other, it will exert pressure, especially on young people, to create a strong culture rooted in the strategy of sustainable development and it will even enhance the public good represented by rural and agricultural areas. Educational visits can also include young people and children's direct participation to recover some of the old-style family farm production, such as homemade bread, jams and crafts. Such activity will also contribute to the maintenance – or at least remind people of – the strength of one's hands. Agricultural areas have always been characterised by skilled activities, some of which have been so well preserved in the European and global diversity of tourism niches that they will bring more and more wealth and power in the future to rural areas.

Territorial Laboratory

The activity of an agricultural enterprise can also be transformed into an instrument acting as a facilitator of social cohesion through the inclusion of groups and individuals who are more vulnerable and marginalised. An agritourism farm may be a real laboratory in which territorial 'locally disabled' activities can find moments of mental and manual presentation within the same range of products and services as a synergistic activity of a traditional enterprise and farm (Fleischer and Tsur 2009). Other new opportunities are represented by:

- farm culture and heritage museums
- training and professional learning
- renewable energy production and use
- short food chain
- cooking and eating slow food
- landscape promotion and fruition
- leisure time.

Case studies: good practice of territorial management

The valorisation of local natural resources is an example of an action taken from the bottom up for the sustainable management and promotion of territory. In order to confirm the proposal of a model and show the approach of this paper it is time to present some practical solutions as a specific demonstration what can be done in rural areas.

Stone Sculpture School of Fallera, Perugia

The Blasi Farm based in Macereto (Piegaro) in the province of Perugia conducted the first Weekend of Spring International Stone Art School in the vicinity of the archaeological site of the town of Fallera and the Field of Grey Stone site within the Blasi Agricultural Company. The initiative was started to activate agritourism on a farm producing excellent wine and olive oil. The farm is located in an area of landscape of great value. The project included a road map leading to the exploitation of local natural resources, with a vision of tradition and innovation and the application of good management practices in the fields of environment and sustainable development. The town of Fallera includes the remains of Roman walls, which, according to some research, date back to the Iron Age. There is a large area in the basement with a field called Grey Stone, which is of particular interest due to sculptures, furniture, wall coverings and fittings. Presumably stone was processed in that area because the name Fallera derives from the Etruscan words *farθan* (genius and creative life force) and *flere* (deity). To sum up, we are in an area where 'the genius of the gods', 'the creative genius' and 'the genius loci' are celebrated in stonework. Therefore, the place is worth being recommended to everybody interested in the problems of the environment, sustainable development, sustainable local development, sustainable management and promotion of territory because it offers outdoor life, creativity combined with a search for one's own hidden artistic inclinations, a unique three-day experience of the life of the Umbrian countryside accompanied with the flavours, colours and sounds of a 'living virtuous green circuit'. The experience offers an opportunity to work for three days on one's own stone that will be delivered upon arrival.

Old mills in the Middle Tiber Valley, Umbria Region

In most Italian valleys there are many old watermills with a long history of the rural population, traditional food production, gastronomy and lifestyle. The Local Area Group surveyed about 15 old mills in the Middle Tiber Valley to propose a rehabilitation plan, especially for activities related to agritourism and rural tourism. The survey was made in 2000 and now promotes a new restaurant and guests' activity combined with educational visits for primary schools.

The Strade del Cantico Wine Route in the Umbria Region

The Umbria Region has a rich tradition of wine production which dates back to the Etruscan, Roman and medieval times. In the last 40 years many different wines produced in the region have been ranked high in the international market, including appraisal by e-commerce. The financial support of the Rural Development Programme of the Common Agricultural Policy 1999–2006 created a development opportunity for wine tourism. Central Umbria near Assisi is the place where St Francis was born and lived. The place became wellknown for poetry and St Francis gained recognition in the Catholic culture as the saint protector of nature through the 'Canticle of the Creatures' (*Il Cantico delle Creature*). The name Strade del Cantico derives from it. During the year there are many events that attract not only a lot of tourists from Italy but also many (about 60 per cent) from foreign countries. Nowadays, many agritourism and rural tourism businesses organise trips along the Strade del Cantico Wine Route.

The scenic region of Todi Municipality

Todi has been called the most sustainable town in the world because it is very rich and has a fascinating rural landscape. In 2010 the town promoted the development of a network of pathways where it is possible to go walking alone or with a tourism guide, ride a horse or a mountain bike, go to a restaurant, or arrange an agritourism expedition taking photos of the landscape.

The TuDER Park Project

The town of Todi, of Etruscan origin (1000 BC), is situated on top of Todi Hill. Different technical and management aspects caused instability in major portions of the slopes and the municipality had to expropriate 900 hectares of land. In recent years the same municipality has been working to improve this land located between the urban (historic and recent) and purely rural area. The authors have conceived the idea of Todi Hill TUDeR Park (Territorial and Urban Development and Rural Areas Park) within a broader development plan. The two basic principles of the Park are a multifunctional approach and a vision as of is as a common good. The aim is to improve the overall image of the town, which can be characterised as an example of advanced sustainable land management, and promotion and modern governance of territory to improve the relationship between urban and rural areas in the concept of Smart City and Smart Community.

The Widespread Hotel of Massa Martana

The small town of Massa Martana has a very interesting Roman origin and rich heritage. About 5000 people live in the town centre that has a prevalent medieval style. In 1997 the municipality was struck by a violent earthquake. Reconstruction was very hard and one of the concepts was to transform the remaining buildings into a network of guestrooms with a central reception and restaurant. This solution adopted the form of the Widespread Hotel. It is the main new activity and provides new prosperity linked to the agritourism and rural tourism potential of the territory.

Sustainable management and promotion of territory (SMPT)

Best practice for sustainable management and promotion of territory

If we manage and promote the territory in joint best practice today, using up-to-date ICT, it is possible for the population in rural areas to achieve all the target of the SDG 2015–2030. Short local food chains; organic farming; management of the water and carbon footprints; small enterprises; agritourism; landscape; biodiversity of rivers, water and forests; smart grids for renewable energy; cooking, handcrafts, tradition and innovation; rural tourism circuits (walking, cycling, horse-riding, fishing, landscape watching, etc.), which derive from the Sustainable Management and Promotion of Territory (SMPT) are concrete elements that contribute to the improvement and enlargement strategy to transform weak traditional rural areas into strong and sustainable smart communities.

The multi-functionality of farm and territorial contract management

The idea of territorial management contracts consists in establishing, within a well-defined normative context, a contract between farmers and local institutions to regulate all the necessary actions for the safety and environmental protection of territory, such as drainage, cleaning of ditches, construction of dykes, soil consolidation and planting of trees – both within the area of their own property and in the areas surrounding particular farms (Ciani *et al.* 2012). Farmers are engaged in these activities, have precise technical parameters and receive payment related to the area involved and to the degree of risk in the zone. In this way permanent or temporary damage caused by landslides and mudslides is avoided and the role of a garrison farmer is reaffirmed; moreover, this kind of contract gives greater functionality to the agricultural sector, improves farmers' cash flow, and stimulates the use and dissemination of ICT for the monitoring and control of activities.

It is important that these contracts be 'strictly localised'. It means that they must be constructed on the basis of the specific characteristics of the territory they refer to. Ad hoc contracts must be established with farmers according to specific environmental problems in a particular zone so that it can be protected. Therefore, territorial management contracts could involve different types of preservation activities, according to the different and specific environmental problems involved.

Having the strength of decentralisation, territorial management contracts – established directly with citizens and farmers – could be the most effective way to guarantee viable production of the ecosystem service, which creates the basis for rural areas attracting tourism movement.

Operators could also link the farm and its multi-functionality by means of Territorial Contract Management (TCM), having an active management role for the defence (avoidance or limitation of risks) and development of the area in an approach where nowadays the territory itself must be considered as a common good.

Green virtuous circuit

When we consider how to stimulate agritourism and rural tourism within the new paradigm and new approach, as discussed earlier, and try to take advantage of new opportunities that the territory can provide in an overall view, it is possible to achieve a very innovative result in each local area and on each farm or in a tourism business activity in rural areas: namely a Green Virtuous Territorial Circuit. We can take advantage of the opportunity to transform a single starting initiative in the field into a catalyst creating more activities, employment and cash flow.

Best practice in Sustainable Management and Promotion of Territory is the way to guarantee a fruitful and innovative, concrete perspective for a future without poverty and with access to all goods and life services in the twenty-first century.

Conclusions

The analysis of the development model in the twenty-first century enabled us to demonstrate that rural tourism and agritourism provided every area of the world with an opportunity to have an interesting future perspective in world tourism. The phenomenon is paradoxically aided by ICT as progressive image transmission stimulates people's curiosity to visit the sites shown in the images they receive.

- Sustainable development is the model that is emerging with new paradigms, the demand for an innovative approach to fruition and for new opportunities that the land itself provides for the sustainable vitality of farm and rural tourism.
- In view of its specific character, agritourism is complementary and related to an agricultural activity. It is the form that must be privileged because the movement of niche tourism in rural areas is mainly based on the supply of ecosystem services. Farmers guarantee a continuous supply of these services.
- The territory should be understood as an intelligent cognitive system that educates. Learning is the cornerstone on which this perspective should be based.

This study presents some practical examples that refer to the wider concept of Territorial Management Agreements. The activation and exploration of good management practices and promotion of the area create a concrete model that can ensure the viability of tourism in rural areas.

Note

1   An acronym for 'Territory, Rural Areas through Development, Innovation, Organisation, Valorisation, user-friendly Technology, ICT sharing, Online Networking'.

References

Allen, R. E. (2010). *Human Ecology Economics: A New Framework for Global Sustainability*. London: Routledge.

BBC News (2012). UN Six billion mobile phone subscriptions in the world. http://www.bbc.com/news/technology-19925506 [Retrieved 23 March 2017]

Brundtland, G. H. (1987). Our common future, chairman's foreword, report of the World Commission on Environment and Development. UN Documents. http://www.un-documents.net/our-common-future.pdf [Retrieved 17 December 2015]

Carson, R. (1962). *Silent Spring*. Houghton Mifflin Harcourt, Boston's Back Bay.

Ciani, A. (2012). The sustainable management and promotion of territory: A strategic operative education plan and training as a result of collaboration between Perugia University, Todi's State Technical Agricultural College and the Local Municipality. In Walter Leal Filho, (Ed.), *Sustainable Development at Universities: New Horizons*, Peter Lang, Hamburg, pp. 235–246.

Ciani, A., Boggia, A., Paolotti, L. & Rocchi, L. (2012). The territorial management contracts (TMC): A practical tool to reduce the risk in land resources management and to improve the multifunctionality of agriculture, *Paper prepared for the 126th EAAE Seminar*, New Challenges for EU Agricultural Sector and Rural Areas. Which Role for Public Policy? Capri (Italy), June 27–29, 2012. http://ageconsearch.umn.edu/bitstream/126052/2/CIANI-BOGGIA-ROCCHI-PAOLOTTI.pdf [Retrieved 10 December 2015]

Coldiretti, Agronotizie. (2014). Consume of land: 82% of the Municipality under the Risk of Landslides and Foods, http://agronotizie.imagelinenetwork.com [Retrieved 26 March 2014]

Delors, J., Al Mufti, I., Amagi, I., Carneiro, R., Chung, F., Geremek, B., Gorham, W., Kornhauser, A., Manley, M., Padrón Quero, M., Savané, M., Singh, K., Stavenhagen, R., Stur, M. W. & Nanzhao Z. (1996). Learning: The treasure within. *Highlights, Report to UNESCO of the International Commission on Education for the Twenty-First Century*. http://unesdoc.unesco.org/images/0010/001095/109590eo.pdf [Retrieved 26 March 2014]

ECA (United Nation Economic Commission for Africa). (2005). *The Millennium Development Goals in Africa: Progress and Challenges*. Addis Ababa, Ethiopia http://repository.uneca.org/pdfpreview/bitstream/handle/10855/5601/Bib.%2041714_I.pdf?sequence=1 [Retrieved 09 January 2017]

Fleischer, A., & Tsur Y., (2009). The amenity value of agricultural landscape and rural-urban land allocation. *Journal of Agricultural Economics*, 60(1), 132–153.

G8 University Summit. (2009). *Torino Declaration on Education and Research for Sustainable and Responsible Development (Turin Declaration)*. http://www.iau-hesd.net/sites/default/files/documents/g8torino_declaration.pdf [Retrieved 6 January 2017]

Hirschman, Albert O. (1958). *The Strategy of Economic Development*. Yale University Press, New Haven, Ct.

IFRC (International Federation of Red Cross and Red Crescent Societies). (2011). World Disasters Report: Data dashboard. http://www.ifrc.org/en/publications-and-reports/world-disasters-report/wdr2011/ [Retrieved 9 January 2017]

Leal Filho, W. (2011). About the Role of Universities and Their Contribution to Sustainable Development. *Higher Education Policy* 24(4), 427–438. DOI:10.1057/hep.2011.16

Meadow, D, Meadows, D. L., Renders, J. & Behrens III, W. W. (1972). *The Limits to Growth*. Universe Books, New York. http://www.donellameadows.org/wp-content/userfiles/Limits-to-Growth-digital-scan-version.pdf [Retrieved 6 January 2017]

Naisbitt, J. (1994). *Global Paradox. The Bigger the World Economy, the More Powerful Its Smallest Players*. William Morrow.

Naisbitt, J. & Aburdene, P. (1990). *Megatrends 2000*, Rizzoli, Milan.

Ohe, Y. (2003). Multifunctionality and farm diversification: A case of rural tourism. 14th International Farm Management Congress, Proceedings CD-ROM, 761–768.

Romero, M. J. R. (1995). The role of the university in sustainable development: Challenge and opportunities. *Higher Education Policy*, 8(4), 26–29.

Romstad, E. (2010). Multifunctional rural land management: *Economics and Policies Journal of Agricultural Economics* 61(1), 202–204.

Rychen, D. S. & Salganik L. H., (2003). *Key Competences for a Successful Life and a Well-Functioning Society*. Hogrefe & Huber, Cambridge, MA.

Sachs, J. (2013). *The Age of Sustainable Development, Project Syndicate*, December 23, 2013. https://www.project-syndicate.org/commentary/jeffrey-d--sachs-proposes-a-new-curriculum-for-a-new-era [Retrieved 23 December 2013]

SDSN (Sustainable Development Solution Network). (2014). A global initiative for the United Nations SDSN: Proposed Sustainable Development Goals (SDGs) and Targets. http://unsdsn.org/wp-content/uploads/2014/04/140417-Goals-and-Targets1.pdf [Retrieved 6 January 2017]

Solow, R. M. (1956). A contribution to the theory of economic growth. *The Quarterly Journal of Economics*, 70(1), pp. 65–94.

Summers, M., Childs, A. & Corney, G. (2005). Education for sustainable development in initial teacher training: Issues for interdisciplinary collaboration. *Environmental Education Research*, 11(5), pp. 623–647. DOI:10.1080/13504620500169841

Tchetchik, A., Fleischer, A. & Finkelshtain, I. (2012). An optimal size for rural tourism villages with agglomeration and congestion effects. *European Review of Agricultural Economics*, 39(4), pp. 685–706.

Tinbergen, J., Dolman, A. J. & Van Ettinger, J. (1976). *Reshaping the international order: A report to the Club of Rome*. Dutton, New York.

ULSF (University Leader for Sustainable Future). (1990). Talloires Declaration. http://www.ulsf.org/programs_talloires.html [Retrieved 7 January 2017]

UN. (1972). Declaration of the United Nations Conference on the Human Environment. Conference on the Human Environment. http://www.unep.org/documents.multilingual/default.asp?documentid=97&articleid=1503 [Retrieved 9 January 2017]

UN. (2002). Report of the World Summit on Sustainable Development; Johannesburg, South Africa, 26 August to 4 September 2002. United Nations, New York. http://www.unmillenniumproject.org/documents/131302_wssd_report_reissued.pdf [Retrieved 7 January 2017]

UN. (2012). Sustainable Development Knowledge Platform Future We Want – outcome document. https://sustainabledevelopment.un.org/futurewewant.html [Retrieved 8 January 2017]

UNCED. (1992). The Global Partnership for Environment and Development. A guide to Agenda 21. Geneva: UNCED – Post Rio Edition. https://www.amazon.com/Global-Partnership-Environment-Development-Agenda/dp/9211004977 [Retrieved 12 January 2017]

UNESCO. (2005–2014). Decade of Education for Sustainable Development, International Launch of the United Nations Decade of Education for Sustainable Development (2005-2014) on March 1 in New York on March 1 in New York. http://unesdoc.unesco.org/images/0013/001399/139937e.pdf [Retrieved 8 January 2017]

UNESCO. (2007). Strong Foundations, Early Childhood Care and Education. Education for All. *EFA Global Monitoring Report 2007.* UNESCO Publishing, Paris. http://unesdoc.unesco.org/images/0014/001477/147794e.pdf [Retrieved 8 January 2017]

UNESCO. (2009). Bonn Declaration, World Conference on Education for Sustainable Development. http://unesdoc.unesco.org/images/0018/001887/188799e.pdf [Retrieved 8 January 2017]

UNGASS. (2000). Resolution 55/2 adopted by the General Assembly: United Nations Millennium Declaration. *Fifty-fifth General Assembly of the United Nations.* http://www.un.org/millennium/declaration/ares552e.htm [Retrieved 9 January 2017]

UNGASS. (2009). Resolution 64/236 adopted by the General Assembly: Implementation of Agenda 21, the Programme for the Further Implementation of Agenda 21 and the outcomes of the World Summit on Sustainable Development. *Sixty-fourth General Assembly of the United Nations.* https://documents-dds-ny.un.org/doc/UNDOC/GEN/N09/475/99/IMG/N0947599.pdf?OpenElement [Retrieved 9 January 2017]

UNSD (United Nations Sustainable Development). (1992). *The UN Conference on Environment and Development:* A Guide to Agenda 21. UN Publications Service, Geneva. https://sustainabledevelopment.un.org/content/documents/Agenda21.pdf [Retrieved 9 January 2017]

WCED (World Commission on Environment and Development). (1987). *Our Common Future*, Oxford: Oxford University Press.

WTTC (The World Travel & Tourism Council). (2013) Economic Impact of Tourism. https://www.wttc.org/research/economic-research/economic-impact-analysis/ [Retrieved 9 January 2017]

7 New rural tourism paradigm in submetropolitan areas

Klaus Ehrlich

Urbanisation as a gradual increase in the proportion of people living in urban areas is a long-lasting worldwide phenomenon that gained speed in the nineteenth century with the industrialisation process. In a worldwide perspective, the urbanisation rate rose from 29.6 per cent in 1950 to an estimated 54 per cent in 2015. In Europe the respective figures are 51.5 per cent to 73.6 per cent and, for Poland, 38.3 per cent to 60.5 per cent.[1] In the process of urbanisation, metropolitan areas around cities of more than 500,000 inhabitants are growing even more rapidly.

Urban population generates the demand for recreation, not only inside the city but also, increasingly, in the surrounding areas. This demand has traditionally caused the development of rural or countryside tourism, especially for short-haul trips or low-cost holidays. However, an increase in income generates a clear demand for high quality facilities and services, where the price is no longer the only criterion. On the other hand, generational and cultural shifts in values provide new opportunities for valorisation of a wider scope of rural assets than in the past: clean and natural environment, authenticity, space for physical activities, or a personal non-massified ambience and attention. All these factors, together with the general phenomenon of digitisation, point to the need for profound revision of the traditional concepts of rural or countryside tourism.

Traditional concepts and definitions

When speaking about rural tourism in Europe, this term is subject to very different and sometimes contradictory interpretations. Three basic concepts can be found most frequently:

1   Rural tourism as an activity directly related to a working farm, usually defined as 'agritourism'. Only active, working farms can be classified under this concept. It was the historic starting point for rural tourism in many countries. Nowadays a wider interpretation of rural tourism prevails, where farm/agritourism is a specific sub-product with a clear-cut profile.
2   Rural tourism as an activity based on the resources and assets of rural areas, with maximum respect for and integration into economic, social and cultural structures and traditions. This classification focuses on rurality as a criterion

distinguishing it from other tourism activities which may use the same rural territory, but are not classified as rural tourism due to their more industrial structure.

3   Tourism in rural space: any tourism activity situated in a rural territory that takes advantage of its resources and characteristics is included in this concept, without considering the social or cultural integration as critical or defining elements of the product. This interpretation finds its limits in sustainability criteria, or when a tourism activity endangers the existence and preservation of resources attracting visitors.

Discussion with advocates of any of the abovementioned concepts is sometimes difficult. Very different points of view and interests of possible stakeholders, such as farmers, tourism professionals, or local authorities influence and strongly bias the perception of rural tourism. In the last 15 to 20 years there seems to have been a majority consent about the second concept. However, general trends of demand and the associated opportunities for profitable business indicate that this concept will merge with the broader interpretation of 'tourism in rural space' into a future joint interpretation of 'sustainable tourism in a rural territory'.

For a global vision and understanding, the definition for rural tourism given by EuroTer 25 years ago is still valid:

> Rural tourism is defined in the overall economy of tourism as the economic use of the countryside, natural resources, cultural heritage, rural habitat, local tradition and local produce through certified products and services illustrating regional identity. It responds to consumers' needs for accommodation, catering, recreation activities, entertainment and other services. It supports local sustainable development and meets the leisure demands of modern society through a new social solidarity of the city and the country.
>
> (EuroTer 1992)

This definition is a good starting point for identifying more individual concepts. In any case, observation of reality usually gives better and more reliable results than abstract concepts. When we imagine a profitable activity in the context of free markets and competitiveness, we must accept that, in the end, it is the customer who decides what rural tourism really means.

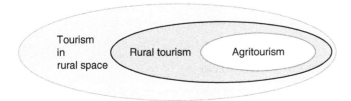

Figure 7.1 Traditional interpretation of rural tourism.

Source: The author's compilation.

Confusion between concept and product

The terms rural tourism and agritourism are frequently used interchangeably, both to describe a technical concept and a tourism product. However, this generic identification is conceptually incorrect because it mixes two dimensions that have little or nothing in common. The result is confusion on both sides and inefficient assignment of public and private resources.

As a *concept*, rural tourism and agritourism are defined as indicated in the previous section: a tourism activity in a rural territory. This definition is valid to describe the technical criteria and parameters needed to frame a tourism policy and support measures in rural territories. Such is the case of different actions taken within the Common Agricultural Policy (CAP) to support recreation and tourism in rural areas, for example, through different rural development programmes since 1991 or national programmes that were implemented by authorities in charge of tourism in many European Union countries.

However, a *tourism product* is something absolutely different. It is based on a corresponding demand pattern in the market, that is, a service or destination will only be successful and sustainable in the market if it offers what a relevant segment of this market wants to consume. This market- and demand-driven approach is not questioned in the traditional tourism industry, but it has rarely been applied to rural tourism and agritourism.

Rural tourism and agritourism services and offers, especially where the development of either of them was strongly supported by public policies, were often created not according to the organic growth of demand, but following largely theoretical considerations. In many cases, they tried to copy successful models in other countries without taking into consideration or understanding their own history and sociocultural background. Consequently, such policies confused the technical concept of rural tourism and agritourism with a market-based product, intending to establish individual technical types of services as a stand-alone product, for example, the case of Spain with the 'casa rurales'. However, similar cases can be found all over Europe.

While it cannot be denied that an individual accommodation service may be a competitive and sustainable product on its own, this is not a general rule. Rural tourism as a technical concept cannot be transformed directly into a tourism product. In fact, a rural tourism product is the result of combining a much wider set of elements, where individual services are only one element among many others. This understanding is still missing or lacking in many countries, even in those where rural tourism and agritourism already have a long tradition.

The situation in submetropolitan areas

Tourism in the countryside surroundings of metropolitan areas is by nature part of the overall concept of rural tourism. It is a clearly visible reality and a consolidated activity in its own right regardless of the three basic concepts, of historic evolution and background, or of development strategies. Furthermore, it is in these areas where recent shifts in demand are more visible and more disruptive to the traditional interpretation.

Like many other services related to recreation, the developmental of rural tourism has been subject to consumer preferences and 'fashions', which have been reflected by periods of more or less dynamic growth or even temporary recession. Nevertheless, the data gathered by EuroGites (the European Federation of Rural Tourism) indicate that in the last 20 to 25 years the mean annual increase in demand and supply has been around 10 to 15 per cent. It is a much higher value than for European tourism in general, where the rate has amounted only to about 2 to 3 per cent per year.[2]

A good part of this growth is caused by an increase in the capacity of countries that only recently have achieved a population with urban characteristics, especially, without family roots in rural areas. In Spain, during the years 1992 to 2010 the accommodation capacity almost doubled every three years. In countries with a longer tradition of rural tourism, quantitative developments are less important or amount almost to zero. In these countries, strong competition still obliges providers to maintain programmes of continuous improvements, innovations and specialisation of services offered.

It is difficult to provide exact figures or even reliable estimates. Definitions and sources of data are very heterogeneous between countries and even within them. In official statistics the majority of rural accommodation facilities simply do not show up because they fall below the threshold of size to be included. EuroGites has established 40 bed places as a tentative upper limit for accommodation facility to be considered Rural Tourism, the mean capacity in Europe would then be around 12-15 beds per unit. Even so, global estimates based on the bed capacity in small, micro, or complementary accommodation in rural areas according to official sources, provide some interesting results for the whole of Europe (28 countries of the European Union plus the rest of continental Europe)[3]:

- more than 500,000 accommodation facilities
- around 6,500,000 beds
- agritourism represents about 15 to 20 per cent of this total
- direct tourism expenses generated by rural tourism greater than 60 billion euros,
- global (direct plus multiplier) effect for the rural economy greater than 110 billion euros.

These values do not include the income generated by excursions (one-day trips without an overnight stay), which is of considerable importance in submetropolitan areas or densely populated areas. Neither do they include the considerable capacities that are offered in the informal market or below the thresholds of statistics, nor the capacity represented by family hotel enterprises with more than 40 beds. Thus, they reflect a cautious and conservative approach to estimates about rural tourism, which in reality may easily generate a total income of more than 200 billion euros per annum for rural areas in Europe. By comparison, at WorldBank figures of 2015 this is similar to the GDP of Finland , or almost duplicates the GDP of Hungary.[4]

It is difficult to establish the share of rural tourism in submetropolitan areas in this total, and further research is necessary. However, with practical knowledge of the sector, it can be estimated at about 50 per cent of the total. The other 50 per cent is located in specific rural tourism destinations, which are attractive for longer distance travel due to high scenic or cultural values.

Within European tourism as a whole, the importance of rural tourism varies largely from 2 per cent to 40 per cent, depending on the country. An intermediate estimate would suggest that rural tourism accommodations represent around 15 per cent of all official beds in the European tourism market, which would confirm the abovementioned capacity of about 6.5 million.

European rural tourism mostly depends on domestic or close-by markets; the available data concerning the origin and occupancy set the following picture[5]:

- 95 per cent of visitors are domestic (they come from the same country).
- 80 per cent of them live less than three hours away, which implies short stays and a concentration of services in wider submetropolitan areas.
- Annual occupancy rates are 20 to 25 per cent, but can be as low as 12 to 15 per cent in many areas In purely touristic regions away from urban agglomerations, accommodation often only operates during a few months of the year.
- 35 per cent occupancy can be considered as a very good result (less than 10 per cent of facilities achieve this result).
- The mean length of stay is between 1.5 days (local markets), 3.6 days (domestic from more than 4-hour travel time), and about 9 days (foreign visitors).
- 85% of visitors prefer independent accommodation (renting the whole house or holiday home). This figure might increase if we included rental agreements for private homes or apartments.
- Only 15 per cent of visitors prefer and use the traditional bed and breakfast (B&B) style of accommodation, which includes additional services such as breakfast and other meals, room cleaning, etc., but this group of clients has a higher spending inclination and capacity.
- Less than 5 per cent expect their accommodation to offer additional or different services other than breakfast and other meals.

In consequence there seem to be two main alternative strategies to obtain an acceptable turnover and profit:

1   Domestic and proximity markets, accessible to wide segments of the population. A relatively reduced investment and a high number of clients give a satisfactory result.
2   Focus on external or minority local niche markets. The limited market size is compensated by a higher profit margin, but requires specialisation and a higher level of professionalism.

At the centre of attention: visitors' needs and expectations

Rural tourism markets are very fragmented. There is no single, unique, or even majority demand pattern. The success of a service or accommodation facility depends precisely on its capacity to attract and satisfy the needs and expectations of specific profiles and market segments within the overall concept of rural tourism:

- strong identification with the typical characteristic of rural areas: agriculture;
- active holidays;
- self-catering accommodation prevails over the traditional concept of a B&B.

The following chart gives a summary of six segments which could be defined in a wider econometric evaluation of consumer surveys in 2005. They combine preference priorities with some additional data regarding age, travel experience, and sociocultural background.

Table 7.1 The six rural tourist segments

No.	Short name	Main characteristics
1	Take it easy and have fun	A 'standard client', with a profile close to mean values across the whole market. These clients do not look for special experiences or intangible qualities, and do not have high expectations about security. Age group: 50+ or young people.
2	Romantic retreat	Give a very high value to equipment standards, but all other factors also receive relatively high valuation, and want to avoid risks. Age group: 20-30, medium-high income, travelling with a partner.
3	Rural idealist	A perfect client for the Bohemian understanding of rural tourism, above all looking for personal contacts and experiences; other factors have little importance. Mostly young people, independent travellers or families with children.
4	Short break	Take short breaks with little anticipation: this requires certainty that there will be no problems. Other factors are close to average. Middle-aged or young visitors, high professional level, frequent travellers.
5	Active and curious	Attach high value active (leisure) with high expectations about other factors except equipment standards. They visit the countryside as active explorers. Middle-aged group, medium-high socioeconomic level, experienced travellers.
6	Enjoy nature	Want to enjoy the location and natural surroundings; not demanding in other aspects, independent and relying on brands and certifications more than others. Middle-aged group, medium socioeconomic level.

Source: The author's compilation.

Demand patterns, preferences and values are undergoing continuous evolution, and so must be all rural tourism products and services. The division presented above is meant as an exercise to show the great variety of markets that can be attracted by rural tourism for different reasons and how to understand them, rather than to establish a definitive or generally valid segmentation.

Some of the segments are contradictory to each other – for example, segments 2 and 5. Some represent a bigger share of the market than others, but none exceeds 25 per cent. The only element that remains stable and with high values is 'location and surroundings'. Therefore, these need to be present in any rural tourism product and confirm the fact that the rural territory is the only factor that unites an otherwise very diverse grouping of products. All the rest can vary considerably and we cannot speak of or define any standard or main profile or product of rural tourism.

Therefore, to be successful the providers of a rural tourism service need to:

- analyse and evaluate their situation, especially strengths and weaknesses;
- specialise in those products that provide the best fit for their strong and weak points;
- improve their product where possible (this is usually easy in terms of equipment or services, but it may be impossible to improve surroundings or recreation offers);
- present their services, with emphasis on those aspects that are of special value or attraction to their target market.

Perspectives and constraints

So far we have analysed the situation of rural tourism in Europe, learnt about the need to know and assess visitors' expectations in order to offer satisfying products and services and we have presented some global views about future perspectives and their bottlenecks. This could help us to improve services, streamline them according to the current demand and prepare for the near future. But what will happen to rural tourism in the long run? What are the trends and tendencies we need to observe in order to anticipate developments that are already around the corner? What challenges will we have to meet? And above all: are traditional definitions and concepts still valid for the future?

General outlook for rural tourism

General perspectives for the future development of rural tourism – both as short-term recreation around bigger cities and as a main holiday product – are very promising. This is due to several reasons:

- Increasing the emotional value given by the urban population to resources such as nature, personal contact and ambience, tranquillity, traditions, or authentic experiences that cannot be found in cities.
- Tendency to split holidays into several shorter trips; instead of one long annual holiday free days are taken all year round and used for short breaks.
- Changes in values regarding lifestyle, health or personal relations transform into a search for Bohemian experiences, wellness, sports, etc. For most of these, rural areas offer almost unlimited possibilities, resources and assets.
- Demographic trends, with an ageing population that has a sound economic background, good health and active attitude without depending on usual seasons or school holidays.

- New technologies (especially Internet applications and functionalities) generate opportunities and a potential (still difficult to estimate to its full extent) even for the smallest and specialised individual offers and products to access niche markets.

Constraints

These promising possibilities are limited by constraints that need to be solved to transform this potential into a tangible success for the rural tourism industry and rural communities as a whole. The most relevant problems of submetropolitan areas are:

- the lack of integration and cooperative management of small products and services, which negatively affects their visibility and positioning under the umbrella of an attractive destination;
- the lack of professional knowledge and capacities amongst small-scale providers;
- a passive attitude to promotion and sales;
- low annual occupancy and price levels that do not provide an opportunity to generate the revenue that is needed for improvement of facilities or services;
- a combination of excessive individualism, sales channels traditionally based on word of mouth communication without commissions or investment in promotion, and low capacities that do not allow for splitting into sales allotments for several parallel channels;
- excessive and ever-increasing regulations and statutory requirements that create additional red tape for small initiatives.

Towards revised understanding and paradigm change

European societies are undergoing a process of profound changes in values and attitudes to life. Traditional patterns of behaviour are no longer valid: the same visitor spends a week in a 5-star resort in Thailand on one holiday but on the next walks the Camino de Santiago, sleeping in bunk beds. As a bottom line, any sort of 'alternative', non-mass recreation offer – in the past almost exclusively provided by rural tourism – now presents good opportunities for growth, while the traditional concepts of standard resort holidays are at most stable or in decline.

This overall picture is the result of several parallel but largely independent developments:

1   Change and shift in tourists' preferences, from standard industrial mass tourism towards concepts that are less 'consumptive' but contribute to the traveller's personal and cultural enrichment and experience: This type of tourist will increasingly substitute the traditional only-sun-and-beach holiday in big complexes, as can be seen in the disruptive success of concepts such as AirBnB.
2   The increase in and availability of free time during the year due to longer holidays, early retirement with decent pension payments, part-time work,

or flexible distribution of annual leave. This type of tourist maintains one 'traditional' holiday per year, but reduces its duration and complements it with a couple of short breaks.

3 Demand for resources, assets and attractions that are available only in rural areas (e.g. nature, environment, clean air, peace and quiet, space for activities). More and more often rural territory is understood as a physical base capable of providing such resources through sustainable exploitation.

Although the first trend offers continuity in the historic concept and understanding of rural tourism as integrating physical, cultural and human assets into a specific comprehensive product of its own, it is already under pressure and competition from similar concepts of the 'sharing econony', as represented by AirBnB. The second trend is neutral, because it simply increases the number of possible clients. Finally, the third trend seems to offer the most dynamic opportunities for growth, it is still in line with the objective to give value to local resources, but it reduces or eliminates the strict and exclusive binding of rural tourism with the sociocultural context of traditional rural communities.

Most concepts of rural tourism, rural development and, in general, urban-rural relationships, date back about 30 to 40 years. The reality of rural areas has changed since then, mostly as a result of concepts and related policies that were generally successful in their intention to transform rural territories and diversify their economic base away from agriculture.

The so-called neo-rural population (internal immigrants of urban origin who resettle into rural areas due to the quality of life or personal motives) is increasingly successful in offering tourism services in rural areas. They frequently attach higher value to the conservation of local assets and resources than the indigenous population. They also have clearer understanding of urban clients' needs and expectations, based on their own experience and, thus, they are more capable of designing adequate facilities and services.

Digitalisation is probably the most disruptive phenomenon, not only for rural tourism. In a short timeframe of 10 years, it changed the rules of the game almost completely, shifting power from providers' stable structures to individual stakeholders' spontaneous decisions, taken both by providers and clients. Easy access to all kind of information through search engines, professional online booking even for the smallest B&B units, or real-time information and unfiltered opinions through social media are examples of these changes. Figure 7.2 illustrates this: in the centre we can see traditional 'strong' and unique characteristics of structures and products of rural tourism, and how they are substituted under pressure from new players and developments.

As urban visitors have an increasingly comprehensive and diverse set of expectations and needs concerning their leisure time, the understanding of rural tourism both as a concept and as a set of products needs to be revised. We propose the following scheme of revised understanding, based on the traditional view but considerably extending it:

In comparison with the traditional understanding shown in the scheme at the beginning of this essay, the new understanding introduces the following changes:

- The overall concept that covers all tourism activities in rural submetropolitan areas, in a situation where sustainability places red tape for industrial or mass tourism, is now defined as sustainable recreation.
- It absorbs the part of what was traditionally understood as rural tourism, where direct binding with rural communities is not the main criterion.
- Both product groups of rural tourism and agritourism in their traditional content remain relevant but with a smaller proportion of the the total.
- All resources of rural submetropolitan areas that have potential for attracting visitors should ideally be unified under 'destination management' with a holistic perspective. It could be either a specific geographic destination or, in an abstract sense, a thematic cluster.

Figure 7.2 Pressure and new competitors to rural tourism structures.

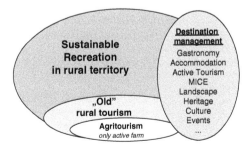

Figure 7.3 New understanding of rural tourism.

Conclusions

Rural tourism is now 'coming of age'. Its further development will depend on market success, in contrast to excessive dependency on public support, as used to be the case in the past. There are some interesting examples in South America and the United States, where rural tourism has been developed by strictly private initiative. They give some perspectives for development in Europe.

The most remarkable tendencies for submetropolitan areas, which make an estimated 50 per cent of total rural tourism, can be summarised as follows:

- high professional knowledge and specialisation, even where services are provided as a complementary activity;
- less philosophy, more business;
- market segmentation, based on the demand for resources and assets that are available in rural territories;
- virtual trust together with structured feedback from customers will be decisive to market success;
- new information and communication technology used at all levels, including real-time online booking and communication;
- integrated sustainable destination management structures with the participation of all public and private stakeholders will be implemented in most rural (territories) under the concept of network of networks.

Notes

1   For all data (world, Europe and Poland), see: UN - World Urbanization Prospects, the 2014 revision   https://esa.un.org/unpd/wup/CD-ROM/WUP2014_XLS_CD_FILES/WUP2014-F02-Proportion_Urban.xls
2   The author's elaboration based on annual surveys, membership development and periodical research 1990–2015.
3   The author's research and calculations based on official or regional statistics and recount of services published on websites and other publicly accessible sources.
4   Reference data: Worldbank, EuroStat and others.
5   A comparative re-compilation of available national and regional statistics, complemented by surveys amongst providers and professional organisations of the sector.

Reference

EuroTer (Commission Européenne DG XXIII). (1992). *Etude Euroter sur les hébergements touristiques de l'espace rural dans l'Europe communautaire.* Commission Européenne – DG XXIII.
Hungary: http://data.worldbank.org/?locations=HU-FI   121 billion USD at ídem = 109 billion EUR
Finland: http://data.worldbank.org/?locations=HU-FI - 232 billion USD at exchange rate 0,9 EUR/USD = 209 billion

8 Normative modelling in coordination of generic and private tourism promotion in submetropolitan areas

Michał Jacenty Sznajder and Sylwia Marek

The problem of normative modelling

Let us assume there is a bundle of consistent goals which a particular community wants to achieve in order to benefit. The members of this community will benefit from these goals to a different extent – some of them will benefit more, others less. For this reason, individual members of this community are interested to a different extent in the achievement of the consistent bundle of goals. Let us further assume that individual goals in this bundle will be financed either from social sources (the community budget) or private sources. In order to ensure the financial transparency of actions, individual goals in the bundle are financed from separate sources. The community budget finances only social goals, and interested stakeholders finance private goals. In spite of the fact that individual goals are financed from separate sources, the finances in a coordinated bundle of goals will result in a synergistic effect. It means that, in consequence of the coordination of goals, each stakeholder receives a greater effect than in the situation without this coordination. The goals become coordinated as a result of normative modelling.

The need to systematise the normative standardisation theory

Normative modelling is applied to coordinate social actions and increases the effectiveness of social actions. However, the scientific literature does not provide a sufficient number of good descriptions of modelling. This chapter presents the authors' concept of normative modelling, which is a synthesis of a literature study and deduction resulting from the research they have conducted, and their analyses and considerations.

Normative modelling results in a normative model, which in practice is applied to increase the effectiveness of social actions. The aim of the model is to achieve maximum effects of social actions as a result of the synergistic effect between public and private funds. Synergy is understood as having a greater effect than regular addition. It can be expressed with the following formula:

synergic effect $2 + 2 > 4$

This synergistic effect does not result from the obligatory combination of public and private funds in the hands of one administrator in order to finance particular social actions together. It results from the voluntary and independent allocation of funds to coordinated aims indicated in the normative model. The model should be efficient and effective and it should stimulate the synergistic effect from social actions. The model should include a market mechanism, with the supply and demand in a particular area of social actions. It is also important to include the stakeholders' needs both in both the short term (1 to 5 years) and the long term (6 to 10 years).

Social actions and their effectiveness

Human nature is characterised by the imperative to take action in order to achieve planned effects. The effects can be achieved by both individual and group actions. If the effects concern a community (family, group, team, parish, commune), they are defined as *social effects* resulting from *social actions*. There may be economic, political, religious, health-promoting, sports and other social actions. Thus, normative modelling may apply to these actions. In normative modelling a social action does not refer to a non-outlay action, as it may sometimes be interpreted. Each action involves both financial and non-financial outlay.

Usually both individuals and a particular community take a wide range of different actions at the same time. These actions are taken both individually and by groups, such as social structures, local governments, institutions, organisations, and enterprises. A list of identified areas of actions (a list of issues) can be set for each community. Normative modelling may apply to all social actions in a community or only to some of these actions. The actions taken in order to achieve a particular goal may be socially uncoordinated or coordinated, and this lack of coordination may be deliberate or unintentional. A deliberate lack of coordination may be a manifestation of individual or group egoism in order to eliminate competitors completely by marginalisation. The aim of normative modelling is to engage all interested parties (stakeholders) in social actions and their effects in a particular area.

As far as a particular area of social actions is concerned, the actions taken by individual people, local governments, institutions, organisations and enterprises may be antagonistic, competitive, neutral or complementary to one another:<list>

- *Antagonistic* or *eliminatory actions* lead to the elimination of other stakeholders from social actions. They are egoistic and generate a wide range of social and economic problems in a particular community.
- The aim of *competitive actions* is to strengthen one stakeholder's position at the expense of other stakeholders (competitors). The most competitive stakeholder gains the benefits.
- *Neutral actions* taken by one stakeholder are neutral to another stakeholder. This means that they do not have any negative influence on another stakeholder's actions.

- *Complementary actions* occur when the actions taken by one stakeholder favour other stakeholders and increase the effectiveness of actions taken by all stakeholders.

The rules of normative modelling

Normative modelling is used to plan and coordinate social actions in a particular community (territorial unit) within a particular range (bundle of goals) in order to increase the effectiveness of these actions. This method promotes the synergy of social actions as a result of coordination of these actions. The following eight rules are used in normative modelling:

- *Generality*: All parties (stakeholders) interested in a particular area of social actions are engaged in the process of normative modelling.
- *Non-exclusion*: Normative modelling is based on counteracting the exclusion of stakeholders for any reason.
- *Stakeholders' independent financing of tasks from the coordinated bundle of goals*: The stakeholders taking social actions are independent business entities and they finance these actions only if they think it is appropriate and up to the acceptable level. Nobody can force any stakeholder to finance anything. Normative modelling shows the stakeholders that it is possible to achieve synergy if the tasks from the coordinated bundle of goals are appropriately financed.
- *The minimum or neutrality of social actions*: Normative modelling excludes stakeholders' antagonistic (eliminatory) and competitive actions and allows only the minimum, i.e. the actions which do not have negative effect on other stakeholders' activity.
- *Synergy*: The main goal of normative modelling is to achieve synergy as a result of stakeholders' social actions.
- *Legal basis*. The normative model must be based on the applicable legal system in a particular community.
- *Competence and procedures*: Normative modelling specifies the competence of individual stakeholders and their actions (sequence and range) are regulated by the formulated procedures.
- *Free access and effective flow of information*: The key element of the normative model is to provide free access to the information concerning modelling and to develop a method (procedure) of the flow of information between the stakeholders. This rule enables the stakeholders who take social actions to retain mutual trust and understanding.

Stakeholders and executors

The persons, local governments, institutions, organisations and enterprises in a particular community that are interested in the coordination of social actions are defined as *stakeholders*. Due to the fact that the fundamental standard of normative modelling is to counteract the exclusion of stakeholders, it is necessary to fully identify them and provide the best information possible about the social actions taken in a particular area. At the modelling stage stakeholders must have the opportunity to express their opinions. Sometimes there are stakeholders who are not ready to finance the tasks from the coordinated bundle of goals, so it is necessary to identify executors. The persons, local governments, institutions, organisations and enterprises in a particular community that finance the coordinated bundle of goals are defined as *executors*.

The pursuit of stakeholders' general understanding of social actions in a particular area is a key element of the normative model. Each group of stakeholders has its goals. Some of these goals may be different but others may be the same. Individual stakeholders develop a chain of communication and information flow, which is imperative for the efficiency, effectiveness and synergy of social actions. A rationally constructed communication model is the fundament of the normative model. Contemporary media, especially the Internet, favour the formation of the communication chain and free distribution of information. This applies both to the hardware (e.g. the Internet, computers, tablets) and software (e.g. social instant messaging systems).

The normative model

The normative model is a document for a coordinated bundle of goals and specific social actions, formulated and approved by the stakeholders in a particular community. It contains a vision and mission for a particular area of social activity. It shows how to avoid financing antagonistic and competitive actions and indicates the procedures and stages of implementation of this vision, which result in a synergistic effect.

Like every model, the normative model is subject to limitations, that is, to boundary conditions. In this case, the legal system that is applicable to a particular community, the executors' assets and liabilities and the social cooperation capacity are the boundary conditions. The rule applied in normative modelling is that the model that is being developed must be based on the system that is applicable to a particular community. A correctly developed model respects international, European Union, national and local laws, as applicable. The development of all procedures for specific social actions must be based on these laws.

Normative modelling: step by step

The normative modelling process is a sequence of the following seven procedures:

- The choice of a social action area for which the normative model will be developed: The local community takes a large number of social actions but some of them are not sufficiently identified. The identification of an action area is the first and most important step in the construction of a normative model and consists of specifying its essence and conditions.

- Formulating a vision for a selected social action area: A vision of the normative model is the same as a vision in the development of a strategy – it is a forward-looking, desirable image of a particular action. However, the fundamental problem is that stakeholders may perceive the vision in different ways, hence the vision should not be the result of individual stakeholders' pursuits but should be formulated in a way that will result in a synergic effect during implementation.
- Formulating a mission for a selected social action area: A mission in the normative model is perceived in the same way as a mission in the development of a strategy – it defines the goals which should be achieved by implementation of the normative model. Due to the multiplicity of stakeholders, goals should be expressed as a coordinated bundle, where the main goal is adjusted to individual stakeholders.
- Identification of stakeholders: When formulating a normative model it is necessary to identify all the stakeholders in order to include their interests. Sometimes the identification process is not sufficient and does not prevent the exclusion of certain groups, therefore a public announcement might be necessary.
- Coordination of stakeholders' interests and synergy from the implementation of the model: The next step involves the determination of individual stakeholders' interests by implementation of the social action in a particular area and coordination of these interests. This step also indicates the synergy resulting from the implementation of the normative model.
- Developing procedures (tactics) for a selected social action: The tactics included in the procedures indicate the ways the implementation will be carried out and the deadlines for the implementation of the vision of a particular social action. The procedures should specify the executors' and stakeholders' tasks and the synergic effects that individual stakeholders might expect to achieve. The appropriate implementation of the procedures guarantees the synergic effect resulting from normative modelling.
- Ensuring legality of the model and procedures: The developed normative model, especially the procedures involved in its development, should be based on the applicable legal system in a particular community.

The peculiarities of normative modelling

Normative modelling might be associated with excessive paper work, legal over-regulation and sluggishness of procedures. However, we live in the epoch of widespread and increasingly abundant consumption of information. Effective and acceptable procedures result in a synergic effect. Normative modelling should be used in these areas of social actions where the outlay for the development and implementation of normative modelling is less than the resulting synergy. Normative modelling may be perceived as less financially effective in the short term than in the long term.

In fact, the whole legal system consists in the formulation of standards at the expense of communities. Normative modelling largely consists in using the existing legal regulations for social actions. However, it is necessary to realise that a badly designed, sluggish and ineffective normative model will be rejected at the stage of its formulation or it will not be financed by stakeholders. In fact, everyday life in a particular community has developed the basis for many social actions, which might be elements of a normative model. When they are combined into a holistic model, they will result in efficiency, effectiveness and synergy.

This reasoning leads to the question: is normative modelling not the same as a business plan or another planning technique. We cannot deny that there is some convergence between them, but there are also considerable differences, which empower us to identify normative modelling as a specific method that deserves further theoretical development. The most important difference in normative modelling is that it refers to the ordering of social actions in a particular area, where the actions must meet the specified rules of modelling so as to achieve the synergy for individual stakeholders as a result of independent financing of private and public outlay.

Financing the promotion of submetropolitan tourism as a normative modelling problem

In vast metropolitan areas there are a lot of people, organisations and institutions interested in the development of local tourism and representing private and social interests.

The parties interested in adequate economic effects from metropolitan tourism must outlay expenses on their development. When we make investments in rural tourism in metropolitan areas, local agritourism is an involuntary beneficiary, and vice versa. This particularly applies to the outlay on promotion. Therefore, it is necessary to distinguish between private promotion and generic promotion. In other words, a private investor financing the promotion of, for example, agritourism or HoReCa, (i.e. their own tourism business), as a consequence finances the generic promotion of tourism in the adjacent metropolitan area. Similarly, when a social investor promotes the development of tourism (generic promotion) in metropolitan areas, as a consequence they also finance the promotion of tourism businesses in this area.

To sum up, generic promotion of tourism encompasses financing the development and maintenance of the tourism infrastructure in its broad sense as well as spreading information about the values and attractions of a particular area. Private promotion involves financing the development and maintenance of an entity and spreading information about its services and products as well as spreading information about the values and attractions of the area where the enterprise is located. This comparison shows that there is a common area for private and generic promotion.

From the practical experience of many countries we can see that, for example, rural tourism is promoted from public funds as part of promotion of the region, whereas agritourism is promoted from farmers' private funds. Despite the promotion of these two forms of tourism being financed from different sources and by independent entities, the funds result in a common economic goal, that is, the maximum return on combined private and public funds invested in promotion.

It is difficult to estimate the annual effectiveness of promotion, because the effects from the funds expended on promotion in a particular investment year are distributed over the following years. The process of financing promotion also took place in previous years, so the final effect for a particular year is the corresponding percentage of the accumulated effect of financing in that year and in several previous years.

Generic and private promotion are financed from private and public funds, which are independent of each other. Therefore, it is necessary to take reasonable actions to at least avoid antagonism or inconsistency between them. In practice, antagonistic actions can be deliberately or unintentionally financed. Local cooperation between private and social stakeholders should eliminate this evident irrationality.

Financing the promotion of tourism in metropolitan areas from social and private sources should result in a synergistic effect. It is a fact that generic promotion as part of the promotion of tourism in a metropolitan area favours the development of private tourism businesses, even those on the fringes of the area, because it concerns the values of the tourism areas where these businesses are located. As a result, there is increased inflow of tourists to these farms. Also, the self-promotion of businesses increases the inflow of tourists to particular metropolitan areas, which results in more rapid development of these areas. In both cases the multiplier effect can be observed. Only generic and private promotion coordinated by appropriate stakeholders results in a synergic effect from private and public funds. Due to the possibility of achieving synergy it is rational that the stakeholders dealing with the development of tourism in submetropolitan areas should be integrated.

The effectiveness of generic and private promotion of tourism in submetropolitan areas

Effective promotion is the way of allocation of the promotional budget leading to rational decisions or to maximal effects of a particular outlay or to a minimal outlay at the assumed level of effects. The area of interest should encompass both quantitative (quantifiable) effects and qualitative (un measurable) effects (Wiktor 2001, pp. 103–108).

The normative model of generic and private promotion of tourism in a particular community should be efficient and effective. The idea of efficiency and effectiveness is expressed in Figure 8.1. The level of efficiency and effectiveness can be expressed in both a measurable and an unmeasurable form, which is defined verbally. The efficiency of promotional actions specifies if and to what extent the goals of the actions were achieved. The funds allocated for these goals are defined as the promotion budget. The effectiveness of promotion is defined as the relation between the expenses of promotion and the effects. An action is regarded as effective if the effects surpass the costs of promotion. A synergistic effect in

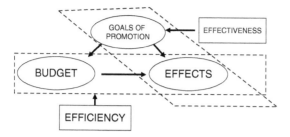

Figure 8.1 The efficiency and effectiveness of promotion.
Source: Wiktor 2001, p. 102.

promotion can be observed when the implementation of solutions in a normative model results in the total efficiency and effectiveness of generic and private promotion being greater than in separate promotion of the two types. Naturally, it is difficult to quantify this synergy, so we limit it only to a verbal description.

The construction of a normative model for generic and private promotion of tourism

Our pilot studies indicate that, for example, the promotion of rural tourism and agritourism is financed ad hoc from the community budget and farmers' budget. It is done without coordination at the local level. As a result, no synergistic effect is achieved. In consequence, uncoordinated promotion may be inadequate, costly and ineffective. This brings us to the question of who should coordinate cooperation in a particular region and how it should be coordinated. Private tour operators may be sceptical about a coordinated promotional action. For some particular reasons institutions and organisations may also be sceptical about coordinated promotion. However, the synergistic effect resulting from the financing of coordinated goals of promotion is tempting enough to undertake such actions.

The formulation of a common model of development of tourism for a particular community in a submetropolitan area usually results in stakeholders' voluntary acceptance of the model and in working on the implementation of the model. If the stakeholders are additionally granted adequate coordinative competences, which they accept, the implementation of the mission and strategy of the normative model will be facilitated. We can expect some the synergistic effect, because actions are oriented in the same direction and there is no overlapping work or double financing of the same outlay.

The identification of stakeholders is a critical element. We can usually distinguish the following six groups of stakeholders interested in the promotion of tourism in a submetropolitan area:

1   Farmers providing agritourism services: They are directly interested in the promotion of their farms and the region, because they expect extra income

from this activity. Promotion will not only let them maintain the current standard of services they provide but will also give them an opportunity to extend their agritourism activity and a possibility to employ members of their families or other people in the village. The agritourism activity provides an opportunity to establish new contacts and to release their farm products on the market, which so far may have been sold through traditional sales channels.

2   Urban and rural inhabitants in a community where the promotional action takes place: They are interested in increasing the inflow of funds to the community, especially by taking advantage of the opportunities provided by the development of tourism (the multiplier effect). They expect greater general interest in their region, which will result in greater employment opportunities and in the local government taking care of the infrastructure in the community.

3   Business entities operating in a particular community (hotels, shops, restaurants, petrol stations): A greater inflow of tourists will provide them with higher turnover.

4   Administration of a particular submetropolitan region: They are interested in general economic development of the community and its welfare. Therefore, they are ready to finance the promotion of tourism values in the region and the development of tourism infrastructure in its broad sense. They have the structures and funds that they can use for general tourism promotion of the region.

5   Traditional and Internet tour operators: They are interested in the promotion of their companies in the region and in providing tourists with the services offered by 1 and 3. They are particularly interested in providing tourism information about the region, which is generated by 4. They expect greater income from tourism by increasing the number of clients in the local tourism market. Tour operators are also interested in the development of the tourism infrastructure in its broad sense, ranging from agritourism farms, through transport infrastructure, and to the Internet.

6   Submetropolitan tourists: They look for specific information generated by other stakeholders. The effective promotion of a particular entity will increase the demand for services offered by the facility. There are also expectations concerning boundary conditions, such as better health care in the region, safety, easy access, and bigger and better-quality shops.

Stakeholders' expectations about the private and generic promotion of tourism in a particular region are both convergent and divergent. The convergent expectations are tourist satisfaction, good service, safety, good promotion. The greatest divergent interest is competition in terms of the number of clients.

Stakeholders should exchange information about tourism in a particular submetropolitan region between each other. If the process of communication between stakeholders is not formalised in any way, and usually it is not, the communication is disorderly and, in consequence, the funds invested in tourism are not used effectively. A rationally ordered flow of information is a fundamental element of the normative model.

The vision is the element of the normative model that should be well formulated and justified, for example, in the form of a paradigm showing the determinants, trends and perspectives of the development of tourism in a submetropolitan area in the long term. Although science might be responsible for the formulation of the paradigm that could be used in normative modelling, it does not provide such long-term indications. The mission specified in the normative model of promotion of tourism in a submetropolitan area is to take actions so as to achieve the maximum effect, including the synergistic effect from the public and private funds invested in the promotion. The implementation of the vision and mission is ensured by a set of legal procedures, applied in a rational sequence and within specific conditions, which must be met by the stakeholders taking actions that are financed from private and social funds to promote tourism.

Conclusion

Normative modelling, which was presented in this elaboration, is a transparent method used to coordinate actions and to finance them voluntarily from public and private funds in order to achieve the efficiency, effectiveness and economic synergy of all stakeholders' undertakings. The method is based on the paradigms of development of individual areas of interest and it ensures long-term solutions. Tourism in submetropolitan areas is a perfect place for the absorption of this method.

References

Gillespie, W. E. (2010). *Strategy Planning in Local Authorities, a Normative Model Consistent with the Principles of Sustainable Development.* PhD thesis. University of Waikato. Permanent Research Commons. http://researchcommons.waikato.ac.nz/handle/10289/4973 [Retrieved 29 December 2016]

Wiktor, J. W. (2001). *Promocja: System komunikacji przedsiębiorstwa z rynkiem*, Wydawnictwo Naukowe PWN, Warszawa.

9 The concept of rural tourism and agritourism

Michał Jacenty Sznajder

Man, nature, tourism

It is a human existential need to have contact with both animate and inanimate nature. This contact causes some effects in people and in nature and these effects should be invigorating for both. Nature provides everything that humans need for survival and people should sensibly use these resources. The long history of humanity shows that nature is a boon to humans and that they usually use it rationally. Alas, this coexistence is also fraught with numerous difficulties. Untamed, powerful forces of nature may cause hundreds of thousands of human beings to perish in a brief moment.

Sometimes people's careless actions cause disorder in nature and increase the likelihood of dangerous revenge taken by nature on humans. Over the last 50 years the Aral Sea in Kazakhstan and Uzbekistan has dried up completely because the waters from the Amu Darya and the Syr Darya rivers had been redirected to farmlands. It is an environmental disaster on an unprecedented scale. Today the Aral Sea occupies only 20 per cent of its original area and as little as 10 per cent of the water resources of the lake in 1960, and its exposed floor has become a desert. Apart from that, in Soviet times a former island on the lake was the location of a military range for biological weapons. At present the place is a sanctuary for various pathogens, for example, anthrax.

It is a challenge for all humanity to minimise threats that result from the nature-human relationship. The dependences and consequences of this relationship are the subject of interest to a wide range of branches of economics and science. They are also reflected by all human activities, including tourism. Humans and nature are supposed to coexist rather than be doomed to war against each other. Everything that humans need for life is provided by nature, starting with sunlight and space for moving around. People need fresh, unpolluted air, clean water, healthy food, and contact with other people, plants and animals. Nature satisfies people's existential, emotional, aesthetic, cultural and cognitive needs, improves the quality of their lives, and promotes health and longevity. Nature enables humans to achieve sustainable development in civilisation.

It is also obvious that, in fact, people are permanently weary, both when surrounded by animate and inanimate nature. Thus, in a way, the need for contact with nature is naturally satisfied in the lives of individuals and societies. Over the centuries the quest for food, from gathering, hunting, fishing, shepherding to modern agriculture, has involved continuous contact with nature and benefits from this contact. Over the years humans have been continuously changing the environment, which had both positive and negative consequences. The most visible anthropogenic effect of this transformation is the current state of global urbanisation, networks of roads, tracks, canals, water reservoirs, agriculture, industry, mining and telecommunication. These transformations have modified the natural environment. On the one hand, it is judged to be desirable progress for civilisation, but on the other hand, it is seen as devastation of the natural environment. It is a relatively common belief that billions of people live in an anthropogenic ally degraded environment, whereas relatively few people live in an unpolluted environment.

The development of civilisation makes people increasingly independent and isolated from animate nature and the natural environment. A large number of human activities have been moved indoors, so now these activities are even more isolated from the natural conditions, especially from the weather and climate. Air conditioning, central heating and car transport are elements that particularly support this isolation. At present, more and more often we can encounter situations where people spend most of the day under artificial weather and lighting conditions. Urbanisation, motorisation and computerisation are three global phenomena which have revolutionised the relationship between humans and nature and which have significantly affected the form of contemporary tourism.

Rapid urbanisation is a phenomenon of the nineteenth, twentieth and twenty-first centuries. The number of cities and urban population have been growing rapidly. In western Europe urban population makes up 80 per cent of the total population. There are more than 509 cities with more than 1 million inhabitants in the world. There are satellite settlements growing around big cities. This is how huge metropolitan areas with populations in the multimillions develop. There are 12 mega-metropolises with more than 20 million inhabitants and there is an increasingly long list of metropolises approaching this number. There are both rich and poor people living in metropolitan areas: The rich are separated from nature by luxury, whereas the poor are separated from it by poverty.

Motorisation is another phenomenon of the twentieth and twenty-first centuries. It is manifested by unprecedented development of transport, especially private transport. Motorisation has a wide range of consequences for human life, people's lifestyles and the economy. Some forms of transport distance people from nature, whereas others bring people much closer to it. Modern mass and individual forms of tourism have developed thanks to air, road and rail transport, including both private and public transport.

Computerisation and digitalisation are also phenomena of the late twentieth and early twenty-first centuries, which are revolutionising all areas of human life and activity to an even greater extent. They enable optimisation of the man-nature relationship. Thanks to computerisation and digitalisation, all tourism undertakings can be perfectly planned, prepared and executed.

The development of civilisation constantly increases the number of people who do not have optimal everyday contact with nature, agriculture and forestry. These people often live in an artificial or even degraded environment. The individual and social negative consequences of devastation and isolation from the natural environment are more and more noticeable. It is especially visible in the development of civilisation-related diseases, such as obesity, depression, and circulatory system failures. In many countries life expectancy is decreasing. Therefore, we urgently need to restore human contact with the natural environment.

Tourism[1] rationally uses the achievements of civilisation for its development. Its main goal is to bring people closer to nature again. However, there are some opponents to this goal. These so-called ecological fundamentalists think that tourism, especially mass tourism, is a serious threat to the natural environment and it should be limited in or even eliminated from some areas. This attitude results from the extreme reply to the essential question in the philosophy of nature: Is man part of nature? Alas, it is not always possible to give a positive answer to this question. Advocates of extreme ecological fundamentalism express the opinion that humans are not only a harmful but also an unnecessary element of nature. In consequence of this attitude, there are attempts to limit people's contact with the natural environment.

While not ignoring the threats to the natural environment resulting from the development of tourism, we can indicate a wide range of solutions which provide tourists with access to the most interesting elements of nature and simultaneously ensure full protection. One example of such solutions is roads that are built especially for car traffic to provide tourists with access to the most attractive places. The Sardinian road SS-125, which is called Orientale Sarda (Sznajder 2014), or the Grossglockner High Alpine Road (Grossglockner Hochalpenstrasse n.d.), enable thousands of tourists travelling by car in Europe to have unparalleled contact with nature, and admire magnificent Sardinian or Alpine views without bringing disorder to the local ecological system. Contemporary nature tourism has developed solutions that facilitate people's contact with nature but do not degrade the natural environment. Future practical solutions will be even friendlier to the natural environment.

Basic definitions

Tourism is not a scientific discipline. On the one hand, it is manifested as a human business activity. As far as demand and supply are concerned, it is defined by people's numerous interests and activities, such as travelling, recreation, relaxation, cognition and achieving experiences. Competent knowledge of tourism requires versatile erudition. Probably there are no areas of knowledge that would be useless for tourism. Tourism phenomena are analysed by different scientific disciplines, which define them according to their specific needs. Therefore there is a great variety of definitions of tourism. The official definition of tourism accepted by the United Nations World Tourism Organisation (UNWTO)[2] reads as follows: 'tourism is a social, cultural and economic phenomenon related to the movement of people to places outside their usual place of residence, pleasure being the usual motivation'.

The same organisation (UNWTO 2010, p.10) defines a visitor as 'a traveller taking a trip to a main destination outside his/her usual environment, for less than a year, for any main purpose (business, leisure or other personal purpose) other than to be employed by a resident entity in the country or place visited'. A visitor (domestic, inbound or outbound) is classified as a tourist (or overnight visitor) if 'his/her trip includes an overnight stay, or as a same-day visitor (or excursionist) otherwise'. There are different enterprises providing services to the act of travel, but tour operators deserve special attention as they plan, offer and execute tourism trips. Tourism is also a human business activity, where the demand side is represented by tourists, and the supply side by tour operators (in a broad sense).

Tourism products, domains and co-domains

The goal of tourism is to provide tourism services and sell tourism products. The services are intangible, whereas the products are tangible results of manufacturing or processing. Apart from that, tourism is connect to imponderables, that is, immeasurable values, which especially refer to space and things like the beauty of the landscape, fresh air or rural architecture. In spite of the fact that imponderables are neither products nor services, they considerably facilitate the market process. Tourism uses the term *attraction*. Products, services, imponderables or their combinations could be tourism attractions. An attraction is something specific that attracts a tourist to visit a particular place. It is not correct to directly identify an attraction with a product or service, because some tourism products and services are regarded as attractions, whereas others are not.

Contemporary tourism offers an enormous range of products and services. Therefore, it is necessary to classify them. In fact, we can distinguish two fundamental classification criteria – the first concerns the seasonal availability of products and services, the other divides products into groups. Due to the seasonal availability of tourism products, services and imponderables, we can divide them into those that are available all year round, and those that are available seasonally. Many tourism products and services have a seasonal character and there is a considerable number of momentary products, services and imponderables among them. They are available now or not for another season, for example, flowers blooming for a short period of time, such as crocuses blooming in spring for a few days on meadows under the mountains. Seasonal products, services and imponderables are more expensive than those that are available all year round. In many regions of the world, for example in Egypt, tourism services can be provided all year round, so they can be relatively inexpensive. In this case tourism is organised like an assembly line, with some people leaving as others arrive. There are trips organised every day and flights, hotels and restaurants are fully booked. In this way, all services on all days of the year are fully used.

The other criterion is the division of products and services into categories, such as hotels, catering services, leisure, sports, therapy, entertainment, specific tourism, direct sales and ethnography. We can identify specific products and services in each category.

The same tourism products and services can be regarded as a domain of a specific type of tourism or as a co-domain of different forms of tourism. For example, the observation of a manufacturing process on a farm is a domain of agritourism, but watching birds in their natural habitats is a co-domain of nature tourism, ecotourism, rural tourism. In fact, most tourism products and services are co-domains.

Nature and tourism

There is a very long list of types of tourism and it is continuously being extended. Human contact with nature is probably noticeable in all forms of tourism even if it is not in the foreground. Nevertheless, there is a whole group of forms of tourism where the main goal is to satisfy the essential human need for contact with nature, called *nature tourism*. It is practised by making trips and staying in the natural environment in its broad sense. The aim of nature tourism is to observe and experience different geological and geographical forms, their flora and fauna, and their cover by forests, agricultural crops, pastures, water areas, wasteland and development. Nature tourism encompasses learning about the world of plants and wild and domesticated animals. Apart from that, it also encompasses tourism in rural and agricultural areas, including human economic, cultural and religious activities related with these areas. The chief motives for nature tourism are recreation and relaxation in the natural environment and the possibility of health promotion through various natural therapies. Therefore, trips to rural and agricultural areas for the purpose of sports and recreation are classified as nature tourism. However, each attempt to define nature tourism is defective and could be undermined, as it is either too broad or too narrow. The range of forms of nature tourism is better characterised by a set of key words grouped into the following categories: nature, ethnography, economy, accommodation, activity, as shown in Table 9.1.

A form of tourism can be classified as nature tourism if it meets the essential conditions of at least one corresponding key word from the Nature or Economy

Table 9.1 Key words characterising nature tourism

Group of key words	Key words
Nature	Nature, landscape, flora, fauna, ecology
Ethnography	Ethnography, rural areas
Economy	Agriculture, forestry, fishing, hunting, food
Accommodation	Camp site, rural accommodation, farm, forester's house
Activity	Journey, stay, learning, observation, pilgrimage, health promotion, leisure, relaxation

Source: The author's compilation.

group and a few words from the Activity group. However, the ranges of different forms of tourism usually overlap, thus making each classification open to dispute. If we assume this limitation as an inalienable element, we can distinguish the following types of tourism within nature tourism:

1   Tourism in rural areas

    a   Sightseeing tourism
    b   Ecotourism

2   Rural tourism

    a   Ethnographic tourism
    b   Culinary tourism, e.g. enotourism (wine tourism)
    c   Agritourism

Rural tourism and agritourism

In the last 25 years of the twentieth century we could observe the emergence of the following neologisms: *tourism in rural areas*, *rural tourism* and *agritourism*. The meaning of these terms has not fully crystallised in practice or in law yet and is still developing. The term *agritourism* is a linguistic and marketing catchword, which has become widely used all over the world. Analysis of European Union law (Kapala 2008) shows that it does not use the term *agritourism* and that the support actions for multidirectional development of farms and rural areas refer to rural tourism only. In practice, the term *agritourism* has been extremely popular recently and has been widely used all over the world.

In fact, *agritourism* is a term introduced by the supply side, that is, by farmers providing tourism services. However, it was also accepted by the demand side, that is, by tourists. This means that tourists interpret and perceive agritourism in a different way than providers of agritourism services. Farmers provide agritourism services in order to increase their income, although sometimes they are guided by other than economic reasons. For the tourist, agritourism is a specific tourism activity that usually takes place in rural areas, in an agricultural environment. Tourists are not particularly interested in distinguishing the differences between tourism in rural areas, rural tourism and agritourism.

Although these terms are not equivalent, they strongly overlap. Ehrlich (2009) defines them in the following way:

> Rural tourism – any tourism activity situated in a rural territory that takes advantage of its resources and characteristics and which is accepted by the concept, without considering the social or cultural integration as critical, defining elements of the product. This interpretation finds its limits in sustainability criteria, or when a tourism activity endangers the existence and preservation of the resources which are assets attracting the visitor.
>
> Rural tourism is an activity based on resources and assets of rural areas, with maximum respect for, and integration into, the economic, social and

cultural structures and traditions. The classification focuses on 'rurality' as the distinguishing criterion, as compared with other tourism activities, which may use the same rural territory but without being regarded as 'rural tourism'.

Rural tourism is an activity directly related to a working farm and the usual term used to describe this is 'agro-tourism'. Only an active working farm can be classified under this concept.

Specialist literature uses two words that hardly differ in spelling from each other: *agritourism* and *agro-tourism*. *Agritourism* is the term used in English-speaking countries and in the Romance languages, for example, *agritourismo* in Italian. However, in other countries, such as Poland, Greece and Cyprus the word *agro-tourism* is used, for example, *agroturystyka* in Polish. Both terms are correct in the corresponding language zones. They result from combining the prefix *agri-* or *agro-* with the stem *tourism*. The prefix *agri-* derives from the Latin word *agricola* (farmer), whereas the prefix *agro-* derives from the Greek word *agros*, which means 'soil' or 'agronomist', that is, a person who is in charge of a land estate.

Contemporary rural tourism and agritourism offers tourists a wide range of products and services. In order to emphasise their specific character and relations with the countryside, agriculture and farm, the prefix *agri-* is added. Hence, we have the following combinations: agri-hotels, agri-catering, agri-recreation, agri-leisure, agri-sports or even agri-therapy. For entities offering agritourism products and services, agritourism is usually a combined activity, which encompasses all or some of the aforementioned activities. Some methods of direct sales of agritourism products are also classified as rural tourism and agritourism.

What sometimes underlies agritourism is the belief expressed in the definition provided by Ehrlich (2009) that the farm is the exclusive entity providing tourism products and services. However, in practice there is an increasing interest by other business entities in agritourism, for example food processing enterprises or specialised capital companies leasing land from farmers and using their work to organise profitable agritourism undertakings. There are cases of international capital penetrating agritourism in order to invest money in the undertakings which guarantee a rapid return on capital, such as maize mazes, and mini-zoos. Soon farmers might be displaced from the market of the most attractive agritourism products and services and from the most attractive areas. They might only be providers of land and labour under the conditions dictated by capital. Farmers might be left with only the least attractive forms of agritourism. Farmers themselves, especially those whose farms are located in areas predisposed to agritourism, often tend to marginalise their farming activity in favour of agritourism activity.

Determinants of rural tourism and agritourism

The analysis of problems of rural tourism and agritourism poses a crucial question: is it reasonable to distinguish them as separate forms of tourism? After all, we might try to prove that there are no substantial reasons to distinguish them as individual forms of tourism. What is more, it might be regarded as unnecessary multiplication of forms of tourism, as the better-known and established forms fully cover the areas of rural tourism and agritourism. Theoreticians make detailed[3] lists of arguments when speaking in favour of distinguishing them as specific forms of tourism. The most important premises could be summarised in the following four determinants.

The determinant of massive, spontaneous and global development: It is amazing to observe the massive, spontaneous and global development of rural tourism and agritourism. There are four layers of this development: language, research, business activity and tourism. In spite of the fact that agritourism is a relatively new term, this neologism has become common in many European languages, for example, *agrotourism* (Greek), *agritourism* (English), *agriturismo* (Italian), *agroturistika* (Czech) and *Agrotourismus* (German). Scientific research on rural tourism and agritourism is developing. Agritourism services are offered by farms all over the world and the rate is increasing rapidly. There are companies being established to support the development of rural tourism and agritourism and this process will be developing dynamically, so it is a convincing argument to distinguish agritourism and rural tourism as forms of tourism.

The agrarian determinant: What distinguishes rural tourism and agritourism from other types of tourism is the fact that leisure and recreation take place in agricultural and rural surroundings in their broad sense and the main tourism attractions require these surroundings.

The cognitive determinant: Rural tourism and agritourism offer specific products, which enable people to satisfy their cognitive needs for contact with nature, the process of food production and life in a rural community.

The emotional determinant: The opportunity to satisfy people's emotional needs is a significant determinant. These needs include the wish to experience the rural idyll: silence, except for the sound of the wind through the trees, the occasional farmyard animal, the smell of the countryside, and being in direct contact with farm animals and plant products as well as processed products.

Functions of rural tourism and agritourism

Similarly to general tourism, rural tourism and agritourism fulfil a wide range of very important leisure, health-promoting, didactic, educational, cultural, social, economic, spatial and environmental functions. Each of these functions has a specific character in rural tourism and agritourism, resulting from the specificity of nature in agriculture and rural areas.

- *Leisure and recreational functions*: to provide tourists with active and passive leisure in rural space by offering a wide range of agritourism products and services.
- *Health-promoting functions*: rural tourism and agritourism offer different forms of health promotion resulting from people's contact with nature and agriculture. They affect human feelings and emotions. They offer specific, advanced-technology products under the common name of agri-therapy.

- *Didactic functions*: Although these are of particularly value to educators and parents, they apply to all tourists. These functions were discussed by Kusztelak, see Chapter 21. Rural tourism and agritourism develop respect for nature and the natural environment, all life forms, native tradition and culture, people living in rural areas, farmers' hard work and the results of their work: that is, food.
- *Educational functions*: concern farmers, tourists and the rural community. Tourists acquire knowledge about nature, plants, animals, food production, the local community and surrounding areas. At the same time, farmers acquire new skills in serving tourists, conducting an enterprise and using foreign languages. They comprehensively extend their knowledge of the area where they live. Rural inhabitants learn new professions and skills.
- *Cultural functions*: concern the renewal of rural traditions, securing and revitalising the material heritage of rural areas. They create a new, cultural image of rural areas. They offer more complete use and animation of some facilities in rural areas (community centres, sports facilities, etc.).
- *Social functions*: For the local community additional employment opportunity is the most important of three social functions resulting from tourism. Employment is offered as a result of demand for direct and indirect services provided to tourists. Indirect tourism service results from the increased demand for various community services. The second social function is a reduction of the stream of emigration from rural areas to cities. This particularly applies to young and well-educated people. The third social function consists of an extension of various social relationships as a result of keeping old and striking new relationships with urban inhabitants.
- *Economic functions*: Here we can distinguish income-generating and infrastructural functions. For farmers the most important thing is to gain an additional source of income by offering tourism services and direct marketing of agricultural and food products. It is possible to use free farm resources and start additional production for tourists, for example, crafts, handicrafts and blacksmithing. The development of local infrastructure, which includes tourism infrastructure, recreational facilities, roads, public transport, waterworks, sewerages, sewage treatment plants and such like, facilitates living in the country, increases living standards and conditions for rural inhabitants.
- *Spatial functions*: These are related to greater care of the aesthetic character of villages, houses, streets, and other public places. Old, interesting constructions, which have perhaps not been used for a long time, are being revitalised and thus, the rural architectural heritage is preserved.
- *Environmental functions*: to develop care of the natural environment and local nature conservation.

Aspects of rural tourism and agritourism

Every farmer or tour operator providing services in rural areas should consider different aspects of tourism, which correspond to various areas of knowledge or skills. These aspects concern law, building, product development, promotion and marketing, financing, enterprise organisation and management.

- *Law*: Some countries have parliamentary laws on rural tourism and agritourism, but most countries do not. In spite of the fact that very often there are no laws on rural tourism and agritourism, this business activity must respect numerous regulations of economic laws, such as those concerning forms of business activity, taxes and safety of tourists and staff.
- *Organisation*: Concerns four individual issues: a) structures functioning in rural tourism and agritourism, especially farms; b) the manner and range of cooperation between these structures; c) organisation of the internal structure of a tourism entity; and d) the process of production or providing services.
- *Management*: To guarantee smooth functioning of an enterprise; it involves planning, organisation, decision making, motivating and controlling. The most important areas of management in rural tourism and agritourism are: a) human resources management; b) management of products and services; c) management of a stream of tourists (the logistics of the current inflow of tourists and planning the yearly inflow of tourists); d) hospitality management, which includes etiquette, management of emotions and management of knowledge transfer; and e) risk management, which involves different sources of risk, from economic and health risks to the risk of death.
- *Marketing*: Agritourism marketing is specifically conditioned by the fact that agritourism entities are territorially scattered and this is a relatively small-scale activity. The Internet has proved to be the best channel for promotion of agritourism. Prices are also very important in agritourism.
- *Economics*: It is necessary to keep accounts according to the tourism entity's relevant accounting act. Not only is accountancy the basis for tax settlements, but it is also a valuable source of data for economic analyses, especially the costs of business activity, threshold point, sources of financing, financial liquidity, return on investments and financial risk.

Recapitulation

This chapter presented the general concept of rural tourism and agritourism and other forms of nature tourism. Different forms of nature tourism, especially rural tourism and agritourism, cater for the essential human need for contact with nature. This contact has been increasingly weakened as a result of major global progress in civilisation, which has taken place in the last two centuries. Rapid development of metropolises, motorisation and computerisation are global determinants of violent and increasingly precise development of general tourism, especially nature tourisms. The group of nature tourisms encompasses various forms. This chapter defined tourism in rural areas, rural tourism and agritourism and discussed them in more detail. The specific determinants of these types of tourism legitimate the use of these names in practice. The increasing range of the term *agritourism* points to the fact that the term is used globally and it will probably cover what scientists define as rural tourism. At the end of this chapter the most important aspects of rural tourism and agritourism were specified.

Notes

1   The films 'Green Tourism' (https://www.youtube.com/watch?v=e2BPorZF71g) and 'Otulina' (https://www.youtube.com/watch?v=3o9xxdUIC9Q), which are available on Michał Jacenty Sznajder's channel on YouTube, complement the subject of this book.
2   UNWTO is a specialised UN agency and leading international organisation in tourism. It is a global forum for issues concerning the tourism policy and a practical source of knowledge about tourism.
3   Lane (1994) provides the following determinants in an analysis of the specific character of rural tourism: it is done in rural areas, chiefly in open spaces; it is adjusted to rural conditions (small-scale undertakings, contact with nature, cultural heritage and tradition); it is rural in terms of the scale of facilities and settlements to which it is related; it supports rather than destroys the rural character of the area; it uses local resources economically.

References

Ehrlich, K. (2009). Perspectives of rural tourism in Europe, In *Tourism in Rural Areas*. Matej Bel University, Banska Bystrica, Slovakia.
Kapała, A. (2008). Agroturystyka w prawie wspólnotowym. *Przegląd Prawa Rolnego*, 2(4), pp.147–161. Publisher: Uniwersytet Adama Mickiewicza w Poznaniu, Poznań. https://repozytorium.amu.edu.pl/bitstream/10593/9101/1/008_Anna_Kapa%C5%82a_ Agroturystyka_w_prawie_wsp%C3%B3lnotowym_148_161.pdf
Lane, B. (1994). What is rural tourism? *Journal of Sustainable Tourism*, 2(1–2), 7–21.
Sznajder, M. J. (2014). *Przepastny masyw Supramonte* [The Cavernous Supramonte Massif – Sardegna]. Part 4, Orientale Sarda. https://www.youtube.com/watch?v=W_ XyaaCYK7w [Retrieved 20 November 2015]

10 Building a tourism palace

Agritourism in metropolitan areas as another stone in the mosaic? The case of Slovenia

Irma Potočnik Slavič

Slovenia: on the European crossroads

Slovenia, with an area of 20,273 km^2 and a population of 2 million, is situated at an important intersection of European traffic corridors, on the crossroads of major European geographical regions (the Alps, the Pre-Alpine region, the Dinaric-Karst, at the edges of the Mediterranean and the Pannonian Basin), where 38 per cent of its area is declared as protected. This provides a solid foundation to attract tourist flows: 3.9 million arrivals (which is 11% more than in 2014) and 10.3 million overnights were recorded in 2015, 2/3 of which were generated by foreign tourists, mostly from Italy, Austria, Germany, Croatia and the Netherlands (SORS 2017).

According to the OECD's Nomenclature of Territorial Units for Statistics (NUTS) methodology, at NUTS 3 level all of 12 Slovenian regions are declared rural. According to the EUROSTAT criteria (that it, with the population density at the municipality level lower than 100 inhabitants per km^2), Slovenia is a poorly urbanised country – the majority of Slovenian municipalities have low population density with the prevalence of dispersed settlement pattern (137 municipalities or 71 per cent). Of the remainder, 54 municipalities are classified as intermediate and there are only two densely populated municipalities: Ljubljana and Maribor (SORS 2014). According to the available statistics, there are two urban centres with broad hinterland, rich in tourist and leisure amenities.

Before we take a closer look at some specific features of agritourism in Slovenian metropolitan areas, several starting points need to be outlined:

- Since only 52 per cent of the total population live in urban settlements, Slovenia is a very rural country, due also to its geographical features and character of its landscape. The residents of urban settlements can spend their recreation and leisure time in diverse rural settings.
- Urban dwellers can (in terms of spatial accessibility and time) practise various forms of recreation and leisure activities, including agritourism. Slovenian urban residents appreciate agritourism on active farms, and spend their time there mostly because of proper home-made food and drinks, but they rarely use the accommodation capacity of agritourism.

- Agritourism businesses (719 registered farms with one service related to agritourism and 401 farms with several services related to agritourism; see Figure 10.1) have developed intensively over the last 15 years, but other services are also available to visitors. Mostly families with children and elderly people are regular guests on agritourism farms.
- The holders of agritourism businesses have to develop services and products that come closer to the tastes and preferences of their potential customers; at the same time, agritourism has an important role in the functioning of local communities and is an important network broker contributing to the development of rural tourism.

Agritourism in metropolitan areas: the re-commodification of farm resources according to the needs of urban visitors

In general, the data on agritourism come from two sources: the Statistical Office of the Republic of Slovenia (SORS), which is focused on continuous and systematic gathering of data on the accommodation capacity and tourist visits; and the Ministry of Agriculture and the Environment which supervises the Register of Supplementary Farm Activities (agritourism is one of 11 categories of on-farm income diversification, see Kigali *et al.* 2013). According to Philip *et al.* (2010),

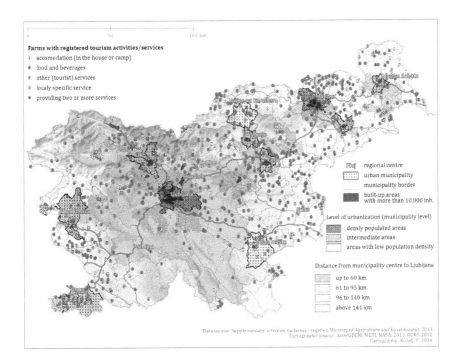

Figure 10.1 Farms with registered agritourist services.

the Slovenian model of agritourism is based on a working farm, where the owner and family members develop products and services that are directly connected with their farm (two-thirds of food and beverages sold on the farm have to be originally produced on the farm). Small operations on the farm are based on individual and authentic agritourism experiences of the family.

The spatial distribution of registered agritourism services in Slovenia is uneven and confirms several inequalities (Figure 10.1). In the western part of the country three clusters are noticeable, that is, the littoral part and its hinterland, the wine-growing regions (the Karst region, Vipava Valley and Goriška Brda region), and the Pre-Alpine hilly and mountainous region. They function as an accessible hinterland of the Ljubljana metropolitan region, access being quick and easy at up to a distance of 60 km by car, mostly via highway. The concentration of agitourism businesses in the Dinaric-Karst region is lower as it has the lowest population density and the highest share of forested land. The distribution is more proportionate in the eastern part of the country, where several mid-sized or smaller urban centres are combined with vastly dispersed rural settlements, and where the attractive mosaic landscape of winegrowing hills meets numerous spa facilities.

The distribution of agritourism services could partly be explained by the accessibility and general population trends. In general, accessibility is a fundamental concern when decisions are made about the provision of recreational space (Pigram and Jenkins 2006, p. 213). Access to a variety of recreational opportunities is generally provided to people with automobiles who are willing to travel a reasonable distance. Such variables as relative location, distance, time and facilities appear to be significant to customers involved in recreational activities. The highest population density can be observed in the central part of the country, where the capital is located. There is an abundance of flat and fertile land and the processes of urbanisation, services, traffic accessibility and suburbanisation are the strongest. The area around the capital of Ljubljana and its daily commuting hinterland of 30-50 kilometres (mostly north of the capital) might be defined as the metropolitan area where about 450,000 people can be seen daily. Other regional centres (e.g. Maribor, Celje, Kranj, Koper, Nova Gorica, Novo Mesto, Ptuj, Murska Sobota) do not have such widespread agritourism hinterlands. Since their hinterlands sometimes overlap, their services are sometimes strongly localised, in some cases regionalised, while some areas (well recognised winegrowing regions or the hinterland of spa resorts, mostly located in the east of Slovenia) have more tourists from all regions of Slovenia and some foreign visitors.

The existing agritourism facilities support the commodification of rural landscapes so that they are accessible to urban visitors travelling by car from the edges of (metropolitan) urbanised areas. Mostly the abovementioned attractive rural landscapes do not have any facilities for agricultural production because farms are characterised by small and fragmented plots of land. The conditions are less favourable for agriculture due to the landscape, climate and mostly part-time character of farming. Over the last 15 years the re-commodification of traditional food and beverage products, and traditional systems of production and consumption of food and beverages (Woods 2011, p. 116) has been intensively developed with individual initiatives, agrarian advisory services and with the support of the state and EU funds. Food tourism, mostly generated by urban residents, seeks the rural experience through taste. Bell (2006, quoted in Woods 2011, p. 116) identifies this as pursuit of the 'gastro-idyll', a nostalgic rendering of the rural as a place in which good, wholesome, fresh food can be eaten according to regional traditions and recipes in convivial surroundings. This movement has promoted the sale and consumption of local food in accessible rural areas, for example, through farmers' markets and the rediscovery of regional recipes and culinary traditions. At the same time, distinctive foods and beverages can command a higher price as 'authentic' rural produce, as indicated in such schemes as Protected Designations of Origin and Protected Geographical Indications in the EU (Woods 2011, p. 116). This re-commodification has become a common strategy for farm diversification as part of the development of agritourism. The latter might include several tourism services: on-farm restaurants, on-farm accommodation, on-farm shops selling produce directly to visitors, farm and vineyard tours, observation rooms, farm museums, provision of cooking courses, or other services. The concept of re-commodification of on-farm resources is evident in the following example.

For most of the twentieth century the Gorenjska region was characterised by early industrialisation, relative nearness of available jobs, growth of the regional centre (Kranj, nearly 40,000 inhabitants), fast and intensive de-agrarisation, prevalence of non-farming households and mostly part-time farmers who cultivated the land. The flat and fertile rural areas functioned as a hinterland for manufacturing industries, which are mostly concentrated in the nearby regional centre. In the last 20 years former rural settlements have become attractive for in-migration residential purposes (suburbanisation). Because of a new highway, improved municipal traffic infrastructure, new employment opportunities (mostly in the field of services), new residential and business areas have flourished. On the other hand, settlements at the edges of those flat and fertile areas, that is, settlements in the hilly thermal belt, were difficult to reach, mostly due to narrow macadam roads and infrequent public transport in the 1960s. This caused the out-migration to move closer to the regional centre (e.g. Kranj). The share of agriculturally utilised areas decreased; only few full-time farmers remained and part-time farmers (mostly owners of small farms) became daily commuters. In the last two decades traffic improvements and the development of other infrastructure have made those areas attractive for in-migration among several social groups (second-home owners, elderly people, young families, returnees). Besides the residential function the area has important landscape amenities and it has become attractive for recreation and leisure activities. Also, the local inhabitants have adjusted to new circumstances, for example, by opening agritourism farms.

An agritourism farmer reported:

I and my husband inherited a small farm from my parents. Both of us were employed in the manufacturing industries in Kranj and for several decades we were part-time farmers. After work in a factory we worked on our farm, where we had up to 5 cows, one horse, small plots scattered around the village and a forest in the hills. Besides, step by step, with our own hands, we started to build a new house next to the old farm house. Ten years ago I lost my job and I decided to do something completely different. We have our own land, we practise farming, we have our own food products, we furnished our new house, I had time, my children grew up and wanted to work with people... There were a lot of daily visitors who went mountaineering, hiking, cycling past our house... And I started with agritourism on a small basis (up to 20 beds, i.e. three apartments). I produce cheese from our milk, sell it on my doorstep, cook by myself. I actively participate in all events in the village. I put a lot of emphasis on direct contact with my guests (we walk in the mountains together). I opened a small tennis court. Young visitors usually pet our dog, cats, hens and horse. My daughter did a master's degree in tourism ... We have daily visitors, mostly from Kranj, Ljubljana, and we mostly provide accommodation to foreign visitors.

(Female, early 50s, agritourism farm holder;
Target research project, 2010–2012)

Agritourism services: a minor role in Slovenian tourism

According to the Slovenian tourism statistics, Slovenian municipalities are categorised into six types: seaside, mountain and spa resorts, Ljubljana, urban and other municipalities. The western part of the country attracts more international and domestic tourists. There are important touristic impacts on seaside and mountainous municipalities. As the capital, Ljubljana, registered approximately 10 per cent of tourist visits; other municipalities have developed either transfer tourism (Postojna cave, sites close to international airports, or Nova Gorica as a gambling resort; see Figure 10.2). On the other hand, the eastern part of the country has more regular distribution of overnight stays – spa municipalities reach between 100,000 and 250,000 overnights per year, whereas other municipalities have a small number of tourist visits.

In the context of Slovenian tourism, agritourism plays only a minor role. Less than 4 per cent of all tourist overnight stays and 1.5 per cent of all tourist arrivals are generated by agritourism facilities. Also, the occupancy of tourist beds on agritourism farms is below the country's average (less than 8 per cent); tourists stay only 2.4 days. From the perspective of tourism, the low take-up of agritourism is also a consequence of the spatial distribution of agritourism facilities. While hotels and similar tourism facilities concentrate in the areas which are very attractive and particularly suitable from the perspective of development of (international) tourism (Cigale *et al.* 2013, p. 343), the majority of agritourism accommodations (approx. 4500 beds and 34,000 seats) is to be found in the 'other municipalities' category. Cigale *et al.* argue (2013, p. 344) that the presence of agritourism is primarily the result of farmers' needs and opportunities, while the demand of the tourism market is secondary. In the case of agritourism, the criteria of economic success are different since tourism is only a

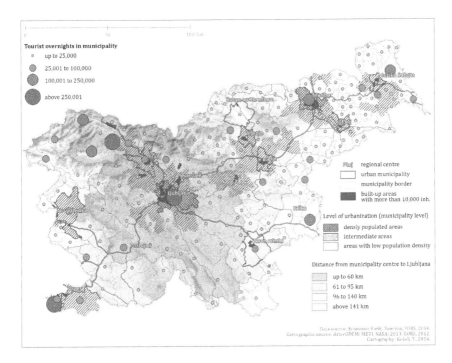

Tourist overnights in municipality
- up to 25,000
- 25,001 to 100,000
- 100,001 to 250,000
- above 250,001

regional centre
urban municipality
municipality border
built-up areas with more than 10,000 inh.

Level of urbanization (municipality level)
densly populated areas
intermediate areas
areas with low population density

Distance from municipality centre to Ljubljana
up to 60 km
61 to 95 km
96 to 140 km
above 141 km

Figure 10.2 Tourist visits to Slovenia (2013).

supplementary (rather than the main or the only) economic activity. Hence, the threshold of economic viability is much lower than in the case of other tourism establishments.

The data of the SORS show the attractiveness of agritourism is less than average in comparison with other types of tourism accommodation. The results from a questionnaire survey that included domestic tourists (440 respondents; Cigale *et al.* 2013, pp. 341, 347–349) and focused on general leisure behaviour and motives for (not) visiting agritourism facilities, showed that the respondents usually stayed at hotels and similar establishments, and only 1 per cent of the respondents chose agritourism facilities for an overnight stay. Only a quarter of the respondents had already spent a night at an agritourism facility (at least once). Among the motives for staying at agritourism facilities two were of greater importance, that is: 'good home-made food and drink' and 'staying in peaceful, rural environment'. The respondents also mentioned 'more personal attitude to the guest' and 'low price'. The most important reason for choosing a particular agritourism facility was attractive landscape (47 per cent of the respondents), followed by location in an area of interest and friendliness of the farm family. As far as the question of why the respondents had not stayed at an agritourism facility yet is concerned, rather surprisingly, it resulted in the following responses: the largest section of the respondents (35 per cent) were not familiar with agritourism offers, or they did not have any particular reason for staying on the farm (33 per cent), or rural areas did not appeal much to them (32 per cent).

The holders of agritourism facilities are usually members of the Association of Tourist Farms of Slovenia (2014), which has approximately 400 members, regularly publishes a catalogue in five foreign languages, has an active web page and central registration system and actively promotes agritourism (fairs, tourism, cultural and sport events). Simultaneously, the majority of holders of agritourism facilities also use their own websites, provide other tourism information or advertise, mostly on website Booking.com. Therefore, the promotion of agritourism should also be more focused on other target groups. Alternatively, there might be some other 'hidden' reasons for not visiting agritourism facilities: Perhaps the agritourism offer is not interesting enough for potential Slovenian tourists, because rural areas are part of their everyday environment (they live in the rural area or in close proximity to it; Cigale *et al.* 2013, p. 349). The fact that might confirm this statement is the size and distribution of second homes in Slovenia. Second homes are often concentrated in coastal and mountainous areas, and in the landscapes conforming to the ideal of the 'rural idyll' located close to major cities. Yet, second home owners are different to tourists – they have invested in a place and return regularly, frequently aspire to be part of the community, and develop a sense of belonging to the locality of their second home (Woods 2011, p. 189). In terms of their number and distribution in Slovenia, second homes have been an important element of landscape development since the 1960s, especially as individual mobility has increased. According to the real estate census (REN 2011), there are 20,740 second homes in Slovenia (the methodology is incomplete and the real number of second homes is much higher), with higher concentrations in mountainous, wine-growing and spa areas, which are usually well connected to a highway and accessible within up to 1.5 hours by car. To get a broader picture, the Slovenes also own approximately 11,000 second homes in the neighbouring coastal part of Croatia (Bobnar 2014, pp. 6, 13–19). The effects of second homes can be seen both in the preservation of cultural landscape and settlement, in the altered settlement structure and in the influence on economy and local community.

Responses to urban visitors' demands: branding agritourism destinations

More and more people are looking beyond the city limits to find their 'activity space' for outdoor recreation. The key elements of attraction are diversity and flexibility. Several fundamental questions need to be asked about urban recreational space (Pigram and Jenkins 2006, p. 206): How much is needed? What form should it take? Where should it be located? How should it be managed? and Who is it for?

According to the statistical data and survey results, we can distinguish two important orientations for the development agritourism in Slovenian metropolitan areas.

- Addressing broader potential urban target groups for agritourism: This might be gradually achieved by product specialisation. Several years ago the Association of Tourist Farms of Slovenia developed a transparent agritourism quality categorisation, indicated by a symbol of 1 to 4 apples and with a clear set of rules. Recently they have divided agritourism products into 7 segments, namely: organic agritourism, organic agritourism with a healthy lifestyle offer, family- friendly, bicycle- friendly and invalid-friendly agritourism, agritourism with a programme for children unaccompanied by parents, and winegrowing agritourism. Domestic and foreign urban visitors might individually adjust their leisure time at agritourism facilities according to their needs and expectations. The majority of agritourism farm holders intend either to enlarge their existing agritourism services (33%), widen their agritourism offer (22%) or keep the status quo (28%). Most investments have been undertaken in the last 5 years (data extracted from the Target Research Project 2012, which included 98 agritourism farms in Slovenia). Therefore, innovation flows and new up-scaling in agritourism 'software', that is, several small investments related to quality and novel offerings, are to be expected in forthcoming years.
- A broader marketing approach needs to be undertaken to guarantee the future development and more stabilised market position of agritourism in metropolitan areas, for example, branding destinations. The brand of a tourism destination consists of several elements, including accommodation, tourism attractions, hospitality, entertainment, cultural and natural resources and wine and gastronomic amenities – all of them could be included into the function of destination branding. Branding is a very detailed and thoughtful process, which is usually related to products or with the creation of a national image and reputation at the international level. Branding a country or region in the world of globalisation is a strategy for gathering wealth or attracting attention, a way of self-affirmation in the promotion of national identity (Scott, Suwaree, Peivi, Ding and Xu 2001, quoted in Kavoura and Bitsani 2013, p. 296).

Williams states on the basis of the UK experience (1995, quoted in Pigram and Jankins 2006, p. 179) that the development of recreation and leisure destinations has undergone three phases: formation, consolidation and expansion. Successful branding of tourism destinations together with a long-term strategy of development of (agri-)tourism is of essential importance to Slovenia (see Figure 10.3). This has been evident in the Goriška Brda region, a typical borderland (next to Italy), close to the regional centre of Nova Gorica, hilly to a height 250 metres. It is a winegrowing region of picturesque cultural landscape, with approximately 5800 inhabitants living in a small municipality, with an extraterritorial road connecting the region to Slovenia, but with very pronounced local identity and strong attachment to land. Features including 100 % grape processing inside the region, the existing trade channels, positive regional image, high quality products, local identity, implementation of innovations (vital wine

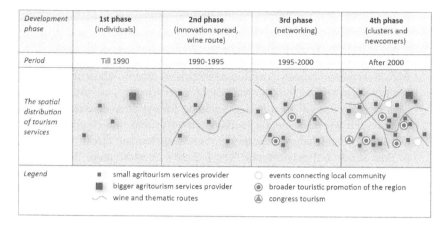

Development phase	1st phase (individuals)	2nd phase (innovation spread, wine route)	3rd phase (networking)	4th phase (clusters and newcomers)
Period	Till 1990	1990-1995	1995-2000	After 2000
The spatial distribution of tourism services				

Legend:
- ■ small agritourism services provider
- ▣ bigger agritourism services provider
- ⌒ wine and thematic routes
- ○ events connecting local community
- ◉ broader touristic promotion of the region
- ▲ congress tourism

Figure 10.3 The phases of development from an agritourist destination to a high-rank rural tourist destination (the case of the Goriška Brda region).

Source: adapted from Sirk M. 2013, design by Koželj T. 2014.

and theme routes have emerged), the co-existence of wine and fruit growing, agritourism and local gastronomy are part of a transparent and well-functioning territorial/regional economic cycle with huge potential, such as for spa developments, hotels in renovated castles, casino approved by locals and conference centres (Potočnik Slavič 2010, 2012; Sirk 2013; Potočnik Slavič and Schmitz 2013).

Conclusion

When the Internet is used, we can talk about e-branding. Since agritourism usually lacks money/means for promotion, the Internet seems to be an appropriate tool. The role of this medium/or promotion material is extremely important if the visitor has not been to the location yet, because it has influence on the image of the destination. E-branding must be informative, well- organised, include opportunities of entertainment, but the emotional component is also important (Kavoura and Bitsani 2013, 296). Thus, it might create a virtual community which is open to many international and domestic tourists. These destinations need to develop e-feelings by means of web cameras as they have impact on emotions. E-branding provides additional help to areas with good urban connections and also to more isolated rural areas, and it helps to develop a positive image (which is also the case of the Goriška Brda region; Kavoura and Bitsani 2013). What are the lessons to be learned from the Slovenian experience? For the future development of agritourism in metropolitan areas, it is crucial to have a prudent combination of various marketing approaches, including tangible and intangible tourism attractions. This should be achieved by the use of both the 'classic' and virtual tourism space, as well as constant innovation, and by simultaneous enhancement of the relationships between agritourism and farming.

References

Association of Tourist Farms of Slovenia (Združenje turističnih kmetij Slovenije). (2014). http://www.turisticnekmetije.si/en/ (Retrieved 22 August 2014)

Bobnar, M. (2014). Vloga sekundarnih bivališč pri ohranjanju poseljenosti podeželja. Diploma thesis, Department of Geography, Faculty of Arts, University of Ljubljana, Ljubljana.

Cigale, D., Lampič, B. & Potočnik Slavič, I. (2013). Interrelations between tourism offer and tourism demand in the case of farm tourism in Slovenia. *European Countryside*, 4, pp. 339–355.

Kavoura A. & Bitsani E. (2013). E-branding of rural tourism in Carinthia, Austria. *Turizam*, 61, pp. 289–312.

Ministry of Agriculture and Environment, Slovenia. (2014). *Register of Supplementary Activities on Farms 2010–2014* (Register dopolnilnih dejavnosti na kmetiji). Ministry of Agriculture and Environment: Ljubljana.

Phillip, S., Hunter, C. & Blackstock, K. (2010). A typology for defining agritourism. *Tourism Management*, 31(6), pp. 754–758.

Pigram, J. J. & Jenkins, J. M. (2006). *Outdoor Recreation Management*. Routledge: London.

Potočnik Slavič, I. (2010). Neoendogenous in- and output of selected rural areas: The case of economic cycles in Slovenia. *Revija za geografijo*, 5(1), pp. 75–90. ISSN 1854-665X

Potočnik Slavič, I. (2012). The significance of the rural web for rural tourism development: The case of Goriška Brda region, *Slovenia. Bulletin – Société géographique de Liège*, 58, pp. 73–82. ISSN 0770-7576

Potočnik Slavič, I. & Schmitz, S. (2013). Farm tourism across Europe. *European Countryside*, 5(4), pp. 265–274. ISSN 1803-8417. DOI:10.2478/euco-2013-0017.

Register nepremičnin (REN: Register of Real-estate). (2011). Statistika pripomb na vrednost nepremičnin po vrstah nepremičnin množičnega vrednotenja. http://www.gu.gov. si/fileadmin/gu.gov.si/pageuploads/novice/Teksti_novic/Statistika_obvescanja.pdf (accessed: 10 May 2014).

Sirk, M. (2013). Razvoj turizma na podeželju v Goriških brdih. Final seminar paper, Department of Geography, Faculty of Arts, University of Ljubljana: Ljubljana.

SORS (Statistical Office of the Republic of Slovenia). (2017). Economy-Tourism. Tourist arrivals and overnight stays, Slovenia, 2015 - final data. http://www.stat.si/StatWeb/en/ show-news?id=6188&idp=24&headerbar=19 (accessed: 13 February 2017).

SORS (Statistical Office of the Republic of Slovenia). (2014). Upravno-teritorialna razdelitev. Projekt statistike razvoja podeželja. http://www.stat.si/tema_splosno_ upravno_podezelje_predstavitev.asp (accessed: 5 August 2014).

Target Research Project 2010–2012 (2012). The potentials of supplementary activities on the farms and entrepreneurship in rural areas. *Final Report of Project Financed by the Ministry of Agriculture (V5-1014)*. Department of Geography, Faculty of Arts, University of Ljubljana, Ljubljana.

Woods, M. (2011). *Rural*. Routledge: London.

11 The forthcoming ICT revolution in tourism in metropolitan areas

Piotr Senkus

Introduction

Alvin and Heidi Toffler (1991) divided the history of the development of civilisation into three substantial parts. They identified them as the agrarian, industrial and information waves m see Figure 11.1. The agrarian wave was the longest of the three. It started when people learnt to cultivate land and breed cattle. It began to decease in the eighteenth century when the industrial wave, which had been growing since the fifteenth century, became more intense. The industrial wave began when Johannes Gensfleisch zur Laden zum Gutenberg invented a movable type in 1450 and, as a result, printing started on its path to becoming widespread. The industrial wave escalated when James Watt improved the steam engine invented by Thomas Newcomen in 1763.

The third wave, which is in progress now, involved the increasing popularity of new technologies, which gave people unlimited communication possibilities. At present this wave is exerting the greatest influence on the functioning of the entire society. It involves a wide range of challenges and threats, which need to be taken into consideration by tour operators providing services in rural tourism and agritourism in metropolitan areas if they want to build their position on the market effectively. The greatest challenge is the revolution in information and communication technologies (ICT), which may be implemented in activities such as virtualisation and mobility, quick response (QR) codes and augmented reality, radio frequency identification (RFID) and the Internet of Things (IoT), or combinations of these activities.

Communication revolution

It is enough to look at a map of Internet penetration to understand the strength of the communication revolution. At present the Internet is everywhere, and it may become either a friend or an enemy of entrepreneurs operating in the sector of rural tourism and agritourism.

The speed with which people have started to use communication technology has increased considerably since the beginning of the information wave. It was about 70 years from the invention of the telephone until there were 50 million users, 38 years for radio, 13 years for television, 15 years for the mobile phone,

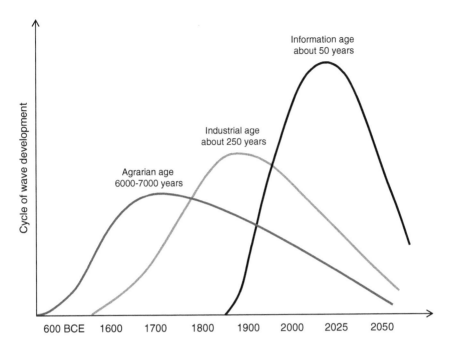

Figure 11.1 Toffler's waves.
Source: Senkus *et al.* 2014.

4 years for the Internet and 3 years for the iPod. Facebook reached 200 million users in less than one year. One billion songs were downloaded to iPods within 9 months. At present more information is globally generated within two days than the amount of information generated in world history so far. On average, one would need twenty-eight years without sleep to watch the videos uploaded on youtube.com within one week. Ten years ago it took as long as 72 hours to download a 2 GB video. At present it takes 10 minutes to download such a video, but we still need 3 hours to watch it. Currently, in developed countries the number of text messages sent daily is the same as the number of text messages sent yearly in 2002. In 1910 news was spread faster by mass media than by means of interpersonal contacts, whereas in 2010 news spread by means of interpersonal contacts was faster than news spread by mass media.

Today the generation of twenty-year-olds does not know the world without the Internet. It is estimated that, by 2017, 7,000,000,000,000 electronic appliances exchanging data will have been interconnected globally, that is, about 1000 appliances per Earth inhabitant. In view of the fact that at present there are about 800 times more sensors, machines and appliances connected to the Internet than there are human Internet users, we should speak of the Internet of Things (IoT) rather than the Internet of humans. There are more than 15,000,000 entries on Wikipedia, where 78 per cent of them are in languages other than English. According to the editors of the scientific journal, *Nature*, the number of mistakes in the English version of Wikipedia is similar to that in *Encyclopaedia Britannica* (Terdiman 2005). The editors of *Nature* conducted an experiment and observed that, on average, there were 3.86 errors per article in the English-language pages of Wikipedia, whereas there were 2.92 errors per article in *Encyclopaedia Britannica*. In 2012 there were more Kindle books than paper books sold (BBC News 2012).

Sir Richard Branson (1999) claims that soon 96 per cent of consumers in the UK will have access to the Internet and this state of affairs will remain stable for the next century. Access to the Internet creates and develops new markets. Their functioning will depend on effective and fast management of information. The situation will be similar in other countries all over the world. Therefore, in the near future the management of information and the use of new technologies will be a determinant for entrepreneurs to gain competitive advantage, including entrepreneurs running businesses in the sector of rural tourism and agritourism in metropolitan areas. This issue becomes even more important as we analyse what is happening on the Internet within one minute.

WEB 2.0 and social networking services

At present one of the most effective tools for quick management of information seems to be communication with potential clients via portals using WEB 2.0 technology. They enable bilateral communication, for example, Facebook, Twitter and blogs. However, it is necessary to remember that there are a few hundred such portals on the Internet. Figure 11.2 shows examples of groups of such services.

Andreas Kaplan and Michael Haenlein (2010) define social networking media as 'a group of applications based on Internet solutions and Web 2.0 ideological and technological fundamentals which enable creation and exchange of user-generated content' (p.). Social networking media are social interaction media using an extended set of communication tools, which go beyond traditional social communication. Thanks to the widespread availability and scalability of communication techniques, social networking media diametrically changed the method of communication between organisations, communities and individual users, and have become natural places for exchanging information.

Recently, 72 per cent of all Internet users reported on their activity on social networking services: 18- to 29-year-olds report that they spend 89 per cent of their time online on social networking services; 30- to 49-year-olds spend 72 per cent of their time; 50- to 60-year-olds spend 60 per cent and people aged over 65 years spend 43 per cent, while 71 per cent of users access social networking services with mobile devices (Bullas 2015).

Research on the use of social media in tourism has been going on since about 2000 and shows that, like other forms of media, this form of communication is highly effective. As results from the research conducted by Tourism Australia, 45 to 80 per cent of tourists are ready to share opinions about their trips or stays at tourism facilities. Very often these opinions are similar to 'live' reports. Participants at different events more and more often 'boast' or describe their experience on

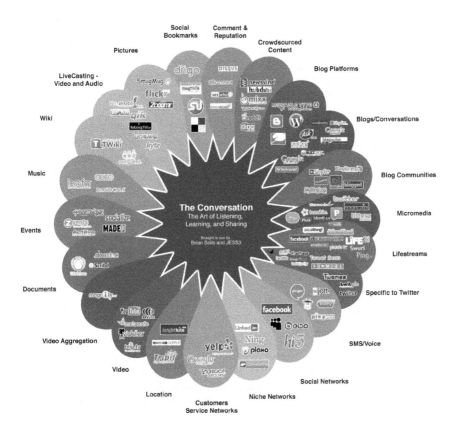

Figure 11.2 The Conversation Prism.

Source: Solis B., Jesse T. https://www.flickr.com/photos/briansolis/2735401175/ [Retrieved 26.09.2016].

social networking portals, such as Twitter, Facebook, Google+, VK. They are also willing to take part in discussions.

This willingness to take part in a dialogue may be used in rural tourism and agritourism in metropolitan areas as a form of activation, encouraging tourists not only to visit attractions but also to develop a habit of regular visits to take part in unique events. Visitors' activity is a perfect database for analyses made by entrepreneurs. It might help them adjust their products and services to visitors' needs and discover their future needs.

Virtualisation and mobility

The increased popularity of personal computers followed by increased popularity of the Internet and mobile devices caused the process of virtualisation, that is, the gradual transfer of traditional manual activities to the Internet.

The influence of virtualisation is particularly noticeable in planning trips and booking attractions. Tourism Australia (2013 pp. 10–12) observes general trend in growth in internet use. In 2012, 46 per cent of total holiday travellers to Australia are booking some aspect of their trip online prior to arrival, retail outlets and the associated distribution infrastructure play a role in converting the other 54 per cent. Apart from facilitation in planning trips and booking, virtualisation improves the quality of functioning of a tourism facility, for example:

- The tourism provider's offer is adjusted to clients' habits thanks to the information in databases, such as the booking database and sales register.
- Better control of tourism traffic – the entrepreneur can read the statistics of clients' expenses on individual attractions and, especially, prevent the situation where the client has to use an attraction in a different place if it is not available at the entrepreneur's facility. In this case, the entrepreneur can use the booking data and either offer the client a different time when the attraction is available or start another identical attraction at their facility. It is necessary to remember that the client who finds an identical attraction at a competitive facility will probably not come back to the original facility where it was not available.
- Management of financial liquidity – booking data enable the entrepreneur to plan finances better and in consequence it may easily result in lower costs for an agritourism business.

The increasing popularity of mobile devices gives unprecedented possibilities – one can install various applications, such as virtual visits, interactive guides or quizzes for people visiting an agritourism attraction. All of these novelties can be used to increase the popularity of an attraction or encourage people to visit the attraction one more time.

Quick response (QR) codes and augmented reality are the latest technologies that are developing particularly rapidly.

Quick Response is an alphanumeric, two-dimensional matrix, square graphic code which was invented by Denso-Wave, a Japanese company, in 1994. It is a modular, fixed-dimensional code which enables Kanji/Kana characters to be encoded, so it is popular in Japan. Additionally, it is possible to encode characters of the Arabic, Greek, Hebrew and Cyrillic alphabets and other user-defined symbols. A QR code may include information such as a website link or business card. When a QR code is read by means of a mobile phone or tablet (with a camera) application, it is possible to view interesting content or to sign up for further information or offers.

QR codes may include the following information:

- sign-up and participation forms
- mobile websites
- videos with films, advertisements, tutorials
- audio recordings – music, Internet radio and other recordings
- electronic business cards
- calendar events

- applications and games
- photographs and drawings
- maps, location, routes – with GPS
- augmented reality (AR)
- making calls and sending pre-set text messages.

Since QR codes proved to be effective solutions used in promotional, advertising and information campaigns, especially in Japan, they began to dominate different sectors of the economy all over the world, including tourism. Neckermann travel agency and Best Western hotel chain pioneered the use of QR codes in tourism.

All over the world there is an increasing number of regions, cities and societies which use QR codes to promote tourism. Not only do they make messages addressed to visitors more attractive, but also they significantly extend information about places such as museums, galleries, castles, churches, as well as tourist actions and attractions organised in a particular region.

QR codes mostly provide benefits to their users:

- Potential customers, because they offer quick and comfortable access to interesting and attractive information
- Companies and institutions promoting tourism products and services, including rural tourism and agritourism in metropolitan areas, as they offer an

Figure 11.3 QR code on hiking trail.
Source: Fotolia.com © Herb – Fotolia.com.

opportunity to convey a multimedia marketing message in a very limited commercial space, for example, travel agencies' posters, mini-stands, hotel flyers, discount and special offer coupons, advertisements in the press or on banners.

QR codes are very often used in combination with augmented reality. This technology combines a real-life picture, usually from the camera of a mobile phone or tablet, with IT-generated elements (e.g. 3D objects, additional information, etc.). When the camera in a mobile phone is directed at a specific object included in the system, the user may receive extra information about the history and functions of the object and visualisations of the object in the past.

The principle of operation of augmented reality systems is simple. They use the GPS module in a smartphone to precisely specify the viewer's position. Next, it is enough to direct the lens at an object, street or building and the program will add information about the object in the form of descriptions placed in speech bubbles in the picture displayed. The information might include facts about a monument, or data showing the location of hotels, cash dispensers and restaurants. Sometimes there are simple drawings added to the picture, as the computing power and quality of graphic images generated by contemporary smartphones corresponds to that of desktop computers about ten years ago. The positioning data enable a smartphone to collect information from the server about all objects around the user so that the program can display it when necessary (Bienkowski, 1991).

As far as agritourism attractions in metropolitan areas are concerned, this technology can be used to give some variety to one's stay on a farm. For example, it could be an educational or informative tool showing visitors the history of the place, handicraft or regional product manufacturing technology.

RFID and Internet of Things

The Internet of Things (IoT) directly refers to a revolution in ICT and telecommunications, which affects the general organisation of the business sector, government sector, non-profit sector and private life. The revolutionary character of this phenomenon is reflected by simple analysis made by means of the Google Trends tool. The analysis of the dynamics of searching for the phrase 'Internet of Things' indicates that in recent years there has been an enormous increase in interest in this term. According to Rifkin (2014), the significance of the Internet of Things is so great that it may involve lesser significance or even the fall of the capitalist era

In general the term 'Internet of Things' is related to the existence of a global network connecting many devices and sensors, which can independently exchange information, usually by Internet transfer. The development of the IoT concept is strictly related to development of the Internet and its new applications. Its great significance was noticed in the US under the 'small planet' programme and in the European Union, which strongly supports the development of the IoT (Rudzikas 2009).

In spite of the evident and obvious relationship between the IoT and interconnected and intercommunicating objects, this phenomenon has not been clearly defined so far (Van Kranenburg *et al.* 2011). In general, we can follow description of Tte IoT as the idea based 'on a worldwide, wireless, integrated network of smart facilities and devices ('things') and a whole range of different sensors and actuators, in which, using standard protocols, the 'things' communicate with each other and with people. This network will connect billions of people' (Rudzikas 2009).

The development of the Internet infrastructure resulted not only in technological innovations but also in social benefits. For some users exchanging e-mail messages, searching for information and establishing new contacts was not enough, so they began to use the Internet as a medium for remote control of different objects.

Although the very concept of the IoT use is relatively new, it is possible to identify milestones in the IoT development (Van Kranenburg *et al.* 2011; Casaleggio Associati, (2011). We can distinguish these milestones in terms of the following waves:

- The first wave – the world as a library: the main use of the Internet infrastructure is preparation of a global glossary of real-life objects, for example, monuments and museums. Apart from the geographical location, we can find a wide range of extra information, descriptions, recordings and photographs. However, the objects do not interact with each other. Thanks to technologies such as Geo-tagging or GPS a wide range of popular services started, such as Google Earth, Google Maps and Wikitude. As far as tourism attractions are concerned, first-wave technology is used to supply information, for example, when an object has been photographed, it is identified and we can read new information about it.
- The second wave – the world online: it is possible to track packages or shipments online. Mobile objects are identified by means of RFID barcodes, visual identification technologies and near field communication (NFC). In fact, the implementation of the World Online concept is unlimited, starting with support given to all types of sports events, through production, trade and all marketing actions aimed at identification of the recipient and ending with contemporary applications of the Internet in social life. As far as tourism attractions are concerned, second-wave technology is used to control traffic in a tourism facility so as to guarantee the maximum occupancy in each attraction, on the one hand, and to reduce the visitors' waiting time, on the other hand.
- The third wave – real-life control of objects: the use of the IoT enables us not only to track but also to search for objects, as many of them have built-in functions identifying their position and transferring this information. In this approach objects are permanently or temporarily connected to the Internet and they can interact with people. The use of this facility can be particularly noticeable in the concept of 'intelligent buildings'. As far as tourism attractions are concerned, third-wave technology is used to automate attractions, such as videos or additional voice information, which will play in the visitor's language when necessary.
- The fourth wave – objects communicating with each other: according to the IoT concept, plants can irrigate themselves when they need it. This

means that objects communicate with each other and they take action under specific conditions. This is known as Machine2Machine communication. iPhone + Nike and Pachube are examples of products using this concept, which are available on the market. As far as tourism attractions are concerned, fourth-wave technology is used to create interactive games and quizzes for visitors.

- The fifth wave – intelligent objects: when we set an alarm-clock, it will ring earlier when the weather or traffic is bad. It is possible that objects communicate via the Internet with different sources of information and adjust their actions to a specific situation. These objects use object generated content (OGC) technologies. The following solutions are some that use fifth-wave technology and are available on the market: WineM, Nike Human Race, GlowCap and Intelligent metres.

Conclusion

The information era has significant influence on the tourism sector. Many tour operators are pioneers in the application of the latest IT achievements. It is possible to offer and purchase accommodation, automate all payments, manage the stream of tourists and provide necessary information at the right time. The information wave is entering rural tourism and agritourism slowly and continuously. Its importance particularly applies to potential tourists who can obtain full information about any undertaking in rural tourism and about agritourism farms. Online purchase of services offered by farms is increasingly important. New information technologies have unlimited potential and are already used in tourism. There will be extremely rapid progress in the use of these technologies, which will bring enormous benefits to many stakeholders.

References

BBC News – Technology. (2012) Amazon selling more Kindle ebooks than print books. http://www.bbc.com/news/technology-19148146 [Retrieved 19 February 2017]

Bienkowski, M. (1991). Augmented Reality – rzeczywistość rozszerzona. Benchmark.pl http://www.benchmark.pl/testy_i_recenzje/Augmented_Reality_-_rzeczywistosc_rozszerzona-4178.html [Retrieved 12 May 2015]

Branson, R. (1999). Branson rushes Net. CNNMoney. http://money.cnn.com/1999/02/17/europe/virgin/ [Retrieved 17 May 2014]

Bullas, J. (2014). 22 social media facts and statistics you should know in 2014. http://www.jeffbullas.com/2014/01/17/20-social-media-facts-and-statistics-you-should-know-in-2014/#I1p7s8HUy18Baqud.99 [Retrieved 12 May 2015]

Casaleggio Associati. (2011). The evolution of internet of things. http://www.slideshare.net/casaleggioassociati/the-evolution-of-internet-of-things [Retrieved 12 May 2015]

Kaplan, A. & Haenlein, M. (2010). Users of the world, unite! The challenges and opportunities of social media. *Business Horizons*, 53(1), 59–68.

Rifkin, J. (2014). *The Zero Marginal Cost Society: The Internet of Things, the Collaborative Commons, and the Eclipse of Capitalism.* New York: St. Martin's Griffin.

Rudzikas, Z. R. (2009). *Internet of Things – An Action Plan for Europe.* European Economic and Social Committee. http://www.eesc.europa.eu/?i=portal.en.ten-opinions.18007 [Retrieved 10 October 2013]

Senkus P., Łuczak M., Skrzypek A. (2014). Internet of Things: Possible usability in agriculture to increase welfare in the rural areas. http://evf.asu.lt/wp-content/uploads/sites/4/2015/03/piotr_senkus_milosz_luczak_adam_skrzypek.pdf [Retrieved 26 September 2016]

Solis, B. (2008). Conversation Prism (1.0). https://www.flickr.com/photos/briansolis/2735401175/ [Retrieved 26 September 2016]

Terdiman, D. (2005). Study: Wikipedia as accurate as Britannica c\net. https://www.cnet.com/news/study-wikipedia-as-accurate-as-britannica/ [Retrieved 19 February 2017]

Toffler, A. (1981). *The Third Wave.* Bantam Book, William Morrow.

Tourism Australia. (2013). Distribution 2020 Situational Analysis p. V. Tourism.australia.com/documents/corporate/Distribution_Final_Fullreport.pdf

Truong, V. D. & Hall, C. M. (2013). Social marketing and tourism: What is the evidence? *Social Marketing Quarterly*, 19(2), pp. 110–135.

Van Kranenburg, R., Anzelmo, E., Bassi, A., Caprio, D., Dodson, S. & Ratto M. (2011). The Internet of things. *Alexander von Humboldt Institut für Internet und Gesellschaft.* Paper prepared for first Berlin Symposium on Internet and Society, pp. 1–83. http://www.theinternetofthings.eu/sites/default/files/Rob%20van%20Kranenburg/Internet%20of%20Things%20Institute%20for%20Internet%20&%20Society%20Discussion%20Paper.pdf [Retrieved 26 March 2015]

Part III

Natural resources in metropolitan and submetropolitan areas

Natural resources in submetropolitan areas.

12 Tourism valorisation of metropolitan areas based on their natural resources

Monika Wojcieszak and Michał Jacenty Sznajder

Natural resources and values in metropolitan areas

The rapid rate of urbanisation was one of the most characteristic processes of the twentieth and twenty-first centuries. As a result, the percentage of urban population increased considerably all over the world. Urbanisation took place at the expense of the rural population and it caused a decrease in the area of forests, grasslands and farmlands which were adjacent to urban areas. Each city and the accompanying metropolitan area includes elements of animate and inanimate nature in its structure, ranging from an individual plant to vast ecosystems and diverse, unique forms of terrain. These elements form territorial and functional systems with diversified utility values. Therefore, it is important that natural resources in cities and metropolitan areas should be appropriately inventoried and used for tourism purposes.

The natural environment is a collection of interrelated natural elements. It develops space indirectly by creating suitable conditions for people to carry out a specific activity or directly, by its features, such as variability and diversity. The diversification of the natural environment (Figure 12.1) means that its specific elements have different ecological potential, which consists of natural resources and the capacity of the environment.

Reference publications use the terms 'resources' and 'natural values'. The term 'natural resources' refers to mineral resources, waters, soils, plant and animal resources, air and forces of nature such as solar energy, water and wind energy. Natural resources are unevenly distributed in space. Meyer (2004) classified natural resources in the following way:

1   Inexhaustible resources: will not be completely consumed in the future, including

   - use-unchangeable resources – water energy, geographical location, insolation
   - use-changeable resources – e.g. water, air

2   Exhaustible resources: may be completely consumed

   - non-renewable resources – e.g. mineral resources
   - partly renewable resources – e.g. soil
   - renewable resources – e.g. fauna and flora.

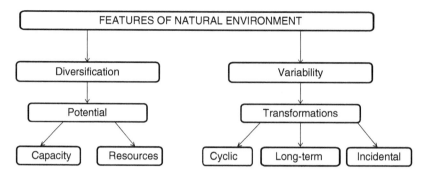

Figure 12.1 Features of the natural environment.
Source: The author's compilation based on Meyer 2004, p. 65.

Another component of the potential of the natural environment is its capacity: its ability to carry the anthropogenic load, that is, the amount of pollution and threats which can be neutralised by the environment. The term 'environment capacity' is used to estimate the degree of pollution of the environment, including underground waters. The combination of all natural resources which are present in a particular space and its capacity determine the ecological potential of this space. It can be graded as maximal, good, moderate, poor or bad. Another trait of the natural environment is its changeability, which is defined as transformations taking place over time. There are short-term, long-term and incidental transformations. Short-term transformations are cyclic, they result from the Earth's rotation about its axis and from the apparent movement of the Sun, and they affect the course of natural processes. Long-term transformations are the transformations which were taking place for millions of years in the Earth's history and formed the present environment. Incidental transformations refer to sporadic, unexpected phenomena, for example, earthquakes, tsunamis, volcanic eruptions, floods, and such like. Incidental transformations often have disastrous effects.

The term 'value' derives from the Latin word *valēre*, which means 'strong, healthy, powerful'. Natural values are the values which potential tourists may find interesting. Thus, they are decisive to the tourism attractiveness of an area. Natural resources are all the elements of the natural environment which can be found in a particular area. When we classify individual values, we need to take different criteria into consideration, especially the degree of human contribution to their formation. The literature uses a division into natural values and man-made or man-transformed values (Wall 1997, following: Lew 1987). The tourism classification of natural values developed by Lijewski *et al.* (2002) is based on this division (see Table 12.1).

The classification of natural values divides them into inanimate natural values, for example, terrain, surface waters and climate, and animate natural values, such as vegetation and animals. Reference publications use the term 'large-space

Table 12.1 Division of natural values

	Natural values	
Non-man-made	*Man-made*	*Partly man-made*
Peculiarities of fauna and flora	Historic parks	Viewpoints
Rocks and groups of rocks	Museums and natural collections	National parks
Gorges, river valleys	Botanic gardens	Scenic parks
Waterfalls, springs	Zoological gardens	
Caves and grottos		
Glacial erratics, talus deposits and other geological objects		

Source: The authors' compilation based on Lijewski *et al.* (2002).

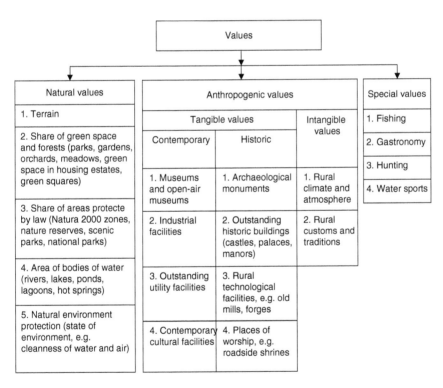

Figure 12.2 A classification of values and their elements favouring and enabling the development of tourist space.

Source: The author's compilation.

natural values', which are defined as the areas which have not been transformed much and which are protected by law due to their scientific, natural and educational values. For example, these are scenic parks, national parks and protected landscape zones. Natural values are the values formed by nature or specific man-made values, which evoke tourists' interest and thus make the basis for the development of tourism phenomena. The definition of values given above presents the essence of the elements which should be taken into consideration when evaluating tourism spaces. Not all elements are equally significant. It is important to place them in a hierarchical order, as shown in Table 12.1.

Considering the classifications provided by the literature and in view of the need to assess the natural values in tourism spaces (Figure 12.2), we developed a classification of values and their elements favouring and enabling the development of tourism spaces.

The division in Figure 12.2 distinguishes three groups of values and their components. These elements may be used as indications to make use of the potential located in a particular area, for example, for tourism purposes. Along with the cultural and tourism infrastructure resources, the resources of the natural environment are an important element of the tourism potential, determining tourism attractiveness. They favour and enable the development of a particular area. Natural conditions have significant influence on the spatial and socio-economic development of a particular area. Local natural resources provide the conditions for tourism, recreation and business activity.

Condensed characterisation of Polish metropolitan areas

In Europe a metropolitan area is very often characterised as the area around the city with a population of about 500,000. In Poland, according to Polish Parliament Law (2003), a metropolitan area is defined as 'the area of a big city and its direct neighbourhood, which is functionally related to it and determined in the concept of spatial development of the country'. There are 12 metropolitan areas of different significance in Poland. Warsaw is the centre of the most important metropolitan area and is followed by Upper Silesia, Kraków, Tri-City, Wrocław, Łódź, Poznań, Bydgoszcz and Toruń, Lublin, Szczecin, Rzeszów and Białystok.

Metropolitan centres in Poland

1   Warsaw Metropolitan Area (WMA)
     Main city: Warsaw
     The capital of Poland
     European metropolis

     a   General information: Consists of 72 communes and is inhabited by about
          3.1 million people. The capital of the metropolitan area is Warsaw, with
          a population of 1.7 million. The metropolitan area is 6.2 thousand km².
     b   Metropolitan functions: National and local administrative centre;
          European political centre; centre of national culture, education, research

and innovation; industrial centre; centre of international road, rail and air transport; international business and financial centre; national tourism centre.

c   Most important natural resources: Kampinos National Park, Warsaw Uprising Mound, Masovian Scenic Park, Natura 2000 zones, Czerniakowskie and Powsinkowskie Lakes, natural monuments.

2   Upper Silesia Metropolitan Area (USMA)
Main cities: Bytom, Chorzów, Dąbrowa Górnicza, Gliwice, Jaworzno, Katowice, Mysłowice, Piekary Śląskie, Ruda Śląska, Siemianowice Śląskie, Sosnowiec, Świętochłowice, Tychy, Zabrze
Coal mining and steel industry region
European metropolis

a   General information: Consists of 43 communes, with a total area of 2.9 thousand km^2. The GMA is inhabited by 2.4 million people. Katowice is the leading city, with a population of 307,000.
b   Metropolitan functions: Local administrative centre; national political centre; local cultural centre; regional centre of education, research and innovation; heavy industry centre; centre of national road transport and international rail, air and inland water transport; international business and financial centre; local tourism centre.
c   Most important natural resources: Katowice Forest Park, Valley of Three Ponds, Regional Culture and Leisure Park, natural monuments.

3   Krakow Metropolitan Area (KMA)
Main city: Kraków
The former capital of Poland; Pope John Paul II's city
Regional metropolis

a   General information: Consists of 51 communes. The total metropolitan area is inhabited by 1.5 million people and occupies a territory of 4.3 thousand km^2. Krakow is the leading city, with a population of 759,000 inhabitants.
b   Metropolitan functions: Local administrative centre; national political centre; international cultural centre; international centre of education, research and innovation; heavy industry centre; centre of international road, rail and air transport; international business and financial centre; global tourism centre.
c   Most important natural resources: a complex of Jurassic scenic parks, Krakow-Częstochowa Upland, numerous reserves and scenic parks, Ojców National Park, Maczuga Herkulesa Monadnock, Niepołomice Forest, natural monuments.

4   Tri-City Metropolitan Area (TMA) – not discussed in the book
Main cities: Gdańsk, Gdynia, Sopot
'Solidarity' and Baltic cities

Regional metropolis

a   General information: Encompasses the cities of Gdańsk, Gdynia and Sopot and consists of 27 communes. The total TMA is 5.2 thousand km² and is inhabited by 1.2 million people. The population of the leading cities is: Gdańsk 461,000, Gdynia 248,000, and Sopot 38,000.

b   Metropolitan functions: Local administrative centre; national political centre; regional cultural centre; regional centre of education, research and innovation; industrial centre; national centre of road, rail, air and sea transport; local business and financial centre; European tourism centre.

c   Most important natural resources: Oliwa Park, Oliwa Brook, wild beach in Oksywie, Donas Hill, Tri-City Scenic Park, cliffs, Kamienna Góra, natural monuments.

5   Wrocław Metropolitan Area (WrMA)
Main city: Wrocław
Beauty on the Oder River
Regional metropolis

a   General information: Consists of 44 communes, inhabited by 1.2 million people. The total area is 6.7 thousand km². The capital of the metropolitan area is Wrocław, with a population of 633,000.

b   Metropolitan functions: Local administrative centre; national political centre; national cultural centre; national centre of education, research and innovation; industrial centre; centre of international road, rail and air transport; inland water transport centre; international business and financial centre; European tourism centre.

c   Most important natural resources: Gajowice Hills, Trzebnica embankment, Barycz River Valley, a fragment of the Oder River Valley, Natura 2000 zones, natural monuments.

6   Łódź Metropolitan Area (ŁMA)
Main city: Łódź
Nineteenth century textile industry metropolis
Regional metropolis

a   General information: Consists of 36 communes with 1.2 million people. The total ŁMA is 3.4 thousand km². Łódź is the leading city, with a population of 708,000.

b   Metropolitan functions: Local administrative centre; regional political centre; regional cultural centre; regional centre of education, research and innovation; industrial centre; local road and rail transport centre; local business and financial centre; local tourism centre.

c   Most important natural resources: the scenic park of the land between the Warta and Widawka Rivers, Sulejów Scenic Park, Łódź Upland Scenic Park, Natura 2000 zones, natural monuments.

7   Poznań Metropolitan Area (PMA)
    Main city: Poznań
    The first capital of Poland
    Regional metropolis

    a   General information: Consists of 22 communes and is inhabited by 1.1 million people. Its total area is 6.4 thousand km^2. Poznań is the leading city, with a population of 549,000.
    b   Metropolitan functions: Local administrative centre; national political centre; regional cultural centre; national centre of education, research and innovation; industrial centre; centre of international road, rail and air transport; international business and financial centre; European tourism centre.
    c   Most important natural resources: Meteorite Morasko and Żurawiniec nature reserve, Sołacki Park, Cytadela Park, Lake Malta, Warta River valley, Greater Poland National Park, oak trees in Rogalin, Rogalin Scenic Park, natural monuments.

8   Bydgoszcz-Toruń Metropolitan Area (B-TMA)
    Main cities: Bydgoszcz, Toruń
    Copernicus' City in a Bipolar Metropolis on the Vistula River Valley
    Local metropolis

    a   General information: Bydgoszcz and Toruń are located in the centre of Kuyavian-Pomeranian Voivodeship. Bydgoszcz is the seat of the government administration and Toruń is the seat of the local government. The Bydgoszcz-Toruń metropolitan area is 2.9 thousand km^2 and is inhabited by 774,300 people. The leading cities are Bydgoszcz with 359,000 inhabitants and Toruń with 204,000 inhabitants.
    b   Metropolitan functions: Local administrative centre; local political centre; local cultural centre; local centre of education, research and innovation; local road and rail transport centre; inland water transport centre; local business and financial centre; local tourism centre (Bydgoszcz) and European tourism centre (Toruń).
    c   Most important natural resources: Tuchola Forest, Forest Culture Park, Bydgoszcz Canal, Vistula and Brda River valleys, Bydgoszcz Forest, Brabarka (a forest settlement), natural monuments.

9   Lublin Metropolitan Area (LMA) – not discussed in the book
    Main city: Lublin
    Local metropolis

    a   General information: Occupies an area of 4.2 thousand km^2, with a population of 717,000 and consisting of 41 communes. Lublin is the leading city, with a population of 314,000.
    b   Metropolitan functions: Local administrative centre; local political centre; local cultural centre; local centre of education, research and

innovation; local road and rail transport centre; local business and financial centre; national tourism centre.

c   Most important natural resources: Polesie National Park, natural monuments,
Roztocze National Park, nature reserves such as Black Forest, Royal Way.

10   Szczecin Metropolitan Area (SMA)
Main city: Szczecin
Between the mouth of the Oder River and lagoon
Local metropolis

a   General information: Encompasses the territories around Szczecin, the
biggest city in northwestern Poland. It consists of 12 communes, with
a total area of 2.5 thousand km² and is inhabited by 621,000 people.
Szczecin is the leading city, with a population of 408,000.

b   Metropolitan functions: Local administrative centre; local political centre; local cultural centre; local centre of education, research and innovation; centre of international road and rail transport and local air transport;
sea and inland water transport centre; local business and financial centre;
international tourism centre.

c   Most important natural resources: Szczecin Lagoon; Lakes: Dąbie,
Miedwie, Jamno; Natura 2000 zones, Szczecin Scenic Park 'Beech
Forest', Wolin National Park.

11   Rzeszów Metropolitan Area (RMA) – not discussed in the book
Main city: Rzeszów
Gateway to the picturesque Carpathians
Local metropolis

a   General information: An urbanised area in the centre of the Sub-
Carpathian region. It encompasses the city of Rzeszów and adjacent territories and consists of 45 communes. The total RMA is 4.3 thousand
km². The metropolitan area is inhabited by 613,000 people. Rzeszów is
the leading city, with a population of 185,000.

b   Metropolitan functions: Local administrative centre; local political centre; local cultural centre; local centre of education, research and innovation; centre of national road, rail and air transport; local business and
financial centre; local tourism centre.

c   Most important natural resources: Lisia Góra Nature Reserve, Olszynki
Culture and Leisure Park, natural monuments such as Errant Stone.

12   Białystok Metropolitan Area (BMA) – not discussed in the book
Main city: Białystok
Northern gateway to Polish forests and lakes
Local metropolis

a   General information: Occupies an area of more than 6.5 thousand km²
and consists of 33 communes. The BMA is inhabited by 560,000 people.
Białystok is the leading city, with a population of 295,000.

b   Metropolitan functions: Local administrative centre; local political centre; local cultural centre; local centre of education, research and innovation; local road and rail transport centre; local business and financial centre; national tourism centre.

c   Most important natural resources: Narew National Park, Knyszyn Forest Scenic Park, natural monuments, Natura 2000 zones.

Although all Polish metropolitan areas were briefly characterised above, due to financial reasons only three of them (Poznań, Szczecin and Wrocław) were selected to present the concept of tourism valorisation of metropolitan areas based on their natural resources.

Natural resources in metropolitan areas

Natural resources are a public good. The quality of the natural environment and its condition is a factor supporting and strengthening the development of a metropolitan area. The natural environment within metropolitan areas is characterised by forest, parks and lakes and they have protected zones and areas of natural value. Surface water resources are also important elements. The elements of the natural environment form scenic values in cities. Table 12.2 shows natural resources in selected metropolitan areas in 2012. The following elements were included with natural resources: natural monuments, protected landscape zones, forest cover and green space.

The following elements were included in protected landscape zones: national parks, scenic parks, nature reserves, other forms of nature conservation in scenic parks and protected landscape zones.

Below is a description of natural resources in metropolitan areas:

1   Natural monuments: individual forms of animate and inanimate nature or clusters of such forms, which are of particular natural, scientific, cultural, historical or scenic value and which are distinguished from other forms by

Table 12.2 Natural resources in three selected metropolitan areas

Metropolitan area ratio	Metropolitan area			Total
	Poznań	Szczecin	Wrocław	
Communes (number)	22	12	42	76
Number of natural monuments per 100 km² of commune area (natural monuments pcs/100 km²)	567	169	338	1074
Share of areas of particular natural value, protected by law in total commune area (% of protected areas)	17.00	6.00	18.00	41.00
Share of forest areas in total commune area (% of forest cover)	19.50	42.00	26.00	87.50
Share of green space areas in total commune area (% of green space)	0.25	0.17	0.30	0.72

Source: The authors' compilation.

their individual traits. This term especially refers to conspicuous trees and shrubs of native or foreign species, springs, waterfalls, karst springs, rocks, ravines, glacial erratics and caves.

2   Protected landscape zone: encompasses areas that are protected due to their distinctive landscape with diversified ecosystems. The areas are valuable because they satisfy a demand for tourism and recreation or due to their function as ecological corridors.

   a   National park: an area distinguished for its particular natural, scientific, social, cultural and educational values. It is not smaller than 1000 ha. All nature and scenic values are protected in this area. A national park is established to preserve its biodiversity, resources, forms and components of inanimate nature and scenic values, to restore degraded natural habitats of plants, animals or fungi.

   b   Nature reserve: an area preserved in its natural or almost unchanged state. These are ecosystems, refuges and natural habitats of plants, animals or fungi. These are also forms and components of inanimate nature which are distinguished for their particular natural, scientific, cultural or scenic values. Depending on the assumed protection goal, we can distinguish the following types of reserves: faunal, floristic, forest, scenic, peatbog, grassland, water, inanimate nature, steppe and halophytic (plants able to thrive in salty conditions). A faunal reserve is an area with habitats of rare or peculiar species of animals or their groups: mammals (wisents, elks, beavers), birds (breeding, nesting and resting sites of different species), reptiles (for example, pond turtles), molluscs (rare snail species) or insects. A floristic reserve is an area with habitats of individual plant species or their groups: shrubs and green plants, endemic and relict species. An inanimate nature reserve is an area with geological opencast sites, karst sites, characteristic soil profiles, examples of erosion, traces of old mining. A scenic reserve is an area with characteristic, leading landscapes of individual regions with natural traits, usually with historic and material culture monuments. A nature reserve may receive a status of international significance, defined by applicable international conventions or resolutions of international organisations. Neighbouring countries may sign agreements demarcating borderland areas of natural value for joint protection.

   c   Scenic park: an area which is protected due to its natural, historic, cultural and scenic values in order to popularise these values under the conditions of sustainable development.

   d   Other forms of nature conservation: are documentation sites, ecological areas and natural scenic complexes in scenic parks.

3   Forests: the least deformed natural formation in the Polish climatic and geographical zone. They are an indispensable factor of ecological balance. Simultaneously, they are the form of land use which guarantees biological production with market value. Forests are a common social good with influence on the quality of human life.

4   Green spaces: areas covered with plants. They have technical infrastructure and buildings which are functionally related with these areas. Green spaces are located in villages with compact development or in cities. They have aesthetic, recreational or therapeutic functions.

In 2012 the largest number of natural monuments per 100 km^2 was noted in the Poznań metropolitan area – 567. By comparison, there were only 169 natural monuments in the Szczecin metropolitan area.

   The highest share (18%) of protected areas in the total commune area is in the Wrocław metropolitan area, whereas the lowest (6%) is in the Szczecin metropolitan area. There is high diversification in the share of protected areas in the total commune area. In some communes there are no protected areas at all. The forest cover was the third element under analysis. The largest forest cover (42%) was in the Szczecin metropolitan area, whereas the forest cover in the Poznań metropolitan area was 19.5 per cent of the total area. Green space includes leisure parks, green squares and green space in housing estates. The highest share of green space was in the Wrocław metropolitan area (0.17%), whereas in the Poznań metropolitan area the share of green space was the lowest.

Valorisation of metropolitan areas

The term 'valorisation' is perceived in two aspects, that is, as a description of values and as a method of space evaluation. In spatial planning valorisation is interpreted as an estimation of the value of a particular area. In order to determine the tourism attractiveness of a region it is important to estimate its natural and anthropogenic values. 'When analysing the significance of values in the development of tourism, we must not fail to include the issue of the quality of natural values, which directly increase or decrease the degree of tourism attractiveness' (Meyer 2004, p. 72). Tourism attractiveness is determined by means of the values and tourism development. Tourism values are often identified with tourism attractions. These elements satisfy the needs of tourists arriving in a particular region. They are means of competition for individual regions. On the basis of the main motives of tourist traffic we can distinguish sightseeing and specialist and relaxation values. Other scientific publications make a division based on the origin of values. They distinguish natural values (created by the natural environment) and anthropogenic values (directly related to human activity). In the process of researching human relations with the cultural, economic, natural and social environment we use evaluation methods, which give specific value to individual traits. Valorisation is the measurement of natural values. The literature provides a few types of valorisation used for the development of tourism, for example, the evaluation of landscape attractiveness. In practice, there are no universal methods enabling objective assessment of the values of natural space, which is distinguished by its diversified resources. There is a large number of traits which are critical to the value of a particular area. These are quantifiable and unquantifiable traits, which are converted into a comparable form.

The use of valorisation enables division of an area into regions with similar conditions for activities such as tourism. Valorisation enables identification of areas, which were homogenous in terms of tourism, with abundant natural environment.

Valorisation method

Complex phenomena are those that cannot be expressed with one trait or which are not directly measurable. Synthetic traits, expressed by simple traits, are used to describe complex phenomena. A simple trait expresses one directly measurable value. We can distinguish the following types of simple traits: stimulants – high shares of these traits are desirable, de-stimulants – lower values of these traits are desirable, and nominants – the traits for which we can determine the optimal numerical value. The degree of development of tourism is an example of a synthetic trait.

The multi-stage method of determination of a synthetic trait goes according to the following scheme (Lira and Wysocki 2004). At the first stage simple traits, which are determinants of the complex phenomenon under analysis, are selected and their value is determined. The selection should be confirmed with factual and statistical premises. Then a data matrix is constructed. It is necessary to check the numerical condition of the matrix by analysis of the diagonal elements of the inverse matrix of correlation matrix R.[1] The next stage is to normalise simple traits. De-stimulants and nominants are converted into stimulants and, simultaneously, their values are converted so as to make them comparable. The process is called unitarisation and is done in the following way:

- for stimulants: $z_{ij} = \dfrac{x_{ij} - \min\limits_{i}\{x_{ij}\}}{\max\limits_{i}\{x_{ij}\} - \min\limits_{i}\{x_{ij}\}}$

- for de-stimulants: $z_{ij} = \dfrac{\max\limits_{i}\{x_{ij}\} - x_{ij}}{\max\limits_{i}\{x_{ij}\} - \min\limits_{i}\{x_{ij}\}}$

- for nominants:

$$x_{ij} \le nom\{x_{ij}\} \quad z_{ij} = \dfrac{x_{ij} - \min\limits_{i}\{x_{ij}\}}{nom\{x_{ij}\} - \min\limits_{i}\{x_{ij}\}}$$

$$x_{ij} > nom\{x_{ij}\} \quad z_{ij} = \dfrac{\max\limits_{i}\{x_{ij}\} - x_{ij}}{\max\limits_{i}\{x_{ij}\} - nom\{x_{ij}\}} ,$$

where:

$\max\limits_{i}\{x_{ij}\}$ – the maximum j-th trait value,

$\min\limits_{i}\{x_{ij}\}$ – the minimum j-th trait value,

$nom\{x_{ij}\}$ – the optimal or desirable j-th trait value.

The third stage consists of determining the method for calculation of the synthetic trait value. It is based on the model method, which consists of calculating the distance of individual units from the development model:

$$q_i = \sqrt{\frac{\sum_{j=1}^{m}(z_{ij} - z_{0j})^2}{m}} \text{ , for (i = 1, 2, ..., n),}$$

where: z_{0j} – the normalised j-th trait value for the model unit.

It is assumed in analyses that $z_{0j} = \max\{z_{ij}\}$ for the traits which are stimulants or which were converted into stimulants. The obtained values will be used for calculation of Hellwig's synthetic measure of development, which is expressed with the following formula (Wysocki and Lira 2005):

$$\tilde{q}_i = 1 - \frac{q_i}{q_0}$$

where: $q_0 = \bar{q}_0 = 2s_0$, $\quad \bar{q}_0 = \frac{\sum_{i=1}^{n} q_i}{n}$, $\quad s_0 = \sqrt{\frac{\sum_{i=1}^{n}(q_i - \bar{q}_0)^2}{n}}$.

The greater the index value, the higher is the degree of development of the phenomenon under analysis. Normally, this measure assumes the values within the interval of (0, 1). By means of the standard deviation (s_q), arithmetic mean ($\bar{q}$) and the calculated measure ($\tilde{q}_i$) it is possible to make a division into four classes:

- class I (very high level): $\tilde{q}_i \geq \bar{q} + s_q$
- class II (high level): $\bar{q} + s_q > \tilde{q}_i \geq \bar{q}$
- class III (medium level): $\bar{q} > \tilde{q}_i \geq \bar{q} - s_q$
- class IV (low level): $\tilde{q}_i < \bar{q} - sq$

In this chapter we use a modified version of Hellwig's model method. We assumed an aggregate index of tourism valorisation, as was proposed by Przezbórska and Lira (2011, pp. 568–579).

These were the following stages of construction of the aggregate index of tourism valorisation:

1 Selecting the set of simple traits
2 Identifying the trend of preferences for simple traits and standardising them into a common comparative system
3 Calculating the synthetic trait value by means of Hellwig's method
4 Identifying and describing typological classes referring to the degree of development of nature tourism.

Ref. 1: The following three diagnostic elements (natural and sightseeing values) classified as stimulants were selected upon analysis of the diagonal elements of inverse correlation matrix R:

- forest cover, that is, the share of forest land in the total commune area
- the number of natural monuments per 100 km² of the commune area
- the share of areas of particular natural value and protected by law in the total commune area.

Ref. 2. The next stage was to standardise the values of diagnostic traits according to Weber's median standardisation (Weber's median was calculated by means of statistical program R).

Ref. 3. A synthetic measure of development was constructed on the basis of a modified version of Hellwig's model method in the positional approach (Lira and Wysocki 2002).

Ref. 4. The communes were linearly ordered according to the synthetic measure value and typological classes were identified (Lira and Wysocki 2004).

Valorisation of tourism space: a case study of the Poznań, Szczecin and Wrocław metropolitan areas

The areas of communes were assumed as weights for the synthetic measure. Table 12.3 shows the basic numerical characteristics of the traits describing the natural values of the communes in individual metropolitan areas in 2012.

The selected traits were characterised by variation in the spatial approach and they were not correlated with each other. In consequence, it was possible to construct a synthetic measure of tourism valorisation in the communes. For example, in 2012 the coefficient of variation ranged from 68.74 per cent for the forest cover to 166.51 per cent for the protected areas.

Table 12.3 The numerical characteristics of the traits describing the natural values of the communes in 2012

Characteristics	Forest cover [%]	Monuments [pcs/km²]	Protected areas [%]
Minimum	0.00	0.00	0.00
Arithmetic mean	21.71	14.13	14.15
Marginal median	19.20	5.95	1.85
Maximum	55.80	78.60	100.5
Coefficient of variation (%)	68.74	135.34	166.51
Weber's median	18.70	8.62	6.10
Diagonal elements of matrix R^{-1}	12.10	6.62	6.10

Source: The authors' compilation based on the data of the Local Data Bank and Central Statistical Office, as of 12 May 2014.

Upon analysis of the values of the natural environment four classes of communes were identified, according to their usefulness for the development of tourism.

As results from the analysis, the communes located in the southwest of the metropolitan areas of Wrocław and Poznań and the communes located in the northeast of the Szczecin metropolitan area are characterised by better natural environmental conditions for the development of tourism. The communes with potentially good natural environmental conditions for the development of tourism are characterised by diversity of their values, for example, a large number of natural monuments, protected areas and high percentage of forest cover (Table 12.4).

Table 12.5 shows the typologies of communes (identified classes of communes) in the metropolitan areas according to the values of the synthetic measure of tourism valorisation in 2012.

The analysis of the data for 2012 reveals that there were 12 communes in the group with the highest synthetic measure value (class I), including one commune from the Szczecin metropolitan area, 6 communes from the Poznań metropolitan area and 5 communes from the Wrocław metropolitan area. There were positive values of the synthetic measure for these communes, ranging from 0.50 to 0.75. Class I included the communes which were characterised by the highest indexes used for the construction of the aggregate measure and included in Table 12.5, that is, the forest cover (32.9%), the share of protected areas (54.6%) and the number of natural monuments per 100 km^2 (24.1%). It is noteworthy that the communes which were included in class I have a rich offer of natural values. These are the areas of interesting scenic parks, forests, reserves, hills, and such like.

Ranked lowest were 13 communes, that is, in class IV. They were characterised by the lowest aggregate index values, ranging from 0.09 to 0.10. This group included one commune from the Poznań metropolitan area, one from the Szczecin metropolitan area and 11 communes from the Wrocław metropolitan area. Class IV was characterised by the lowest values of all the traits used for the construction of the synthetic measure (for example, there were very few natural monuments). The values of these traits in these communes are much lower than the average values in the communes included in class I or II. For example, it is noticeable in the data concerning protected areas – 0.02 per cent (class IV). In terms of natural

Table 12.4 The inter-class diversification of natural values in the communes in 2012 (harmonic mean values in the classes)

2012	Classes			
	I	*II*	*III*	*IV*
Forest cover [%]	32.9	27.1	22.2	21.5
Natural monuments [pcs/km^2]	24.1	24.5	6.6	1.2
Protected areas [%]	54.6	17.6	3.0	0.02

Source: The authors' compilation based on the data of the Local Data Bank and Central Statistical Office, as of 12 May 2014.

Table 12.5 The typology of metropolitan areas according to the values of the synthetic measure of tourism valorisation in 2012

Class	Measure value	Number of communes	Communes in class*
I	0.50–0.75	12	Stare Czarnowo (2), Wrocław (3), Czerwonak (1), Międzybórz (3), Milicz (3), Mosina (1), Luboń (1), Murowana Goślina (1), Poznań (1), Suchy Las (1), Krośnice (3), Żmigród (3)
II	0.22–0.49	18	Sobótka (3), Śrem (1), Puszczykowo (1), Tarnowo Podgórne (1), Kornik (1), Pobiedziska (1), Trzebnica (3), Prusice (3), Stargard Szczeciński (2), Wisznia Mała (3), Komorniki (1), Brzeg Dolny (3), Mietków (3), Stęszew (1), Kobylanka (2), Oborniki (1), Wołów (3), Katy Wrocławskie (3)
III	0.11–0.21	33	Swarzędz (1), Dobra (2), Przeworno (3), Stargard Szczeciński (2), Cieszków (3), Syców (3), Rokietnica (1), Kołbaskowo (2), Jordanów Śląski (3), Skoki (1), Szamotuły (1), Dopiewo (1), Kostomłoty (3), Gryfino (2), Buk (1), Goleniów (2), Wińsko (3), Kobierzyce (3), Szczecin (2), Twardogóra (3), Oleśnica (3), Kondratowice (3), Stepnica (2), Długołęka (3), Jelcz – Laskowice (3), Udanin (3), Czernica (3), Strzelin (3), Kostrzyn (1), Miękina (3), Oława (3), Police (2), Żórawina (3)
IV	0.90–0.10	13	Nowe Warpno (2), Kleszczewo (1), Oborniki Śląskie (3), Zawonia (3), Dobroszyce (3), Środa Śląska (3), Dziadowa Kłoda (3), Bierutów (3), Borów (3), Domaniów (3), Malczyce (3), Święta Katarzyna (3), Wiązków (3)

* The values in brackets refer to the metropolitan area where the commune is located: (1) the Poznań metropolitan area, (2) the Szczecin metropolitan area, (3) the Wrocław metropolitan area.

Source: The authors' compilation.

and sightseeing values these communes may be less attractive for potential tourists. For example, in class IV there is a high share of farmland in the territorial structure. Classes II and III include intermediate communes in terms of their usefulness for the development of nature tourism. Class II consisted of 18 communes: 8 communes from the Poznań metropolitan area, 2 communes from the Szczecin metropolitan area and 8 communes from the Wrocław metropolitan area.

There are 33 communes in class III: 8 communes from the Szczecin metropolitan area, 7 communes from the Poznań metropolitan area and 18 communes from the Wrocław metropolitan area. The communes belonging to classes II and III can be described as areas with natural values that have average favourable effect on the development of tourism, although they are characterised by a relatively high percentage of forest cover, that is, 27.1 per cent in class II and 22.2 per cent in class III. The communes in classes II, III and IV are characterised by a low share of protected areas (ranging from 17.6% to 0.02%). The assumption of this valorisation was that all of the traits under analysis had equal, positive effect on the tourism attractiveness of these areas due to the presence of various natural and sightseeing values. Potential tourists may differently perceive the values included by the author of this study.

Conclusions

Each metropolitan area has valuable natural resources, which determine its tourism value and the flow of tourists. Geographical location is also critical to attractiveness. Protected areas, green space, forests and natural monuments play an important role in valorisation. The method of tourism valorisation of an area presented in this book has not only cognitive aspects, but can also be used in practice to indicate potential locations of tourism investments in the area valorised.

Note

1   If the elements are greater than 10, the trait is excessively correlated with other traits and it should be eliminated from the set.

References

Bank Danych Lokalnych. (n.a.). https://bdl.stat.gov.pl/BDL/dane/podgrup/temat. [Retrieved 10.02.2014]

Lew, A. A. (1987). A framework of tourist attraction research. *Annals of Tourism Research*, Elsevier Scencie, 14(4), pp. 553–575.

Lijewski, T., Mikułowski, B. & Wyrzykowski, J. (2002). *Geografia turystyczna Polski*. Publisher: PWE, Warszawa.

Lira, J. & Wysocki, F. (2002). Mediana w zadnieniach porządkowania obiektów wielocechowych. In J. Paradysz (Ed.). *Statystyka regionalna w służbie samorządu terytorialnego i biznesu*. Publisher: Akademia Ekonomiczna w Poznaniu, Poznań.

Lira, J. & Wysocki, F. (2004). Zastosowanie pozycyjnego miernika rozwoju do pomiaru poziomu zagospodarowania infrastrukturalnego powiatów. *Wiadomości statystyczne*. Publisher: GUS, No. 9, pp. 39–49.

Meyer, B. (2004). *Turystyka jako ekonomiczny czynnik kształtowania przestrzeni*. Publisher: Wydawnictwo Naukowe Uniwersytetu Szczecińskiego, Szczecin.

Polish Parlament Law. (2003). Ustawa z dnia 27 marca 2003 r. o planowaniu i zagospodarowaniu przestrzennym, (Dz. U. 2003 nr 80, poz. 717 z późn. zm.).

Przezbórska, L. & Lira, J. (2011). Walory Środowiska przyrodniczego jako czynnik rozwoju turystyki wiejskiej w Polsce. In *Polityka Ekonomiczna*. Publisher: Wydawnictwo Uniwersytetu Ekonomicznego we Wrocławiu, Wrocław, 2011, pp. 568–579.

Wall, G. (1997). Tourism attractions: Points, lines, and areas. *Annals of Tourism Research*, Elsevier Scencie 24(1), pp. 240–2431.

Wysocki, L., Lira J. (2005). Statystyka opisowa. Pub. *Wydawnictwo Akademii Rolniczej im. Augusta Cieszkowskiego*, Poznań, pp 45–63.

13 Kampinos National Park as a tourism attraction for Warsaw metropolitan areas

Katarzyna Mikrut

Kampinos National Park in a nutshell

Kampinos National Park is the second largest national park in Poland. It occupies an area of 38.5 thousand ha, including 27.5 thousand ha of forests, 7.5 thousand ha of farmland and nearly 0.2 thousand ha of water. The area of the park buffer zone is almost the same as the protected area, that is, 37.7 thousand ha. The park is situated in central Poland. It stretches latitudinally west of Warsaw, in a strip which is 10 to 15 km wide and 45 to 50 km long. It is an example of one of a few parks in the world whose area neighbours or is contained within the limits of the country's capital city. It borders Warsaw directly northwest of the city. The park was established on 16 January 1959 to protect both the natural values of Kampinos Forest and rich monuments of Polish history and culture.

There are about one thousand names used all over the world to define territorial forms of nature conservation. For this reason, it is in practice impossible to make any comparison on a global scale. For example, in the UK the national park is an area with a relatively poor protection regime, extensively used and sometimes even densely populated. On the other hand, in Poland the national park is regarded as the highest form of conservation, with very limited human activity. The development of a system of typology and classification of protected areas was an important step taken by the International Union for Conservation of Nature (IUCN) to standardise protection categories. The classification system, which has been effective since 1992, distinguishes six categories: I to VI. According to this system, Kampinos National Park was classified as Category II – a high degree of protection. On 21 January 2000 the park and the buffer zone were recognised as a World Biosphere Reserve. Since 2004 it has been part of the Natura 2000 network, PLC 140001.

As far as nature conservation is concerned, the main statutory goal of Kampinos National Park is to preserve the complex of inland dunes and wetlands together with their biological and scenic diversity, and their geological, geomorphological, hydrological and soil properties. It is a unique complex both in Poland and Europe.

Kampinos Forest is a unique reservoir of inanimate nature, especially inland dunes and swamps. It has abundant fauna and flora. The flora includes pines,

Figure 13.1 A view of Warsaw from Kampinos National Park.

Source: Photo by G. Okołów.

oaks, birches, ashes, alders and poplars. The forest is the habitat of elks, beavers, lynxes and many other species of animals. The elk is an animal that was successfully reintroduced in the forest.

At present there are only about 1800 people living in the park. The number of inhabitants has been decreasing systematically due to the scheme of purchasing land for the state treasury, which was introduced in 1979. We can observe the opposite tendency in the buffer zone, where the number of inhabitants is growing continuously. The population of the park buffer zone is about 65,000. The inhabitants of Warsaw, which is nearby, should also be added to this number, that is, nearly 2,000,000 people.

Kampinos Forest: a protagonist of tourism in metropolitan areas

The interest of Warsaw tourists in Kampinos Forest dates back to the nineteenth century. At the time well-known and meritorious inhabitants of Warsaw and Masovia toured the forest. Some of them were Kazimierz Władysław Wójcicki, a literary historian, folklorist, collector of folk tales and legends; Oskar Kolberg, an ethnographer and musicologist; Karol Kurpiński, a composer, co-author of the national style in Polish music and Frederic Chopin, a world-famous pianist and composer, who spent his childhood there.

The first scientific tours of Kampinos Forest were organised in the mid-nineteenth century by Wojciech Jastrzębowski, a naturalist, pedagogue and sightseer, professor of the Agronomic Institute in Marymont near Warsaw (now a district of Warsaw). He used illustrative methods in the teaching process. He conducted field researches with his students and engaged them to collect botanical and mineralogical specimens.

Kampinos Forest was the place where the first organised tourism trip took place on a Polish lowland, on 2 June 1907. Previously, this type of tourism had been practised only in the Polish mountains. The trip was guided by the founders of the Polish Sightseeing Society and Nature Conservation League: Aleksander Janowski, a sightseeing pioneer and Kazimierz Kulwieć, a pedagogue and naturalist. The trip was an implementation of the statutory provisions of the Polish Sightseeing Society, which obliged its members to make trips around the country, learn about natural curiosities and take care of them. The excursionists set off from Warsaw on two steamboats, 'Kopernik III' and 'Nadwiślanin', sailing on the Vistula. They reached the harbour in Gniewniewice near Kazuń (see Figure 13.2), where they left the boat and went walking together with the guides. They walked via the villages of Leoncin and Teofile to reach the edge of Kampinos Forest, where they rested. The strongest continued walking through the forest towards Stara Dąbrowa. As the records show, there were as many as 387 excursionists. It was an extraordinary event for the Warsaw inhabitants, as they wore formal clothes, which were absolutely unfit for tourism. The women were dressed in elegant dresses with long trains and they were holding parasols in their hands. This must have made hiking difficult. The excursionists were accompanied by wagons carrying the participants' luggage. It was possible to buy souvenirs commemorating the event: a postcard with a wisent and a map of Kampinos Forest. The forest inspectorate delegated two men to guide the hikers. The whole event was described in an illustrated weekly magazine *Świat*, which discussed social problems, literature and art. In those times it was a significant and extraordinary undertaking, which was widely commented upon and described by reporters.

Varsovians' weekend tourism destinations

Inhabitants of Warsaw (Varsovians) can choose between a number of interesting weekend tourism destinations, such as Zegrze Lake, Chojnów Forest, Kampinos Forest, Bolimów Forest, Masovian Scenic Park and many others. Research by Cieszewska (2009) showed that 42 per cent of Warsaw inhabitants choose areas within a radius of 25 km of their place of residence, 65 per cent within a radius of 50 km and as many as 86.6 per cent of weekend trips are made to destinations which are not further than 100 km from the city centre. The most popular destinations are Zegrze Lake – 13.1 per cent, Chojnów Forest – 12.7 per cent, Kampinos National Park – 12 per cent and Otwock region – 10.8 per cent.

Every year about one million people visit Kampinos National Park. Of these visitors, 73.1 per cent live in Warsaw and as many as 43 per cent of the tourists

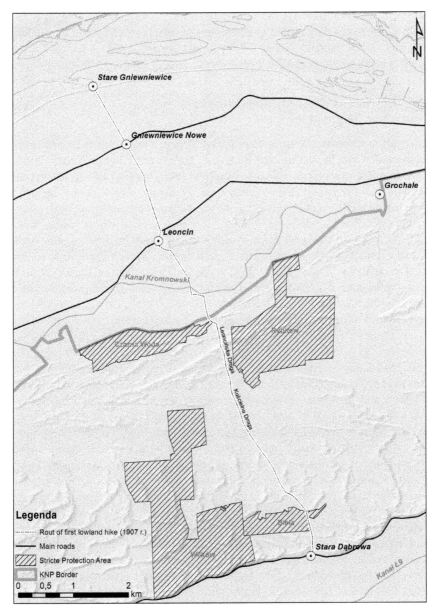

Figure 13.2 The route of the first excursion in the Polish lowland.

Source: The author's compilation on http://www.kampinoski-pn.gov.pl, accessed in 2015.

come from three districts of Warsaw which are closest to the park: Bielany, Bemowo and Żoliborz. Of the remainder, 11.1 per cent live in Masovia and 9.4 per cent live in the park buffer zone. The inhabitants of other regions of Poland rarely choose Kampinos National Park as a destination – only 2.1 per cent. Other tourists make up the final 4.2 per cent (Prószyńska-Bordas *et al.* 2005).

Tourism versus nature conservation in Kampinos National Park

The staff of Kampinos National Park face a difficult challenge to reconcile nature conservation and increasing tourism traffic. On the one hand, it is their duty to protect nature in the park, which is a national good. On the other hand, they are supposed to satisfy the human demand for relaxation, recreation and spending time surrounded by nature. In order to reconcile these conflicting interests, access to the national park must be regulated so as to give everybody interested a chance to learn about the diversity of ecosystems and, at the same time, minimise the negative effect of tourism on nature. Access to the park is granted in a planned manner, which is reflected by orders, regulations and other documents. Zoning is also important. The park areas of higher natural value are characterised by a higher protective regime and lesser interference by technical elements of tourism facilities. Traffic monitoring, reception, appropriate information and educational actions are also important elements of tourism order in the park. There are three types of protected areas in the park: strict protection zones, active protection zones and scenic protection zones, which have different protection regimes. Strict (passive) protection consists in leaving the selected area completely to the forces of nature and, in practice, is the abandonment of any human interference. Actions taken in strict protection zones enable an undisturbed course of ecological processes. These actions include ecosystem monitoring, fire protection, controlling invasive species, renaturalisation of water relations. Active protection consists of enabling and facilitating the course of natural bioprocesses, including the processes of ecosystem regeneration, succession and naturalisation. These actions include protection and restoration of biodiversity, controlling invasive species, mowing meadows, and reconstruction of the stands of trees. Scenic protection zones were established in order to preserve the traditional Masovian landscape, with a mosaic of fields and pastures, knotted willows and haystacks erected for winter. Traditional farming is the condition which must be met in order to preserve the agricultural landscape characterised by a considerable degree of naturalness. This type of landscape is disappearing dramatically in the surroundings of the Warsaw agglomeration. Table 13.1 shows the dependence between the protection regime and tourism development intensity.

Tourism attractions within the park

The tourism attractions within the park are impressive, but limited because of nature conservation. There are hiking and bicycle- and horse-riding trails. Tourists

Table 13.1 The dependence between the protection regime and tourism development intensity

Functional protection zone	Natural value	Access for tourists	Permitted tourism infrastructure
Strict	Very high	Low	Hiking trails only
Active	High	Medium	Trails, footbridges, observation towers, information boards, shelters
Scenic	Medium/low	High	Trails, footbridges, observation towers, information boards, shelters, car parks, recreational areas, reception and educational centres

Source: The author's compilation

can walk along about 360 km of marked hiking trails or cycle along 200 km of bicycle trails. Apart from that, there are footbridges, observation towers, information boards, shelters, car parks, recreational areas, and reception and educational centres available for tourists.

Admission to the park is free. According to surveys conducted by Józef Piłsudski University of Physical Education in Warsaw and the Warsaw University of Life Sciences, tourists visiting Kampinos National Park are chiefly motivated by relaxation, scenic values, contact with nature, peace and quiet, monuments and the location's short distance from their home (Dzioban 2012). The park offers possibilities and facilities for admiring the beauty of nature, and visiting historic places as well as other places related to material culture. It has clear rules concerning management of the park and providing access to it. The park gives information and it has a legible image and the conditions of development of the local community. However, it cannot provide tourists with access to any place at any time, nor can it provide space for the development of infrastructure or selected services, such as accommodation or food outlets. Hiking, bird watching, cycling, cross-country skiing, ecotourism and picnicking are considered to be nature-friendly activities.

The park buffer zone is an area of very high economic and tourism activity. It offers various forms of business activity and attractions of rural tourism, agritourism and culinary tourism. The Otulina agritourism farm, which is described in this book, is situated on the edge of the park in the buffer zone. As the park is an area of natural value and it is located in the neighbourhood of a big city, we should ask the question of how it is perceived by visitors. It is tempting to say that subconsciously it may be treated as a city park. This thesis may be suggested by the following arguments: most visitors live close to the park, they visit it frequently, their visits are rather short and independent of the season of the year (Dzioban 2012).

The presence of humans and their influence on the natural environment involves the need to limit their negative effects. For this reason the park stakeholders need to pay attention to appropriate planning, zoning, traffic direction and implementation of clearly defined rules for the use of particular areas. Visitors and tourists need to be provided access to different elements of nature and landscape, with small infrastructure, such as shelters and benches, which will facilitate relaxation or access to information. It is particularly important that local governments, non-governmental organisations, entrepreneurs and institutions involved in nature conservation, tourism, finance and scientific research should exchange information and cooperate with each other at the local level. If there is high pressure from the number of visitors, it is a good idea to provide offers which are alternative to this destination, the so-called honeypots.[1]

The neighbourhood of such a large area of natural value and the greatest metropolis in Poland creates the need for very careful planning and implementation of tourism facilities in this national park. Kampinos National Park offers the people who live in the nearby metropolis an opportunity to have contact with nature – the most valuable elements, which make the park so attractive.

Note

1   This is a location that attracts a lot of tourists who, due to their great number, can exert pressure on the environment and other people. Honeypots are often used to manage tourist numbers in the tourism industry. The use of honeypots may help to protect sensitive zones and simultaneously provide tourists with satisfactory substitute experiences. Honeypots are alternative destinations distracting tourists from the most valuable areas, but at the same time they are attractive and well prepared for receiving tourists with plenty of facilities like car parks, toilets and shops.

References

Cieszewska, A. (2009). *Ocena ruchu turystycznego w Kampinoskim Parku Narodowym w latach 2005–2006.* In A. Andrzejewska & A. Lubański (Eds.). *Trwałość i efektywność ochrony przyrody w polskich parkach narodowych.* Report available in headquarters of Kampinos National Park, Izabelin, Poland.

Dzioban, K. (2013). Wielkość ruchu turystycznego w Kampinoskim Parku Narodowym. *Studia i Materiały Centrum Edukacji Przyrodniczo-Leśnej.* Publisher: SGGW Leśny Zakład Doświadczany w Rogowie, Poland, No 37, pp. 90–96.

Prószyńska-Bordas, H., Dzioban, K., Kęsicka, E. & Gajewski, A. (2005). Wycieczkowicze z Warszawy i ich opinie o przystosowaniu Kampinoskiego Parku Narodowego do turystyki. *Kultura Fizyczna*, 3–4, pp. 2–9. Publisher: Akademia Wychowania Fizycznego w Warszawie, Warszawa.

14 Kampinos National Park as a place of recreation for Warsaw inhabitants

Katarzyna Dzioban

Introduction

National parks and other protected zones are the most attractive areas of recreational and tourism activity due to their natural values. Each of them plays a different role in the Polish nature conservation system and is used for different purposes. Due to their character and the preservation of unique natural values, they are particularly attractive places for tourism penetration (Lahti 2008). Bedimo-Rung *et al.* (2005) also note the significance of parks for the physical activity and public health of society. Apart from that, from the point of view of national parks, it is recommended that they should be actively promoted. This promotion should be concentrated on elements of the natural environment and sustainable tourism products (Stevens 2002). Ważyński (1997) notes urban inhabitants' need for leisure, which is best realised in a forest environment. In this context, forests located within city limits or in their close neighbourhood become particularly important, as is the case with Kampinos Forest. Moszyńska (2000) also notes the areas of everyday and public holiday leisure within the city – in the suburban zone. In her opinion, it is Kampinos National Park, being 'the lungs of Warsaw', and the Vistula River valley, where recreational and tourism functions should take the lead (quoted in Kozłowski 1997). This area is characterised by a variety of forest and brushwood communities and it has particular natural values, which are useful for tourism and leisure (Krzymowska-Kostrowicka 1991).

Recreation and tourism in Kampinos National Park

Kampinos Forest, which has been a UNESCO-MaB international biosphere reserve since 2000, is one of the biggest protected zones in Poland. Being a national park, it is subject to legal forms of protection which regulate area development and the manner of granting access to visitors. These regulations are expressed in the applicable Nature Conservation Act, other legal acts and park by-law.

The boundary of Kampinos National Park runs in the neighbourhood of urbanised areas of the Warsaw agglomeration, that is, the districts of Bemowo and Bielany, where new estates are approaching the forest, and close to the developing town of Łomianki. The park is surrounded by busy main thoroughfares.

It is possible to drive a car on asphalt roads and reach the villages of Truskaw or Wiersze, which are relatively deep in the park interior. The dense network of roads, which is dangerous to nature in the park, is a facility for tourists, who can relatively quickly arrive near the park or even drive inside. The only problem is where to park cars safely and legally.

The abundant natural values of the park are accompanied by numerous cultural values, which are chiefly located in the zone surrounding the park. The inter-penetration of nature and history proves that Kampinos National Park has a unique and specific character, which distinguishes it from other Polish national parks. There are many monuments in the park and its protective zone; some of them are world famous, for example, the birthplace of Frederic Chopin in Żelazowa Wola. There are numerous cemeteries, graves and war memorials in the park. Many visitors come to see the cemetery mausoleum in Palmiry with contains the graves of the victims of the Nazi terror of 1939–1941 and the branch of the History Museum, Palmiry Memorial.

It is estimated that every year the number of people visiting Kampinos National Park ranges from more than half a million to almost one million (Dzioban 2012). Visitors usually arrive at weekends. The development of tourism culture is one of the main – and important – trends in the educational and popular activity of the park. It is practised in the Jadwiga and Roman Kobendza Didactic and Museum Centre in Granica and in the Educational Centre in Izabelin. Thanks to enthusiasts and specialists who can directly teach people to appreciate nature and to develop appropriate tourism attitudes, Kampinos National Park is becoming an area of active and qualified tourism and ecotourism for an increasing number of tourists from the nearby urban agglomeration.

Due to the proximity of the Warsaw urban complex, the location of Kampinos National Park is rather unfavourable, because the functions of some adjacent areas are incompatible with tourism functions. Some demand for suburban recreational areas has been taken over by neighbouring forest areas, such as Młociny Forest and Bemowo Forest. They have picnic clearings, bonfire sites and playgrounds for children.

There is a considerable stream of walkers and others seeking recreation arriving at Kampinos National Park. They can use hiking routes and picnic sites in the Warsaw suburban zone of mass tourism. Some of these places were incorporated into the park and afforested a few years ago. They look neat and attractive for tourists, because they are protected from damage. Providing people with access to Kampinos National Park involves facing the challenge of negative consequences of tourism. Nature is threatened by visitors' inappropriate behaviour. Tourists leave tracks, cyclists damage dunes, drop litter and tread on the surrounding terrain, cars damage roadsides, people enter and cause anxiety in animal habitats, walk dogs in the park, but do not always keep them on a lead.

National parks are developed according to slightly different rules than other recreational and tourism areas. Because of previous construction, many national parks have accommodation and terrain transport facilities, such as cable cars and ski lifts. At present the accommodation, sports and recreational infrastructure is being located in less protected areas, for example, in the buffer zone, which protects the park from the harmful effects of external factors. The park interior is often divided into zones with different tourism functions. Tourists can move around national parks only along special routes. These are usually marked on information boards, which show a site plan of the park with the routes marked, and describe natural curiosities and provide warning information.

The following types of tourism are predominant in Kampinos National Park: sightseeing, chiefly hiking and cycling, cross-country skiing and, to a lesser extent, horse-riding (with or without permission). There are sleigh rides organised in winter. Recreational and tourist access of the park can only be done along marked routes. Kampinos National Park is the place with the longest hiking trails (Styperek 2001). Apart from hiking trails, there are also cycling routes in the park, The network of hiking trails (about 360 km), which cross the most attractive places in the park, is roughly arranged in a grid. The routes correspond to belts of the chief landforms (dunes and marshy depressions) and they are connected with main villages located on the edge of the forest, from where tourists set off on their trips (bus stops, car parks). Camping in tents is allowed only in special places and with a permission given by the park management, who specify the number of tents and the length of time allowed. Due to natural terrain obstacles (such as sandy or muddy roads) cross-country hiking is not recommended for disabled people in wheelchairs. Educational trails are recommended to disabled people, for example, from Izabelin to the Forest Botanic Garden in Laski. There is a particularly dense network of short tourism routes (a few kilometres in length) in the part of the park for walking, which is located nearest to Warsaw. Tourists on bicycles can also use the Kampinos Cycle Route, which surrounds the forest, connecting cycle routes and other roads for local inhabitants.

Visitors arriving at the park can satisfy their essential existential, social and cognitive needs in small spaces with basic infrastructure: car parks, rain shelters, footbridges (which enable tourists to cross difficult terrain), observation towers and platforms, resting places with playgrounds and bonfire sites. Tourists can use 19 car parks and 12 resting fields and recreational clearings. There are 7 educational routes to provide information about the park and its values, and there are guidebooks and brochures about the park. There are shelters and resting places located along most of the routes and also other tourism facilities, such as benches, tables, rain shelters, information boards and signposts. There are no bars or restaurants along the routes and only small catering outlets near some car parks, for example, in Dąbrowa Leśna, Truskaw, Roztoka and Granica. There are playgrounds for children in some clearings, such as in Opaleń (Markowski and Okołów 2009). In the buffer zone there are some accommodation facilities for organised groups and a few facilities for individual tourists, including a few agritourism farms.

Similarly to other national parks, Kampinos Forest can be entered in a linear manner. There is a consistent system of tourism routes to see and learn about the most beautiful and interesting tourism values. The routes are equipped with signposts, recreational facilities (benches, rain shelters) and technical facilities (footbridges), where necessary. The management of the park marks tourism routes in this area in accordance with the marking conventions specified by the Polish Tourist Sightseeing Society so as to use consistent markings on the national scale.

Due to the natural area of Kampinos National Park, its closeness to a large urban agglomeration – closeness to places of residence, beautiful nature, specific terrain and diversified morphology (dune embankments) there is increasing tourist and recreational traffic, chiefly from Warsaw. Convenient transport facilities are a big advantage of the park location. On the one hand, a dense network of roads enables relatively easy access to selected places on the edge of the park. At the same time, many public roads, such as Palmiry Road or the road from Kazuń to Leszno, cross the interior of the park. Thanks to the well-developed city transport (public transport) network it is possible to explore the park from the east, that is, from Warsaw.

Socio-demographic characterisation of park visitors, frequency of visits and method of transport

As results from the survey of 4670 people moving around Kampinos National Park show, it is not an area visited by tourists from all over Poland. Only few respondents live far away from the park. The park is not promoted among individual and foreign tourists as a tourism attraction on a national scale. It is treated as a specific big park for people living in Warsaw and nearest surrounds of the city.

The park is mostly visited by Warsaw inhabitants, especially from the districts which are nearest the park, that is, Bielany, Bemowo, Żoliborz and Wola. Other visitors arrive at the park chiefly from Masovian Voivodeship (11%) and the park buffer zone (9%). There are very few people from other voivodeships (provinces) who come to the park. As far as individual tourism is concerned, the tourism function of Kampinos National Park has regional character. In view of the fact that the park is located in the immediate neighbourhood of a large urban agglomeration, the results of the survey are not surprising.

Most of the people visiting the park are aged 30 to 44 years (32% of visitors), while people aged 45 to 64 are the second largest group (25%). However, we cannot neglect the fact that there are visitors aged over 75 or even 90 years. There are various reasons why the park is not very popular among elderly people. The mobility of elderly people is limited and they tend to have health problems more often. It is interesting to note that there are more male visitors in each age group. Thus, we can see an unfavourable phenomenon, where fewer women participate in tourism and recreation. We can observe this situation even in a national park with very good access, as it can be reached not only by car but also by city (public) transport. Undoubtedly, this phenomenon reflects differences in the amount of free time is at the disposal of men and women and it shows the lesser popularity of this form of leisure among women. More than 93 per cent of visitors coming to the park completed post-secondary education, including 52 per cent of visitors with higher education. The park is mostly visited by employed people (more than 63%). There is a relatively low share of students (14%) and pensioners (13%). It is noteworthy that there is only a minimal percentage of unemployed visitors (5%)

among the population surveyed. This effect is chiefly characteristic of Warsaw and the Masovian region, where the unemployment rate is lower than in other voivodeships. The fact that the majority of visitors are employed proves that they have health-promoting habits, they are aware of the fact that excursions outside the city can have a favourable influence on their health and that they want to compensate for their usual lack of movement and contact with the natural environment.

Visitors usually come to Kampinos National Park with their friends (37.4%) or family (33%). Every fourth tourist walks alone around the park. A vast majority of visitors come to the park by car rather than city transport (public transport) (54%). There is a statistically significant greater number of women t coming to the park by their own means of transport than men. In the group of visitors who ride bicycles to the park (27%), there are more men. They are more active and more determined to ride on sandy roads in the park. Apart from that, it is necessary to ride a long distance from the city to the park. In spite of the close proximity, there is a relatively small number of people coming to the park on foot (4%).

An analysis of the frequency of arrivals at Kampinos National Park reveals that it is usually visited by regular tourists. Nearly 53 per cent of the tourists visit the park more than six times a year. More than 80 per cent visit the park twice or more times a year. They are mostly men. There is a relatively small number of people visiting the park once a year. There are more women coming to the park once a year.

The fact that most of the visitors live in Warsaw and that they come to the park more than six times a year indicates that the inhabitants of the capital of Poland treat Kampinos National Park as a city park. Perhaps it should be called a suburban park as city parks are visited by urban dwellers much more often than six times a year. Apart from that, city and suburban parks located close to visitors' homes are particularly important for elderly and young people, whose access to more distant parks is usually limited (Bell 2007).

For Warsaw dwellers the park is a place for their recreational activity and a destination for excursions lasting a few hours to all day. It is due to a few elements, including the size of the park, its values, tourism development or even the time that people planning trips can spend there. Most tourists coming to Kampinos National Park spend 2 to 3 hours there (39%) or 4 to 5 hours (33%). There is a small number of tourists who spend more than 5 hours in the park, as well as a few who stay for less than 2 hours. Apart from that, in each time range men stay longer in the park than women. Mostly tourists do not stay overnight, they arrive for short walks and go back to other activities in the city. In the summer season mosquitoes are a nuisance, and they very strongly discourage people from longer hikes in the forest.

Purpose of visit, preferable forms of park penetration, benefits from staying

For more than a half (55%) of people arriving at the park, active leisure is the main purpose of their visit, and contact with nature is the second. In comparison with men, women significantly more often declare contact with nature as the purpose of their visit to the park. On the other hand, more men than women (7% and 2%, respectively) come to the park to exercise and improve their physical fitness. Easy access is the most popular reason (32%) why tourists visit the park. Slightly fewer people (29%) found the forest and nature to be the main reason for their visits to the nearby national park.

The respondents indicated that physical activity was definitely the most important benefit resulting from spending time in the park. More than a half (59%) of the group under analysis indicated physical benefits and active recreation as the main benefit from staying in the park. Interpersonal benefits were found to be of secondary importance. More than 13 per cent of the respondents thought it important to stay in the park in the company of another person. As it turned out, 12 per cent of the people coming to the park declared that aesthetic benefits and contact with beauty of nature were important for them.

Most visitors coming to Kampinos National Park move around on foot (53%) and by bicycle (47%). They tend to choose the eastern (52%) and southeastern (5%) parts of the park. A considerable number of visitors (15%) declare that they visit the whole park, but do not specify which part of the park it usually is. Every second person moves around the park along well-known routes. Only a minimal number of visitors (5%) choose nature trails. Regular visitors significantly more often declare that they walk along well-known routes.

Preparation of the park for tourism and recreation: assessment

The respondents think that there is good access to the park, with 84 per cent of them ranking the access as good or very good. Visitors coming to Kampinos National Park usually think that it is well prepared for tourism and recreational activity. The respondents expressed their positive opinion about the following elements: quality of information on boards, marking of routes, cleanness of the park and general preparation of the park for tourism and recreation. Nearly a half of the respondents think that the quality of information on boards at the main entrances to the park and car parks is average (46%). Slightly fewer people thought that the quality of information was good. Only 7 per cent of the visitors expressed their negative opinion about the quality of information about the park. It is interesting to note that there was a higher percentage of men who expressed their negative opinion (8% of men and 6% of women) and a higher percentage of women who expressed their positive opinion (47% of women and 43% of men). Most tourists (63%) think that the routes are marked well. Only 4 per cent of the respondents said that the routes were marked badly. A considerable percentage of the respondents (31%) thought that the marking of the routes was average. In this case it was also men who significantly more often stressed that the routes were marked badly.

More than a half of the respondents (60%) think that the park is clean. Despite this opinion there is a considerable group of people (27%) who think that the park is dirty. The divergence in the responses to the question about cleanness may have resulted from differences in the condition of different parts of the park where the tourists were surveyed. It also depends on the season of the year, vegetation, tourism traffic intensity, recreational use of a particular place, the availability of dustbins and the time that has passed since the last cleaning. In consequence of the respondents' positive opinions about the preparation of the park for tourism, a vast majority of them (78%) say that there is nothing that would cause problems during their stay in the park. Only a small group of the respondents (7%) declared dirt, litter and insufficient development (4%) to be problems.

Visitors' tourism and recreational behaviours

Educational trails are an important element supporting implementation of the educational function in national parks. As results from the survey, in spite of the information a considerable number of visitors coming to the park (47%) do not use educational trails. Only 29 per cent of the tourists walk along educational trails, whereas nearly 24 per cent are ignorant of their existence. The situation looks much better as far as places of national remembrance are concerned. Most of the respondents (79%) know places of national remembrance and they stop there. There is only a small percentage of the respondents (4%) who are ignorant of their existence.

There is no doubt that, above all, the park should have a protective function. It is possible that there are some limitations to recreational and tourism activities. If visitors do not understand the conditions under which tourists have access to the park, they may cause damage to the ecosystems, which are protected by law. A vast majority of visitors coming to Kampinos National Park (98%) declared that they abide by the rules of nature conservation. Simultaneously, there was a relatively large group of the respondents (17%) who failed to behave appropriately in a protected zone. They admitted that they picked plants and mushrooms in the park. However, a vast majority of the respondents (82%) declared that they did not. Most of the visitors coming to Kampinos National Park were convinced that they abide by the rules of moving around the park and nature conservation, which are specified in the regulations. In fact, almost 50 per cent of the people in Kampinos Forest walk off the routes. As it turned out, men tend to walk off the routes more often. It is even worse to note that not all tourists realise that complying with the rules of nature conservation involves a ban on picking plants, forest fruit, mushrooms and walking off the routes.

Maps are the main source of information for visitors coming to Kampinos National Park (37%) as they help those who do not know the area to walk around the park. Information boards (16%) are a supplementary source of information for those who do not have other materials. A large number of people (29%) do not use any materials about the park.

All over the world protected zones, including national parks, are increasingly burdened with tourism traffic. This fact has significant influence on the implementation of nature conservation schemes (Freimund and Cole 2001; Jackson *et al.* 2003). The following illegal behaviours are particularly dangerous: picking flowers and mushrooms, walking pets, riding off-road vehicles and above all, walking off the routes, that is, illegal dispersion (Witkowski *et al.* 2010).

Tourism is an important function in every national park. It is a factor which may create more dynamic economic and cultural development for an area. Conversely, uncontrolled development may be dangerous to the natural environment. However, we need to remember that protection of the natural environment must be the first priority, as it is necessary to preserve its natural values. Further development of different forms of the natural environment depends on its protection and causing minimal harm. Simultaneously, this protection will result in benefits for people seeking contact with the natural environment located as close to their homes as possible.

References

Bedimo-Rung, A. L., Mowen, A. J. & Cohen, D. A. (2005). The significance of parks to physical activity and public health: A conceptual model. *American Journal of Preventive Medicine*, 28, pp. 159–68.

Bell, S., Tyrväinen, L., Sievänen, T., Pröbstl, U. & Simpson M. (2007). Outdoor recreation and nature tourism: A European perspective. http://www.livingreviews.org/lrlr-2007-2 [Retrieved 15 September 2015]

Dzioban, K. (2012). *Studia nad ruchem rekreacyjno-turystycznym w Kampinoskim Parku Narodowym*. Doctoral dissertation typescript. Warszawa: AWF.

Freimund, W. A. & Cole D. N. (2001). Use density, visitor experience and limiting recreational use in wilderness: progress to date and research needs. *USDA Forest Service Proceedings*, pp.

Jackson, S. A., Haider, W. & Elliot, T. (2003). Resolving inter-group conflict in winter recreation: Chilkoot Trail National Historic Site, British Columbia. Elsevier *Journal of Nature Conservation*, 11, pp. 317–328.

Kozłowski, S. (1997). *W drodze do ekorozwoju*. Publisher: PWN, Warszawa.

Krzymowska-Kostrowicka, A. (1991). Przydatność rekreacyjna środowiska przyrodniczego województwa stołecznego warszawskiego. In A. S. Kostrowiecki (Ed.). *Kształtowanie układów ekologicznych w strefie podmiejskiej Warszawy*. Publisher: SGGW, Warszawa, pp. 60–66.

Lahti, K. (2008). Protected areas as a destination for recreation. *Outdoor Sports and Environmental Science*. 23, pp. 19–24. German Sports University, Cologne.

Markowski, M. & Okołów, G. (2009). Działalność Kampinoskiego Parku Narodowego i oferta dla społeczeństwa. *Proceedings of the conference* Materiały z konferencji popularno – naukowej '50 lat Kampinoskiego Parku Narodowego – funkcje oraz znaczenie w środowisku przyrodniczym i społecznym'. Kampinos National Park, Izabelin, Poland.

Moszyńska, B. (2000). Walory zdrowotne zbiorowisk leśnych w turystyce i rekreacji w strefie podmiejskiej Warszawy. In K. Pieńkos (ed.). *Problemy turystki i rekreacji w lasach Polski*. Publisher: Polskie Towarzystwo Leśne, Akademia Wychowania Fizycznego, Warszawa, pp. 72–83.

Stevens, T. (2002). Sustainable tourism in national parks and protected areas: An overview. *Scottish Natural Heritage Commissioned Report F01NC04*. Inverness, UK.

Styperek, J. (2001). Piesze szlaki turystyczne w polskich parkach narodowych. *Turyzm*, 11/1. Publisher: Wydawnictwo Uniwersytetu Łódzkiego, Łódź.

Ważyński, B. (1997). *Urządzanie i zagospodarowywanie lasu dla potrzeb turystyki i rekreacji.* Publisher: Akademia Rolnicza Poznań, Poznań.

Witkowski, Z., Mroczka, A., Adamski, P., Bielański, M., Kolasińska, A. (2010). Nielegalna dyspersja turystów – problem parków narodowych i rezerwatów przyrody. *Folia Turistica*, 22, pp. 35–65. Publisher: Akademia Wychowania Fizycznego w Krakowie, Kraków.

15 Otulina

Agritourism in the Warsaw metropolitan area

Ewa Tyran

The Warsaw metropolitan area

Warsaw is one of eleven Polish metropolises and the centre of the Warsaw Metropolitan Area (WMA) with the neighbouring towns and villages. The area is not clearly defined and there are different divisions. According to a statistical division of Poland at the European Union Nomenclature of Territorial Units for Statistics (NUTS) 3 level, it encompasses subregions PL-126 and PL-127. According to the GUS (Central Statistic Office) Regional Data Bank, on 31 December 2006 the metropolitan area of those two subregions was over 8600 km^2 with over 3 million inhabitants. The population density was 3,355 per km^2.

Of the population of the whole Warsaw Metropolitan Area, 20.8 per cent live in rural areas. The Warsaw Metropolitan Area is a place of dynamic tourism development, including rural tourism and agritourism, as the area encompasses several unique values.

It is easy to notice that agritourism farms are concentrated in the most attractive areas of the agglomeration (in terms of natural values), that is, the areas surrounding Bolimów Scenic Park and Kampinos National Park.

Kampinos National Park

Kampinos National Park was established on 16 January 1959 thanks to the efforts of Roman and Jadwiga Kobendza. It is located in the Central Lowland, between the left bank of the Vistula and Bzura Rivers, off the northwestern outskirts of Warsaw. The park area is 38,544.33 ha, of which 72.40 ha belong to the Bison Breeding Centre in Smardzowice. Around the park extends the protected zone of 37,756 ha. Forests cover more than 73 per cent of the park, while the rest of the area is occupied by all kinds of non-forest communities. Kampinos National Park is one of the most important wildlife refuges in the Polish lowlands.

Due to the natural and social significance of the Park, in 2000 Kampinos National Park and the protected zone were recognised by UNESCO as a World Biosphere Reserve under the name 'Kampinos Forest'. The park is an important recreational area for the capital, as discussed in Chapter 14. There are several unique species of flora and fauna in the park. The moose is the largest of

50 species of mammals and it is a symbol of Kampinos National Park. During the World War II the park witnessed partisan actions and battles. Cemeteries scattered throughout the forest are testimony to those dark times. There are graves of 2,115 victims of mass executions at the cemetery mausoleum in Palmiry.

The Park is visited by over one million tourists yearly. Visitors can enjoy 350 km of hiking trails, 200 km of bicycle trails, horse trails and 19 parks and 12 resorts located on the outskirts of the park. There are three educational centres in the park: the Centre for Education in Izabelin, the Centre for Teaching and Museum and the Bison Breeding Centre.

Otulina: agritourism

The Otulina Agritourist Farm was chosen for the venue of the editorial team of this book in June 2014 (see Sznajder 2014 for video of Otulina). The Otulina (meaning 'forest buffer zone') Agritourist Farm is situated within the buffer zone of Kampinos National Park, 45 km from Warsaw, the capital of Poland, and 6 km from Żelazowa Wola, the birthplace of Frederic Chopin, where his parents' manor house in a beautiful garden is open to visitors. The location gives the farm very specific advantages – within less than one hour the inhabitants of, or companies located in or near, the biggest Polish city and the whole metropolitan agglomeration can find a place to rest, celebrate different events or participate in courses and workshops.

The farm is rather small, with an area of 2.8 ha consisting mostly of meadows and a small lake (pond). The farm is situated on the edge of the forest. As there are only meadows rather than arable land on the farm, the grass or hay is sold to the horse hotel in the neighbourhood.

The owner of the Otulina Farm graduated from Warsaw Business School. For fourteen years she was a successful employee, the head of the Human Resources Department for IKEA. Her job involved organising training, seminars and integration events for IKEA staff – some of these were held in different venues than the IKEA headquarters. She strove to find pleasant, quiet places surrounded by nature for these events. In the meantime she and her husband bought a small meadow farm with a small lake. There was an old house and a barn on the farm. In the beginning they stayed on the farm at summer weekends, so they started renovating the buildings. Although she liked working for IKEA, her total engagement in the job made her feel that she neglected her family and it was difficult to remain in the position. She realised she had to change something in her life. The farm gave her an opportunity to start a new business – an agritourism activity. Her previous organisational experience motivated her to take the final decision to give up her steady, safe but very demanding job and start from scratch. Step by step she established the agritourism farm named 'Otulina', which opened in June 2007. There are 14 beds in double rooms with en-suite bathrooms in the guesthouse. The barn was reconstructed into a place for meetings and training. Now there is a spacious and very nicely decorated dining room and kitchen on the ground floor and a lecture room with full multi-media equipment upstairs. The owner speaks

English, which helps foreigners to communicate. The owner is a member of the Local Action Group.

Clients: The owner's previous experience and relations with different companies enabled her to relatively easily find clientele for her new business. Now she offers an ideal place for all kinds of field events, ranging from family celebrations to seminars and training for companies from the Warsaw agglomeration. The close proximity to the biggest Polish airport is important for foreign tourists, who would like to stay close to the National Park and other places worth sightseeing. As was mentioned before, the farm usually receives groups – on weekdays groups from different companies and corporations arrive for training and seminars, whereas weekend visitors want to relax in a quiet place, surrounded by nature. The owner cooperates with several companies, including IKEA, her previous employer, and these are her regular clients.

The Offer: The rooms are not rented individually – the building can only be rented as a whole. Regardless of the number of guests, the price is 900 to 1000 zlotys per day, depending on the season. The owner offers full board or individual meals on request. The meals are very tasty and prepared mostly from local products she buys from local farmers. She also offers small parties for family reunions, birthdays, and other celebrations. Tourists visiting the farm have access to a private beach and a small pier on the lake. Next to the barn is a barbecue and two shelters, where tourists can eat meals al fresco, especially barbecued delicacies. Those who want a bonfire can use a specially prepared area with benches. A tennis court is offered free of charge. In bad weather a separate TV room, a room with a fireplace or the dining room offer enough space for indoor activities. A safe car park is important for tourists arriving by car or bus. The farm also offers its own transport.

Promotion, mission and future: The information about the farm and its specific offer can be found on its webpage (www.otulina.com) and on Facebook. Because the rooms are not rented to individuals, the owner does not want to use any other promotion platforms. It is most important that companies and their employees have a very high opinion of her services.

The owner used her own resources to finance most of the investments in renovation and adaptation of the farm building for agritourism. To improve the conditions and offer entertainment in 2011 the owner invested some EU funds she received for transformation from farming activities to non-agricultural activities. She is also a beneficiary of direct payments to grasslands, as the farm has no arable land. As the owner says, the mission of the farm is to provide the best possible services to her visitors according to the purpose of their visit – mainly either rest and relaxation or participation in training and workshops, or both. Her ambition and vision are to constantly improve the quality and scope of her services to satisfy guests.

The owner says that the location close to the Warsaw agglomeration, where many companies have their headquarters, and close to Kampinos National Park makes her farm a very special place. At present she is not thinking of expanding her agritourism activity. The number of people and events on her farm give her enough work that she can manage and enough income to say it is a good business. She changed her lifestyle to have more time for her family and the range and amount of her present business give her what is most important. Her present situation could be at risk if there are more farms with similar offers and scope of activities. However, to her knowledge, now there are no other farms or plans to offer the same kind of services. Thus, in a way her farm offers unique services.

References

Otulina Agritourism farm. (2011). http://otulina.com/ [Retrieved 8 September 2015]

Sznajder, M. (2014). Rural and agritourism in metropolitan areas. Video. Seminar presentation. https://www.youtube.com/watch?v=3o9xxdUIC9Q

Part IV

Types of tourism and tourism segments in the metropolitan commuter belt

Cycling along a metropolitan pathway.

16 Forms of rural tourism in metropolitan areas

Janusz Majewski

Introduction

This part of the monograph is an analysis of the potential for the development of rural tourism in metropolitan areas. The starting point is the concept of rurality, which includes the criteria that should be met by the areas so that they can be regarded as rural. The criteria were developed by researchers and form the basis for the demarcation of areas that are suitable for rural tourism. Nonetheless, rurality is a value defined by consumers, who have their own image of it. These approaches are not always fully convergent, which is particularly noticeable when both are applied to create a tourism product, because from the marketing point of view rurality is the core of products in rural tourism and a unique selling proposition.

While the issue of rurality in remote areas does not arouse much controversy, we may wonder if we can talk of any form of rural tourism in more urbanised areas. If so, which forms of tourism have the greatest chances in the market and what should their specificity be like? In order to answer these questions we will analyse the types of space in metropolitan areas and examine them with the criteria of rurality. In consequence, on the basis of the author's observations we will suggest the forms of tourism in metropolitan areas which will retain the criteria of rurality.

Spatial transformations caused by urbanisation

The processes of urbanisation have caused enormous spatial, social and economic changes both in cities themselves and in adjacent areas. New types of space have emerged and are intermingling. There are various new functions in relationships between the centre, suburban and rural areas (Glaeser & Kahn 2003). The spaces located closer to cities are being absorbed, whereas more distant areas are trying to retain the status of self-sufficient units. On the other hand, the high prices and small size of building plots in cities and their surroundings push people to choose more distant locations. It is not rare to see commuters travelling from places as far as 50 or more kilometres from the centre of the metropolis. A new category of ruralists has emerged – people leave cities, because they enjoy the rural climate.

This phenomenon is known as counter-urbanism. It goes together with the organic lifestyle, close contact with nature and healthy nutrition, which are in fashion (Gulinck 2004). These migrations also have an impact on villages, which are being transformed into residential districts, with predominant single family housing, high share of green space and completely new social structure.

These changes are also noticeable in Poland. Farming is disappearing from villages located near big cities. Rural inhabitants are being employed outside agriculture. Traditional rural lifestyles are becoming things of the past while villages are often being transformed into isolated clusters of single family houses with a shopping centre (Zębik 2011). Rural areas used to be mentally, scenically and culturally separated from cities even though they were not located far away from each other. At present it is necessary to travel a much longer distance or even go abroad to find such rural areas.

The concepts of a metropolitan area and region in response to new problems

The new functional relations of cities and adjacent areas caused the emergence of common problems, such as transport and handling waste, and searching for forms of organisation to solve these problems. Big cities form coalitions with suburban and rural areas, which are defined as metropolitan regions or metropolitan areas. The essence of such coalitions is the partnership of its members. Although the literature makes a distinction between these two terms, in practice they are used interchangeably. However, we might try to find some important differences. The metropolitan area encompasses the space of the functional influence of the core city, whereas the policy of urban–rural partnership includes the urban sprawl and merger of cities, small towns and villages. On the other hand, in a metropolitan region there are one or more core cities. Their relationships with rural areas are less intensive than in a metropolitan area and they are oriented towards functional complementarity. According to the European Association of Peri urban Parks (FEDENATUR), the main goal of the partnership is the policy of cohesion, which is implemented by building the socio-economic solidarity and development of the regions including mutual benefits (FEDENATUR 2014).

Thus, the concept of a metropolitan region is broader and more general than that of a metropolitan area, because its space may encompass several metropolises with their adjacent areas. This approach to partnership and territorial cohesion can be shown by the example of MORO North – a project implemented in Germany. The project participants were the following north German cities concentrated around the Hamburg metropolis: Kiel, Heide, Hamburg, Lübeck, Hannover, Lüneburg, Bremen, Rostock, Flensburg and Wismar. The metropolitan region also encompassed the adjacent areas and together they created model proposals of the cooperation and management structure in the form of urban–rural partnership. As a result, rural partners implemented their own projects and became partners in the network. Less developed areas benefited from the cooperation with more developed areas and vice versa (Köhler 2011).

Urban–rural partnerships are also called functional urban regions (FUR). In this case the term 'region' may refer to an area that is smaller not only than a metro-politan region but also smaller than a metropolitan area, for example, a partnership between a small town with 10,000 inhabitants, being the centre, and the rural areas related to the town. Some metropolitan areas have clearly demarcated boundaries, which do not always fall in line with the FUR. Sometimes they encompass a few such units, but a metropolitan area is a form of a functional urban region. To order the terminology the European Union's Statistical Agency, Eurostat, introduced the term 'larger urban zone' (LUZ), which attempts to harmonise the definitions of the metropolitan area with the FUR (Peeters 2011; OECD 2013).

The idea of the metropolitan area results not only from the awareness of the benefits from the partnership in terms of internal relations but also from the new approach to the cohesion of areas. Very often even big cities are too small to individually compete on a national or international scale. Therefore, alliances with rural areas are necessary to be noticed on the market. For this reason that the organisations PURPLE and ESPON were established. PURPLE (Peri-urban regions platform Europe) is a platform for the exchange of know-how and good practices in peri-urban regions to correlate and coordinate existing projects and to promote new trans-European initiatives (PURPLE n.d.). ESPON (European Observation Network for Territorial Development and Cohesion) is a research programme within the spatial development of Europe, which deals with all of the problems which have been discussed so far (ESPON n.d.).

The criteria of demarcation of spaces suitable for rural tourism

In rural tourism the character of space is of greater significance than in confer-ence tourism, for example. In the former type many activities take place in open space and they depend on it, whereas conference events are usually located in closed spaces and the surroundings (city, village, forest) usually play a secondary role. Therefore, the starting point for our analysis will be to determine the types of space that enable the location of activities which are specific to rural tourism. The issue seems to be simple if we assume a polarised approach, where we make a division into either urban or rural areas (Scott *et al.* 2007).

However, the reality of metropolitan areas is much richer and more compli-cated, which does not always result in greater potential to build interesting tourism offers. There is a multitude of intermediate areas between the core city and rural areas. They have their specific names: 'suburban', 'semi-urban', 'peri-urban', 'rur-urban' and there are no clear boundaries between them (Grazuleviciute-Vileniske and Vitkuviene 2012; Carril and Vila 2012). On the one hand, rural areas might have enclaves with urban development (residential districts in an open field, colonies of warehouse and industrial facilities). On the other, typical rural spaces are made in cities (urban agriculture).

Additionally, there are new concepts, such as: 'rurality near the city', 'rurality in the city' and 'rurality in the city countryside', which might be considered to be log-ically self-contradictory (Bryant and Johnston 1992). These concepts result from urban inhabitants' demand for rurality, which is expressed not only by travelling to the 'real countryside', but also in the development of quasi-rural spaces in cities. This phenomenon can be demonstrated by examples of urban agriculture and peri-urban agriculture, which are gaining great popularity. Peri-urban agriculture (especially horticulture) is a natural phenomenon, which has been observed around big cities for a long time. However, the development of cities causes inevitable absorption of the areas which have so far been used for farming and it also causes their transformation into suburban areas. Therefore, the advocates of sustainable development propose returning to the maintenance of agriculture near big cities, because the high costs of transport can be reduced. In consequence, the greenhouse effect will be reduced and the landscape and biodiversity will be retained (Paul and McKenzie 2010). Scientists noticed these phenomena and organised a special conference to discuss them (Dewaelheyns and Gulinck 2008).

Urban agriculture is interpreted very broadly. The Food and Agriculture Organisation (FAO) of the United Nations has defined urban agriculture as:

> the growing of plants and the raising of animals for food and other uses within and around cities and towns, and related activities such as the production and delivery of inputs, processing and marketing of products, subdivision in intra-urban and peri-urban agriculture, (...) an industry that produces, processes and markets food and fuel, largely in response to the daily demand of consumers within a town, city, or metropolis, on land and water dispersed throughout the urban and peri-urban area, applying intensive production methods, using and reusing natural resources and urban wastes to yield a diversity of crops and livestock.
>
> (FAO 2007, p. 1)

In view of this, it is a good idea to ask the following questions: Can these ideas be taken into consideration when building offers for rural tourism? Which intermediate areas (neither completely urban nor rural) can be classified as rural areas? The answers depend on the criteria assumed for the delimitation of these areas. In turn, these criteria depend on the perspective assumed to define the identity of rural tourism, which will distinguish it from other forms of tourism. So, what factors in metropolitan areas favour the development of this identity or cause its loss?

In order to answer these questions it is a good idea to return to the classic criteria of rurality, which have been well established in scientific literature. It is rurality that is the key distinguishing element both for researchers of different forms of tourism and for consumers, who often associate rurality with idyllic images. When confronted with the reality, though, there should not be too great a divergence from this idyllic picture.

Twenty years ago Bernard Lane formulated three main criteria for the identification of areas suitable for the development of rural tourism::

- Geographical: employment density and size of village, small settlements located at a distance from each other, more natural environment than developed areas (farmlands, meadows, forests);

- Economic: land use and economy (agricultural areas, forest areas, non-agricultural areas in natural and semi-natural state, wildlife, non-industrial areas), low percentage of developed areas;
- Socio-cultural: lifestyle; strong, direct social bonds; specific culture; work ethic; agrarian community; influence of tradition. (Lane 1994, p. 16)

Thus, a question arises whether we can find rural areas when we apply all the three criteria to metropolitan areas. When we add one more element, which is particularly important in rural tourism – authenticity – the range rural spaces will be strongly narrowed. The enclaves of rurality in cities, which have been increasingly popular recently, for instance, urban agriculture, will have to be excluded. When we apply these criteria, quasi-rural spaces in many cities and on their outskirts will not be classified into rural tourism, because they are isolated, artificial enclaves and they can be regarded as rural curiosities in urban space. For a tourist, they temporarily substitute rurality, but do not offer full rural experience during the visit, because the tourist will leave the rural enclave and enter a crowded street in the city. Thus, urban agriculture is not a base for the development of agritourism, because it lacks rural facilities with rural landscape and inhabitants. It is absolutely unjustified to use the term 'farming in the city countryside', because it blurs the real differences between urbanity and rurality (Shaw and Williams 2002). On the other hand, neither residential suburban areas nor estates with second homes will be classified as places of rural tourism, because in spite of the rural surroundings, they are urban spaces as such.

However, as far as peripheral areas (even with open non-urbanised space) are concerned, the answers are not so obvious. As a result, there are a lot of situations when it is not possible to give a definite answer to the question about the rurality of an area. Therefore, each specific space should be individually analysed and the criteria of rurality should be matched to each real space rather than simply assigning a general space category. Each of the criteria results in the situation where tourists escaping from the noise and congestion in cities have an opportunity to follow the activities which are specific to rural areas.

Rural tourism in urban neighbourhood (in metropolitan areas)

Tourism plays a less important and different role in urban neighbourhood than in forest areas, rural areas and in city centres. The peripheral areas in big cities are often industrial, providing services or residential spaces. In view of this fact, tourists are not strongly motivated to pay a visit unless there is a special attraction in the location. However, there are such spaces within metropolitan areas which can be taken into consideration when preparing tourism offers with rural identity. Below we discuss three types of space which meet the criteria of rural tourism.

The following types of space in metropolitan areas can be taken into consideration when preparing an offer of rural tourism:

Natural areas: National parks (in Poland there are national parks near three agglomerations: Poznań – Wielkopolska National Park, Warsaw – Kampinos

National Park, Krakow – Ojców National Park). All three parks are situated in close proximity to these cities, because their boundaries are only 20 km from the city centre. There are scenic parks not far away from almost all other agglomerations. They provide a natural recreational base. Additionally, there are natural peripheral urban spaces, which do not receive any form of protection, but are attractive recreational and educational resources. In view of the fact that rural tourism and nature tourism are related to each other, though they are not identical, natural areas can be taken into consideration. Accommodation facilities are often located in the buffer zones of national and scenic parks. The study on the Poznań metropolitan area confirms this thesis, because most rural accommodation facilities (including agritourism facilities) can be found near protected natural areas (Majewski and Zmyślony 2014).

Small towns with facilities strongly related to villages and agriculture: (e.g. food processing, trade). Small towns should be classified under urban tourism because of their name. Therefore, it seems to be paradoxical to classify them under rural tourism. However, in spite of the fact that some small towns have urban space (usually it is only the market and adjacent streets), they are socio-economically strongly related to rural areas and individual farms can be found less than one hundred metres away from the market. A typical small rural town has urban development in the form of a small centre. It usually has traditional houses (though not necessarily historic buildings), an urban system, and shops and services which are available within walking distance. There are not only economic bonds with rural areas (food processing, trade, rural services) but also social bonds (common family celebrations, parish festivals and other festivals). All these elements create a unique atmosphere in the place where the rural lifestyle is predominant. It is the space for small, family-owned hotels and guesthouses, small training and conference centres, wedding houses and wellness centres. In combination with the rural attractions in the area, they make an interesting offer for short stays. Small towns generate more tourism income than villages, because they tempt tourists with shops, restaurants and services (Harshbarger 2012).

Classic (traditional) rural area. There is no controversy about the third type of space, because it is generally situated several dozen kilometres away from the core city, although classic rural spaces can also be found closer to the city. Apart from that, these are typical rural spaces, because there are animal breeding, farming, beekeeping, crafts, direct sales and roadside stands. The tourist will find an authentic rural sense of place or even elements of the rural idyll there.

The factors of competitive advantage of rural tourism in metropolitan areas

The identification of the three types of space which are suitable for building rural tourism products in metropolitan areas ask the question about the type of offers and their main recipients. Before we conduct a detailed analysis of the character of tourism offers on a larger scale than that of one metropolitan area, it is worthwhile to determine the categories of products with the greatest chances in the market.

A product category is interpreted as a form of tourism that guarantees competitive advantage. The starting point for determination of the factors of competitive advantage will be the reasons why tourists make a decision to make a trip to places near cities rather than more distant areas. The most important reasons are:

Transport accessibility: Refers not only to the distance measured in kilometres but also to time distance, which is determined by the transport capacity. Both factors are significant in this category. facilities located in metropolitan areas are usually available within one hour's drive. A lot of them are available by public transport. The development or revitalisation of railways, whose original purpose was to facilitate access to the metropolitan centre, enables the core city dwellers use them to reach attractions located on the outskirts. Thus, accessibility is the main factor taken into consideration when clients compare similar offers in terms of their character, quality and price. This also affects affordability, because a shorter distance usually involves much lower costs of transport.

The diversity and authenticity of attractions The competitive advantage can be gained when the attractions are different from urban attractions. This is another reason why clients may choose them. There may be different aspects of diversity, such as wildlife, architecture, climate, forms of activity, landscape, open space, locality, slower pace of life. It is impossible to replace these elements in cities, because they are assigned to a place and they often result from a long tradition.

Competitive prices and high quality of the offer: Prices of services in smaller towns and villages are very often much lower than in big cities. Therefore, some clients are ready to pay the costs of transport to enjoy less expensive offers. This particularly applies to medical services (including rehabilitation and dental services). However, it also applies to cosmetic, automotive and many other services. In view of the fact that some services are time-consuming they can be combined with a recreational visit to a village or small town.

Forms of rural tourism specific to metropolitan areas

Culinary tourism has become very popular recently and sometimes cuisine might even be the main motive for travelling rather than the necessary component of the offer, which, like an overnight stay, cannot be avoided. Culinary tourism involves not only dining at restaurants and consumption of food on its own, but it also involves table manners and accompanying activities in their broad sense. Culinary tourism also includes the sales of local products, participation in shows and tastings, culinary courses and schools, culinary festivals, visits to the places where food is produced and processed, such as agricultural and horticultural farms, participation in harvesting and fruit picking, thematic trips, fairs and education. The increasing popularity of organic food and local products creates great opportunities for the development of various forms of culinary tourism in rural areas.

Shopping tourism: For centuries big city centres contained the commercial function and were full of life. Now they have turned into bank and office districts. This transformation has made city centres deserted (especially in the evening and at weekends) and they may even be dangerous. Trade has moved to shopping centres in suburbs, but these facilities cannot create the traditional shopping atmosphere, which can still be found in small towns. It is a chance for small towns, which can offer slow shopping or slow food, such as fresh food products purchased directly from producers. The gastronomic offer, farm stores and road-side stands established by farmers and local processing plants will be a good supplement to the shops. There is increasing interest in shopping towns or villages, which specialise in one type of merchandise, as has been proved by the market success of antique villages or book towns.

Educational tourism: Educational offers are mostly addressed to organised groups of students, schoolchildren and kindergarten children. The main advantage of this form of tourism is its non-seasonal character and repeatability, because every year new age groups of students can use the same offer. When the segment of clients is clearly determined, it is relatively easy to prepare the offer that will meet their expectations. The identification is also simple, because it is a precisely defined 'corporate client', that is, teachers and child-minders, who have address details. Rural areas, especially farming and forest areas, provide great opportunities for various offers, such as outdoor schools, processing demonstrations, collections of old farm machinery, arts and crafts demonstrations, farm schools, living history farms and miniature villages (Adam 2004).

Recreational tourism: The city cannot provide the forms of recreation which require large natural areas or open spaces, such as nature playgrounds or harvesting and crop processing. However, the forms of recreation which require regular visits at least once a week have the greatest chance for market success, because the short distance from the city is the main reason why a particular offer is chosen. This situation takes place when one does a sport, not necessarily professionally, such as taking horse-riding lessons, or adopting an animal or plant.

Agritourism stays: This category includes most of the recreational activities listed above, but we will concentrate on a longer stay, lasting at least a few days. Although the agritourism offer of villages situated further away from one's home may be more interesting than the offer of villages located closer to cities, that is, in metropolitan areas, the distance factor may be a decisive criterion to the choice of the latter offer. For example, sometimes the whole family cannot spend their holiday together, because one person has to go to work and stay in the city. However, rural accommodation facilities located near the core city enable one parent to spend their holiday with the children staying at that rural facility all the time, while the other parent can commute to work from there or spend weekends.

Business tourism: Small conferences, training sessions, integration events or small business meetings may take place at rural accommodation facilities adapted for these purposes. Especially as far as one- or two-day events are concerned, the short travel time factor may be critical to the attractiveness of a particular place. In view of the fact that rurality and nature are trendy, rural facilities are an alternative to small urban hotels and conference centres.

Health tourism: Rural offers cannot compete with spas, but they follow the trend of wellness and well-being and they provide chiefly short-term stays lasting one or a few days. The range of services includes both those of an urban character and those of a rural character. As far as urban services are concerned (hairdresser, beautician, dentist, physiotherapist), the price and quality may be decisive factors. As far as rural services are concerned, their character is a specific value added (herbal therapies, animal therapies, hydrotherapies, etc.), which is difficult to copy in an urban environment.

Conclusions

Rural tourism in metropolitan areas has its specific character, which results both from the type of resources and from market factors, which influence the expected offers. When both of these factors are taken into consideration, both the demand and supply will be favourable to the future of rural tourism. Some metropolitan areas meet the conditions of rurality and they have large potential for the development of rural tourism. There are non-urbanised spaces in metropolitan areas and they are of great value to city dwellers, because they have retained their authentic character. If we plan the development of tourism in these areas, we should definitely try to maintain all aspects of rurality. Otherwise, rural tourism will lose its unique character. As a result, its Unique Selling Position (USP) will be blurred and its market attractiveness weakened.

References

Adam, K. L. (2004). Entertainment farming and agritourism, NCAT. https://attra.ncat.org/attra-pub/viewhtml.php?id=264 [Retrieved 26 June 2014]

Bryant, C. R. & Johnston, T. R. R. (1992). *Agriculture in the City's Countryside.* University of Toronto Press, Toronto.

Carril, V. P. & Vila, N. A. (2012). Agritourism in peri-urban areas: Lessons from a vegetable tourism initiative in the Baix Llobregat Agrarian Park (Catalonia). *Cuadernos de Tourismo*, 29, pp. 281–296, Universidad de Murcia, Murcia.

Dewaelheyns, V. & Gulinck, H. (Eds.). (2008). Rurality near the city. Editorial paper for conference, Division Forest, Nature and Landscape, Department of Earth and Environmental Sciences, K. U. Leuven, Leuven.

ESPON. (European Observation Network for Territorial Development and Cohesion) (n.d.). www.espon.eu [Retrieved 10 July 2015]

Eurostat. (2012). http://ec.europa.eu/eurostat/documents/345175/501971/EU-28_2012.xlsx [Retrieved 1 January 2017]

Eurostat. (n.d.). Larger urban zones (LUZ). epp.eurostat.ec.europa.eu

FAO. (2007). Profitability and sustainability of urban and peri-urban agriculture. Food and Agricultural Organisation. Agricultural Management, Marketing and Finance Occasional Paper No 19, pp. 1–108. ftp://ftp.fao.org/docrep/fao/010/a1471e/a1471e00.pdf [Retrieved 6 July 2015]

FEDENATUR. (2014). *The place of peri-urban natural spaces for a sustainable city*, Fedenatur report to the European Commission, DG Environment, Brussels.

Glaeser, E. & Kahn, M. (2003). *Sprawl and Urban Growth*. Harvard University, National Bureau of Economic Research, Tufts University.

Grazuleviciute-Vileniske, I. & Vitkuviene, J. (2012). Towards integration of rural heritage in rurban landscapes: The case of Lithuanian manor residencies. *American Journal of Tourism Management*, 1(2), pp. 53–63, DOI:10.5923/j.tourism.20120102.04

Gulinck, H. (2004). Neo-rurality and multifunctional landscapes. In J. Brandt and H. Vejre (Eds.). *Multifunctional Landscapes*. Vol. 1 Theory, Values and History. WIT Press, Southampton, UK, pp. 3–73.

Harshbarger, B. (2012). Small town tourism: Building the dreams. *Rural Research Report*, 22(6), pp. 1–8. Illinois Institute for Rural Research.

Köhler, M. (2011). Hamburg metropolitan region. Regional cooperation – facts and practice. Secretariat of the Hamburg Metropolitan Region, Hamburg. http://english. metropolregion.hamburg.de/contentblob/2420824/6ecef6b1f04ca942a27142d644149 d0e/data/facts-and-practice.pdf [Retrieved 16 July 2014]

Lane, B. (1994). What is rural tourism? *Journal of Sustainable Tourism*, 2(1–2), pp. 7–21.

Majewski, J. & Zmyślony, P. (2014). Wiejski charakter – podmiejska lokalizacja. Turystyka wiejska na obszarze metropolitalnym Poznania. (Rural Character – Suburban Location. Rural Tourism in the Poznań Metropolitan Area). *Turystyka I Rekreacja*, 1/2014(1), pp. 120–126. Publisher: Akademia Wychowania Fizycznego w Warszawie, Warszawa.

OECD. (2013). https://www.oecd.org/gov/regional-policy/Definition-of-Functional-Urban-Areas-for-the-OECD-metropolitan-database.pdf [Retrieved 1 January 2017]

Paul, V. & McKenzie, F. (2010). Agricultural areas under metropolitan threats: Lessons for Perth from Barcelona. In G. W. Luck. D. Race & R. Black (Eds.). *Demographic Change in Australia's Rural Landscapes: Implications for Society and the Environment*. Springer, Dordrecht, pp. 125–152.

Peeters, D. (2011). The functional urban areas. Database. ESPON, European Union, Brussels. Retrieved from https://www.espon.eu/export/sites/default/Documents/ToolsandMaps/ ESPON2013Database/3.7_TR-FUAs.pdf [Retrieved 17 June 2015]

PURPLE (Peri-urban regions platform Europe) (n.d.). Peri-urban open space: How multi-functional land use can bring multiple benefits. Topic Paper. http://www.purple-eu.org/ uploads/TopicPapers/updates/peri-urban/paper.pdf [Retrieved 11 June 2015]

Scott, A., Gilbert, A. & Gelan, A. (2007). *The Urban–Rural Divide: Myth or Reality*. Macaulay Institute, Aberdeen.

Shaw, G. & Williams, A. N. (2002). *Critical Issues in Tourism*. A Geographical Perspective. Blackwell. Oxford.

Zębik, G. (2011). Typology of suburban communities in Poland. *Bulletin of Geography, Socio-economic Series*, No 16, Jagiellonian University, Cracow. DOI:http://dx.doi. org/10.2478/v10089-011-0021-x

17 Holiday tourism in metropolitan areas

Andrzej Piotr Wiatrak

Introduction

We can observe the process of space metropolisation in contemporary society. As a result, the relation between the central city and other areas is changing and this causes changes in the structure of space use and development. This applies to the entire socio-economic activity, starting with housing, through different productive functions and ending with service functions, especially the tourism and recreation. Usually the main focus is on housing, because it concerns the essential needs of local and immigrant population and these needs mostly increase in consecutive years. Productive and service functions are also widely discussed due to the development of a metropolitan area and people inhabiting this area. On the other hand, although tourism and recreation concern the whole metropolitan area and its entire community, in practice it is not discussed in much detail, nor are plans implemented. This situation results from the fact that the needs concerning tourism and recreation are not essential. Apart from that, due to limited finances, developing metropolises first make building and housing investments, followed by investments in the productive and service activity, usually leaving investments in tourism and recreation to the end.

Tourism activity plays various roles in society, so we will consider what conditions are necessary to run this activity, which factors stimulate and which destimulate it and how we should strengthen the former and limit the latter. These issues involve strategic thinking and choosing how to run a tourism activity in the future, which priorities the activity will have, which of its resources will be used and how, who will prepare and implement the plans of its development, and such like. This applies to all types of tourism activities, especially to holiday tourism, which is of particular importance in a metropolitan area due to the proximity and short timeframe for a tourism trip and due to the increasing needs in this field. As the metropolitan area develops, the burden of work and living conditions usually increase and, simultaneously, there is a greater demand for regeneration of the inhabitants' physical and mental strength.

Due to the topical character of the issues under discussion and due to social expectations concerning the development of tourism in metropolitan areas, this discussion attempts to approach the issues systemically. This part of the chapter sketches the conditions and needs of holiday tourism in metropolitan areas and presents the following issues: the metropolis and metropolitan area, the essence and character of holiday tourism in a metropolitan area and the conditions of the development of holiday tourism in Piaseczno County, Poland.

The issues presented and analysed in this discussion were based on the reference literature, on the development strategy for Piaseczno County and on the author's considerations. The aim of this discussion is to indicate that:

- the metropolitan area is predisposed to the development of holiday tourism;
- the character of the development of tourism activities may be diversified in metropolitan areas, but should be based on holiday tourism combining different types of tourism and the motives for this type of tourism;
- strategies of metropolises, districts, associations of communes and individual communes should be used as tools for the development of holiday tourism if we take into account the social character of preparation of these strategies and the tools of the implementation strategy.

The metropolis and metropolitan area

The *metropolis* is an element of a settlement network, which determines its influence on neighbouring areas. This influence concerns both specialisation of that area in a particular activity and engagement of the community in business and social activity. This can be expressed by living in one settlement system and working in another settlement system within a particular metropolis. These conditions affect the definition of metropolis according to the assumed traits and identification criteria. At present there is no homogenous definition and the metropolis is usually defined as:

- a city of one million or more inhabitants, but for regional metropolises this limit is usually lowered to 500 thousand inhabitants;
- a large urban centre with specific spatial and functional structures and spatial development, with the centre of administration and economy, trade, culture and science, transport, etc. (Chmiel 2006; Korcelli-Olejniczak 2010, 2012; Smętkowski *et al.* 2009)

Another term is the *metropolitan area*, which comprises a spatially continuous settlement system composed of separate administrative units and consisting of three complementary areas:

- the *metropolitan nucleus* – comprises a big city or compact urban area,
- *suburbs*;
- the *suburban zone* – from a dozen to several dozen kilometres away from the metropolitan nucleus. (Smętkowski *et al.* 2009)

The metropolitan area is a functional entity, which integrates the component settlement units and which influences their functioning regardless of administrative borders. The interrelation and interaction of the three complementary areas listed above concern all the types of activities which complement each other. This is particularly noticeable in tourism and especially in holiday tourism. On the one hand, this activity is diversified in individual areas of the metropolis, while on the other, it is specialised and oriented towards different groups of people.

The essence and character of holiday tourism in metropolitan areas

All types of tourism may develop in a metropolitan area. However, due to the service-providing character of the suburban zone, holiday tourism plays a particular role. It comprises the following elements:

- short-term leisure near one's place of residence;
- 0 to 3 nights spent in a cottage, flat or house located away from one's place of permanent residence, usually in a place attractive to tourists;
- passive or active leisure;
- diversified character: cognition, sports, entertainment, health, meetings, etc.;
- staying close to nature, with relaxation, cognition, activity, etc.; and above all staying outdoors.

There are different forms of holiday tourism in metropolitan areas. The most important of them are:

- weekend tourism;
- suburban tourism, urban tourism and rural tourism;
- cognitive and sightseeing tourism;
- cultural tourism.

Individual forms of tourism are interconnected, such as suburban tourism and rural tourism. Therefore, it is necessary to segment clients of holiday tourism, taking the motives of their tourism activity into consideration. Clients of holiday tourism in metropolitan areas can be divided into three groups:

- Inhabitants of a large urban centre.
- Inhabitants of the suburban zone, who work at their place of residence or nearby, usually use local facilities in their area and find it attractive to make a trip to a big city.
- Inhabitants of the suburban zone who work in a big urban centre, commute to work and do not use local facilities in the area every day.

The basic group which uses or may use the offer of holiday tourism is the inhabitants of a large urban centre who make short-term tourism trips to:

- regenerate their physical and mental strength;
- rest and temporarily change their living environment;

- relax and do therapeutic activities, including wellness and visiting spas;
- spend their leisure time actively, starting with walking and cycling sight-seeing tours with exploration of the region and ending with doing different sports;
- spend their leisure time actively and have entertainment, such as at sports competitions, boar roasting, etc. (Faracik 2008; Gaworecki 2003)

This type of tourism is usually based on natural values, especially those related to water and forest areas that facilitate bathing, water sports, fishing, mushroom picking, riding and walking. This type of tourism usually does not require intensive development of the tourism infrastructure, but it is recommended to develop specialised infrastructure (e.g. to facilitate sailing) in metropolitan areas.

Various tourism values are used for this purpose, not only natural values but also anthropogenic values). They provide tourists with an opportunity to learn more about the region where they live and its history. This understanding may concern various issues, including the following:

- Settlement landscape and land development –

    - residential houses, manors, palaces, castles, etc.;
    - industrial structures and livestock buildings;
    - public buildings;
    - churches, chapels and other places of worship;
    - museums, open-air museums and halls of memory;
    - parks, gardens, orchards, etc.

- The method of management and production in a particular area –
    - history of management in a particular area;
    - craft, handicraft, folk art;
    - traditional processed food and dishes, etc.;
    - spiritual heritage in a particular area;
    - historical events and legends;
    - customs and rituals;
    - fairs;
    - dialects, etc. (Wojciechowska 2003)

It is necessary to take into consideration the fact that for many people, especially newcomers in the metropolis, the history of the region is unknown and therefore learning about it may be an interesting educational experience.

On the other hand, inhabitants of the suburban zone, who work at their place of residence or nearby, are interested in city tourism. There are diverse motives for visiting cities, including metropolises, in free time. Usually these motives are related to:

- visiting a city and learning about its cultural heritage;
- participating in cultural events at theatres, cinemas, festivals, museums, etc.;

- participating in sports events;
- participating in religious rites and celebrations;
- education;
- entertainment;
- shopping. (Mika 2008)

This group of inhabitants is chiefly characterised by the intellectual motive of their trips and cultural values are the main reason for their trips. On the other hand, inhabitants of the suburban zone who work in a big urban centre have more diversified motives for holiday tourism, because they can be found both in the city and in the suburban zone. For this reason, their motives for holiday trips depend largely on their individual preferences and on the degree of binding to a particular area. It is necessary to consider the fact that some of the suburban population are immigrants. This should favour intellectual tourism, especially cultural tourism, both at their place of residence and place of work.

Diversified motives for holiday tourism make the basis for distinguishing types of tourism. In order to do so it is necessary to segment tourism services, considering the following criteria:

- preferences concerning the form of spending free time, including tourists' passions and hobbies;
- preferences concerning the standard of tourism services, including satisfying essential needs;
- preferences concerning the place of stay (e.g. guesthouse, hostel, farm);
- type of tourism (excursions, hiking, water tourism, etc.);
- tourists' occupational qualifications and their readiness to use the offer of active or passive leisure. (Pizło 1998)

According to the assumed segmentation criteria and diversification of motives for tourism trips, we can distinguish the following types of tourists using the services provided by holiday tourism:

- leisure type;
- cognitive type;
- nature-oriented;
- culture-oriented;
- people-oriented;
- task type – oriented to a specific task, e.g. fishing, hunting,
- competitive type (e.g. sports-oriented);
- 'health' type – oriented to health care;
- entertainment or entertainment-recreational type. (Przecławski 1997)

It is necessary to recognise types of tourists to prepare a tourism offer, which is diversified not only in terms of the demand but also in terms of the supply, that is, tourism and scenic values of the metropolitan area, the state of the natural environment and its general and tourism-oriented development. The main idea is to use the existing resources and values of a particular area and adjust them to the current and predicted demand. In view of this, the actions described above and the preparation of tourism products should result both from the development strategy in a metropolis, voivodeship (province), county or commune and from the tasks and goals of environmental policy, taking tourism values and resources into account, that is, environmental factors (clean environment), cultural factors (culture, monuments, history, folklore, etc.) and the specific character of the metropolitan area. These factors should be the basis for preparation of tourism products, which should be adjusted to different groups of clients and which should provide a broad spectrum of services with distinct character, for example:

- weekends in a place surrounded by nature and greenery;
- lessons in history and natural science (especially for children);
- culture and folklore;
- local crafts and souvenirs;
- food from organic farms;
- regional open-air festivals (bonfires, ram roasting, sleigh rides, etc.).

Individual products should be well prepared in each metropolitan area and should be adjusted to the current conditions in individual communes. Local spatial development plans and regional and local development strategies play an important role in these actions. The plans and strategies are qualitative concepts concerning the future, which order the social and business activity. They are a consistent plan of actions in a particular area (e.g. a county), which was deliberately developed on the basis of current resources and values and their relationships with the external and internal environments. They also designate the way to achieve the goals (for example in the tourism activity interrelated with other forms of actions in a metropolitan area) (Wiatrak 2011).

Trends in the development of holiday tourism in Piaseczno County: a case study

Piaseczno County is situated south of Warsaw. It has agricultural and residential character. The county has good road and rail connections and is located close to Warsaw Okęcie Airport (15 km from the centre of Piaseczno). The terrain is flat. It is located on Warsaw Plain and is intersected with the valleys of the Jeziorka, Czarna and Utrata Rivers and their tributaries. There is an extensive forest complex (especially Chojnów Woods) and vegetation characterised by a high degree of naturalness and biodiversity. The county has the following natural values:

- Chojnów Scenic Park – more than 10,000 ha, comprises forests and the Jeziorka River valley with abundant scarp and marshy meadow vegetation;
- Warsaw Protected Landscape Area – 20,000 ha;
- 14 nature reserves, e.g. Lake Czerskie;

- Other natural areas, e.g. Dworski Park in Wola Gołkowska and a protected spa zone in Konstancin-Jeziorna. (Strategia 2003)

The county features the following anthropogenic values:

- The Fairy-Tale Museum and the Papermaking Museum in Konstancin-Jeziorna;
- Exaltation of the Holy Cross Church, the Tzadik Manor, synagogue and house of prayer in Góra Kalwaria;
- The fourteenth century castle of the Dukes of Masovia in Czersk;
- The graves of insurgents from the January Uprising (1863) and World War I cemeteries in the Commune of Piaseczno;
- The late nineteenth century Piaseczno Narrow-Gauge Railway. (Strategia 2003)

Due to the location of the county and its scenic, natural and cultural values the following types of tourism are the most popular:

- cycling;
- hiking;
- horse-riding;
- fishing. (Strategia 2003)

Tourists usually ride bicycles and hike along delineated routes. The most popular cycling routes in the county are:

- the Chojnów Yellow Cycling Route (7 km);
- the Chojnów Black Cycling Route (13 km);
- the Chojnów Green Cycling Route (24 km);
- the Vistula Blue Cycling Route (32 km). (Strategia 2003)

The most popular hiking routes in the county are:

- the Warsaw Ring Route;
- the Nature Reserves Route;
- the route from Konstancin to Góra Kalwaria and Czersk;
- the Historical Architecture Route around Konstancin;
- the Chojnów Main Forest Route. (Strategia 2003)

The authorities of the county see the role of tourism in its development. The follow-ing statements are contained in the Piaseczno County Sustainable Development Strategy (Strategia 2003):

> Due to the abundance of natural and cultural values in Piaseczno County it is predisposed for the development of recreation and tourism in the Warsaw Metropolitan Area and Region. Tourism services provide an opportunity for socioeconomic development in the southern part of the region. It is necessary

to provide an attractive tourism offer, which is competitive to other counties in the outer zone of the Warsaw agglomeration and which will increase Warsaw inhabitants' interest in the county. The development of the tourism and recreational function should correspond to the local conditions and guarantee protection of natural and cultural resources. The historic route Wilanów–Konstancin-Jeziorna–Góra Kalwaria–Czersk–Warka will be an important tourism area.

The following goals were adopted to implement the strategy:

- promote natural and cultural values and tourism and recreational facilities;
- renew tourism and recreational facilities in existing centres;
- develop new areas for tourism and recreation;
- implement accompanying measures, e.g. improve the sanitary condition, strengthen the natural condition, facilitate public and private transport in the county. (Strategia 2003)

These plans are appropriate, but they have not been fully implemented in the last decade. On the one hand, we can observe improvement in the sanitary condition, natural condition and transport in the county. Nevertheless, the actions taken to develop tourism facilities and prepare an offer for holiday tourism are still insufficient. We can observe actions taken by local governments mostly in the commune and county, but they are not always sufficient. This situation results from budget limitations and can be observed regardless of European Union subsidies, which can be received according to the rule of additivity. However, the actions taken by investors (inhabitants of the county and others) are still insufficient. This means that the adopted strategy lacks instruments for its implementation, such as support given to investors and propagation of the goals and tasks in the strategy. This situation might also result from the fact that the preparation of the strategy has not been socialised and there have been no consultations concerning the preparation and implementation of the strategy (Wiatrak 2011). If inhabitants are involved in particular goals and tasks, the strategy is effective. For example, Piaseczno Narrow-Gauge Railway is the biggest tourist rail carrier in Masovia. It is operated by the Piaseczno-Grójec Narrow-Gauge Railway Society, which was established in 1988 by a group of enthusiasts who wanted to save historical railway technology. Every Sunday individual tourists can undertake train excursions, travel around areas of natural and scenic values and admire views of historic railway stations, buildings and manors. They can stop, have a meal and enjoy a wide range of other attractions in Runów (Kolej Wąskotorowa n.d.). There are positive effects of such actions and they should be popularised.

Conclusions

It is justified to prepare development schemes of holiday tourism in metropolitan areas. Programming trends in the development of holiday tourism should be based on natural values in the area and combined with actions in other spatial and functional zones. Development plans should receive social support at the stage of preparation and there should be clearly defined instruments for their implementation. These should include finding investors from the metropolitan and other areas. The preparation of development plans should include one's own outlay and involvement, for example, from different organisations such as the abovementioned Piaseczno-Grójec Narrow-Gauge Railway Society or the local action group, Pearls of Masovia.

The development of holiday tourism in metropolitan areas should be based on development strategies and plans, resulting from the general development strategy in the area and allowing for the interests of individual groups of stakeholders, including tourists. It is important to combine the strategies of metropolises, counties, commune associations and communes to integrate actions taken at individual levels. The absence of combined strategies may be a barrier to development, increase costs of actions and prolong the time of their implementation.

There are numerous and diversified benefits of tourism development strategies and plans (including holiday tourism). The most important of them include a complex approach to a specific issue (e.g. combining the development of an area and its functions with tourism infrastructure) and combining individual types of tourism. The preparation and implementation of an effective system to manage the development of tourism in metropolitan areas should be based on the participation of the local community. This should include both setting goals and their verification against current and predicted conditions. It is important that the participation should encompass a relatively wide range and include tourists' needs. Social support given to prepared strategies, the acceptance of approved schemes and involvement of the community in the implementation process improves the effectiveness of actions taken to prepare specific tourism products according to the existing demand, resources and tourism values.

References

Chmiel, M. (2006). Co to znaczy obszar metropolitalny i do czego jest nam potrzebny. http://www.malgorzatachmiel.pl/aktualnosci/przymorze-male/co [Retrieved April 2006]

Faracik, R. (2008). Turystyka podmiejska. In W. Kurek (Ed.). *Turystyka*. Publisher: Wyd. Naukowe PWN, Warszawa, pp. 328–330.

Gaworecki, W. W. (2003). *Turystyka*. Publisher: PWE, Warszawa, pp. 79–90.

Kolej Wąskotorowa. (n.d.). Kolej Wąskotorowa Piaseczno, Tarczyn, Grójec [Narrow-gauge railway Piaseczno, Tarczyn, Grójec]. http://www.kolejka-piaseczno.pl [Retrieved 6 June 2014]

Korcelli-Olejniczak, E. (2010). Kształtowanie się regionu metropolitarnego Warszawy w świetle analizy zasięgu działalności przedsiębiorstw sektora zaawansowanych usług. *Przegląd Geograficzny*, Book 4. Publisher: Instytut Geografii I Przestrzennego Zagospodarowania Polskiej Akademii Nauk, Warszawa, pp. 573–592.

Korcelli-Olejniczak, E. (2012). Region metropolitalny – pojęcie, struktura przestrzenna, dynamika. *Prace Geograficzne*, 235. Publisher: Instytut Geografii I Przestrzennego Zagospodarowania Polskiej Akademii Nauk, Warszawa.

Mika, M. (2008). Turystyka miejska. In W. Kurek (Ed.). *Turystyka*. Publisher: Wyd. Naukowe PWN, Warszawa, pp. 319–328.

Pizło, W. (1998). Kanały dystrybucji na rynku usług agroturystycznych. In A. P. Wiatrak (Ed.). *Marketing i produkty markowe w turystyce wiejskiej*. Publisher: SGGW, Warszawa, pp. 33–42.

Przecławski, K. (1997). *Człowiek a turystyka. Zarys socjologii turystyki*. Publisher: Wyd. ALBIS, Kraków, pp. 38–44.

Smętkowski, M., Jałowiecki, B. & Gorzelak, G. (2009). Obszary metropolitalne w Polsce – diagnoza i rekomendacje. *Studia Regionalne i Lokalne*, 1, pp. 52–73. Publisher: Centrum Europejskich Studiów Regionalnych i Lokalnych UW, Warszawa.

Strategia. (2003). *Strategia zrównoważonego rozwoju powiatu piaseczyńskiego* [Strategy of sustainable development for Piaseczno Community]. Publisher: Starostwo Powiatowe w Piasecznie http://www.piaseczno.pl/pliki/58/Strategie%20 rozwoju/79/Strategia%20Zrownowa%C5%BConego%20Rozwoju%20Powiatu%20 Piaseczy%C5%84skiego%20-%20diagnoza%20.doc [Retrieved 3 January 2017].

Wiatrak, A. P. (2011). *Strategie rozwoju gmin wiejskich. Podstawy teoretyczne, ocena przydatności i znaczenie w przemianach strukturalnych obszarów wiejskich*. Publisher: Wyd. IRWiR PAN, Warszawa.

Wojciechowska, J. (2003). Turystyka kulturowa regionów jako element produktu turystycznego. In T. Burzyński & M. Łabaj (Ed.). *Turystyka rekreacyjna oraz turystyka specjalistyczna*. Publisher: Biuro Ekspertyz Finansowych, Marketingu i Consultingu Uniconsult, Warszawa, pp. 152–159.

18 Social farming-based tourism from the perspective of metropolitan areas

Elżbieta Kmita-Dziasek

Metropolitan areas: social challenges

The European Union's (EU) ESPON[1] programme defines a metropolitan area as a territory consisting of an individual city or urban agglomeration and adjacent communes: the surroundings. The definition stresses the interdependence between the centre of the metropolitan area and its surroundings. The metropolitan centre concentrates workplaces and public services to which the inhabitants of surrounding areas commute from an area within a 1-hour radius. As time passes, the process of metropolisation usually limits the functions of the surrounding areas to being a residential and recreational base for the metropolis inhabitants.

In recent decades the percentage of the urban population has increased dramatically in Europe. The census of 1921 in Poland revealed that 24.6 per cent of the population lived in cities. In 1966 the urban population exceeded the rural population and at present more than 60 per cent of the Polish population live in cities (MRR 2010). The urbanisation ratio in western and northern European countries is even greater, exceeding 80 per cent in the United Kingdom, Sweden, Finland and Denmark, and exceeding 90 per cent in Belgium, Luxembourg, Holland and Iceland (UN 2014).

Urbanisation is accompanied by disagrarisation. Only from 2002 to 2010 in Poland the total number of farms larger than 1 ha dropped by more than 20 per cent and there was a simultaneous decreasing tendency in areas of arable land, which exceeded 8 per cent (Central Statistical Office 2011). This phenomenon particularly applies to rural areas located in the neighbourhood of big cities. They surround metropolitan areas and are strongly transformed due to changes in their functions and infrastructural needs.

Apart from the benefits of metropolisation, that is, dynamic development; economic, scientific and technological potential; labour market and sociocultural infrastructure, metropolitan areas are subject to the intensified negative effects of urbanisation and globalisation. The process of metropolisation significantly influences lifestyle, causing stratification, social and spatial segregation among the inhabitants in the area. It also intensifies social pathologies, leading to social exclusion and alienation. In most urbanised areas of Europe and other continents one can observe weakened or even broken social relations caused by increasing migration, consumerist approach, rivalry, competitiveness, meeting the standards and keeping up the pace of life. The crisis in social relations causes the loss of the sense of identity and undermines the individual's sense of safety, which is a natural need. It is estimated that every year one third of adult Europeans experience at least one of the symptoms of a negative mental state, anxiety and depression being the most common (WHO 2013). Since the early 1990s there has been increasing incidence of mental diseases in Poland. Between 1997 and 2009 the total number of outpatients treated for mental disorders nearly doubled, whereas the number of patients receiving 24-hour care increased by half. Among the patients treated for mental disorders the number of city dwellers is about 12 per cent greater than the number of rural inhabitants. However, as far as some categories of mental disorders are concerned, the percentage of patients living in cities is three times as high as the percentage of patients living in rural areas, for example, patients suffering from disorders induced by psychotropic drugs (Wojtyniak and Goryński 2012).

The turn of the twentieth century was a period of radical change in the demographic structure. According to the UN report, since the early 1950s human life expectancy has increased by nearly 20 years on average and it will have increased by another 10 years by 2050. According to the forecasts of the Central Statistical Office, in 2050 the number of retired people in Poland will exceed one third of the population (GUS 2009). As a result of the extended life expectancy, which is a positive and expected phenomenon, and due to the prolonged ageing process, there is an increasing demand for leisure services and health care, especially long-term care, for senior citizens.

In metropolitan areas the abovementioned demographic and social problems are combined with the instability of social structure, intensity of migration, unemployment, economic polarisation, family crisis, endangered safety and crime. In addition, the spontaneous urbanisation of suburban zones causes spatial chaos and degrades landscape and, in consequence, the zones lose their recreational and investment attraction (Lendzion 2004). Sustainable development of metropolitan areas, ensuring fair division of the benefits and costs of economic development in the centre of the metropolis and its surroundings, is a challenge to be faced.

The concept of social farming: a call to global society

Social farming, also known as green care or farming for health, is an innovative approach integrating social services into the trend of multifunctional farming. Social farming encompasses actions taking advantage of the opportunities provided by the agricultural activity to support therapy, rehabilitation, social integration, lifelong learning and social services in rural areas. The idea combines two worlds, that is, agriculture and social affairs, or, to be more specific, the farm and professional social services. Social services include education and nurture, health care, social assistance, resocialisation, culture, recreation, leisure and social housing.

Small farms, which are predominant both in Poland and in the European Union, are particularly predisposed to providing green care services. Farms with an area up to 5 ha make up 69 per cent of the total number of farms, whereas in the EU, the share of farms with an area up to 10 ha on average reaches 80 per cent

(GUS 2012, Eurostat 2010). Small farms have unique conditions not only to fulfil the commodity-providing function but also to provide public goods related with health, leisure, education and care. Especially small farms, which usually have free social capital and technical potential, can fulfil new social functions better than global educational, social or health care systems.

Social farming faces a wide range of problems of contemporary civilisation and responds to social challenges linked to social stratification, ageing, development of civilisation-related diseases including mental disorders and addictions, increasing pathologies, social dysfunctions and problems of the labour market. Preventatives and balancing of civilisation deficits are as important as therapy, re-integration and social inclusion. It has been scientifically proved that contact with the authentic rhythm of a farm, plants and farm animals as well as participation in the food production cycle positively influence the human emotional and mental development (Figure 18.1).

According to the assumptions of social farming, the traditional structures of a multigenerational family and natural self-help networks are typical of rural local communities. The tasks of care and support, which used to be the natural competence of the members of a multigenerational family or local neighbourhood, need to be replaced by external service systems in global societies.

In addition, we cannot neglect the importance of social farming for the agricultural sector as such. Social ideas open the sector to new possibilities and practical implementation of multifunctionality in agriculture. They contribute to the extension of the range of possible additional services, increase the number of rural entities interested in them and generate income. In general, society has an

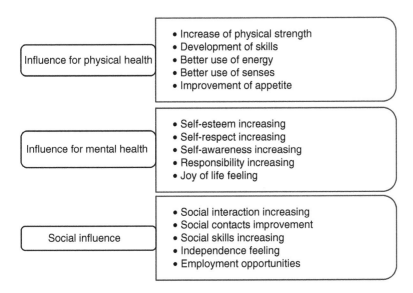

Figure 18.1 A summary of the benefits of social farming for service users.

Source: The author's compilation based on Di Iacovo and O'Connor 2009, p. 41.

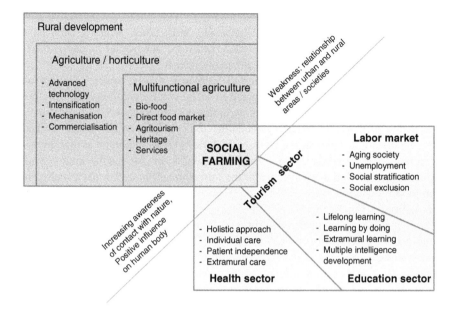

Figure 18.2 Social farming by sector.

opportunity to change its attitude to agriculture and farmers, as well as an opportunity to build new relationships between farmers and consumers and to promote farm products. New challenges cause the development of farmers' entrepreneurial attitudes towards increased social responsibility, including the introduction of pro-ecological solutions. The awareness of the farmer's role in the protection of the rural cultural landscape is strengthened.

There are social farming projects undertaken all over the world. Usually they are the initiative of private entities or charity, church or third-sector organisations. Pioneers of the idea in a particular region have different motivations, such as:

- the wish to help specific groups of disadvantaged people, e.g. initiatives started by disabled children's parents;
- the wish to share rural life with disadvantaged people;
- deliberate search for alternatives to industrial agriculture;
- the wish to participate in the implementation of goals of social justice and social solidarity as one's personal, family or group lifestyle;
- the pursuit of professional development, e.g. initiatives concerning social affairs, care or education, undertaken by professionals;
- a chance for new potential sources of income combined with the wish to be open to problems of the local community, e.g. undertakings initiated by farmers.

Highly urbanised countries are the most experienced in the development of social farming. This points to the correlation between the demand for social farming services and the metropolisation process. For example, according to the latest report of the Dutch National Support Centre for Agriculture and Care, at the end of 2012 in Holland, where the degree of urbanisation reaches 90 per cent, there were more than 1,100 care farms. This number had tripled over a period of ten years (Jaarverslag 2013).

Social farming-based tourism: new opportunities for metropolitan areas

The importance of natural rural environment for relaxation is recognised all over Europe. Tourists associate rurality with agricultural landscapes, therapeutic values of the environment and food products as well as local culture, customs and traditions. We can observe the increasing importance of direct contact with a rural family and farm resulting from the interest in relaxation in rural areas. The attractiveness of relaxation in rural areas is also determined by the values of traditional farms. Farming activities and animals are particularly important to children relaxing in rural areas in the company of their parents or visiting the countryside as a school activity. There is growing importance of the role of rural areas as places of creative management based on knowledge, where experiences, impressions and emotions become particularly significant. The specificity of family farms with multidirectional production, extensive cultivation and breeding methods and intimate homestead atmosphere fully corresponds to the image of rural tourism, which is based on farming traditions, the cultural identity of a region, family, hospitality and high quality in all European countries.

Having a social mission, agriculture is at the crossroads of a few economic branches, where apart from the agri-food sector, health care, education and labour market, tourism is also important.

According to the data of the European Commission published in 2012, the infrastructure of rural tourism, which is measured by the number of accommodation facilities, is the best developed in the following European countries: France (17%), Italy (16.5%), Germany (11.9%) and Spain (11.8%). In Poland this index is 2.3 per cent and it encompasses nearly a quarter of the total number of accommodation facilities in new EU member-states, except the EU-15. From 2007 to 2012 in the whole European Union the supply of accommodation facilities in rural areas increased by 4.9 per cent. The increase was much greater in new EU member-states (EU-N12), – 11.7 per cent (European Commission 2013).

The increase in the supply of offers of rural tourism simultaneously involves the increase in competition, both in international markets and in domestic or even regional markets. The search for competitive advantage leads rural tourism towards the development of regional offers, creation of brand-name products and the offering of specialised services addressed to specific target groups of visitors and niche markets. Social farming-based tourism can be found among other different trends of specialisation in rural tourism, such as: heritage tourism, qualified tourism, nature tourism, culinary tourism, spa and wellness tourism and adventure tourism. Farm stays combined with social services or extension of the business by the offer for one-day visitors is a chance for agritourism farms to prolong the tourism season, attract new clients, improve quality standards and gain a stable source of income.

The current trends favour or even force the development of individual forms of care, a holistic approach to charges, extracurricular, active methods of education and lifelong learning. The following people may be potential target groups in social farming-based tourism:

- schoolchildren and kindergarten pupils;
- active senior citizens;
- people with physical, mental or emotional disabilities;
- the socially disadvantaged;
- young offenders or people with learning difficulties;
- the long-term unemployed.

Although the general definition of social farming has not been agreed upon around Europe yet, farms undertaking a social mission can be divided into the following four types, depending on the target group and diversified purposes: care farms providing care services, therapy farms undertaking therapeutic and re-educational activities, inclusive/social farms concerned about social and employment inclusion and educational/didactic farms undertaking pedagogical activities (Official Journal of EU 2013).

Care farms – providing short-term and long-term care chiefly to elderly people.

The increasing percentage of retired people poses a challenge to the social policy of the state, where it is a duty of the state to guarantee appropriate quality of life to elderly people and to provide access to specialist social and health services. Apart from that, the members of the current older generation are increasingly aware of their health and have growing expectations concerning their old age, that it should be characterised not only by fitness but also by independence, and occupational and social activity.

Therapy farms – providing re-educational and therapeutic activities.

Therapy provided by farms can be based on activities, rehabilitation and individual support. Therapy farms also provide occupational education. However, it is not their aim to help their charges enter the labour market or to offer employment. The therapy is supposed to compensate for deficits, assist mentally disabled people to become fitter, and help people with mental disorders or social deficits integrate with society. There are gardening therapies, specialist therapies with animals, green exercise, eco-therapies and activity therapies, which involve participation in everyday farm work.

Social farms – for integration in the world of work and for social inclusion.

Social services are directed to people convicted of criminal offences or who are on the margins of society. This type of activity provides occupational integration or employment, including professional trainings, to marginalised groups on the open labour market. The socially disadvantaged, including the disabled, are employed on social farms as volunteers, trainees or workers.

Educational farms – undertaking pedagogical activities.

The modern approach to education makes a farm an attractive place for teaching classes and integrating theory and practice in many subjects. Direct contact with a rich agricultural, natural and socio-economic environment on a farm favours holistic development. We can distinguish two types of educational farms addressing their programmes to children and youth:

- Farms concentrated on the education of schoolchildren, familiarising them with farm life, providing knowledge about the origin of food and offering contact with the natural rural environment.
- Farms offering educational visits with a special programme for children with various dysfunctions (e.g. attention deficit hyperactivity disorder) or for children from pathological, broken and dysfunctional families.

Free rural space, the presence of animals, the abundance of smells, tastes and sounds provide a variety of cognitive stimuli and emotional benefits to participants of didactic programmes on educational farms, regardless of their age. The offer of educational farms also includes programme profiles addressed especially to adult participants, including exclusive oenological workshops on wine farms.

Social farming-based tourism: Best practice

The National Educational Farms Network is a pioneer social farming enterprise in Poland.[2] The establishment of the network was based on the assumption that:

- it is necessary to familiarise people with the farmer's work and the origin of food;
- the farm has the right potential for attractive educational activities;
- educational services provide farmers with an opportunity to gain extra income, motivate them to continue the farming activity and to maintain the viability of rural areas.

The concept of an educational farm and its market identification under the name of 'Educational Farm' was defined as a result of a national project. An educational farm is a facility located in a rural area and providing educational activities based on agricultural and rural potential, especially in crop production, animal production, crop processing, ecological and consumer awareness, rural material-culture heritage, traditional professions, handicrafts and folk arts. The facility should have farm animals or crop plantations for presentation to groups of children and youth, who visit the farm as part of their school curriculum or as part of their extracurricular activities, or the animals or plantations should be shown as a tourism attraction to families with children or to individual adult travellers.

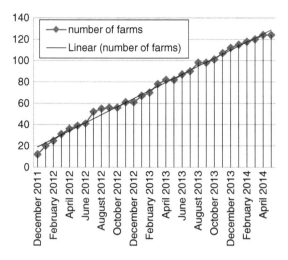

Figure 18.3 The dynamics of development of the National Educational Farms Network in Poland from December 2011 to June 2014.

Source: The author's compilation.

Since the very beginning development of the National Educational Farms Network has been trending steadily upwards and it has exhibited a noticeable and steady increase. The concentration of dispersed activities under the common brand name guarantees a transparent image distinguishing the educational services of member farms on the market, favours better use of resources, orients the qualitative development of educational programmes, attracts external funds and increases the efficiency of promotional actions.

Both the agricultural and educational sectors are beneficiaries of the network. It is important for the agricultural sector to have an opportunity to meet future consumers. It brings a change to the farmer's daily routine, provides the joy of work with children and teachers, and offers farm families creative development, new employment opportunities and extra income.

The educational sector finds variety and an enrichment of the teaching process through guaranteed quality curricula oriented to practical activities, workshop exercises in different subjects, alternative places of education and rural culture experience.

Educational programmes are written by hosts on the basis on their own potential and the potential of their farms. Most programmes last up to 3 hours and they are managed by the hosts. The largest target group is children beginning their school education.

Educational programmes in crop production help participants to discover, feel and experience the biodiversity of the world of plants, learn about traditional and modern cultivation methods, lifecycles and the interdependence of farming systems and natural ecosystems. This involves a wide range of discoveries of shapes, forms, colours, smells and tastes as well as lifecycles and metabolisms.

Education in animal production encompasses learning about the life of animals, sightseeing tours of farm buildings, learning about appliances and tools, breeding systems, the use of animals and their vital functions. The programme is adjusted to schoolchildren's age. Contact with animals teaches children to be sensitive and selfless, trains them how to take on responsibilities and stimulates their cognitive needs.

Education in crop processing encompasses presentations and workshops showing milk, meat, cereals and, seasonally, vegetables and fruit and their journey from the production and harvesting of the raw material to the final attractive or utility item. The activities teach not only the processing methods, but they also teach respect for the producer's work by providing some experience of the production effort.

Education in ecological and consumer awareness provides information about the origin and nutritional value of the farm products. This type of education teaches participants how to distinguish between natural and highly processed industrial products and it develops their consumer habits.

Education in rural material-culture heritage, traditional professions, handicrafts and folk arts is based on the richness of material and spiritual culture of rural areas. It offers attractive activities involving artistic, culinary or even entertainment practice.

At the *national level*, the National Educational Farms Network is coordinated by the Agricultural Advisory Centre (AAC), Krakow Branch. The AAC implements its statutory rural development tasks by propagating the idea of

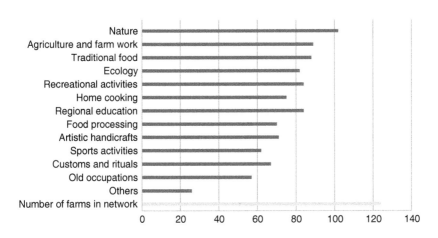

Figure 18.4 The educational activities subjects offered by members of the National
Educational Farms Network at the Agricultural Advisory Centre in
Brwinów, Krakow Branch.

Source: The author's compilation.

education on farms and promoting the activity of educational farms in the Network. The AAC qualifies and admits new members to the Network, organises periodical trainings for Network members and advisors–coordinators from individual voivodeships (regions), and prepares and approves the programmes of field trainings organised by Voivodeship Agricultural Advisory Centres. The AAC also organises promotional stands at tourism and agricultural fairs, and maintains a database of educational farms on the website of the Network, which is available to a wide group of recipients. It manages the brand 'ZAGRODA EDUKACYJNA [educational farm]', which has a coherent

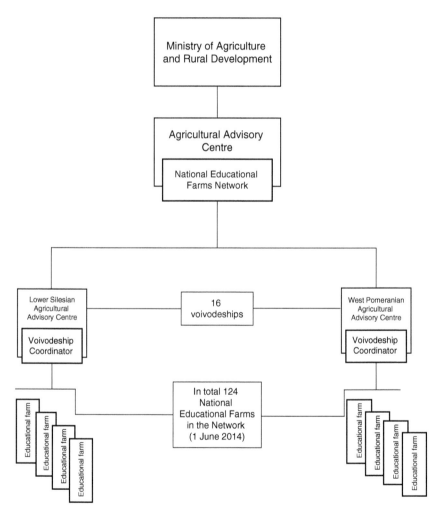

Figure 18.5 The functional structure of the National Educational Farms Network.

Source: The author's compilation.

Figure 18.6 The logotype of the National Educational Farms Network.
Source: CDR, Krakow Branch.

visualisation. According to the decision of the Patent Office of the Republic of Poland, since 2014 the word mark 'ZAGRODA EDUKACYJNA' and its logo have been protected by law.

At the *regional (voivodeship)* level, the Voivodeship Agricultural Advisory Centres in all of the 16 voivodeships are partners of the AAC in the management of the National Educational Farms Network. In each centre there is at least one qualified advisor, who acts as a voivodeship coordinator. The coordinator's task is to recommend facilities in the voivodeship to the Network. Coordinators advise how to adapt the farm for educational services, help farmers to develop pro-grammes and fill in an application form for the Network. They take promotional and training actions in the voivodeship.

At the *local level*, farms which start to provide educational services according to the assumptions of the National Educational Farms Network submit an application with a description of suggested educational pro-grammes. Membership in the Network is voluntary and free of charge. The Network members are obliged to abide by the regulations. Farms admitted to the Network has the right to be identified with the logotype of the Network (Figure 18.6).

There are member farms of the National Educational Farms Network in all voivodeships in Poland (Figure 18.7). The largest number of such facilities can be found in the voivodeships whose capitals are strongly urbanised metropolitan centres, such as Warsaw, Krakow, Tri-City and Wrocław.

Figure 18.7 The distribution of educational farms on an administrative map of Poland
(as of 1 June 2014).

Source: The author's compilation.

Conclusions

Social farming-based tourism, as a unique combination of agritourism and professional social services, is dynamically entering rural areas. It brings a new quality
to agritourism and new part-time employment opportunities for farmers. It also
brings hope for the maintenance of agriculture and rural landscape in metropolitan
surroundings as a space for relaxation, physical exercises, therapy, care, education
and re-integration for the inhabitants of metropolitan centres with civilisation-
related problems.

From this perspective, rural areas in the surroundings of metropolitan centres
gain a new value for city dwellers. The areas also become important due to the
improvement of urban inhabitants' quality of life, which they may not have been
aware of. It is their interest to ensure that the metropolitan centre should not develop
at the expense of its surroundings. It should develop according to a plan and should
guarantee effective, easily accessible, high quality social service functions.

Notes

1 ESPON: The European Observation Network for Territorial Development and Cohesion under Objective 3 'European Territorial Cooperation' of the EU Cohesion Policy concerning spatial development and territorial cohesion of the EU countries, Iceland, Liechtenstein, Norway and Switzerland. The programme has been under implementation since 2000 and its results significantly influenced the inclusion of the territorial aspect into the EU cohesion policy in the Lisbon Treaty.
2 The concept of the National Educational Farms Network was developed between 2010 and 2011 by the Agricultural Advisory Centre in Brwinów, Krakow Branch, as a project financed by the EU under the European Agricultural Fund for Rural Development (EAFRD) 2007–2013.

References

Dessein J. (ed.) (2008). *Farming for Health. Proceedings of the Community of Practice Farming for Health.* Merelbeke.

Di Iacovo, F. & O'Connor, D. (Eds.) (2009). *Supporting Policies for Social Farming in Europe: Progressing Multifunctionality in Responsive Rural Areas.* ARSIA – Agenzia Regionale per lo Sviluppo e l'Innovazione nel settore Agricolo-forestale, Firenze, Italy.

European Commission. (2013). Rural development in the European Union – statistical and economic information 2007–2013. https://ec.europa.eu/agriculture/statistics/rural-development_en [Retrieved 3 August 2014]

Eurostat. (2010). Agricultural census 2010 – main results. Acquired from http://ec.europa.eu/eurostat/statistics-explained/index.php/Agricultural_census_2010_-_main_result-son 28 March 2014

GUS. (2009). *Prognoza ludności Polski na lata 2008–2035* [Population projection for Poland 2008–2035]. Central Statistical Office, Warszawa. http://stat.gov.pl/cps/rde/xbcr/gus/L_prognoza_ludnosci_na_lata2008_2035.pdf [Retrieved 3 August 2014]

GUS. (2011). *Powszechny Spis Rolny 2010–2011.* Central Statistical Office, Warszawa. Acquired from www.stat.gov.pl on 3 August 2014.

GUS. (2012). *Rocznik Statystyczny Rolnictwa* [Statistical Yearbook of Agriculture 2012] Central Statistical Office, Warszawa. http://stat.gov.pl/cps/rde/xbcr/gus/rs_rocznik_rolnictwa_2012.pdf [Retrieved 3 August 2014]

Jaarverslag Ferderatie Landbouw en Zorg 2012. (2013). Ferderatie Landbouw en Zorg Voorthuizen. http://www.landbouwzorg.nl/jv_flz/Jaarverslag_FLZ_2012_web.pdf [Retrieved 3 July 2014]

Lendzion, J. (2004). *Znaczenie obszarów metropolitalnych i ich otoczenia oraz współczesnych procesów metropolizacyjnych w kształtowaniu polityki regionalnej Państwa.* Publisher: Departament Polityki Regionalnej Ministerstwa gospodarki i Pracy, Warszawa. http://www.platforma.org/media/dokumenty/znaczenie_obszar_w_metropolitalnych.pdf [Retrieved 28 March 2014]

MRR. (2010). *Rozwój miast w Polsce.* Ministerstwo Rozwoju Regionalnego [Ministry of Regional Development], Warszawa. http://eregion.wzp.pl/sites/default/files/rozwoj_miast_w_polsce_0.pdf [Retrieved 9 June 2014]

National Educational Farms Network. (2014). Logotype. www.zagrodaedukacyjna.pl [Retrieved 3 August 2014]

Official Journal of the European Union. (2013). Opinion of the European Economic and Social Committee on 'Social farming: Green care and social and health policies' (own-initiative opinion) (2013/C 44/07). Acquired from http://eur-lex.europa.eu on 28 March 2014.

UN. (2014). World urbanization prospects, 2014 Revision. New York. http://www.com-passion.com/multimedia/world-urbanization-prospects.pdf [Retrieved 3 August 2014]

WHO. (2013). The European mental health action plan. Regional Committee for Europe Sixty-third session. EUR/RC63/11. http://www.euro.who.int/__data/assets/pdf_file/0004/194107/63wd11e_MentalHealth-3.pdf [Retrieved 3 August 2014]

Wojtyniak, B. & Goryński, P. (Ed.). (2012). *Sytuacja zdrowotna ludności Polski i jej uwarunkowania*. National Institute of Public Health – National Institute of Hygiene, Warszawa. [Retrieved 3 July 2014]

19 Pilgrimaging and religious tourism in metropolitan areas

Michał Jacenty Sznajder

Since the dawn of time people have been going on pilgrimages to sacred places. The adherents of archaic religions, such as animism or druidism, see the existence of magic powers and spiritual world in animate and inanimate nature. Mountains, seas, lakes, rivers, trees, are full of good and evil spirits. People have been visiting these places of animistic spiritual world and shamans have been facilitating their contact with the after world. Animism is present even among Christians and Muslims. Buryatia and Yakutia in Eastern Siberia are the centres of contemporary animism, but it can be encountered on all continents. Polytheism is the belief in many gods. It developed particularly strongly in ancient Egypt, Hellenic Greece and ancient Rome. Gods dwelled in special places, such as Osiris in the after world, Zeus on Mount Olympus and Hephaistos in Vesuvius. Polytheism attracted crowds of pilgrims to certain places, where it was possible to receive grace from gods or know one's future. Monotheism strengthened the tradition of pilgrimages. It is not surprising to say that pilgrimaging is the oldest form of tourism.

All over the world there are places where people think they can experience a specific form of encounter with God, prophets, saints and gods. Usually these are secluded places: deserts, high mountains, deep forests, wetlands or other desolate areas away from human settlements. We could give numerous examples for each of these locations, such as the mounts Sinai, Hebron or Nebo. When we analyse today's locations of sacred places, we can see that they are either in the city proper city (e.g. Allahabad, Mecca, Guadalupe) or in the metropolitan belt (e.g. the Basilica of Sainte-Anne-de-Beaupré near Quebec City, Shrine of St Maximilian Maria Kolbe next to Warsaw or Canterbury Cathedral in the city of Canterbury, about 70 km southeast of London). We might pose the thesis that 'sacred' locations have the capacity to become a magnet for urbanisation, which means that former desolate religious areas develop urban or even metropolitan structure. Initially all types of religious services develop. Next, we can see the development of transport, medical and services such as hotel, restaurant and catering and the café sector (HORECA) and the production of devotional objects. They are followed by the development of other branches of economy. The case of Cova da Iria proves this thesis. What used to be a pasture is a lively town now. The higher the rank of a pilgrimage destination is, the longer the distance pilgrims travel to reach it. The term 'pilgrimage' comprises a wide range of religious, cognitive, organisational, financial, legal, pedagogical and sociological aspects, which go far beyond the scope of this monograph.

Pilgrimaging and religious tourism are synonymous terms, but they are not identical. A pilgrimage is a trip motivated only or mainly by religious aspects, whereas religious tourism also includes cognitive and recreational purposes. Religious tourism is a broader term than pilgrimaging, which is thought to be the oldest type of tourism, and which is still developing (Kroplewski and Panasiuk 2011, p. 7). This type of tourism is a significant area of interest for representatives of tourism sciences. Although pilgrimaging is usually done for religious reasons, it is also conditioned by numerous personal, family and social motives. Long social and political marches can also be included in this category.

The flow of pilgrims is not equal throughout the year. Some pilgrimage destinations attract people all year round (Mecca, Jasna Góra, Guadalupe, Fatima), though the flow of visitors is the most intense in the summer. Other places are visited only in the summer or on religious holidays. It is justified to pose the thesis that the lower the rank of a shrine, the shorter the distance that pilgrims are prepared to travel to visit it.

Modern pilgrimage tourism additionally includes many other cognitive and recreational elements in its programme. Contrary to some people's opinions, pilgrimaging is not a marginal and disappearing phenomenon, but it is developing dynamically, contributing to the growth of national income and providing employment to local inhabitants. It is estimated that as many as a few hundred million people are involved in pilgrimaging every year, of whom nearly 200 million are Christians. Thus, pilgrimaging is not only a religious phenomenon but it is also an important social and economic phenomenon. Contemporary pilgrimaging uses all possible means of transport, ranging from walking to chartering planes. There are natural and numerous connections between pilgrimaging and religious tourism and nature tourism, ecotourism, rural tourism, agritourism and culinary tourism in metropolitan areas.

As a result of various events that took place in the history of humanity, over the centuries the number of places of worship, which are visited by pilgrims, has been increasing continuously. At present there are bigger and smaller pilgrimage centres scattered all over the world, especially in well-known metropolises. Believers of different religions visit them. Probably pilgrimaging can be observed in all religions all over the world. The followers of world religions visit the following destinations:

- Baha'is: Haifa and Acre in Israel.
- Buddhists: places related with Buddha's life, such as his birthplace in Lumbini, Nepal, his awakening place in Bodh Gaya, the place where he started teaching in Sarnath, and his death place in Kusinara in north-eastern India.
- Hindus: many places related to legendary events involving different Hindu gods; almost any place can be a pilgrimage destination, but these are usually rivers, lakes and mountains. There is a long list of pilgrimage destinations in Hinduism.

- Muslims: Mecca, Medina, Jerusalem, Karbala and Kufa; pilgrimage (al-Hajj) is one of the fundaments of this religion. There are 15 sacred places in Islam and they attract more than 10 million pilgrims a year, including 5 million pilgrims visiting Mecca.
- For Jews, the most important pilgrimage destination is the Western Wall (Wailing Wall) in Jerusalem, which is a remaining fragment of Solomon's Temple. Jews go on pilgrimages to many places all over the world, for example, Chasids visit Lelów in Poland.
- There are also 'lay pilgrimages' to the graves or mausoleums of well-known people who spread different ideologies or to the graves of celebrities, for example, Elvis Presley.
- Christian pilgrimage traffic is especially popular among Catholics (of whom there are nearly 1.2 billion worldwide). It is concentrated around such pilgrimage destinations as Rome and Guadalupe: 12 million visitors each a year, San Giovanni Rotondo: 7 million, Lourdes: 6 million, Fatima: 5 million and Jasna Góra: 4.5 million.

The Holy Land seems to be the world's most important pilgrimage centre. It witnessed the events described in the Old and New Testament. It had different historic names, ranging from the Promised Land, through Canaan, Judea and Samaria, Palestine, up to the contemporary names of political structures, such as, Israel, the Palestinian National Authority and Jordan, and included parts of Syria and Egypt. No matter how broadly we mark the Holy Land area and whatever the name we call it, it will never be precise. There are Jewish, Christian and Muslim pilgrims flowing continuously to the Holy Land from all over the world.

There is an enormous number of pilgrimage centres in Poland. According to Mróz (2011), at the end of 2010 there were more than 800 pilgrimage centres of the Catholic Church in Poland, where Marian shrines were predominant – about 550. There are 97 shrines devoted to Jesus Christ, whereas saints and the blessed are particularly strongly revered in more than 160 centres. Mróz (2011) divides pilgrimage centres into those of international, national, supra-regional, regional and local ranks. The most important pilgrimage centres in Poland are: Jasna Góra, Krakow, Licheń, Kalwaria Zebrzydowska, Wadowice, Niepokalanów, Góra Św. Anny, Trzebnica and Św. Krzyż. Apart from that, there are also Orthodox pilgrimage centres, for example, Grabarka, and Jewish centres, for example, Lelów and Auschwitz.

Religious tourism is very often observed both in submetropolitan and metropolitan areas. Therefore, it is closely related to rural tourism and agritourism. The relation is proved by the examples of pilgrimages at the Hindu festival Kumbh Mela, the Shiite pilgrimage to Karbala and the Christian Way of St James. Nature tourism favours non-agricultural development of rural areas. The closeness of a pilgrimage centre enables the rural community to gain income from services provided to pilgrims. Local inhabitants provide accommodation and prepare meals, offer guided tours, provide car parks, and manufacture and sell souvenirs and religious merchandise. There are numerous examples of the positive influence of pilgrimage centres, pilgrimages and religious tourism on the economic recovery in small towns and villages. Finally, we can look at examples of three extreme pilgrimages in three world religions. The first example refers to Kumbh Mela, a Hindu festival; the second example concerns Arbaeen, a Shiite walking pilgrimage from Basra to Karbala, while the third describes an individual pilgrimage to Santiago de Compostela, usually undertaken by Catholics.

Kumbh Mela: a Hindu festival

The ancient city of Prayag in India is situated at the junction of three sacred rivers, the Ganges, Yamuna and Sarasvati. Later kings renamed it Allahabad (now in Uttar Pradesh State). Hindus believe that it was the place where Brahma, a Hindu god, offered his first sacrifice after he had created the world. Sangam, the confluence of the three rivers, has been a sacred place for centuries. One can see the silty, light yellow waters of the Ganges meeting the green waters of the Yamuna. However, the third river cannot be seen. Some people say that it flows underground, whereas others say that it is a mythical river. At the confluence the Ganges is only 1.2 metres deep, but the Yamuna is as deep as 12 metres. Hindus believe that by taking a bath in that place they can be cleansed of all their sins. The place is the destination of the world's greatest pilgrimage as part of the Kumbh Mela festival. It is considered to be the world's largest congregation of people. It is estimated that in 2013, during the 55 days of this pilgrimage about 100 million people took a ritual bath (Knowledge of India 2005). On 10 February, when the sun is thought to begin its northward journey, there were about 30 million pilgrims. The Kumbh Mela pilgrimage is organised at 3-, 6-, 12- and 144-year cycles. Hindus set a wide range of goals of their pilgrimage, ranging from the remembrance of saints, through spiritual development and the forgiveness of sins, to reflection and contemplation. During the pilgrimage the adherents carry out various activities – eat a special diet, participate in religious rites, make donations, shave their heads, maintain abstinence, listen to teachings and advice and walk around sacred places. Hindus believe that if one makes a pilgrimage to four sacred places during Kumbh Mela, one will be liberated from the cycle of birth and death.

Arbaeen: a Shiite walking pilgrimage from Basra to Karbala

Every year many Shiites go on a pilgrimage from Basra in southern Iraq to Karbala in the central part of the country. There are religious mourning ceremonies in memory of Hussein, who was Muhammad's grandson. He is revered by Muslims as the Prince of Martyrs. He was killed in Karbala on a day which became known as Ashura, the tenth day of the Islamic month of Muharram, having refused to pledge allegiance to the corrupt and tyrannical caliph, Yazid. Shia is a branch of Islam, which is common in Iran, Azerbaijan and Iraq. The Shiites are a minority in other Islamic countries. Over the centuries they have been persecuted and massacred by the Sunni majority and their leaders. Even now the Shiites are victims of organised discrimination. In some Islamic countries like Afghanistan, Bahrain, Iraq, Pakistan and Saudi Arabia they are banned from practising Islam, building mosques or even reading the Quran. This conflict has been going on for nearly 1,400 years and there are no signs of it coming to an end. On the one hand, there are peaceful forces of Shi'ism. On the other hand, there are the belligerent forces of Daesh (ISIS).

The Arbaeen pilgrimage consists of two parts: a trek from Basra to Karbala and a visit to the tomb of Hussein. Today there are specific circumstances affecting the Shia Muslims' pilgrimage to Karbala. The pilgrims are in constant danger of suicide terrorist attacks made by competitive branches of Islam. Thus, on the one hand, it is a political march that takes a few days; on the other hand, it is a religious pilgrimage. Shia claims it is the world's most populous gathering. Not only does the congregation exceed the number of visitors to Mecca, it is more significant than Kumbh Mela. According to Sayed Mahdi al-Modarresi (2014), 'Arbaeen reached twenty million last year [2014] – that is a staggering 60% of Iraq's entire population'. From the tourist point of view, the description of the long trek from Basra to Karbala is the most interesting, as there is an enormous group of nearly 20 million pilgrims walking. Below are fragments of the description of the pilgrimage provided by al-Modarresi (2014).

An avalanche of men, women and children, but most visibly black-veiled women, fill the eye from one end of the horizon to the other. The crowds were so huge that they caused a blockade for hundreds of miles (...)

The 425 mile distance between the southern port city of Basra and Karbala is a long journey by car, but it's unimaginably arduous on foot. It takes pilgrims a full two weeks to complete the walk. People of all age groups trudge in the scorching sun during the day and in bone-chilling cold at night. They travel across rough terrain, down uneven roads, through terrorist strongholds, and dangerous marshlands. Without even the most basic amenities or travel gear, the pilgrims carry little besides their burning love for 'The Master' Hussein. Flags and banners remind them, and the world, of the purpose of their journey.

One part of the pilgrimage which will leave every visitor perplexed is the sight of thousands of tents with makeshift kitchens set up by local villagers who live around the pilgrims' path. The tents (called 'mawkeb') are places where pilgrims get practically everything they need. From fresh meals to eat and a space to rest, to free international phone calls to assure concerned relatives, to baby diapers, to practically every other amenity, free of charge. In fact, pilgrims do not need to carry anything on the 400 mile journey except the clothes they wear.

More intriguing is how pilgrims are invited for food and drink. Mawkeb organisers intercept the pilgrims' path to plead with them to accept their offerings, which often includes a full suite of services fit for kings: first you can get a foot massage, then you are offered a delicious hot meal, then you are invited to rest while your clothes are washed, ironed, then returned to you after a nap. All complimentary, of course.

Everything, including security is provided mostly by volunteer fighters who have one eye on Daesh, and the other on protecting the pilgrims' path.

The Way of St James: pilgrimage routes

Santiago de Compostela is a city in northwestern Spain with a population of about 100,000. Cape Finisterre is situated slightly further west, on the Atlantic Ocean. These are the destinations of the famous pilgrimage route, the Way of St James. The tradition of pilgrimages to St James's grave is more than 1000 years old. St James the Greater was one of the Twelve Apostles of Jesus Christ. He was the first of the Apostles to die as a martyr, when he was beheaded by Herod in Jerusalem in 44 AD. St James spent some time in Spain, where he preached the Gospel. Therefore, his disciples transported his remains to Spain and buried them in Compostela. Later, when Spain was in the hands of the Moors, the grave of the Apostle was completely forgotten. The grave was rediscovered in the ninth century and it became the destination of individual pilgrims from all over Europe. Although the grave of the Apostle was the pilgrims' destination, they went further west to the beaches on Cape Finisterre to collect a shell, which was a proof or a sort of certificate confirming their pilgrimage. Over the centuries there was built a complex system of roads leading to Santiago de Compostela and further, to Cape

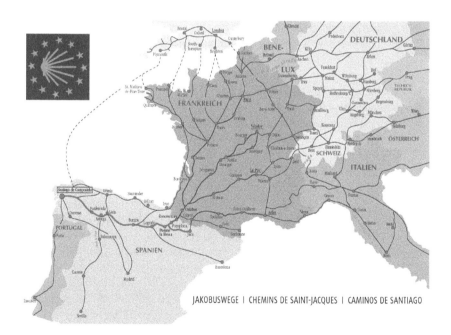

Figure 19.1 The system of St James's pilgrimage routes in western Europe.

Finisterre, from different corners of Spain, Portugal, France, Holland, Belgium, the United Kingdom, Switzerland, Germany, even from as far as Poland, Ukraine and North Africa. The French Way (Camino Frances), which is about 800 km long, is the best developed route.

The routes are described and marked with a characteristic shell logo. Walking for many days or even weeks along the Way of St James is an unforgettable experience where pilgrims encounter nature. The Way of St James is available to individual pilgrims. They can visit churches and chapels on the way and stay for the night at convenient pilgrim hostels or agritourism farms.

References

al-Modarresi, S. M. (2014). World's biggest pilgrimage now underway, and why you've never heard of it! *The Huffington Post*, 24 November. http://www.huffingtonpost.co.uk/sayed-mahdi-almodarresi/arbaeen-pilgrimage_b_6203756.html [Retrieved 8 May 2016]

Knowledge of India. (2005). History of Kumbh Mela : The Largest Human Gathering on Earth http://knowledgeofindia.com/the-kumbh-mela/. [Retrieved 12.02.2017]

Kroplewski, Z. & Panasiuk, A. (2011). Wstęp. *Zeszyty Naukowe Uniwersytetu Szczecińskiego. Ekonomiczne problemy usług.* No. 65. Publisher: Uniwersytet Szczeciński, Szczecin, Poland.

Mróż, F. (2011). Sanktuaria Świętych i błogosławionych w Polsce – zarys problemu. *Zeszyty Naukowe Uniwersytetu Szczecińskiego. Ekonomiczne problemy usług.* No. 66. Publisher: Uniwersytet Szczeciński, Szczecin, Poland, pp. 233–250.

20 Agritourism in Kraków metropolitan areas

A case study

Józef Kania and Małgorzata Bogusz

A case study is an analysis of a particular case, which consists in analysing descriptions of selected, specific events in a particular branch, in this case – the events occurring in rural tourism and agritourism in metropolitan areas. It is based on the analysis of an individual case with a detailed description leading to the conclusion about the causes and results of the course of this case. The knowledge acquired through case analysis enables us to better understand the phenomena which are similar to the phenomenon under analysis and thus, it helps us improve real actions.

As a method of presentation, a case study provides an opportunity to understand in detail how an organisation functions and what dependences there are. It describes creativity, uniqueness, innovativeness and context. It also describes a real-life situation and gives an opportunity to discuss the case and understand specific tasks, relations and processes, so it provides answers to a wide range of questions, such as: how, when and why.

Case study method: according to Nowak (2012, p. 21), the case study is treated as a research method

> where the researcher attempts to provide a possibly comprehensive description of a particular community or individual, including a wide range of variables. The researcher is interested both in the value of the variables and in the dependences between them. The research object has individual character. The researcher starts investigations without initial hypotheses and intends to investigate the phenomenon in detail in its real context ....

The essence of the case study method is that it includes a holistic approach to the observation, reconstruction and analysis of the phenomena under study. Apart from that, it enables inclusion of the 'actor's' view into the study (Zonabend 1992). The case study method does not require a specific minimum number of cases or randomisation. The researcher works on the situation presented in the case study. The case study method may consider an individual case or a multiple case. As far as the latter is concerned, this means that there was replication of the study based on specially selected cases rather than on a sample selection. When replication is impossible, the researcher is limited to the analysis of an individual case.

Yin (2003, p. 10) notes that the generalisation of the results of an individual case analysis or multiple case analysis is used to develop theories, but it is not referred to a population. The results of a multiple case study will be more reliable methodologically if they have been replicated by pattern-matching. This means that the explanation of a case study must closely match the facts it is supposed to explain and various implications that can be drawn from the study. Thus, the descriptive and predictive power of the theory resulting from the study becomes stronger.

To sum up, we can say that the case study is a summary or synthesis describing real-life situations or events on the basis of investigations, analyses and data collected. The task of the case study is to provide information and experience to the people who are not involved in the situation described.

The aim of the case study is not to encourage people to copy the existing models or to set best practice universal standards. The case study should provide support to practitioners and encourage them to seek appropriate solutions to the specific situation in which they have to act and make use of other people's experience and considerations (Hurrell *et al.* 2010). This method can be used to make a detailed description of the best agritourism farms representing different types of farms.

A case study might have the following aims:

- to create a situation in which students have to make a decision on the basis of a critical analysis of data;
- to look at real rather than theoretical examples of other people's activities,
- to draw conclusions which are significant to one's own undertakings;
- to show concepts which are worth copying;
- to indicate potential mistakes to be avoided;
- to gather described experience so as to avoid stress in the future, to avoid copying somebody else's mistake or even to apply proven solutions.

It is necessary to stress the fact that the aim of case studies, including the ones presented in this chapter, is not to encourage people to copy the existing solutions or to set best practice universal standards. Case studies should provide support to practitioners and encourage them to seek appropriate solutions to the specific situation in which they have to act and make use of other people's experience and considerations.

Krakow: a metropolitan centre in the Krakow agglomeration

The Krakow agglomeration comprises the central city of Krakow and the surrounding urbanised communes, including Wieliczka, where the agritourism farm under study is located. The number of inhabitants in the agglomeration ranges from 1 million to 1.4 million, depending on the concept and assumed area delimitation criteria. Krakow (Latin: *Cracovia*, German: *Krakau*) situated in southern Poland on the River Vistula. It is the second most populated city with the second largest area in Poland [Population, size and structure by territorial division 2008]. Krakow was the capital of Poland and a coronation city. It is a necropolis of the kings of Poland. It is one of the oldest Polish cities, with more than one-thousand-year history and numerous valuable examples of architecture and many cultural institutions with collections of priceless monuments. The city is also an administrative, educational, scientific, economic, service-providing and tourism centre.

In 2000 Krakow was listed among the five most popular cities in Europe. In 2007 it was named 'the most fashionable city in the world', according to Orbitz, an American Internet agency setting trends in global tourism (Kursa and Romanowski 2006).

In 2012 nearly 9 million people visited Krakow, including 2.35 million foreign tourists, who chiefly came from the United Kingdom, Germany, Italy, France, Spain and Russia. The number of tourists has been increasing systematically since 2003 (5.5 million people) (PAP 2012). In the last decade there has been increasing significance of religious tourism, pilgrimages, tourists following the Jewish culture and congress tourism (www.krakow.pl 2014). Tourists are also very interested in Lesser Poland Voivodeship (region), with the capital in Krakow. It is visited by 14.5 per cent of the total number of tourists spending their holidays in Poland. It is the second most visited voivodeship, following West Pomeranian Voivodeship.

The Amigówka: an agritourism farm

> If you have come here, you must know why Krakow and Wieliczka are worth visiting, but after the effort of sightseeing you might like to relax in a terrace, on the grass or in a gazebo, have a bonfire or feel the warmth of a fireplace. That's why it's a good idea to stay at the Amigówka. That's where you can breathe fresh air in the countryside. Our house is at the end of the village – there are only meadows and woods further. Roe deer and pheasants make themselves feel at home in our garden.

This is how Piotr, who is the farm owner, uses his website to welcome visitors who would like to relax at the Amigówka. The agritourism facility Amigówka is a settlement located in the village of Mietniów, at the Wieliczka Foothills, the first heights in the Carpathians, 18 km from Main Market Square in Krakow and only 4 km from the centre of Wieliczka. Piotr is the owner of the Amigówka. Since 2011 he has been running this agritourism business with his daughter. Piotr is a qualified guide and courier. He has great experience in tourism, having gained his experience working in his profession and attending trainings in rural tourism and agritourism, which were organised by the local action group: Wieliczka Countryside.

As he stresses, as far back as a few years ago he did not realise that there was a place like Mietniów. He was charmed by the place and he decided to buy a 4.3 ha farm. There used to be an old house made of wicker and thatch in the place where the Amigówka is located now. The original house was pulled down and a simple, wooden house made from pine logs was built in its place. Experience in agritourism, cooperation with local tourism organisations, the location of the farm near

Figure 20.1 Agritourism house.
Source: Fotolia.com © helmutvogler.

the metropolitan centre – Krakow with about 760,000 inhabitants and Wieliczka with 21,000 inhabitants – and the willingness to gain new experience were the main factors which influenced the owner and his daughter to start running a farm and receiving tourists in 2011. The owner started his agritourism activity at the Amigówka by offering 2 rooms for rent. Later he used financial aid from the European Union to furnish another 3 rooms. At present there are 5 guestrooms with 12 beds on the farm. There is a double bedroom, kitchen, bathroom and living room with a fireplace and 4 beds on the lower ground floor. On the upper ground floor there are 2 bedrooms (with 2 or 3 beds), a bathroom and a kitchenette. There is a big terrace, partly covered with a roof, overlooking the south and there is a rural gazebo to the east. There are several hectares of meadows and woods around the house. There is an independent entrance to both floors of the house.

The price of beds ranges from 40 zlotys per night in the summer to about 50 zlotys per night in the winter season and at Christmas time (in 2014). The prices vary depending on the time of one's stay on the farm, and are lower for visitors staying longer than 4 days. The host of the Amigówka also provides board to his guests. He usually serves breakfast and sometimes dinner. As he stressed in the interview, guests do not have lunch on the farm, because they spend the whole day away from the farm, visiting Krakow and the surrounding areas. The owner cooperates with different organic farms, which provide products that he serves to his guests.

Figure 20.2 Old-time farmhouse.
Source: Fotolia.com © ermess.

The area of the farm is 4.3 ha. There are only extensively used meadows and a multi-fruit orchard on the farm. Piotr cooperates with beekeepers and lets them use the flowery meadows.

All year round the farm offers rooms for rent to Polish and foreign tourists, who usually come to visit Krakow and Wieliczka. As Piotr stresses, this was the reason why the Amigówka was established – to cater for tourists coming to visit Krakow and the surrounding areas. This is why the close proximity of the metropolitan centre is so important. Foreign visitors come to see Krakow and Wieliczka and they are the chief consumers of agritourism services (90%). They come from almost all countries around the world.

The owner says: 'We do not receive many tourists, but those who visit us usually become our friends, because this is the Amigówka, that is, a friendly place'. It is noteworthy that pets are welcome on the farm – tourists have arrived with their dogs, cats or even with a parrot which once came with guests from Germany. It is important to note that the farm does not offer any additional services. However, the owner closely cooperates with local institutions, for example: the Local Action Group (LAG) Wieliczka Countryside, Galician Guest Farms, Friends of Wieliczka Club, the Wieliczka Tourist Organisation and the Wieliczka Rural Housewives' Section. As a result of this cooperation a wide range of additional services are provided.

Piotr is a member of the LAG Wieliczka Countryside. As a result of cooperation with the group they developed the following six tourism packages under the common name 'Wieliczka Wins!':

- Package I: The town of Wieliczka – an uphill route;
- Package II: Mehoffer in Jankówka and Kantor in Hucisko;
- Package III: The Morsztyns – following the footsteps of the Arians in Wieliczka;
- Package IV: Dancing Rural Wieliczka;
- Package V: Sculpture workshop;
- Package VI: The flavours of Wieliczka.

All these packages are offered by the Amigówka agritourism farm in cooperation with the LAG Wieliczka Countryside and the Amigo Tourist travel agency.
 The Amigówka also offers additional services:

- guided tours of Krakow, Wieliczka, Niepołomice, Dobczyce and Bochnia lasting a few hours;
- sightseeing tours of the house of Tadeusz Kantor (an outstanding Polish artist) in Hucisko;
- booking of tickets to the salt mine in Wieliczka, to concerts, performances and events in Krakow and Wieliczka;
- culinary workshops;
- holidays for elderly people;
- accommodation, board and transport for visitors to the Spa Salt Mine in Wieliczka.

The rich offer of tourism services and regular cooperation with local institutions resulted in the owner making 80 per cent of his income from the tourism business. It is his main source of income at the moment. Only 10 per cent of his income comes from farming and the same amount from casual work. In spite of the fact that the farm is oriented towards tourism, it is not categorised. However, the high standard of services provided by the farm and good promotion provide new clients for the owner. Tourists staying on the farm who are satisfied with the standard of services are the best promotion, because they recommend this charming place to others. Apart from that, Piotr promotes his farm and region by taking part in tourism fairs. As he says, most clients make reservations on the Internet sites Booking.com and Airbnb, chiefly being guided by positive opinions about the Amigówka farm that they read at these websites.
 As far as cooperation with local societies is concerned, Piotr stressed the considerable role of the Local Action Group Wieliczka Countryside in the development of agritourism in the entire Wieliczka region. He also stressed the activity of the Friends of Wieliczka Club, which makes monthly presentations of the tourism potential in Wieliczka and shows how to use it. As far as agritourism activity is concerned, there is only one farm providing such services in the village of

Mietniów, that is, the Amigówka. There are three agritourism farms in the commune and five farms in Wieliczka County. Piotr emphasises the fact that, despite the few agritourism farms in the region, they cooperate with each other regularly. In the interview Piotr also pointed to the convenient location of the Amigówka to nearby Krakow and Wieliczka, which is of primary importance for this type of agritourism activity. However, what is absolutely decisive to success is the fact that the Amigówka is not only an oasis of peace but it is also a place of friendly meetings, where the door is always open to visitors.

All the information in this case study comes from the interview with the owner and from the text uploaded on the website of the farm (Amigówka Farm n.d.).

References

Amigówka Farm. (n.d.). Welcome page. http://amigowka.pl/ [Retrieved 4 August 2014]

Hurrell, S., Hussain-Khaliq, S. & Tyson, R. (2010). *Studium przypadku – Poradnik* [Case Study Project] Studia przypadku współpracy partnerskiej jako instrument zmian. Fundacja Partnerstwo dla Środowiska, Kraków. English version – http://thepartnering-initiative.org/research-and-learning-2/case-study-project/ Polish version – http://www.fpds.pl/media/filemanager/publikacje/partnerstwo/studia_przypadku.pdf [Retrieved 15 May 2012]

Kursa, M. & Romanowski, R. (2006). Kraków najmodniejszym miastem Świata. Publisher *Gazeta Wyborcza*, 2006.

Nowak, S. (2012). *Metodologia badań socjologicznych*. Publisher: Wydawnictwo Naukowe PWN, Warszawa.

PAP. (2012). Kraków odwiedzi 9 mln turystów w 2012 roku. www.propertynews.pl [Retrieved 4 September 2014]

Population, size and structure by territorial division. (2008). Central Statistical Office, Warszawa

Yin, R. K. (2003). *Case study research: Design and methods*. Sage, Thousand Oaks., California.

Zonabend, F. (1992). The monograph in European ethnology. *Current Sociology*, 40(1), pp. 49–60.

21 A pedagogical and psychological exegesis of tourism

Andrzej Kusztelak

Terminology

Every year millions of people leave their places of permanent residence and take holiday trips. Sometimes they travel to different countries around the world, being encouraged by colourful offers of travel agencies, audio-visual commercial spots and other forms of marketing. Sometimes they travel to selected places in their own country and sometimes they visit their family and friends living in the country. Thus, a question arises why some of them choose a quiet holiday at the seaside, on a lake or in a forest where they can enjoy the beauty of nature in their homeland, whereas others plunge into social life in attractive and fashionable resorts in their country or abroad and yet others travel around their country and the world seeking risk and adventure. What attracts the people who return to the same places every year like proverbial birds of passage? What makes others choose new, unknown places every year?

It is impossible to provide definite answers to any of these questions because each beneficiary of a holiday trip has their own, subjective hierarchy of values in this respect.

Free time, holiday, travel, tourist expeditions, exercise and recreation, relaxation, leisure are areas of scientific reflection comprising a broad spectrum of terms, phenomena and processes. Some people/researchers claim that these areas are subject to freedom and optionality of choice or, as others indicate, these are obligatory actions, which are alternative to the daily routine. Due to the changing reality of modern-day life, physical recreation and exercise result from the need to adopt a specific, balanced and healthy lifestyle. At the same time, considerate and proper planning of one's leisure chiefly results from the fundamental precepts of ecology and psychophysical hygiene (Kwilecka 2006).

Tourism is one of these areas of human activity which are at a stage of great confusion or even amorphousness. It is even possible to completely agree with the thesis posed by Krzysztof Przecławski, who said that after 1989 the popularity of tourism in Poland could be described with the term 'touristification' (Przecławski 1997).

As we concentrate on the concept of tourism in this elaboration, we should be aware of an extremely broad range of meanings, which sometimes renders us helpless. The variety of situations in which the term 'tourism' is used in the media and especially in colloquial speech, not excluding the definition developed by the United

Nations World Tourism Organisation (UNWTO), makes the term very blurred, indefinite and incompatible with its range of meanings. When we take these facts into consideration, we can even observe that many experts on tourism and touring do not pay so much attention to this or other terms used in this field of knowledge. However, from the pedagogical point of view, it is necessary to have some definitions ordering the knowledge due to the increasing penetration of tourism and touring into the didactic and educational theory and practice (Denek, 2012 p. 120).

The terms 'tourism' and 'tourist' became popular only in the nineteenth century. It is assumed that the term 'tourism' was first introduced into literature by Marie-Henri Beyle (Stendhal) in his book titled *Memoirs of a Tourist* published in 1838 (Kulczycki 1977, p. 18). The tourist described in the title is a young man who tries to find the sense of his life while travelling. The term 'tourism' appeared in Polish when it was used by Xawery Łukaszewski (in Denek 2012, p. 120). Several decades later the term 'tourism' was entered into a well-known encyclopaedia of the French Academy, where its author, E. Littre, defined it as 'a trip made out of curiosity and to kill time' (Libera 1969, p. 183). The professional literature often quotes the definition of tourism formulated by Walter Hunziker and Kurt Krapf, which is now a classic. According to the definition, tourism is 'the whole of relations and phenomena resulting from strangers' travelling and staying as long as it does not involve permanent settlement or commercial activity' (quoted in Winiarski and Zdebski 2008, p. 14). The definitions of tourism have been changing continuously as the phenomenon has been evolving. Therefore, the holistic approach seems to be the most justified, at least due to the fact that, in general, everybody is right because tourism may mean something different to every person. Krzysztof Przecławski's position is a weighty approach to the essence of the problem. He considered tourism to be an interdisciplinary, psychological, social, spatial, economic and cultural phenomenon (Przecławski 1997, p. 31). Thus, the factor distinguishing a real tourist is his or her deliberate activity undertaken for 'the very pleasure of travelling with due consideration of the aims to satisfy his or her needs and aspirations' (Winiarski and Zdebski 2008, p. 15).

The term 'tourist' will be interpreted as a person for whom the trip and staying away from the place of their permanent residence are more important than their consequences. Thus, it is the subjective assessment and the willingness to be a tourist that matter rather than formal criteria. This approach clearly emphasises the inner mechanisms of the activity and the mental processes which accompany the activity. Simultaneously, these processes and mechanisms focus on changes in the personality and relations with other people in a local community. This approach to tourism lets us treat it as an activity with subjective, humanistic character.

It is necessary to define the terms 'recreation' and 'free time' in our considerations. These terms are specifically interrelated. Free time can be defined in two ways: first quantitatively, that is, it is part of the daily time budget which remains after all one's occupational and non-occupational duties have been done and after the basic needs of one's organism have been satisfied; and second qualitatively, that is, it is the time which is at one's disposal for one's enjoyment and satisfaction (Pięta 2008, pp. 11–12). One of the precursors of free-time pedagogy and the author of the canonical definition of free time, Joffre Dumazedier, a French sociologist, lists three basic functions of this time: leisure, entertainment and development (Dumazedier 1962, p. 26; Czerepaniak-Walczak 2011, p. 222). In relation to this concept of free time some authors see the term 'recreation' as various 'forms of activities undertaken besides all duties for relaxation, entertainment and self-improvement' (Demel and Humen 1970, p. 7).

From the perspective of the humanities it is important that recreation should be treated as a human activity which satisfies one's needs and aspirations and which provides entertainment and relaxation on the one hand, and premises for the development of one's personality on the other. Recreation should be treated both as a

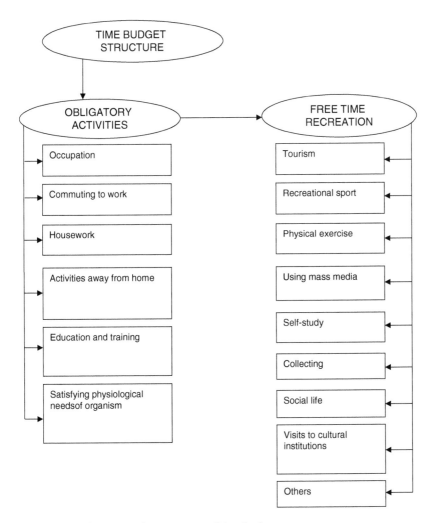

Figure 21.1 The structural components of time budget.

Source: The author's compilation.

psycho-pedagogical phenomenon due to the experiences it provides and as a social phenomenon, which is set in a particular place and time in the historical and cultural context. Figure 21.1 shows the relationship between free time and recreation.

When we classify recreational activities, we should remember that it is one's subjective assessment rather than the form of these activities that is decisive to their recreational character. The same activity may be done voluntarily in a specific situation and thus it can be a form of recreation, whereas in a different situation it will be an obligatory activity and it will be treated as one's occupation.

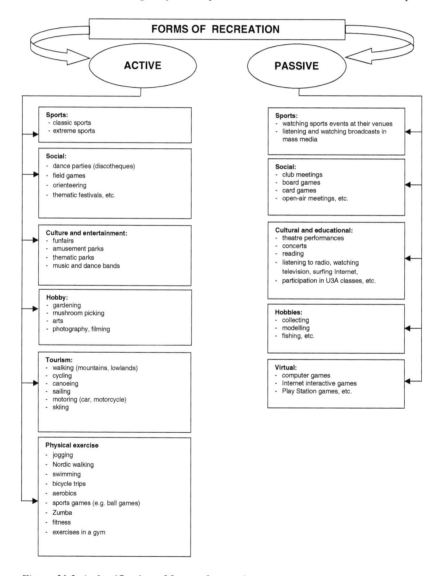

Figure 21.2 A classification of forms of recreation.

Source: The author's compilation based on Winiarski 2011, p. 16.

In view of this suggestion we can adopt the following classification of forms of recreation, as can be seen in Figure 21.2.

Tourism, free time and recreation from the pedagogical perspective

Reflection upon time, its essence and axiological dimension is an intrinsic element of human awareness. The duality of time as an effect and as a factor of culture is particularly noticeable in upbringing, especially in the perspective of its evaluation.

Time management is a factor that affects the personality of an individual and the human community. Last century 'time became a commodity', Denek (2006, p. 121) stated, and therefore it is necessary to manage it rationally. Thus, the inclusion of time into the field of pedagogical reflection and consideration and didactic practice became the natural consequence of seeking and updating the conditions of intentional, individual development and transformations in social life (Czerepaniak-Walczak 2011, p. 201). This issue will also be an important premise in the development of metropolitan areas. Considering the categories of interdisciplinary social needs and conditions of the development of the entire metropolitan area is an important problem in the formation of the metropolitan area.

Discovering and experiencing educational benefits resulting from different forms of free time is a significant task for pedagogues and educators. At present nobody doubts the fact that free time is an area of an individual's life that is mostly influenced by personal needs, dispositions, habits, patterns of conduct and that it affects other areas and is influenced by them (Zawadzka and Ferenz 1998, p. 11).

The personality-developing potential of free time with all its possible forms of use makes it an important subject of pedagogy as a science focusing on intentionally organised conditions for personal development and social change. If an individual induces permanent and desirable changes in the personalities of the people subordinated to this individual in consequence of social interactions and deliberate actions, this effect can be regarded as a process of education. The education of a human within their lifetime is the subject of pedagogy in broad terms. However, we need to be aware of the fact that pedagogy encompasses a wide range of definitions of education, which emphasise different aspects of the entire process of education. Stefan Kunowski gathered all these definitions into four groups: praxeological, evolutionary, situational and adaptive (Kunowski 2000, pp. 167–168).

In order to better position tourism from a pedagogical perspective we will recount only two specific definitions of education. Roman Schultz considers education to be a planned human activity, whose aim is to achieve specific goals, that is, concrete, desirable and permanent changes in human personality (Schultz 2011, in Jaworska and Leppert 2011, p. 253).

We can also find it useful to recount the interpretation of education provided by Heliodor Muszyński. He defined education as controlling the processes of socialisation and enculturation and teaching an individual to comply with the aims of developing specific personality-related dispositions (Muszyński 1988; Łobocki 2003, p. 34).

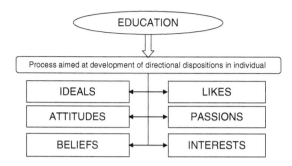

Figure 21.3 The structure of the process of education.

Source: The author's compilation.

Following these premises, we can assume that the aim of the process of education is to develop specific directional dispositions in an individual, which are desirable from the social point of view. Figure 21.3 shows a graphic representation of this approach to the process of education.

The aim of human education is to support the development of an individual's personality. The process of education is intentional. In the aspect of practical educational activity this boils down to the accomplishment of specific goals. As far as education is concerned, these aims are usually derived from the ideal of education. The adoption of a specific ideal, that is, a full description of human integrated traits, which are valuable from the point of view of the interest of society or groups, involves the choice of methods and measures.

Without going into detailed consideration of the concepts of ideal education, which can be found in the theory of education, we can take full responsibility for our reasoning and assume that a human educated at the beginning of the twenty-first century can coexist with other people, respects other people' belief systems, people, their products and the natural environment where they live. When we indicate the characteristics of a human whose education standard meets the requirements of contemporary times, we can define them in a language of attitudes, that is, an individual's relatively stable and consistent cognitive, emotional, motivational and behavioural organisation of attitudes towards particular objects or classes of objects (Mądrzycki 1977, p. 18). To be more specific, an educated human has internalised desirable attitudes towards:

- supreme values (ideological attitudes);
- society, where they live and work (social attitudes);
- themselves (intrapersonal attitudes);
- other people with whom they interact (interpersonal attitudes);
- personal life and finding their own way of life (existential attitudes);
- cultural goods and national heritage (attitudes towards culture);
- the natural environment on a global and local scale (attitudes towards nature).

Bearing in mind the abovementioned list of attitudes, which encompass the content of our lives, we can notice that the entire course of human life is the time of complementarity of obligatory and voluntary activities. It is the time of mutual diffusion of duties and leisure activities, starting with children's games, through school education, youth interests, adult hobbies and ending with the passions of retired people (at their third or even fourth age). The right to free time must not be limited by one's intellectual or physical condition, one's state of mind, energy or health. 'As far as these people are concerned, the management of free time for education is of particular importance, not only in the sense of recreation and entertainment but also compensation and therapy' (Czerepaniak-Walczak 2011, p. 216).

This interpretation of pedagogy of free time in its broad sense fulfils different functions, where the following 4 functions are of particular importance: descriptive, interpretative, explanatory, and teleological and designing.

The *descriptive* function expresses itself in making pictures illustrating the subject of this pedagogy. The fulfilment of this function boils down to examining free-time budgets, the content of activities which fill this time, forms of organisation and the entire institutional structure which enables spending free time. The *interpretative* function of pedagogy of free time consists in giving meanings to facts, phenomena and the contexts of their occurrence. The *explanatory* function leads to understanding why the existing facts and phenomena adopt this rather than another form of free time. The last function, the *teleological and designing* function, has evident axiological premises. The following 2 perspectives can be observed in this function:

- education *for free time*, rational management of free time, effective realisation of the functions of free time to one's own benefit and to the benefit of the environment;
- education *in free time*, that is, in educational situations which are characterised by their voluntary and non-commercial nature, and which are the source of subjective satisfaction (during weekends and holidays) (Czerepaniak-Walczak 2011, pp. 228–229).

The aims of education for free time and in free time are integrally related to the concept of the education ideal. However, due to the specific character of the educational process itself it is possible to distinguish such directional dispositions that can be most effectively developed in free time. The dispositions include: independence, creativity, responsibility, finding the limits of one's capacity, courage, prudence, and so forth. All these qualities can be developed in all environments in human life: in one's family, at home and school, in peer group or social group. The local environment plays an important role in education for free time and in education in free time, because there are specific patterns and traditions of free-time behaviours and there is a specific infrastructure which enables one to realise individual functions of free time.

Because there are numerous traps and dangers connected with spending free time, there is a widespread sense of deficit of free time and – due to the personal and collective consequences of the increase in the deficit and to the fact that free time is usually filled by mass media, chiefly by television and the Internet – it is a problem of particular concern that people, especially the young generation, should be prepared for rational management of free time.

Tourism, free time and recreation in the psychological perspective

In the analysis of the pedagogical aspects of recreational activity there was strong emphasis on the role of deliberately organised social activity based on interactions between the educator and pupil, where the aim is to induce changes in the pupil's personality according to the plan. Personality is also a primary area of interest in psychology. Therefore, let us have a look at recreational activity and activity from the perspective of another important social science.

The genesis and development of the term 'personality' creates the situation where it is still used with different meanings. What is the relation between human personality and recreational activity? This important question must be preceded at least with a short theoretical reflection. Personality is a complex of relatively stable qualities and inner mechanisms with which a person is different from other people and which have influence on the organisation of one's behaviours, that is, they have influence on stability in one's acquisition and ordering of knowledge, skills and experience, on emotional reactions in interactions with other people and on stability in one's choice of goals and values.

At present neither psychologists nor pedagogues are unanimous about a compact and closed structure of personality. As personality is regarded as a complex of individual human traits, which are both inherited and acquired in the process of education, internal and external personalities are often distinguished (Pięta 2008, p. 191).

Przecławski correctly states that tourism itself is a psychological phenomenon, because it is a permanent and increasingly important element in the structure of contemporary people's needs (Przecławski 1997, p. 31). It is the human that is the most important in tourism, because as a being who is capable of thinking, feeling, learning, creativity and making choices the human is the subject of travelling. Humans feel the need to travel, they are motivated to do so, they have specific aims related to travelling and there is always a relationship between travelling and their system of values (among others, Shepard 1988). Thus, we have strongly emphasised such structural components of personality as motives, needs and attitudes, which undoubtedly belong to the internal personality.

To sum up this analysis as a premise for further reflection, we can assume that the components of internal personality will be significant elements presenting the role of personality in the field of tourism. Pięta (2008, p. 192) included these 6 components of internal personality: motives, needs, attitudes, values, temperament and intelligence.

We shall focus our attention on 3 selected components only: motives, needs and attitudes.

The problem of *motivation* is one of the most important problems concerning tourism activity. According to Wiesław Łukaszewski, the theory of motivation describes all mechanisms which are responsible for triggering, directing, sustaining and ending one's behaviour. This applies to the mechanism of simple and complex behaviours, to internal and external mechanisms, as well as to affective and cognitive mechanisms (Łukaszewski 2000, p. 427).

What causes the decision to start a tourism activity? According to the aforementioned interpretation, it is motives that are decisive to the causes of human behaviour, direction of activity and the degree of determination in pursuit of one's goals. Motives are very clearly accounted for by the theories of motivation: theories of instinct, theories of attitudes/personality, drive/learning theories, theories of development and self-improvement, humanistic theories and cognitive theories (Franken 2005, pp. 24–44).

Each human is born with a certain set of *needs*, which are modified through learning processes. Abraham Maslow's hierarchy of needs is a particularly important and useful theory for the analysis of human tourism behaviours. The theory distinguishes deficit needs and development needs. Each tourism trip involves changes in the daily routine and social environment and it provides opportunities to experience things and have different impressions. At the same time, it might be a source of strong emotional experience.

Maslow's concept also provides a theoretical basis for tourism to be treated as an activity where people can achieve self-accomplishment. The values humans adopt direct their personalities and designate the sense of their lives (Maslow 1990, p. 154–159).

The theory of needs was used by theoreticians of tourism to classify the motives for travelling. Przecławski developed an interesting classification in this area. It includes the following 9 categories of motives for tourist trips:

- the willingness to go to a particular place in one's own country or abroad;
- the willingness to leave one's place of permanent residence for a short time;
- the willingness to strike up a new acquaintance;
- the willingness to spend a particular period of time with a close member of family or friends away from one's place of permanent residence;
- the willingness to comply with the stereotypes and standards in one's environment;
- satisfying one's emotional and aesthetic needs;
- satisfying one's creative needs;
- satisfying one's biological needs;
- following tourism as such because of the diversity of goals (Przecławski 1996, following: Winiarski and Zdebski 2008, pp. 50–51).

The genesis of tourism activity should be sought in human innate propensities for exploration and domination of the natural environment, which resulted from human's need to struggle for survival (Franken 2005). In contemporary times tourism activity has chiefly been based on the imitation ritual. In consequence, this has become a civilisation standard.

Apart from motives and needs, some reflection upon *attitude* cannot be ignored as part of the explanation of people's tourism activity. The concept of attitude is an ambiguous term, because it is used in different fields of science. Psychology uses different approaches in order to classify attitudes. A major classifications was based on the attitude factor, which is predominant in a particular concept. According to this rule, the concepts of attitudes can be divided into 5 main groups (Mądrzycki 1977, pp. 16–17). These concepts:

- see the essence of attitude in the cognitive factor;
- regard feelings as the most significant element of an attitude;
- stress the evaluative factor;
- consider motives to be the substantial element of an attitude;
- consider behavioural reactions to be the main element of an attitude.

However, the holistic approach seems to be justified, where personality is perceived in the aspect of the relation between the human and outer world. Therefore, in our considerations of the relationship between the subject and object we will interpret attitude as a relatively stable organisation of the subject's knowledge, beliefs, feelings, motives, certain forms of action and expressive reactions related to a particular object or a class of objects, where this organisation was developed in the process of satisfying one's needs under specific social conditions (Mądrzycki 1977, p. 20). In other words, attitude is a permanent predisposition to be motivated by something (Newcomb *et al.* 1970, p. 61).

Because all motivational processes also encompass an individual's feelings, thinking, perception and behaviour, we can say that attitude always involves a certain state of readiness for experiencing the relationship of feelings, thinking, perception and behaviour towards a particular object or state of the matter, which is defined as the object of this attitude.

When we consider an individual's activity in the aspect of tourism, it is necessary to note the attitude towards nature, that is, the love of the beauty of nature, respecting all aspects of the life of the fauna and flora, rational use of nature, taking care of the natural environment, and so forth, as well as the attitude towards the world of culture and national heritage, for example, an attitude with respect for cultural values, creative cultural expression, perception of works of culture and such like.

When we indicate specific attitudes, it is necessary to remember that each of them can be characterised by such traits as: the content of the object, its range, direction, strength, complexity, permanence and position in the system of attitudes (Mądrzycki 1977, pp. 27–30).

Summary

When we describe the situations which may be experienced by a person undertaking different forms of recreational activity, it is necessary to remember that there are always specific time, environmental and social conditions of this activity. Therefore, contemporary recreational activity encompasses the aforementioned various forms of activity and for broad public opinion it may be the object of evaluation and development of interest. All these external, situational dimensions of recreation closely interact with all components of the subject's internal

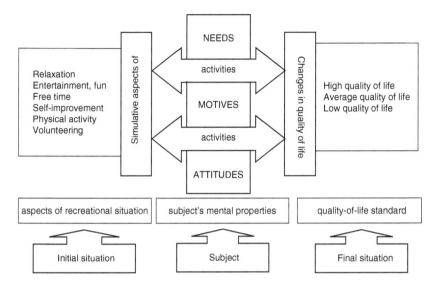

Figure 21.4 An interactive model of the activity.

Source: The author's compilation based on Winiarski 2011, p. 192.

personality. Well-integrated mental properties of a person undertaking a recreational activity and appropriate interaction with the situational conditions of recreation will be decisive to the final recreational effect, that is, to the sense of increased quality of life of the person undertaking the recreational activity. The interactions in recreational activity are fully illustrated in Figure 21.4.

An example of a event from an axiological perspective

Given the different location of the areas of supply and demand for tourism activity, they can generally be separated into 2 types of autonomous regions. The first of them will be metropolitan touring area, which is formed in surroundings of large cities and big urban agglomerations as a natural, nearest to them relaxing (leisure) areas particularly suitable for daily, weekends or longer period of vacation. The second type is tourism of the peripheral region, or the entire suburban area. Note, however, that the demand for suburban recreation is becoming an important driving force for development of tourism in the metropolitan region. Both these types of tourism can powerfully affect the structural components of the inner personality. Described below is an example of such a tourism offer in the metropolitan area as well as in a peripheral areas from an axiological perspective: an expedition trail in Poznań and the Wielkopolska Region.

Following the monuments of technology in Greater Poland

Subject of event: The knowledge of an average inhabitant of Greater Poland about the industrial heritage in this region is minimal. Old structures, machines, appliances and technological production lines are very rarely found in the register of monuments. As a result, they are not protected by law and they are usually in a state of decay. There are chiefly monuments related to agriculture in Greater Poland, such as: sugar factories, mills, breweries, slaughterhouses, distilleries, dairies and brickyards. There are also old gasworks, railway stations with interesting architecture, roundhouses, water towers, narrow-gauge railways and interesting bridges. Some of them have been restored and therefore they are worth seeing.

Route 1: Poznań–Szreniawa–Jaracz

Didactic aims: the following places are worth visiting:

- Poznań: the Old Brewery (remains of old elements integrated into a new shopping, business and cultural complex), the Cegielski Factory (a 1924 traction engine, Hipolit Cegielski's office), the Gasworks (the water gas house, power plant, filter hall and boiler room), the Automobile Museum (about 40 vehicles, a collection of unique parts, accessories and souvenirs), the City Transport Museum (old trams and buses, uniforms, ticket validators, seats, a ticket machine, timetables, a mock-up of the Poznań Fast Tramway).
- Szreniawa: the National Museum of Agriculture and Agri-Food Industry (an 1895 traction engine, presentations showing the history of bread production, oil extraction and milk processing; tools used in pottery, carpentry, saddlery, blacksmithing, cooperage, weaving and tanning).
- Jaracz: the Museum of the History of Milling and Water Appliances in the Rural Industry (the mill on the Wełna River, where one can learn about the whole process of flour production, and monuments related to grain processing).

Educational aims:

- learning about the history of development of the region;
- learning about the inventors of modern technological solutions;
- developing local patriotism;
- developing respect for work;
- learning about rural life in previous times and learning about the job of a farmer and other jobs;
- developing respect for national heritage.

Route 2: Sielinko–Rakoniewice–Wolsztyn–Śmigiel

Didactic aims: the following places are worth visiting:

- Sielinko: the Meat Industry Museum (appliances used in the meat industry, guild banners, documents, wagons for animal transport, refrigeration compressors).

- Rakoniewice: the Greater Poland Firefighting Museum (heavy equipment and fire engines, a collection of uniforms, helmets, medals, banners, posters, books).
- Wolsztyn: the Roundhouse (about 30 steam locomotives, including the 'Beautiful Helen' made in the 1930s, draisines [small, light rail vehicles], carriages, railway accessories, uniforms, ticket offices).
- Śmigiel: the gasworks (all the gasworks equipment, a collection of gas meters and gas lamps).

Educational aims:

- learning about the old technological infrastructure in the Greater Poland region and about its role in the industrialisation of Poland;
- learning about the history of selected walks of life in Poland from the perspective of the quality of life;
- developing pride and respect for people's intellectual and organisational efforts in previous times;
- developing local patriotism;
- developing cognitive inquisitiveness.

Route 3: Jarocin–Nowe Skalmierzyce–Kalisz–Opatówek–Zbiersk–Turek–Kłodawa

Didactic aims: the following places are worth visiting:

- Jarocin: the train station;
- Nowe Skalmierzyce: the train station;
- Kalisz: Stone Bridge from 1825;
- Opatówek: the Industrial History Museum, the 1824 iron bridge,
- Zbiersk: the sugar factory;
- Turek: weavers' houses and the Weaving Museum located in the nineteenth century Town Hall;
- Kłodawa: the salt mine, walking along the Underground Tourist Route.

Educational, aims:

- developing respect for the work of salt miners and weavers;
- developing local patriotism;
- developing respect for the contribution of the towns and villages in Greater Poland to the social development of the region and country;
- developing cultural sensitivity;
- developing cognitive inquisitiveness.

Route 4: along the Noteć River, Czarnków

Didactic aims: the following places are worth visiting:

- locks on the Noteć River;
- Czarnków brewery;
- the steel and concrete bridge near Chrzypsko Małe, built over the Oszczynica Stream in 1907–1908;
- a trip by Gniezno Commuter Rail from Gniezno to Anastazewo;
- a trip by Środa Narrow Gauge Rail from Środa Wlkp. to Zaniemyśl;
- a trip by Śmigiel Commuter Rail from Stare Bojanowo to Wielichowo;
- a trip by Wyrzysk County Rail from Białośliwie to Łobżenica.

Educational aims:

- developing local patriotism;
- developing cognitive inquisitiveness;
- developing respect for cultural heritage;
- developing respect for people's work in the entire region;
- developing the attitude of sensitivity towards nature;
- developing the attitude of rational use of nature and the technological heritage of past generations of Poles.

References

Czerepaniak-Walczak, M. (2011). Pedagogika czasu wolnego: schole w szkole i poza szkołą. In R. Winiarski (Ed.). *Rekreacja i czas wolny*. Publisher: Oficyna Wydawnicza Łośgraf, Gdańsk.

Demel, M. & Humen, W. (1970). *Wprowadzenie do rekreacji fizycznej. Elementy historii, teoria i metodyka*. Publisher: Sport i Turystyka, Warszawa.

Denek, K. (2006). *Edukacja dziś-jutro*. Co-publishers ŁWSH, WSH, UAM, Leszno-Poznań-Żary, Poland.

Denek, K. (2012). *Filozofia życia*. Publisher: Wyd. WSPiA im. Mieszka I w Poznaniu, Poznań.

Dumazedier, J. (1962). *Vers une civilization du loisir?* Edition du Seuil, Paris.

Franken, R. E. (2005). *Psychologia motywacji*. Publisher: GWP, Gdańsk.

Jaworska T. & Leppert R. (Ed.) (2011). *Wprowadzenie do pedagogiki. Wybór tekstów*. Publisher: Impuls, Kraków.

Kulczycki, Z. (1977). *Zarys historii turystyki*. Publisher: Sport i Turystyka, Warszawa.

Kunowski, S. (2000). *Podstawy współczesnej pedagogiki*. Publisher: Wyd. Salezjańskie, Warszawa.

Kwilecka, M. (Ed.). (2006). *Bezpośrednie funkcje rekreacji*. Publisher: AlmaMer Wyższa Szkoła Ekonomiczna, Warszawa.

Libera, K. (1969). *Międzynarodowy ruch osobowy*. Publisher: PWE, Warszawa.

Łobocki, M. (2003). *Teoria wychowania w zarysie*. Publisher: Impuls, Kraków.

Łukaszewski, W. (2000). Motywacja w najważniejszych systemach teoretycznych. In J. Strelau (Ed.). *Psychologia*. Podręcznik akademicki, T. II. Publisher: GWP, Gdańsk.

Mądrzycki, T. (1977). *Psychologiczne prawidłowości kształtowania się postaw*. Publisher: WSiP, Warszawa.

Maslow, A. (1990). *Motywacja i osobowość*. Publisher: PAX, Warszawa.

Newcomb, M. T., Turner, H. R. & Converse, E. P. (1970). *Psychologia społeczna.* Publisher: PWN, Warszawa.

Pięta, J. (2008). *Pedagogika czasu wolnego.* Publisher: AlmaMer Wyższa Szkoła Ekonomiczna, Warszawa.

Przecławski, K. (1997). *Człowiek a turystyka. Zarys socjologii turystyki*, Publisher: Albis, Kraków.

Shepard, R. (1988). Sport, leisure and well-being: An ergonomics perspective. *Leisure Sciences*, 31, pp. 1501–1517.

Strelau, J. (Ed.). (2000). *Psychologia.* Podręcznik akademicki, T. II. Publisher: GWP, Gdańsk.

Winiarski, R. (2011). *Rekreacja i czas wolny.* Publisher Łośgraf Warszawa.

Winiarski, R. & Zdebski, J. (2008). *Psychologia turystyki.* Publisher: WAiP, Warszawa.

Zawadzka, A. & Ferenz, K. (1998). *Społeczne aspekty wypoczynku młodych kobiet*, Publisher: Wyd. Uniwersytetu Wrocławskiego, Wrocław.

Part V
Portfolio offer for tourism in submetropolitan areas

Yachting: *metropolitan* tourism options for Auckland.
Source: Fotolia.com © Lukas Skup, Fotolia.com.

22 Traditional and modern tour operators in agritourism

Jarosław Uglis and Joanna Kosmaczewska

Introduction: tour operator issues

Tour operators play a vital role in the travel and tourism industry (Middleton and Clarke 2001; Gountas 2005). Their presence is necessary to effectively convey the product from the producer to the consumer, that is, the tourist.

According to the OECD (2008, p. 546) tour operators are defined as 'businesses that combine two or more travel services (e.g. transport, accommodation, meals, entertainment, sightseeing) and sell them through travel agencies or directly to final consumers as a single product, called a package tour, for a global price'. They are often called trip organisers.

As far as where tour operators function is concerned, it must be stressed that they operate in a specific environment, which includes political, legal, economic, geographical and cultural dimensions. However, there are other factors which influence the functioning of this business: competitors, shareholders, competitive products, agents, distributors, clients behaviour, demographic changes climate and other framework (see Holloway 2004).

First, the tour operator must know the nature and extent of competition, that is, other companies doing similar business. Who is the biggest competitor for the company, what is its market share or what are its strategic plans? For example, in Poland there are 3793 businesses providing tourism services (as of 18 July 2014) in the central register of tour operators and tourism brokers.

Second, the functioning of tour operators depends on the political situation in a particular country, especially on legal regulations, for instance, being registered as a tourism organiser or agent.

The literature often refers to two different types of intermediaries in tourism: tour operators and outgoing travel agencies. For example, there is an interesting division of agencies organising trips and tourism in Poland, where the travel and tourism industry is regulated by the Tourist Services Act of 29 August 1997 (Tourist Services Act 1997). According to the current legislation, there are three types of companies organising tourism trips:

- tour operator – an entrepreneur who organises tourism events;
- tour broker – an entrepreneur who looks for an offer on behalf of a client, or who completes and signs contracts for the provision of tourism services;

- travel agent – an entrepreneur who leads mediation in contracts for the provision of tourism services for authorised tour operators in a particular country or for other providers established in this country.

Tour operators are often called wholesalers since they buy large amounts of services such as accommodation, board and transport from providers of individual services and combine them into one tourism package. The main characteristic of this type of product is one price for all the services included in it. On the other hand, travel agents are often called retailers since they sell the tour operator's services in exchange for commission which they receive after the transaction is completed.

Therefore, it is noteworthy that due to the legal conditions mentioned above, there is a term 'travel agency' which is used in business practice and in everyday language in Poland. This term defines the three types of enterprises listed above.

Distribution channels in tourism

A tourism product may be prepared and promoted but it does not guarantee that customers will buy it if the operator does not deliver it to the right place or at the right time. Therefore, the distribution of tourism products and services is a very important activity in the chain of tourism. From the marketing point of view, distribution in tourism includes all activities which involve overcoming time and spatial differences connected with the creation of a tourism product, its payment and consumption. As Halloway (2004) emphasises, distribution is vital if the product is to reach selected markets.

At this point, it should be noted that the distribution of products offered by tour operators and travel agents is absolutely different from the distribution of tangible property. This is due to the fact that the conclusion of a contract to use a specific package of tourism services at a specific time in the future means buying the right to use it rather than buying ownership. Thus, the distribution system in tourism involves slightly different aspects. Moreover, product/service distribution is supported by all reservation systems in tourism, which continuously monitor the supply and demand.

As far as tour operators and travel agencies are concerned, the essence of distribution is to provide customers with convenient access to the offer in a specific place or places and to enable them to obtain detailed information about the offer and how to purchase it (Michalska-Dudek and Przeorek-Smyka 2010).

The distribution channel is a term that is inextricably linked with distribution. It refers to the way in which the product comes from the producer to the final consumer (Figure 22.1). Moreover, the distribution channel in tourism can be defined as any organised and serviced system, created or utilised to provide convenient points of sale and/or access to consumers, away from the location of production and consumption (Middleton and Clarke 2001).

The main aim of the distribution channel is to sell prepared products and provide information to customers and brokers (Buhalis 2000). Reference publications provide many different criteria of division of distribution channels. In general, two

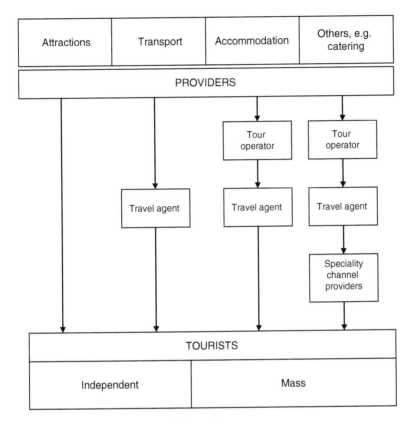

Figure 22.1 Distribution channels in tourism.

Source: The author's compilation.

types can be distinguished: direct and indirect. Another division is made according to the number of intermediaries: short and long, or according to the technology used: traditional and modern channels – using the Internet and television.

Distribution channels are dependent on target markets. Travel companies can distribute their products individually or they can find professional intermediaries. Brokerage is currently a common form and it has been popular practice in the travel and tourism industry for years. The main benefit resulting from this cooperation is increased sales through entering new markets, where the company was not present before. The choice of a broker is very difficult and it chiefly depends on the kind of product offered and the market segment to which the product is addressed. In practice, most producers choose one or a few brokers to sell their products. Moreover, they can use both channels – individual distribution or professional intermediaries – at the same time.

The direct sales channel refers to sales without brokers, which provides full control of the marketing instruments employed. It may be done by personal contact with customers, when they buy the product directly from the provider during a telephone call or on the Internet, which is very important nowadays. This channel is very effective with small local or regional tour operators, travel agencies with well-known brands and with high-loyalty customers (Michalska-Dudek and Przeorek-Smyka 2010).

The indirect sales channel refers to selling products to customers by specialised brokers. There are wholesalers, who are tour operators, and retailers, who are travel agents. When choosing indirect channels of distribution two parameters must be taken into consideration: length and width. The former refers to a large number of direct sections (vertical layout), whereas the latter refers to the number of brokers in this section (horizontal layout). As far as the scope of brokers' cooperation in the distribution channel is concerned, two conventional types of channels can be distinguished. In the first, individual brokers are loosely related to each other, whereas in the other brokers are vertically integrated, where a chosen participant is the leader who coordinates work in the channel. This coordination is based on savings developed through shared operation, owing to the satisfactory level of profit.

As was mentioned above, tour operators buying all package components and then selling the prepared package act as wholesalers in the distribution system. Additionally, tour operators can act as retailers selling their products directly to the customer. Therefore, their role has increased rapidly in the tourism distribution system. Nowadays, the businesses of Internet tour operators and online travel agents are developing quickly since they sell their products both online and by call/contact centres. Some examples of such ventures are Expedia Inc., Lastminute.com, Travelplanet.pl, Wakacje.pl and easygo.pl. The activity of the Internet intermediaries becomes a more and more significant sales channel for big tour operators because there is a growing number of consumers who prefer buying tourism trips online.

Previous considerations concerned the general rules of functioning of the distribution system in tourism, and showed its multifaceted character. For companies offering tourism services which operate in metropolitan areas, it is important to choose an effective distribution system for their products. Therefore, it is important to determine the number of tour operators and travel agencies functioning in these areas. Moreover, it is worth trying to refer to the tour operators from the nearest big towns such as Bristol, Cracow, Lyon, Poznań, Valencia or Warsaw. What is more, starting a destination management company (DMC) could be a perfect solution. The company would play the role of a local tour operator, specialised in inbound tourism in its own area (Migdał 2012). Good knowledge of local specificity in all fields and the chance to contact the company in order to coordinate cooperation would be big advantages for the company. The establishment of this entity should be initiated by local tourism organisations (LTOs), which are the main elements creating tourism in regions. LTOs adopt many forms and shapes, including informal networks of tour operators.

In short, the DMC should be a commercial company, and local tourism organisations would be some of the most significant shareholders. The range of operation of this company would include cooperation with local providers of tourism services, preparation of product offers and a database of local tourism products, service providers, outer tour operators and tourists. Additionally, the goals of this company would be to take care of the image of the offered tourism product and the region, to keep the service reservation system and to start and maintain cooperation with outer tour operators.

Agritourism: distribution issues

In choosing a distribution method, each accommodation provider operating in the agritourism business should make a decision whether they want to promote and sell their services themselves, or whether they would rather use paid or free services offered by various agencies (see Figure 22.2).

The following factors usually influence the choice of distribution channels for agritourism products:

- the farm's economic situation;
- experience in offering this type of tourism services;
- the farm owners' education level and their individual traits of personality;
- the number of co-operators and competitors in the local market of tourism services;
- the unique features of the services offered.

A tourism product is usually sold through a direct distribution channel when it is viewed from a narrow perspective, that is, understood as the offer of a single farm. This situation is probably caused by the farm owner's lack of readiness to share the profits with any agencies. Limiting the distribution channels to direct sales

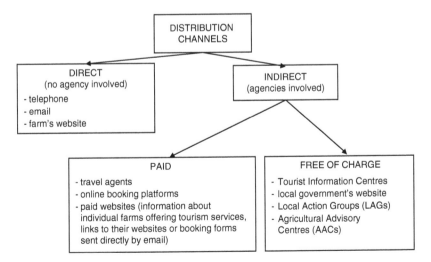

Figure 22.2 Agritourism service distribution channels.

Source: The authors' compilation.

only gives the farm owners an opportunity to strike up a closer and more familiar relationship with their guests. It is also much easier and quicker to modify the offer and adjust it to customers' current needs and expectations. It additionally reduces the risk of guests' possible disappointment that might appear due to the incomplete or slightly embellished information about a particular farm and its offer presented by an agency. The employment of an agency to sell a tourism product usually results in potential customers' increased access to the information about the product and purchase possibilities. On the other hand, though, it may cause inappropriate information flow (too many channels extend the information flow time and may cause misinterpretation) and additionally, it extends the time of payment for the services provided. The agencies supporting providers of agritourism services by selling their offers can be divided into two groups: those charging fees for their support and those providing support free of charge. In most channels of indirect distribution of agritourism services travel agents charge fees, either in the form of a margin added to the price or in the form of commission, which depends on the amount of services sold. In return they sell agritourism offers as independent, separate products (travel agents act as intermediaries or agents) or include them (usually as an accommodation database) into their own offer in order to provide more complex and interesting tourism products. However, it must be clearly emphasised that the price of the agritourism product remains exactly the same regardless of its seller. By making the decision to use chargeable distribution channels the owner of an agritourism business agrees to reduce their profit by the sum paid to the agent as remuneration. Therefore, agritourism businesses, especially those beginning their market activity, hardly ever decide to use chargeable indirect distribution channels for their services, usually because they are afraid of making too little profit in comparison with the margin and/or commission they would have to pay the agents in the first years of their business activity. Agritourism businesses usually start cooperating with travel agents when they want to expand their offer and/or address it to the customers (e.g. foreign tourists) who remain beyond the range of their marketing activities. However, providers of agritourism services can easily reduce the risk resulting from the use of agents' chargeable services if they decide to sign an allotment agreement. This agreement is usually signed between travel agents (tour operators) and, for example, hotels. The agreement describes the conditions of availability of a specific number of hotel beds at a particular time, their price and the possibility to cancel the booked accommodation according to the conditions accepted by both parties who signed the agreement. The same agreement can be successfully signed between a travel agent and the owner of an agritourism business, allowing the latter to decide who remains temporarily in charge (and to what extent) of the decisions concerning the number of beds offered in a particular place.

Online channels of distribution of agritourism services

All the transformations caused by the development of information and communication technologies, though most frequently occurring in cities, can also be observed in rural areas, especially those situated close to big cities. This involves a large number of changes in most sectors of the economy, especially in the sector providing tourism services, including agritourism. The application of new technologies to transmit information in the process of selling services often creates a new virtual space, where the agritourism business not only should appear, but should also know how to compete. This virtual space also provides cooperation opportunities, for example, presenting various offers together on the same website. For customers the space is the source of information about potential tourism destinations and opinions on the range and quality of the services offered as well as the relationship between the price and quality in a particular offer.

Nowadays, the Internet is one of the most important mediums of communication. In Poland access to the Internet is relatively strongly determined by the place of residence – whether it is an urban or a rural area. However, common access to the Internet is a matter of time. Nowadays, show that the difference in access to the Internet between urban and rural areas has significantly decreased (*Społeczeństwo informacyjne* 2012).

Moreover, the use of the Internet depends on the potential user's age, sex, education, and social and professional status (Troszyński and Bieliński 2010). The results of research published by the Rural Development Foundation indicate that the following factors are likely to decrease the use of the Internet among rural inhabitants: aged over 45, low education level, running a farm as the only source of income and professional inactivity (Troszyński and Bieliński 2010).

Taking into consideration the fact that the services offered to tourists should be rendered by active farms (or farms operating as agritourism accommodation only), we should admit that the owners of agritourism farms belong to the above-mentioned group. In this case no access to the Internet or the inability to use its potential should be regarded not only as a loss of potential profits but also as a sort of exclusion from modern civilisation. Nevertheless, in such situations the agritourism offer can be directed to a narrow circle of customers, for whom the lack of new communication technologies is an undeniable asset. However, we must assume that the choice of a particular target group of consumers should be the agritourism farmer's conscious choice, unaffected by any of the deficits listed above, such as education or finance.

Nowadays, it seems essential for each agritourism farm to have its own website since this allows its owner to be ahead of any local or regional competitors and additionally, it is very likely that the range of the offer will be extended on a global scale.

Moreover, the website may become a very effective distribution channel for the services offered, because it would present them in a very attractive way, and the use of modern communication tools, such as blogs, Facebook or Skype, might act as a 'promotional speaking tube'.

Some companies and associations constitute another group of agents that act as broker and in return for a fee (usually a flat rate) agree to make their website available for advertising agritourism services on the Internet. In this case the fee is charged either directly for each single booking made or for the presence of the agritourism service in the database. The choice of this channel for the distribution of agritourism offers turns out to be relatively favourable for farm owners, because the agent's role is limited to the information distribution function only. Thus, further contact between the service provider and customer/guest takes place online (including all payments) or personally by phone, fax, email or the farm's website.

Two different types of online booking platforms can be distinguished: those whose offer is limited to accommodation based on agritourism (e.g. www.goscinnawies.pl) and those whose offer includes traditional hotel accommodation, though supplemented by the agritourism offer (e.g. Booking.com). Both booking platforms sign agreements with the owners of agritourism businesses to represent them in contact with potential agritourism holidaymakers. Therefore, the platform administrators act as travel agents representing service providers. They serve customers on behalf of the agritourism businesses and, in return for their service, they charge a commission on each accommodation unit sold. They enable online booking, payment and transfer of the money, reduced by commission, to the owners of agritourism businesses.

As far as the 'goscinnawies' platform is concerned, cooperation between the platform administrator and service provider is also possible free of charge, but it is restricted to uploading only a short piece of information about the business and one photograph.

At the moment (2016), the portal presents 1159 businesses labelled as agritourism farms and potential customers can look for them according to the province they are located in, the farms' specialities and the facilities they offer. However, the disadvantage of this booking platform is the use of its own categorisation symbols, which are very similar to those used by the Polish Rural Tourism Federation *Gospodarstwa Gościnne*. Customers might mistake them. Only a thorough and detailed study of the rules and regulations concerning service providers rather than clients will let us understand the internal assessment system used for the agritourism businesses that are presented.

The Booking.com platform is an example of an online agent offering traditional hotel accommodation, supplemented by the offer of accommodation in different facilities, including agritourism facilities. Currently the users of this portal can make online bookings, choosing from among 506,677 accommodation offers, where agritourism accommodations makes up only 1 per cent (5,270 households) of the total offer. There are 9,301 businesses offering accommodation in Poland that can use the services provided by this online platform, but only 1.2 per cent of them are agritourism businesses (108 households). Undoubtedly, the main advantage of cooperation with this booking platform is its wide range of operation. The website of Booking.com is available in 42 languages and thanks to positioning and paid commercial banners displayed in social media it is easily recognisable. Moreover, thanks to the Android application for mobile devices it is possible to make bookings while travelling. The GPS (global positioning system) module enables travellers to find accommodation on smartphones and tablets. It can be done according to 3 criteria: the traveller's current location and a given radius, the destination and a given radius, and accommodation address details.

Additionally, the module calculates the route between the user's current location and the destination.

A new geo-targeting mobile application, which contains a database of over 1,000 tourist farms (available at www.stokrotka.com) seems to be an interesting and very useful facility for the promotion of agritourism offers, as it enables the owners of agritourism businesses to send information about their offers directly to their customers' mobile phones in the form of text messages or emails. The system can also send web banners to online locators and tourism services.

All of the abovementioned facilities make it hard to imagine effective online sales of agritourism services without booking platforms. In view of the quality and scope of information provided by most agritourism businesses on their websites, we must assume that they do not treat the Internet as a tool giving them a competitive advantage or helping them to sell their offers, but only as a means of sharing information about their businesses with the general public. This seems to explain why the owners of agritourism businesses so willingly upload free information about their activities and offers on websites administered by local action groups, associations and local governments. The owners of agritourism businesses should also bear in mind that the Internet is not only the medium people use invariably in order to find information about particular products and services, but also the medium used to share opinions and experiences. Meanwhile, the most popular online service, TripAdvisor, grouping 83.4 million registered users from 188 countries, includes the offers of only 58 agritourism businesses from Poland. Facebook seems to have already gained much more popularity among accommodation providers. The phrase 'agritourism + Poznań' entered into this social network search engine results in about 30 website addresses of agritourism businesses that are immediately displayed. A fan page with an offer from an agritourism business apparently provides better opportunities to reach a wider group of potential guests, keep in touch with former guests, and make friends and acquaintances of former guests interested in the business offers. It also provides an opportunity to organise various promotional campaigns and numerous competitions.

Conclusion

To conclude these deliberations it is necessary to analyse the effectiveness of the Internet as a sales-stimulating medium or as a source of passive or active knowledge.

Generally speaking, all marketing and selling activities carried out online are believed to have only one disadvantage – they need time to be dealt with regularly and appropriately and knowledge to be dealt with effectively. Therefore, having analysed in detail the opportunities created by the Internet, owners of agritourism businesses should make their independent decisions which tasks they would like to carry out themselves and which they would ask professionals to do. At the same time, they should precisely determine the fundamental criteria of the choice they are likely to make – the amount of time they can spend handling the offer presented online and the main features characterising the basic segments of the market where they are going to provide their services, such as the age and education of their potential customers.

References

Buhalis, D. (2000). Relationships in the distribution channel of tourism: Conflicts between hoteliers and tour operators in the Mediterranean region. In J. Crotts, D. Buhalis & R. March (Eds.). *Global Alliances in Tourism and Hospitality Management*. Haworth Press, New York, pp. 113–139.

Gountas, S. (2005). Tour operations management. In L. Pender & R. Sharpley (Eds.). *The Management of Tourism*. SAGE, London, pp. 47–66.

Holloway, J. C. (2004). *Marketing for Tourism*. 4th ed. Pearson Education, Harlow.

Michalska-Dudek, I. & Przeorek-Smyka, R. (2010). *Marketing biur podróży*. C.H. Beck, Warszawa

Middleton, V. T. C. & Clarke, J. R. (2001). *Marketing in Travel and Tourism*. 3rd ed. Butterworth-Heinemann, Oxford.

Migdał, M. (2012). *Poradnik Lokalna Organizacja Turystyczna*. Publisher: Forum Turystyki Regionów, Szczecin.

OECD. (2008). Glossary of Statistical Terms. ISBN: 9789264088023 (EXTERNALHTML); 9789264055087 (PDF); 9789264025561 (print); DOI:10.1787/9789264055087-en.

Społeczeństwo informacyjne w Polsce. (2012). The Statistical Office in Szczecin, available http://stat.gov.pl/cps/rde/xbcr/gus/nts_spolecz_inform_w_polsce_2007-2011.pdf.

Tourist Services Act. (1997). Tourist Services Act of 29 August 1997. (Official Journal). Act on Tourism Services, of 29 August 1997 (Dz. U. of 2004, No. 223, item 2268, as amended) Ministry of Sport and Tourism of the Republic of Poland, http://en.msport.gov.pl/ministry.

Troszyński, M. & Bieliński, J. (2010). *Internet na wsi 2009. Wykorzystanie Internetu na terenach wiejskich w Polsce. Stan na rok 2009*. Publisher: Fundacja Wspomagania Wsi, Warszawa.

23 A model of agritourism offer polarisation in metropolitan surroundings – the Łódź Metropolis

A case study

Jolanta Wojciechowska

Selected model approaches to Polish agritourism

Agritourism has been developing in Poland for nearly 25 years.[1] The first inventory was made in 1996 and it showed that there were 15.6 accommodation places on farms receiving tourists (Report on the state of 1997). Since that time a mainly increasing tendency observed. In 2007 there were more than 87 thousand beds and about 8.8 thousand agritourism facilities. There was a noticeable decrease noted in 2009, when there were about 5.5 thousand agritourism facilities and 57.1 thousand beds. However, in 2010 the Central Statistical Office registered 7 thousand agritourism facilities providing 82.7 thousand beds. There has been no change in these numbers since that time.

There are agritourism facilities in 55 per cent of all communes in Poland (Bednarek-Szczepańska 2011). According to the statistics, they can be found in every second commune, but there are only individual or a few facilities in them. There are few villages with a high density of agritourism farms. Over the 25 years of agritourism, farm accommodations have made up 3 per cent to 4 per cent of the total tourism accommodation in Poland. This group of agritourism accommodation fills a specific niche in tourism and it noticeably contributes to numerous positive changes in rural space, both in the appearance of rural space and the mentality of local community (Wojciechowska 2009).

The distribution of agritourism in the geographical space of Poland is determined by various factors. Over the period of 25 years of the development of agritourism a relatively significant distribution has crystallised, as can be seen in Figure 23.1, showing the distribution model. The distribution encompasses three zones of intensity in the development of agritourism: low, medium and high. The areas with high intensity of development are marked by the latitudinal arrangement and they show noticeable convergence with the location of tourism zones in Poland, especially those which are rich in natural and scenic values. Thus, agritourism facilities can chiefly be found in the mountainous zone (in the south), in the uplands (in the southeast), in part of the lake districts and in the coastal lowland (in the north). There is a much lower number of agritourism facilities in the agricultural strip of lowlands in central Poland, which is characterised by poorer tourism values.

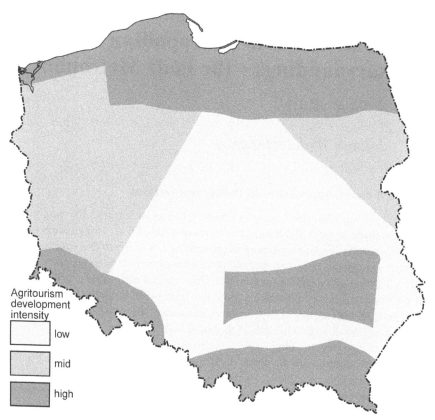

Figure 23.1   The geographical variation of agritourism development intensity in Poland.

When we take an even more simplified approach to the problem of distribution of agritourism in Poland, we can assume that a model of external concentration of agritourism farms can be observed in the geographical space of Poland, as can be seen in Figure 23.2. The model was based on the main geographical units in Poland, regarding them to be an important criterion of the location of agritourism facilities. Such units sketch the framework of tourism regions and their names can be associated with the type of landscape that is characteristic of the region. Being a landmark, landscape affects human imagination and stimulates contemporary tourism traffic (Liszewski 2003). Thus, the proposed model shows how agritourism farms are distributed in the geographical spaces of Poland and Switzerland, for comparison. In Switzerland – contrary to Poland – agritourism farms are concentrated in the central part of the country. Such farms can mostly be found on the Swiss Plateau, which is characterised by favourable access to transport, scenic values and a rich network of rural settlements. Thus, it is a model of internal concentration of agritourism farms within the space of that country. In Switzerland agritourism farms are situated close to urban centres, within the zone

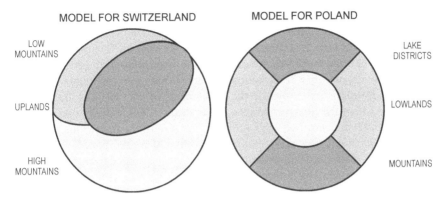

Figure 23.2   Models of the location of agritourism farms in Poland and Switzerland.

of travel time of 'up to one hour', whereas in Poland they are situated more than one hour away (Wojciechowska 2011). These two examples of countries with different locations of agritourism farms confirm the strong relationship between geographical units and tourism regions.

These models provide the inspiration and background for another model approach, which is the aim of this chapter. It concerns the polarisation of agritourism in the metropolitan areas of Poland. The concept of a metropolitan tourism and recreational region (developed by Liszewski 2005) makes special reference to the model. The region is understood as geographical space used by a big city with metropolitan functions, including its facilities. The space is the destination of tourism migrations and it is noticeably segmented. The centre of the region, the metropolitan city, is the destination or transit place for tourist arrivals, which contribute to the development of cognitive, business, cultural and other types of tourism. The outer areas of the region are the destinations for the city inhabitants' weekend and holiday trips. These two main functions of the metropolitan region provide a good reason to call it a tourism and recreational region. This chapter identified such a region in the metropolis of Łódź. 'There are two forces which take part in the tourist and recreational development of the metropolitan region, i.e. the forces which attract and eject people from the metropolitan city and which are connected with the tourist function in its broad sense' (Liszewski 2005, p. 136). As a result of the influence of these two forces geographical space is occupied for tourism and recreational purposes. The space which is the closest to the metropolitan city undergoes the most intensive transformations for recreational purposes. Simultaneously, these processes are transferred to more and more distant outer zones or even to the outskirts of the region.

This concept has provided inspiration for the determination of the forces and processes which are responsible for the development of agritourism in metropolitan areas. These considerations let us pose a thesis that the agritourism offer in metropolitan surroundings is clearly polarised. This means that the space surrounding the metropolis is marked by differences, which let us identify two zones of different types of agritourism offer. The first zone encompasses the direct neighbourhood of the metropolis, its outskirts and the suburban area, which are strongly influenced by the metropolis. The other zone encompasses more distant areas, which are much less influenced by the metropolis. Both zones are characterised by the presence of agritourism offers with its own, individual features, which are diversified according to the components of the zone and the types of tourists to whom the offer is addressed. The distance between the two zones is different and it depends not only on the rank or size of the metropolis, which is defined by its population, area and functions, but it also conditioned by the tourism values of nature and culture and by tourism and recreational development.

Łódź is an example of a metropolis which will let us explain and prove the universal character of the thesis. It will be the subject of further considerations. It is noteworthy that Łódź is the third largest city in Poland, with a population of 718,960 in 2012 (Central Statistical Office).

An outline of a tourist arriving in the metropolis of Łódź

Studies of tourist arrivals in Łódź show that in 2011 about 780.5 thousand tourists visited the city, including 121.8 thousand foreign tourists (15.6%) (Włodarczyk 2012). Thus, domestic visitors prevail in the tourist traffic. They usually come to Łódź from the towns (especially from big cities) in Łódź and Masovian Voivodeships (administrative units) and from other neighbouring voivodeships. Foreign tourists usually come from the United Kingdom, Germany and other European Union countries, where they usually live in cities.

The questionnaire survey[2] revealed that the domestic tourist visiting Łódź is usually a young man under 30. He has a job, higher education and good financial situation, in his opinion. He has been to Łódź before and he will stay longer than for one night (usually 2 or 3 nights). He stays at a hotel, but every third person stays with friends or family. He organises his trip individually and arrives in the city in his own car, usually in the company of friends (every fourth tourist) or family (every fifth tourist). The main purpose of the visit is business. During his stay the tourist wants to visit his family, take part in a cultural event, go sightseeing and shopping. He visits the most popular places in the city – Piotrkowska Street, the high street of Łódź and Manufaktura, a revitalised nineteenth century post-industrial area with a complex of commercial and cultural services, located north of the city centre. He wants to come back to Łódź and he recommends the city to his friends. He finds out about the city from his friends, family and on the Internet (29%).

The foreign tourist visiting Łódź is usually a young man aged about 30, with a job, higher education and good financial status. He has been to Łódź before and he wants to stay for 2 or 3 nights. He stays at a hotel, but every third person stays with friends or family. He organises his trip individually and arrives by plane or car. He travels with a partner or friends. The main purpose of the visit is business and visiting friends (every fifth tourist). During his stay the tourist wants to go sightseeing and shopping and to see his friends or relatives. He visits the most popular places in the city – Piotrkowska Street and Manufaktura, but he also visits the Jewish Cemetery, Old Town and Księży Młyn (a largely revitalised nineteenth century post-industrial complex situated south of the city centre). He uses gastronomic offers and visits Łódź museums more often than the domestic tourist. He finds out about the city from his friends and on the Internet. A large number of the respondents (a quarter) could not make a decision if they would recommend the city to their friends.

The outlines of the domestic and foreign tourists did not differ much from each other. As experts on questionnaire surveys indicate, this results from the fact that Łódź is an example of the city where most tourists arrive on business to take part in conferences, fairs, and so forth. This fact is also confirmed by the seasonal character of the tourist influx to Łódź. There are two peaks, from April to June and from September to October, and two slumps, from December to January and from July to August. The situation looks different when we consider visitors arriving in tourism and recreational areas in the Łódź region. One season of arrivals is noticeable in Łódź Voivodeship: from May to October. The structure of using accommodation facilities has a different distribution. There is a higher percentage of people using unregistered accommodation facilities and a lower percentage of people staying at hotels (about 29%) (Włodarczyk 2012). It is possible to observe more tourists using agritourism accommodation facilities among visitors arriving in the region. It is a rare situation among visitors to Łódź. This means that agritourism facilities and other providers of tourism services compete with each other for tourists visiting the region.

Łódź is a city of regional importance on the tourist map of Poland. This fact is confirmed by the following data: 69 per cent of one-day visitors and 21 per cent of tourists come from Łódź Voivodeship (region), whereas 23 per cent of tourists come from the neighbouring Masovian Voivodeship (Włodarczyk 2012, p. 203). Łódź Voivodeship is considered to have no clear tourism image (Włodarczyk 2012, p. 204). In comparison with other regions of Poland it occupies distant positions (among 16 voivodeships it is in the second ten) in rankings of tourism traffic.

Agritourism in Łódź Voivodeship

Agritourism in Łódź Voivodeship began to develop more intensively in the second half of the 1990s. According to estimates, there were about 250 agritourism farms in 2009 (as compared to 1500 agritourism farms in Warmian-Masurian Voivodeship, which was the leader at the time) (Wojciechowska 2009). At present the number of agritourism farms is estimated at 218.[3] Figure 23.3 shows the distribution of agritourism farms in individual counties. Agritourism facilities are mostly located in places with the most interesting natural values. Such values can be found along river valleys, which are distant from Łódź, such as the Pilica River valley in the east and the Warta River valley in the west, including its southern stretch. They can also be seen north of the city in areas of diversified terrain and landscape (the so-called Łódź Heights). These areas form a rhombus-like

The number of agritourist
farms in the counties
of Łódź voivodeship

- 1 – 5
- 6 – 10
- 11 – 15
- 16 – 20
- 21 – 25

- - - - - - One-dayofferzone
·········· Residential offerzone

0   20   40 km

Figure 23.3   A model of spatial polarisation in agritourism offers around the Łódź
metropolis.

quadrangle around the metropolis. The metropolitan city is situated at its north
side. This quadrangle of tourism and recreational values of the Łódź metropolis
affects the distribution and form of agritourism offers.

At present there are 6 agritourism societies in Łódź Voivodeship, of which
95 owners of agritourism facilities are members, that is, less than a half the total
number of all such facilities in the voivodeship. The locations of the societies
correspond to the distribution of agritourism farms and tourism and recreational
values enclosed in the aforementioned quadrangle. There are 3 societies on the
western side, 2 on the eastern side and 1 on the northern side, which is in close
proximity to the metropolis. None of the societies is a member of a national organisation, the Polish Federation of Rural Tourism, which was established in 1996.
Agritourism is also the subject of interest for Local Action Groups. There are 20
such groups in the voivodeship and their activity covers nearly the entire region.
An action group usually consists of a few owners of agritourism facilities.

Since the 1990s Łódź Voivodeship has been at the bottom of the list of voivodeships with agritourism farms and accommodation facilities. As can be seen, the entities interested in the development of agritourism in the region are characterised by considerable individuality of their actions, which results in poor consolidation of cooperation.

A model of agritourism offer polarisation in the surroundings of the Łódź metropolis

According to the thesis posed in this chapter, the recreational offer of agritourism farms is noticeably diversified in the surroundings of the Łódź metropolis. This observation has been proved by long-term and latest research.[4] The main findings will be presented here to confirm the thesis.

Within Zone 1, the zone immediately surrounding the Łódź metropolis and up to 15 km from its limits, there are agritourism facilities whose owners usually provide an offer which will attract guests to spend a few hours or the whole day there, without an overnight stay. This can be observed on the farms which belong to the Zgierz Land Agritourist Society (see research by Retelewska 2011). It is one of the oldest societies in the Łódź region; established in 1999, at present there are 20 members. Their farms are located in the northwest and north of the metropolis limits.[5] Their arithmetic mean distance from the metropolitan city is 7.5 km. These are small and medium-sized farms; 18 farms are smaller than 15 ha, including 4 which are smaller than 5 ha. The farm owners mostly breed horses. Only 8 farms are ready to provide beds to tourists. Usually these are guestrooms in a separate part of the building inhabited by the farmer's family. There is a campsite on only 1 farm. The farms provide the following recreational and leisure facilities: a place for a barbecue or bonfire (13 farms), fishing place (8), leisure garden (6), football pitch or volleyball court (5) and playground for children (5). There is a mini zoo on 3 farms and a farming equipment exhibition on 2 farms. Board is definitely a secondary offer. Only 2 farms offer full board to their guests and 6 farms provide access to the kitchen. The owners of 2 farms offer 1 meal (dinner) or drinks and homemade pastries. However, the offer of additional services is much richer: 14 farms offer trips around the neighbourhood, 12 offer a barbecue or bonfire including roasting sausages or potatoes, 11 offer sleigh rides in winter, 6 provide rides on a horse-drawn wagon or coach, 5 offer horse riding lessons, and 5 offer the picking of forest fruit and exploration of the fauna and flora in nearby forests. On 5 farms one can rent sport and leisure equipment, for example, bicycles or balls, while 3 farms offer lessons in folk crafts. On 3 farms it is possible to take part in farm works, which let guests experience how animals are bred or crops are grown.

The agritourism offer of these farms is chiefly based on different attractions which are available on the farm itself and in its nearest surroundings. This type of offer attracts guests to farms for a short time, that is, for a few hours (10 farms) or a whole day without staying overnight (7 farms). These services are mostly used by groups of schoolchildren and students or adult groups of friends. The Society planned and drew up an agritourism bicycle trail (in 2003 it was recognised as the first trail of this type in Poland and in 2005 a guidebook for the trail was published) and a few other thematic trails. These and other actions were possible because the Society participated in several different projects. One of them, the Regional Education Programme, was based on the potential of 5 agritourism farms. The programme enabled the construction of a 1-day offer in the form of an 8-hour trip during which the participants are shown traditional farming procedures, disappearing jobs (blacksmithing), crafts (products made from tissue paper and straw). They also learn about the history, nature and culture in the region. Visitors are transported by wagon or sleigh (in winter) between the places of different attractions. Each trip ends with a bonfire. The activity of the Society, which has been briefly described here, is considered to be a great success, not only on a regional scale.

The agritourism offer of residence is marked by a wide range of different properties. In the Łódź region it is mostly offered in tourism reception areas, that is, in the areas which are rich in natural values, such as forests, rivers and water reservoirs. The places are located at a distance of about 60 to 120 km from the metropolitan city and they make up Zone 2 in the presented model (Figure 23.3). Both the metropolis dwellers and residents of the Łódź region and other regions of Poland use this zone. As results from field research show, the agritourism offer in this zone is chiefly based on overnight stays. For example, all of the surveyed agritourism farms in the Pilica and Warta River valleys (about 90 farms, i.e. 70% of the total number of farms in Zone 2) offered beds (among others, Pukosz 2007; Sobala 2013). Guestrooms are the most common form of accommodation in the zone (75–97% of the total offer), but there are also holiday lodgings (10–15%) and campsites (5–10%). The role of the board offer is also different. Guests are usually offered breakfast and dinner, but there is also a considerable offer of full board or access to the kitchen. In all, 26 per cent of the farms located in the Pilica River valley offered full board. As can be seen, it is important in the offer, but it is not the predominant service. There is generally an extended offer of extra services. For example, 53 per cent of the farms located in the Pilica River valley offer between 6 and 10 different attractions(Sobala 2013). More than 10 attractions are offered by the owners of the facilities which won awards in the competition for the best agritourism farm in the Łódź region (Reczyńska 2013). However, all these attractions are standard and they do not differ much between competitors. It is estimated that between 45 per cent and 55 per cent of the total number of attractions offered on agritourism farms in this zone are based on breeding (stud) or keeping horses. A large number of attractions are based on fishing, whereas the educational offer is estimated at 6 to 12 per cent.

It is significant that the agritourism offer in the zone under analysis is available all year round. The visitors who use this offer, usually in the summer season, though, are families with children (23% of the tourists surveyed in the Pilica River valley), elderly people (19%), visitors with pets (19%) or people with health problems (10%) (Sobala 2013). Tourists staying on agritourism farms usually spend time relaxing passively (20%), having short walks (26%) or watching nature (13%). When they were asked which attraction they missed during their stay on the farm, most of them answered: 'It's hard to say.' Some of them gave a very diversified spectrum of examples, which clearly depended on their age or interests. Mostly they did not give very original responses (Sobala 2013). As results from the survey show, and similarly to Zone 1, in Zone 2 small and medium-sized agritourism farms are predominant. They offer 14 to 18 beds to tourists. This means that there is usually 1, or possibly 2 or 3 families who are friends on the farm and thus, tourists can relax in a small group.

To sum up this analysis, it is necessary to note the spatial distribution of the identified types of agritourism offer. Figure 23.3 shows a simplified diagram of the distribution. Two radial zones can be drawn on the basis of differences in the number of agritourism farms in the counties of Łódź Voivodeship. The first zone refers to agritourism facilities concentrated near the metropolis, whereas the other zone encompasses the facilities which are more distant from the metropolis. Both zones are characterised by specific agritourism offers.

The first type of offer enables one-day visitors, who usually live in the metropolis, to satisfy their demand for recreation and leisure. The offer addressed to this group of tourists is based on recreation and regional education. It is available at places which can be reached by suburban transport. Due to the fact that children and students are a large group of recipients of this offer, it is also popular among adult inhabitants of the metropolis. Children inform and persuade their parents and grandparents to spend their leisure time in the country. Thus, they extend the group of potential recipients of the offer.

One might ask how attractive this offer is to a domestic or foreign tourist arriving in Łódź. As results from the outlines presented above show, there are great chances to attract potential tourists on the Internet, which is one of the major sources of information. However, in order to make sure that tourists can find information about the possibilities to stay on agritourism farms located near the centre of the metropolis, the information about regional agritourism offers must be appropriately transmitted to the Internet and it must also be positioned and updated. Regional institutions should be more engaged in the execution of this concept, because it entails both financial outlay and advanced technologies, which are not always available to individual owners of agritourism facilities.

The other type of agritourism offer, which can be found in the more distant zone of the metropolitan area, is based on a longer (more than 1 day, or a weekend) leisure stay, not only for the inhabitants of the Łódź metropolis but also for those from the neighbouring metropolises, Warsaw and Silesia (as a conurbation) and for other tourists.

Universality of the model: conclusion

Figure 23.3, which shows the diversification of agritourism offers in the Łódź metropolitan area, presents a model that also applies to other metropolises. In their surroundings two zones of agritourism offers can also be identified: the 1-day offer and the residential offer. The offers function in a different way and, in consequence, they have different components and types of tourists as recipients of the offer. In Zone 1 there is a majority of agritourism facilities with an offer for visitors staying for a short time: a few hours, 1 day or a weekend. In Zone 2 there are mainly facilities with an offer for tourists staying for a longer leisure time, for some or all of their holiday. It is noteworthy that in both zones the offer may be influenced by the specific character of a particular metropolitan city, but on the whole they retain the principles of the presented model. For example, agritourism farms located within the administrative limits of the city of Cracow (in Zone 1) are used to a great extent by domestic tourists arriving for short touring and leisure stays. Thus, the agritourism offer in the zone near the city is developed both for the inhabitants' need of recreation and leisure and for numerous tourists arriving in the city. The situation in Poznań is similar due to regular events such as fairs for different branches of the economy. It is also noteworthy that in seaside metropolises the zones identified in the model are shaped like semi-circles. In the Łódź metropolitan area the zones are shaped like circles, though not concentric. The concentric arrangement of circles would be the most desirable in the universal model.

The main forces which are responsible for the form of agritourism offers and their diversification in the metropolitan area are the ejective and attractive forces (following Liszewski 2005). Figure 23.4 includes these forces and shows the model of polarisation of the agritourism offer around the metropolis. Zone 1 is chiefly characterised by the forces pushing the metropolis dwellers to the outskirts for recreational purposes (for a few hours, 1 day or a weekend). These forces trigger the processes which develop an appropriate agritourism offer in this zone of the metropolitan area. The offer usually includes facilities and appliances used for recreational and educational purposes. In this zone the forces attracting tourists can also be observed, depending on the scale of development of tourism functions in the metropolitan city.

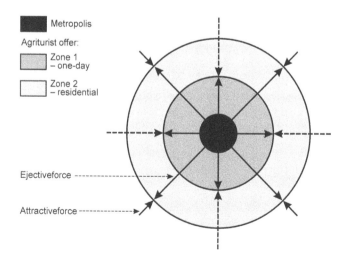

Figure 23.4 A model of polarisation of agritourism offers surrounding the metropolis.

In Zone 2 the ejective and attractive forces act simultaneously and have comparable power. The former force pushes metropolitan dwellers for a longer stay, leisure or holiday. Simultaneously, the latter force attracts other visitors from the region or country to come and tour the countryside and to enjoy leisure. Thus, these forces trigger the processes which develop residential agritourism offers. There are numerous factors which influence these offers in metropolitan areas. Above all, the factors include visitors themselves, fashion in tourism, general type of development in the area, and so forth.

In order to further develop the identified types of agritourism offer in each metropolitan area it is important that the owners of agritourism facilities as well as supporting organisations and institutions diversify their approach, cooperate with each other, coordinate tasks and systematically monitor their offers. Agritourism is a branch of the economy where success depends on cooperation between different entities, both those related to tourism and those which are not directly related. It is not only necessary to seek cooperation but also to learn constantly how to use it.

Notes

1   Agritourism, both as a term and as a phenomenon in tourist traffic. Its beginnings are attributed to the establishment of the Suwałki Chamber of Agritourism in 1991. It started national agritourism symposiums, which are still the events where theoreticians and practitioners of agritourism exchange their views. The Suwałki Chamber of Agritourism also became one of the first representatives of regional, and later, national self-government in agritourism (Wojciechowska 2009).
2   The survey was conducted from 2009 to 2011 in an original methodological convention by a team of experts from the Institute of Urban Geography and Tourism, University of Łódź. The findings were published in the article 'Tourist Traffic in Łódź and Łódź Voivodeship' (in Polish) by S. Liszewski (2010) and B. Włodarczyk (2011 and 2012).
3   www.ziemialodzka.pl (22 April 2014).
4   Research on agritourism is systematically conducted by the Institute of Urban Geography and Tourism, University of Łódź. This chapter is chiefly based on theses by Pukosz (2007), Reczyńska (2013), Retelewska (2011) and Sobala (2013).
5   The number of these farms is estimated at 60 per cent of the total number of farms in Zone 1 of the metropolitan area of Łódź.

References

Bednarek-Szczepańska, M. (2011). *Mit o agroturystyce jako szansie rozwojowej dla polskiej wsi* [The Myth of Agritourism as a Development Opportunity for Polish Rural Areas]. *Czasopismo Geograficzne*, 82(3), pp. 249–270. Publisher: Polskie Towarzystwo Geograficzne, Warszawa.

Central Statistical Office (n.d.). www.stat.gov.pl

Liszewski, S. (2003). Region turystyczny/A Tourist Region. *Turyzm/Tourism*, 13(1), pp. 43–54. Publisher: Wydawnictwo Uniwersytetu Łódzkiego, Łódź.

Liszewski, S. (2005). Metropolitalny region turystyczno-wypoczynkowy. Przykład miasta Łodzi/A Metropolitan Tourist and Leisure Region: The City of Łódź – a Case Study. *Turyzm/Tourism*, 15(1–2), pp. 121–138. Publisher: Wydawnictwo Uniwersytetu Łódzkiego, Łódź.

Pukosz, A. (2007). *Monografia Stowarzyszenia Agroturystycznego Ziemi Wieruszowskiej.* Bachelor's thesis, Wydział Nauk Geograficznych, Uniwersytet Łódzki, Łódź.

Raport o stanie wiejskiej bazy noclegowej w Polsce. (1997). (A report on the condition of rural tourist accommodations in Poland). Projekt PL.-0310-02-02, Turystyka Wiejska: Rozwój wiejskiej bazy noclegowej, Program Phare Tourin II, DG Agroprogress International AL. Publisher: Centrum Doradztwa i Edukacji w Rolnictwie, Kraków, p. 62.

Reczyńska, K. (2013). *Konkurs 'Złota Grusza' czynnikiem rozwoju gospodarstw agroturystycznych w województwie łódzkim.* Master's thesis, Wydział Nauk Geograficznych, Uniwersytet Łódzki, Łódź.

Retelewska, A. (2011). *Specyfika działalności Stowarzyszenia Agroturystycznego Ziemi Zgierskiej.* Master's thesis, Wydział Nauk Geograficznych, Uniwersytet Łódzki, Łódź.

Sobala, A. (2013). *Zróżnicowanie oferty agroturystycznej w nadpilicznych parkach krajobrazowych.* Master's thesis, Wydział Nauk Geograficznych, Uniwersytet Łódzki, Łódź.

Włodarczyk, B. (Ed.). (2012). *Ruch turystyczny w Łodzi i województwie łódzkim w 2011 roku.* Publisher: ROT Województwa Łódzkiego, Łódź.

Wojciechowska, J. (2009). *Procesy i uwarunkowania rozwoju agroturystyki w Polsce* [The Processes and Conditions of Agritourist Development in Poland]. Publisher: Wydawnictwo Uniwersytetu Łódzkiego, Łódź.

Wojciechowska, J. (2011). Agroturystyka w Szwajcarii. In B. Włodarczyk (Ed.). *Turystyka. Księga jubileuszowa w 70. rocznicę urodzin Profesora Stanisława Liszewskiego.* Publisher: Wydawnictwo Uniwersytetu Łódzkiego, Łódź.

24 The basket of tourism products and services offered on the Internet by agritourism farms in selected European countries

Michał Jacenty Sznajder and Milena Malinowska

The Internet as an ideal medium for promotion of agritourism farms

The Internet is a commonly used medium. According to Seybert and Reinecke (2014),

> a large majority of Europeans make use of the Internet. In 2014, half of the EU population aged 16–74 used the Internet on portable computers or hand-held devices through a mobile phone network or wireless connection when not at home or at work. About one sixth of Europeans has never used the Internet.

If we add the use of the Internet at home and school, its significance will be even greater. It is natural that agritourism farms use the Internet for self-promotion. By using their own websites, business portals like Booking.com, Google-Earth or social networking media like YouTube and Facebook, agritourism farms can present their offer in an attractive way and sell their products and services even to tourists from distant corners of the world. Thus, the Internet has become a global medium enabling tourists to obtain information about the agritourism offer of any farm around the world. Undoubtedly, individual websites of agritourism farms and special vertical portals have become perfect tools to provide information about products and services offered by agritourism farms. Individual websites are more and more often a direct channel for marketing one's own products and services as well as food products offered by neighbours or even local manufacturers of folk products. Apart from that, websites are a perfect advertising tool, presenting agritourism farms in an attractive way (Kosmaczewska 2010). For these reasons websites of agritourism farms are widely available on the Internet. Apart from that, the information contained on the websites is a valuable research material, enabling analysis of different aspects of farms' activity, for instance, the basket of products and services offered by farms in a particular region. The characterisation of this basket includes both the number and frequency of the products and services in the offer.

Many factors affect both the number and frequency of products and services offered by agritourism farms, for example, the legal and economic environment in a particular country, its economic development and geographical location.

The influence of these factors will be discussed upon the results of a study of the Internet offers of 500 European agritourism farms located in four countries and in northern Scandinavia. The latitude, which is surely decisive in regards to types of products and services, is expressed by the following sequence: Italy, Austria, the United Kingdom, Poland, Scandinavia. Italy represents the southern European belt, Austria – the central European and Alpine belt, the United Kingdom – the western-central European belt and an island country, Poland – the eastern-central European belt, northern Scandinavia – the northern European belt. We selected 100 websites of agritourism farms from each country. Scandinavia was treated as one unit comprising farms situated in central and northern Norway, Sweden and Finland. The farms selected for the analysis were evenly distributed in each country.

New classification of products and services offered by agritourism farms

Running an agritourism business consists in offering and selling tourism products and services related to a farm or agricultural production. An agritourism product is a tangible product made or processed on an agritourism farm. Agritourism products include meals, food products, such as milk, meat, fish, bread, fruit and vegetables, as well as souvenirs made on a farm. Agritourism services are intangible. For example, these are different forms of accommodation, observation of a production process or cooking lessons. Natural and recreational values are the most significant elements in the creation of agritourism products and services. They are particularly important for tourists arriving from metropolitan areas.

When browsing the Internet offers of agritourism farms from the aforementioned countries, we can see that many products and services go far beyond the limits of what we traditionally associate with agritourism or even rural tourism. These products are chiefly offered by other types of tourism. Many items offered by agritourism farms do not have anthropogenic origin and are classified as non-anthropogenic natural values.

There is a long list of products and services offered by agritourism farms all over the world. Some of them are very popular, whereas others are niche products. They can be grouped. Since 2006 the literature has been using a division into 9 classes: accommodation, catering services, agri-sport, ethnography, agri-therapy, agri-recreational services, agri-entertainment, specific agritourism and direct sales (Sznajder *et al.* 2009, p. 134). When we browse the websites of 500 agritourism farms from the aforementioned European countries, we can see that they offer a much wider range of products and services than in the package prepared in 2006. It is absolutely necessary to include all products and services offered by agritourism farms. It is also necessary to prepare a new classification of products and services offered by agritourism farms. The classification is based on the following four grouping levels:

- Level 1 – *category of tourism*, marked with capital letters (Table 24.1);
- Level 2 – *types of products and services*, marked with Arabic numerals;
- Level 3 – *kinds of products and services*, marked with small letters;
- Level 4 – *varieties of products and services*, marked with dashes.

The new classification of tourism products and services provided by farmers consists of nine categories: sightseeing tourism, ecotourism, sports and recreation, rural tourism, agritourism, agri-therapeutics, ethnographic tourism, food tourism and pilgrimage tourism. In addition, the classification lists 28 types, 20 kinds and 11 varieties of products and services offered. The new classification includes products and services offered on the Internet by the European agritourism farms under study.

The process of creating an offer of an agritourism farm involves selection of products and services, appropriate exhibition of the offer and selection of the target segment of recipients. It is also necessary to adjust the offer to recipients' changing preferences. Owners of agritourism farms should update their offer to maintain their competitive capacity and the individual character of their products and services. Also, these actions usually extend the offer (Świetlicka 1997).

The most important components of the offer of agritourism farms are accommodation services (beds in guestrooms, bungalows, tents) and board (full board, self-catering, thematic meals, regional meals), access to natural space, guiding services (such as horse rides, tractor rides), sports and recreational equipment rentals (bicycles, canoes, nordic walking poles), sports equipment and caravan storage services, access to gardens and orchards, contact with farm animals (feeding animals, milking cows, collecting hens' eggs), crafts lessons (weaving baskets, making local culture products), participation in housework (making fruit and vegetable products, baking, preparing milk products), participation in farm work and field work, opportunity to observe unique species of plants and animals. It is extremely difficult to make an appropriate classification of such a rich and diversified list of agritourism products and services. The list should be updated as new products and services develop.

The basket of products and services

The term *basket of products and services* refers to products and services purchased by consumers and is used in macroeconomic studies to determine the currency inflation level, whereas *portfolio* refers to goods and services offered by a producer or service provider and is widely used by enterprises for their marketing actions. The basket of products and services characterises a list of products and services purchased by consumers in a particular period of time. The basic basket of expenses on products and services includes expenses on essential living needs, that is, food, hygiene, medication, education and upbringing, whereas the basket of higher-order needs includes secondary needs, such as culture, sports and leisure. According to this classification, expenses on relaxation on agritourism farms belong to higher-order products.

This elaboration uses the term *basket of agritourism products and services* to characterise the number and types of products and services that can be purchased on agritourism farms or in their direct neighbourhood. The basket includes all products and services listed in Table 24.1. The basket is characterised by two parameters: the number of products and services offered by an agritourism farm and the frequency of the offer. The frequency parameter reflects consumers' demand for individual tourism products and services.

The next part of this chapter presents the basket of agritourism products and services offered by farms in the aforementioned European countries. The basket of agritourism products and services refers to the list of products and services and the frequency at which they are offered. It is important to learn if the contents of the basket changes depending on the country and latitude. Therefore, it seems justified to pose the initial hypothesis that the latitude and country of origin significantly influence the contents of the basket. It will be important to discover if the number of products and services offered by agritourism farms depends on the country of origin (latitude). It is tempting to say that in more economically developed countries agritourism farms offer a smaller number of products and services than in less developed countries. Many farmers entering the market of agritourism and rural tourism might be convinced that their economic success is directly proportional to the number of products and services offered.

Rural tourism is developing dynamically. This fact is proved by a constant increase in the number of people running agritourism businesses, private accommodation and businesses providing access to facilities located in rural areas. This situation encourages farmers to extend their offer of products and services and improve their quality to make them competitive. This competitiveness should result in diversification and a high quality of products and services on offer so that they can meet tourists' demands and expectations rather than be a one-time 'bait' for arriving tourists (Balińska 2010; Meyer 2010).

The theoretical approach to assessment of the influence of the number of agritourism products and services offered by farms on their economical results is not clear enough. It is always possible to indicate the advantages and disadvantages of extending or limiting the number of products and services offered. On the one hand, one can argue that extension of the offer lowers the quality of these products and services and the agritourism farm does not know in which fields it should specialise. The extension of the number of products and services may also cause higher costs and result in low cost-effectiveness of the enterprise. On the other hand, one can indicate that reducing the number of agritourism products proves the market maturity of an agritourism farm and the products it offers are characterised by high quality. It is difficult to theoretically solve the dilemma of the influence of the number of products and services offered on the economics of an agritourism farm.

Table 24.1 A new classification of tourism products and services offered by agritourism farms, according to categories (capital letters), types (numerals), kinds (small letters) and varieties (dashes)

A Sightseeing tourism
  1 Terrain
  2 Panorama
  3 Monuments in rural areas
B Ecotourism
  1 Silva-tourism
  2 Flora and fauna watching
    a Safari
    b Bird watching
    c Whale watching
    d Diving
    e Collecting specimens
C Sports and recreation
  1 Hiking
  2 Horse riding
  3 Cycling
  4 Canoeing
  5 Sports and recreational games
D Rural tourism
  1 Holiday stay in the country
  2 Holiday stays in the mountains
  3 Holiday stays by the sea
  4 Holiday stays at lakes
  5 Holiday stays by rivers
E Agritourism
  1 Farm stay
    a (LARP):
      • Outdoor games
      • Paintball
      • Straw towns
      • Maize mazes
      • Quads
    b Farm observations:
      • Production process
      • Educational trail
      • Farm zoo
  2 Direct sales
    a Catering services
      • Picnic sites

      • Readymade food
      • Canteen
      • Restaurant
    b 'Pick your own' sales
    c Stalls
    d Souvenirs
  3 Holiday farm
  4 Conference farm
F Agri-therapeutics:
  1 Zootherapy:
    a Hippotherapy
    b Feline therapy
    c Canine therapy
    d Dolphin therapy
  2 Drugs made from plants and animals:
    a Aromatherapy
    b Apitherapy
  3 Special diets
  4 Mini-sanatoriums
G Ethnographic tourism:
  1 Folk art
  2 Historic farms
  3 Historic villages
  4 Museums
  5 Open-air museums
  6 Living open-air museums
H Food tourism
  1 Culinary tourism:
    a Regional cuisine
  2 Product tourism:
    a Wine tourism
    b Bakery tourism
    c Dairy tourism
I Pilgrimage tourism
  1 Pilgrimage routes
  2 Participation in rites

Source: Compiled by Michał Sznajder.

The number of products and services offered by European agritourism farms

The analysis of the Internet offers indicates that the number of products and services offered by one agritourism farm ranges from seven (the UK) to forty (the UK and Italy). The average number of products and services offered by all of the agritourism farms under study was 20.6. The lowest average number was in Austria: 18.6, followed by the UK: 19.2, Scandinavia: 20.3 and Italy: 22.5. The highest average number was in Poland: 22.7. Figure 24.1 shows the distribution of the number of products and services offered by agritourism farms in the countries under study at an interval of 5 products.

The data in Figure 24.1 clearly indicate differences in the distribution between the countries. The most favourable distribution is in the UK, followed by Austria, Italy and Scandinavia. The least favourable model of distribution is in Poland. The model distribution of the number of products and services offered by individual agritourism farms should range from 11 to 20. These are optimal limits. This number of products guarantees sufficient possibilities to diversify the agritourism offer and simultaneously maintain a high quality of the products on offer. As far as the farms offering not more than 11 products are concerned, their offer is relatively poor and insufficiently diversified for potential clients. In spite of the high quality of products on offer, the list is too short and thus, it may limit the group of recipients. If many agritourism farms offer the same number of identical products in one region, it is justified to conclude that the area is characterised by

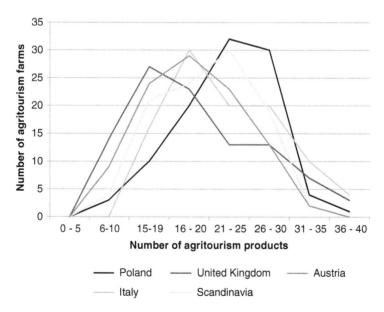

Figure 24.1 The distribution of the number of products and services offered by agritourism farms in selected European countries.

a poor agritourism offer and it may discourage potential visitors. The opposite situation may be observed if there are farms whose list of products is too rich and too diversified. The agritourism farms which offer more than 20 products and services to tourists are usually unable to guarantee high quality of all their products in the long-term. As a result, tourists will not be interested in low-quality products. Figure 24.2 is a radar chart comparing the number of products and services offered by agritourism farms in individual countries with the arithmetic mean of the number of products in the whole group under study.

The orange broken line is a model of the resultant mean values. The analysis points to the fact that British agritourism farms fall within the mean model, which means that the number of products is more compacted than the mean value for Europe. The Italian and Austrian model oscillate around the European mean model, whereas the Scandinavian model and, especially, the Polish model are contained outside the model resulting from the mean value, so they can be called uncondensed models.

Frequency of individual products, services and attractions offered

We analysed the frequency of nature tourism products and services offered according to the new classification shown in Table 24.1. Tables 24.2 to 24.10 show the results of the analysis.

In the *sightseeing tourism* category, terrain is the most significant, whereas historic buildings are the least significant element offered by agritourism farms. The

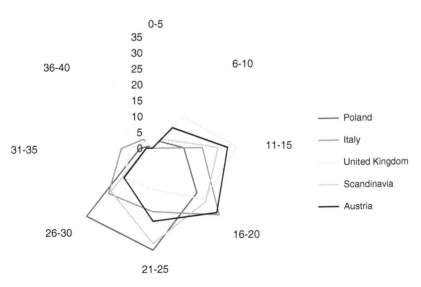

Figure 24.2 The number of products offered by agritourism farms in the countries under analysis.

Table 24.2 The frequency of the offer of *sightseeing tourism* products and services – percentage

Specification	Italy	Austria	United Kingdom	Poland	Scandinavia	Percentage
Sightseeing tourism including:	86	74	89	77	92	83.6
Terrain	70	67	68	50	71	65.2
Panorama	24	18	39	18	14	22.6
Monuments in rural areas	63	20	35	17	9	28.8

Source: The author's research.

Table 24.3 The frequency of the offer of *ecotourism* products and services – percentage

Specification	Italy	Austria	United Kingdom	Poland	Scandinavia	Percentage
Ecotourism, including:	89	44	55	55	51	58.8
Silva-tourism	58	51	89	78	86	72.4
Flora and fauna watching, including:	78	73	86	83	74	78.8
Safari	3	0	4	7	2	3.2
Bird watching	38	28	61	52	28	41.4
Whale watching	0	0	1	0	0	0.2
Diving	0	0	3	0	1	0.8
Collecting specimens	5	3	6	1	1	3.2

Source: The author's research.

Table 24.4 The frequency of the offer of *sports and recreation* products and services – percentage

Specification	Italy	Austria	United Kingdom	Poland	Scandinavia	Percentage
Sports and recreation, including:	59	84	85	78	91	79.4
Hiking	96	98	100	97	99	98
Horse riding	28	35	36	39	34	34.4
Cycling	54	48	59	51	47	51.8
Canoeing	14	14	11	28	39	21.2
Sports and recreational games	44	33	46	49	36	41.6

Source: The author's research.

Scandinavians stress the significance of terrain most often. The significance of monuments decreases along with the latitude. Monuments are the most important in Italy, but they are the least important in Scandinavia.

Table 24.5 The frequency of the offer of *rural tourism* products and services – percentage and location

Specification	Italy	Austria	United Kingdom	Poland	Scandinavia	Percentage
Rural tourism, including:	71	63	63	61	38	59.2
Holiday stay in the country	43	31	37	16	12	27.8
Farm location						
Mountains	48	91	15	36	28	43.6
Sea	15	0	19	3	5	8.4
Lakes	28	8	27	35	51	29.8
Rivers	29	25	18	37	24	26.6

Source: The author's research.

Table 24.6 The frequency of the offer of *agritourism* products and services – percentage

Specification	Italy	Austria	United Kingdom	Poland	Scandinavia	Percentage
Agritourism, including:	72	69	62	59	46	61.6
Farm stay, including:	75	75	59	50	54	62.6
LARP, including:	8	3	13	10	2	7.2
Outdoor games	37	17	20	19	17	22
Paintball	0	0	0	3	1	0.8
Straw towns	0	0	0	0	0	0
Maize mazes	0	0	0	1	0	0.2
Quads	1	0	4	3	4	2.4
Farm observations, including:	78	83	69	63	78	74.2
Production process	79	77	61	46	56	63.8
Educational trawl	59	52	54	34	45	48.8
Farm zoo	57	77	63	38	51	57.2
Direct sales, including:	23	25	11	7	20	17.2
Catering services, including:	36	79	31	67	75	57.6
Picnic sites	12	17	28	36	35	25.6
Readymade food	1	0	4	3	0	1.6
Canteen	32	78	51	51	67	55.8
Restaurant	53	11	13	16	12	21
'Pick your own' sales	23	2	4	4	0	6.6
Stalls	1	0	0	0	0	0.2
Souvenirs	10	9	4	1	8	6.4
Holiday farm	51	58	43	21	20	38.6
Conference farm	14	7	18	15	9	12.6

Source: The author's research.

Table 24.7 The frequency of the offer of *agri-therapeutics* products and services – percentage

Specification	Italy	Austria	United Kingdom	Poland	Scandinavia	Percentage
Agri-therapeutics, including:	57	77	67	47	62	62
Zootherapy, including:	41	64	66	37	53	52.2
Hippotherapy	21	27	24	19	15	21.2
Feline therapy	10	1	11	2	2	5.2
Canine therapy	9	0	13	1	3	5.2
Dolphin therapy	0	0	0	0	0	0
Drugs made from plants and animals, including:	10	5	0	3	3	4.2
Aromatherapy	7	0	0	1	1	1.8
Apitherapy	5	1	0	1	0	1.4
Special diets	1	0		1	3	1
Mini-sanatoriums	6	1	1	3	1	2.4

Source: The author's research.

Table 24.8 The frequency of products and services offered by agritourist farms in the countries under study in the *culinary tourism* category – percentage

Specification	Italy	Austria	United Kingdom	Poland	Scandinavia	Percentage
Culinary tourism, including:	68	77	37	62	61	61
Regional cuisine	39	38	24	46	42	37.8
Product tourism, including:	85	71	42	34	54	57.2
Wine tourism	39	0	1	1	1	8.4
Bakery tourism	51	37	14	22	19	28.6
Dairy tourism	31	61	47	20	47	41.2

Source: The author's research.

In the *ecotourism* category, products and services are significant in all the countries, but in Italy their significance is decisive. Agritourism farm owners in the UK, Scandinavia and Poland pay attention to the products and services of silva-tourism. In the UK and Poland they also pay attention to bird watching. Other forms of flora and fauna watching are of minor importance.

Products and services in the *sports and recreation* category are very popular and almost equally offered in the countries under analysis. Almost all agritourism farm owners point to the possibility of hiking in the surrounding areas. Cycling is the second most popular product on offer. Apart from that, the research revealed that many farms offer the opportunity to rent sports equipment. Every third agri-tourism farm offers horse riding to its clients.

Table 24.9 The frequency of the offer of *ethnographic tourism* products and services – percentage

Specification	Italy	Austria	United Kingdom	Poland	Scandinavia	Percentage
Ethnographic tourism, including:	14	0	7	10	9	8
Folk art	13	3	3	12	6	7.4
Historic farms	37	19	28	9	23	23.2
Historic villages	26	5	13	3	5	10.4
Museums	25	12	6	15	16	14.8
Open-air museums	28	21	27	31	26	26.6
Living open-air museums	1	1	2	5	1	2

Source: The author's research.

Table 24.10 The frequency of the offer of *pilgrimage tourism* products and services – percentage

Specification	Italy	Austria	United Kingdom	Poland	Scandinavia	Percentage
Pilgrimage tourism, including:	14	26	1	1	0	8.4
Pilgrimage routes	14	22	1	1	0	7.6
Participation in rites	3	7	1	1	0	2.4

Source: The author's research.

The frequency of products and services offered by agritourism farms in the *rural tourism* category is presented in Table 24.5. Owners of agritourism farms in Italy and the UK often emphasise the holiday character of their farms, whereas owners of agritourism farms in Scandinavia and Poland rarely stress this fact. The terrain surrounding an agritourism farm is also emphasised. In each country the smallest number of agritourism farms was located in coastal areas. In Austria agritourism farms are located mostly in mountainous areas. In all the countries mountains and rivers are some of the attractions offered by agritourism farms. In Poland and Scandinavia many farms are situated on lakes.

Products and services offered by agritourism farms in the countries under study in the *agritourism* category is presented in Table 24.6. Observation of the production process is of high significance in the offers of the farms under study. More than half of Italian, Austrian and British farms declare that they have educational trails. The fewest educational trails are in the offers of Polish farms. Catering services are also important elements of agritourism. Among the farms in Austria, the UK, Scandinavia and Poland, the most popular form of serving meals on the farm

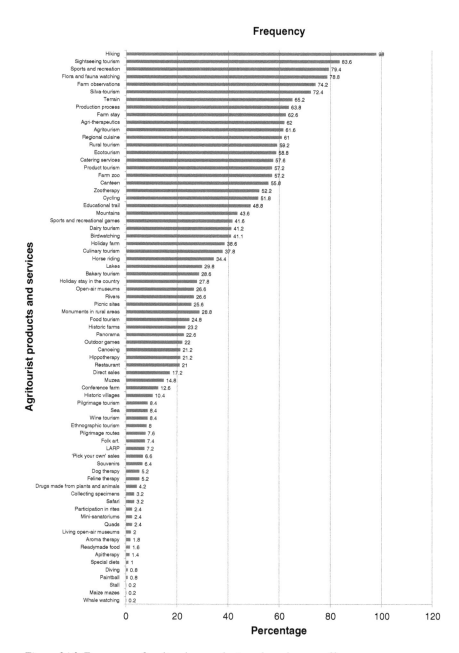

Frequency

Agritourist products and services	Percentage
Hiking	98
Sightseeing tourism	83.6
Sports and recreation	79.4
Flora and fauna watching	78.8
Farm observations	74.2
Silva-tourism	72.4
Terrain	65.2
Production process	63.8
Farm stay	62.6
Agri-therapeutics	62
Agritourism	61.6
Regional cuisine	61
Rural tourism	59.2
Ecotourism	58.8
Catering services	57.6
Product tourism	57.2
Farm zoo	57.2
Canteen	55.8
Zootherapy	52.2
Cycling	51.8
Educational trail	48.8
Mountains	43.6
Sports and recreational games	41.6
Dairy tourism	41.2
Birdwatching	41.1
Holiday farm	38.6
Culinary tourism	37.8
Horse riding	34.4
Lakes	29.8
Bakery tourism	28.6
Holiday stay in the country	27.8
Open-air museums	26.6
Rivers	26.6
Picnic sites	25.6
Monuments in rural areas	28.8
Food tourism	24.8
Historic farms	23.2
Panorama	22.6
Outdoor games	22
Canoeing	21.2
Hippotherapy	21.2
Restaurant	21
Direct sales	17.2
Muzea	14.8
Conference farm	12.6
Historic villages	10.4
Pilgrimage tourism	8.4
Sea	8.4
Wine tourism	8.4
Ethnographic tourism	8
Pilgrimage routes	7.6
Folk art.	7.4
LARP	7.2
'Pick your own' sales	6.6
Souvenirs	6.4
Dog therapy	5.2
Feline therapy	5.2
Drugs made from plants and animals	4.2
Collecting specimens	3.2
Safari	3.2
Participation in rites	2.4
Mini-sanatoriums	2.4
Quads	2.4
Living open-air museums	2
Aroma therapy	1.8
Readymade food	1.6
Apitherapy	1.4
Special diets	1
Diving	0.8
Paintball	0.8
Stall	0.2
Maize mazes	0.2
Whale watching	0.2

Figure 24.3 Frequency of agritourism products and services on offer.

is the canteen. By contrast, in Italy restaurants are predominant. 'Pick your own' service is possible on every fourth farm in Italy, whereas in the other countries there is minimal percentage of farms offering this form of sale.

The frequency of products and services offered by agritourism farms in the countries under study in the *agri-therapeutics* category is in Table 24.7. In all the countries agri-therapeutics is strictly correlated to zootherapy. Zootherapy is chiefly based on hippotherapy (horse therapy), but feline therapy and canine therapy are also important. Other types of therapies are minimal. Hippotherapy is the least popular and the least developed item in the agritourism offer of Polish and Scandinavian farms. Italian agritourism farms offer not only agri-therapy with animals, but they also try to develop this branch of agritourism by providing drugs made from plants and animals and mini-sanatoriums.

Table 24.8 shows the offer of farm owners in the *food tourism* category. Regional cuisine offers are very important everywhere. Product tourism reflects food processing traditions. Offers related to wine and bakery production are predominant in Italy, whereas dairy production is the predominant offer in Austria, the UK and Scandinavia. There is no specific profile of the product offer in Poland.

Ethnographic tourism category is presented in Table 24.9. Contrary to our expectations, ethnography is not a particularly frequent area of the offer of agritourism farms. These products are mostly offered by agritourism farms in Italy. They chiefly offer visits to museums and open-air museums.

Table 24.10. shows the share of *pilgrimage tourism* in the farms under study. In fact, there are no products of pilgrimage tourism in the offer of agritourism farms in the UK, Austria or Scandinavia. The Polish offer is significantly different to the other countries. Every fourth Polish agritourism farm makes reference to pilgrimage routes.

Figure 24.3 shows a synthetic diagram of the frequency of products and services offered by the 500 European agritourism farms under study. The most popular products were hiking and sightseeing tourism. The frequency of these products is 98 per cent and 83 per cent, respectively. The rarest products are whale watching, straw structures and maize mazes. This means that farmers offer less expensive and safer tourism products at low investment and operating costs. This is usually related to free gifts of nature that are of high scenic and recreational value.

Summary

The offers of agritourism farms published on the Internet are a perfect database for analysis of complicated processes related with the market of agritourism products and services. The analysis revealed that agritourism farms in European countries offered not only typical agritourism products and services but also those which were poorly or completely unrelated to agritourism. Classification of products and services has high cognitive significance. Therefore, in this chapter we propose a new classification of products and services provided by farmers. This updated classification has four levels: category, type, kind and variety.

The analysis of the Internet offers reveals that the number of products and services offered by one agritourism farm ranges from seven (the UK) to forty (the UK and Italy). The average number of products and services offered by all of the agritourism farms under study was 20.6. The model distribution of the number of products and services offered by individual agritourism farms should range from 11 to 20. This number of products enables both sufficient diversification of the agritourism offer and simultaneous maintenance of high quality of the products on offer. The Italian and Austrian models are concentrated, whereas the Scandinavian model and especially the Polish model are uncondensed.

The long list of products and services offered by agritourism farms on the Intern*et al*so includes the most and least popular products and services. Hiking tourism was the most popular and frequent product, with a frequency of 96 to 100 per cent, depending on the country. The second most popular product was sightseeing tourism, with a frequency ranging from 74 to 92 per cent, the mean value being 83 per cent. Whale watching was the least frequently offered product. It was listed by only one farm in the UK, while equally unpopular was the maize maze, listed by only one agritourism farm in Poland.

The analysis of the Internet offers of 500 European agritourism farms from five European countries indicates that some of the products on offer depend on the latitude, terrain, the economic development of a country, its history and tradition. As was observed, agritourism offers are hardly ever related to the sea. This means that relaxation at the seaside is dominated by other types of tourism. In Austria almost all agritourism farms are located in the mountains. In Italy offers are considerably influenced b: ecology and cultural, culinary and product heritage (wine and bakery products). The development of agri-therapy depends on the economic status of a country. Agri-therapy is the least developed in Poland, because domestic tourists cannot afford this service. Canoeing is usually offered in Sweden. Pilgrimage tourism is the most frequently listed item in Poland. Many products and services in Europe are offered equally frequently. This applies to walking and observation of production processes.

The popularity of products and services offered by agritourism farms on the Internet depends on the latitude to a certain extent. The following product are latitude-dependent: visiting monuments in rural areas, bakery and wine tourism, which is usually offered by Italian agritourism farms. There are many products whose presence in the basket of products and services is not influenced by latitude or the economic development of the countries under study. Some of these products are flora and fauna watching, hiking, sports and recreational games, farm observations and culinary tourism.

References

Balińska, A. (2010). Konkurencyjność produktu turystyki wiejskiej w opinii turystów. *Acta Scientarum Polonorum, Oeconomia*, 9(4), pp. 5–14. Publisher. SGGW w Warszawie, Warszawa.

Kosmaczewska, J. (2010). Witryny internetowe jako narzędzie kreowania konkurencyjności w agroturystyce. *Acta Scientarum Polonorum, Oeconomia*, 9(4), pp. 225–232. Publisher: SGGW w Warszawie, Warszawa.

Meyer, B. (2010). Nowe trendy w kształtowaniu produktów turystycznych. *Acta Scientarum Polonorum, Oeconomia*, 9(4), pp. 313–322. Publisher: SGGW w Warszawie, Warszawa.

Seybert, H. & Reinecke, P. (2014). *Internet and Cloud Services – Statistics on the Use by Individuals*. Statistics in focus 16/2014. Eurostat. http://ec.europa.eu/eurostat/statistics-explained/index.php/Internet_and_cloud_services_-_statistics_on_the_use_by_individuals [Retrieved 10 May 2016].

Świetlicka, U. (Ed.). (1997). *Agroturystyka*. Publisher: SGGW, Warszawa, pp. 490–498.

Sznajder, M. J, Przezbórska, L. & Scrimgeour, F. (2009). *Agritourism*. Publisher: CABI,.

25 Internet product and service offers by agritourism farms located in four metropolitan areas in Poland

Michał Jacenty Sznajder and Damian Dudziak

Poland is a country with serious demographic problems. Some people even speak of a demographic disaster. This situation has been caused by the Poles' economic emigration to the European Union countries, the USA and Canada and by a very low fertility rate. In spite of this situation, following global trends, there is a dynamic process of urbanisation in Poland. In fact, only Warsaw and Upper Silesia Metropoly can be regarded as the centre of a metropolis of European significance. The other metropolitan areas, such as those of Kraków, Łódź, Poznań or Wrocław are thought of as regional metropolises. The number of metropolitan areas in Poland ranges from 8 to 12, depending on the criteria used. There is still agriculture, agritourism farms and rural tourism in the metropolitan areas that used to be typical rural areas. Each of the 12 metropolitan areas in Poland is unique, but share some common traits.

We can ask if the offer of products and services presented by farmers running agritourism farms in individual metropolises is homogenous, poor or diversified. In order to answer this question we analysed the Internet offers of agritourism farms located in 4 selected metropolitan areas in Poland: Bydgoszcz-Toruń, Poznań, Szczecin and Wrocław. The metropolises are characterised by a diversity of tourism values. The Bydgoszcz-Toruń metropolitan area includes 19 administrative units (communes), the Poznań metropolitan area 23, the Szczecin metropolitan area 12 and the Wrocław metropolitan area 44. The research was conducted on a small but exhaustive sample.

The Union of Polish Metropolies (2003) provides comprehensive information on legal, demographic and economic status and the metropolises development in the country. The selected metropolitan areas are diversified in population. There are about 1.2 million inhabitants in both the Wrocław and Poznań metropolises; there are 0.62 million inhabitants in the Szczecin metropolis and about 0.77 million in the Bydgoszcz-Toruń metropolis. The terrain is one of the significant factors differentiating agritourism and rural tourism in these areas. The Wrocław agglomeration offers hilly areas for tourism. In the Poznań agglomeration tourists can spend time on the plains with a relatively large number of lakes. The Szczecin agglomeration is situated in the Oder River valley and delta and the Oder Lagoon. The Bydgoszcz-Toruń agglomeration lies in the Vistula River valley. Consumers are an important element diversifying the development of agritourism and rural tourism in metropolitan areas. The demand observed in the abovementioned metropolitan areas is created by the inhabitants of these agglomerations and by a specific inflow of tourists. In the Szczecin agglomeration, apart from the native inhabitants of the metropolis, people from Germany, especially from Berlin, use the offer of agritourism and rural tourism. In the Poznań agglomeration the services are also used by transit tourists from eastern Europe travelling west and those from western Europe travelling east (international tourism) as well as by tourists from southern Poland travelling north and those from northern Poland travelling south (seasonal, domestic holiday tourism). In the Wrocław metropolis the offer of agritourism and rural tourism is used by the inhabitants of Wrocław and surrounding areas and by transit tourists from southern Poland travelling north and those from northern Poland travelling south (seasonal, domestic holiday tourism). The Bydgoszcz-Toruń metropolitan area is not a tourist centre and it is more oriented towards local tourist traffic. In the Szczecin agglomeration the demand for tourism can chiefly be observed in the summer, whereas in the Poznań agglomeration it is the most balanced throughout the year and more intensive in the summer season (due to domestic tourism).

We analysed the basket of products and services offered by all agritourism farms in the aforementioned metropolitan areas that have a website indexed by maps.google.pl. The analysis investigates the basket and specifies the number and frequency of individual products and services. In total, the Google search engine indexed 196 agritourism farms in these areas, but as many as 114 of them did not yet have their own websites and only their contact details were indexed. This means that as many as 58 per cent of the agritourism farms in these areas do not use the full potential of promotion on the Internet. Of the total number of identified entities, 42 per cent had their own websites. Products and services were grouped into categories according to the scheme proposed by Sznajder (2015, see Chapter 24). The basket of products and services offered by agritourism farms in the Bydgoszcz-Toruń, Poznań, Szczecin and Wrocław metropolises includes 43 items of the 60 items listed in Sznajder's classification.

Figure 25.1 shows the structure of products and services offered by agritourism farms according to tourism categories (Level 1). One farm could provide many products and services in a particular product-and-service category. The comparison in Figure 25.1 confirms the fact that agritourism farms offer tourism products and services in most categories rather than in the agritourism category only. Non-agritourism products and services make up 67 per cent of all farmers' offers. It is necessary to enrich the offer of products and increase the competitiveness of agritourism farms. Thus, we cannot expect agritourism farms to offer only agritourism products and services. Sports, recreation and sightseeing were the products and services that were most often offered in other categories.

Figure 25.2 shows the total offer of products and services in all 4 metropolises by their occurrence frequency. The most common products and services in the offer are picnic spots, hiking and the panoramic location of the farm (panorama). The next positions, with more than 40 per cent occurrence frequency, include cycling and silva-tourism (forest tourism). There are individual offers of wine tourism, pilgrimage routes, folk art and safari.

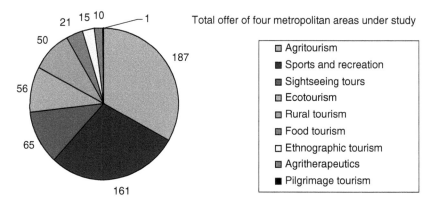

Figure 25.1   The structure of the basket of products and services in all metropolises by category.
Source: The authors' research.

On the other hand, one might ask how diversified the offer of agritourism farms in individual metropolises is in terms of the product and service categories. The analysis of the data shown in Figure 25.3 reveals that as the popularity of a particular product and service category decreases, we can observe diversification in the offer between the metropolitan regions. This particularly applies to sightseeing and ecotourism, where the Wrocław metropolitan area is in first place and the Poznań metropolitan area is in fourth place. For historical reasons, the Poznań metropolitan area is the leader in culinary tourism, ethnography and agri-therapy.

There are 36 different attractions in the basket of products and services offered by agritourism farms in the Poznań metropolitan area, 31 attractions in the Wrocław metropolitan area, 30 attractions in the Bydgoszcz-Toruń metropolitan area and 24 attractions in the Szczecin metropolitan area. Although the Poznań metropolis is not the most attractive area for agritourism, the offer of the agritourism farms in the region is the most diversified.

The most popular products and services in the Poznań metropolis are picnic spots, hiking and horse riding, where the frequency of occurrence exceeds 50 per cent. The least popular elements in the offer are pilgrimage routes, folk art, quads, educational trails and mini-spas. The offers of this region did not include 5 attractions which were offered in the other 3 metropolises: holiday countryside stays, paintball, 'pick your own' sales, sea, mountains, safari and special diets.

The most popular products and services in the Szczecin metropolis are picnic spots, panorama, hiking, cycling and lakes. The least popular elements in the offer are regional cuisine, rivers, holiday countryside stays, canoeing, bird watching, restaurants, paintball, educational trails, production processes, farm zoos, holiday farms and conference farms. The offers in this region did not include 19 attractions which were offered in the other 3 metropolises.

The Wrocław metropolitan area offers 31 different attractions. The most popular products and services are picnic spots, panorama, cycling and silva-tourism,

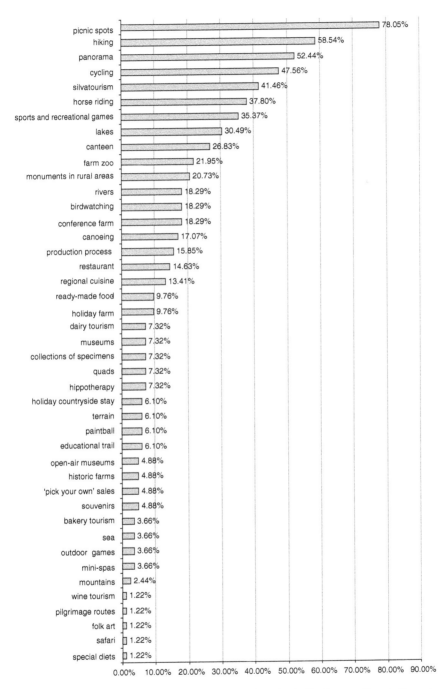

Figure 25.2 The total offer of products and services in the Bydgoszcz-Toruń, Poznań, Szczecin and Wrocław metropolises by their occurrence frequency.

Source: The authors' research.

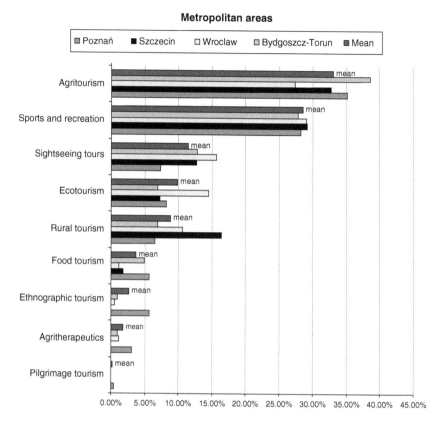

Figure 25.3　A comparison of the basket of agritourism products and services in individual metropolises.

Source: The authors' research.

where the frequency of occurrence exceeds 50 per cent. As results from individual listings on the websites show, the least popular elements in the offers are historic farms, safaris, restaurants, outdoor games, special diets and mini-spas. The offers of this region did not include 12 attractions which were offered in the other 3 metropolises.

The basket of products and services of nature tourism in the Bydgoszcz-Toruń metropolitan area includes 30 different attractions offered by agritourism farms. The most popular products and services are picnic spots and panorama, where the frequency of occurrence exceeds 50 per cent. As results from individual listings on the websites show, the least popular elements in the offer are bakery tourism, holiday countryside stays, monuments in rural areas, museums, collections of specimens, paintball, educational trails, holiday farms and mini-spas. The offers in this region did not include 13 attractions which were offered in the other 3 metropolises.

The analysis reveals that only 42 per cent of the agritourism farms in the agglomerations under study used the cheap form of promotion provided by the Internet. Apart from the products and services which are typical of agritourism, the offers also include attractions which belong to categories other than agritourism. Agritourism products and services make up 33 per cent of all tourism attractions offered by farmers. In the areas under study the number of attractions in the offers ranged from 20 to 36, which points to considerable diversification between the metropolises under analysis. The diversification can be explained in terms of historical and natural conditions. The most popular elements in the offers were picnic spots, hiking and panorama, whereas folk art, safaris and special diets were the least popular.

References

Aglomeracja wrocławska. (n.d.). http://aglomeracja.wroclaw.pl/ [Retrieved 30 June 2014]
Stowarzyszenie szczecińskiego obszaru metropolitalnego. (n.d.). http://www.som.szczecin. pl [Retrieved 30 June 2014]

26 Risk in rural tourism and agritourism

Jan Sikora

Risk: causes and types

The dynamic development of globalisation in societies causes significant transformations in the economy, culture and politics. It changes the way people think and behave and it contributes to more open and reflective ways of life and management, according to accepted values and ethical standards (Giddens 2004). On the one hand, it is difficult to predict these changes, plan them and control their course. On the other hand, they cause an increasing risk in human activity. The risk cannot be clearly determined, nor can its causes or effects be indicated. Being the effect of changes, risk needs to be calculated in each human action, for example, in decisions about to live, how to behave or how to run a business.

The changes caused by economic, social, demographic and political processes mean that the activity of people and societies face new forms of risk, which are different from the risk they confronted in the past. Contemporary processes of globalisation, especially in economics, involve risk caused by humans. This risk results from people exerting influence on the natural environment by means of modern technology, new knowledge and information. This risk is called ecological risk and it also entails danger to people's health. Different categories of risk emerging widely as a result of human activity cause people and society to face new challenges and choices.

According to Beck, a German sociologist investigating risk in the context of globalisation, a risk society is developing (Beck 2004). A risk society is not limited to nature and health risk, but it also encompasses other changes taking place in contemporary socio-economic life, such as unstable employment, increasing unemployment, decreasing importance of traditions and customs in the development of human identity and social communities and the disappearance of a traditional family model. According to Beck, it is significant that a risk society is characterised by the absence of spatial, time and social limits of risk and by the precarious nature of decisions. Therefore, it applies to all actions taken by individuals and social groups in all societies. Conversely, the minimisation of omnipresent risk in human activity in a modern society should involve the development of different forms of human activity and people's cooperation. The responsibility for risk control cannot be left only to authorities and politicians. Other social groups need to join them (Beck 2004).

In view of these considerations we should assume that risk can be defined as the possibility of loss or damage in view of the precariousness of consequences of future events or the circumstances of these events. Each individual human, social group, organisation or business entity is endangered in their activity by different types of risk, such as financial risk (loss of money), injuries suffered by employees or legal responsibility. Each risk may also influence the effectiveness of a business, social or political activity. It may affect the profitability of an organisation, cause problems in the accomplishment of goals or lead to stagnation and bankruptcy. Risk may be perceived as high or low, depending on the likelihood of an unfavourable result.

Risk that can be estimated quantitatively or measurably on the basis of previous experience may be subject to insurance. Thus, it is impossible to be insured against the risk which cannot be calculated quantitatively.

Examples of risk in rural tourism and agritourism

Running a non-agricultural business, such as rural tourism and agritourism, involves the processes of economic and social transformations. An example of such transformations is the implementation of requirements included in European Union strategies in rural areas, for example, the strategy of multifunctional rural development, sustainable development strategy and multifunctional agriculture strategy (Sznajder and Przezbórska 2006). These strategies approach rural tourism and agritourism as businesses determined by external and internal conditions. Objective external conditions are the components of the aforementioned rural development strategies. They guarantee that rural inhabitants can freely choose the types of non-agricultural enterprise. They point to the choice of rural tourism and agritourism as forms of non-agricultural activity according to the entrepreneur's economic, social and personal situation. Objective external conditions refer to the rules of market economy, regulations concerning certain business activities, and rules concerning crediting, taxation and independence of tourism business entities. Subjective external conditions involve social attitudes in different communities; other people's attitudes, including the attitudes of local authorities; human mentality and cooperation between people. All these conditions may either favour or inhibit the tourism activity in rural areas.

On the other hand, objective internal conditions concern the economic and organisational situation and the technical and utility infrastructure and social infrastructure in rural areas, rural tourism enterprises and farms. By contrast, subjective internal conditions concern the personality of the people starting tourism and agritourism enterprises in rural areas. These conditions include the traits of the human capital of rural inhabitants, the owners and staff of tourism entities, such as knowledge, qualifications, motives and personality traits (courage, hard work, honesty, optimism, solidarity, readiness to take risk).

In view of the aforementioned conditions of the tourism and agritourism activity in rural areas, we can notice that anyone who starts a business in tourism must meet these conditions (Sikora and Wartecka-Ważyńska 2014). Not only do they motivate one to start an enterprise from the position of making a profit, but they also encourage one to invest their finances, assets and human capital. These actions involve not only taking the right decisions about the tourism and agritourism activity in a situation of continuous precarious factors but they also lead to taking the risk resulting from this activity. Running a non-agricultural business, including rural tourism and agritourism business, is also determined by ethical rules, which are included in two global codes: *The Manifesto for a Global Economic Ethic* (Global Ethic Foundation 2009) and *The Global Code of Ethics for Tourism* (UN 1999).

Running a tourism business as such, including businesses in rural areas, forces people to adopt more open and reflective lifestyles, according to accepted values and ethical standards. *The Manifesto for a Global Economic Ethic*, which was adopted by the United Nations in 2009, assumed the 'principle of humanity' as the superior, universal value recommended to states and business entities. According to the principle, each human being has inalienable and absolutely inviolable dignity, regardless of their age, sex, race, colour of skin, physical and mental capacity, language, religion, political views, nationality and social origin. This means that people must always be the subjects of rights and actions and it is unacceptable that people should become the objects of commercialisation in social life. As a fundamental rule of global ethics in business, humanity is supported by other ethical values, such as respect for humans, moral duty pointing to the support of good, the values of justice, solidarity, honesty and tolerance.

The other document, *The Global Code of Ethics for Tourism*, which was adopted by the World Tourism Organisation in 1999, contains the values and standards for the implementation of these values, oriented towards people's cognitive, leisure and recreational needs. The document lists such values as 'sustainable and generally available tourism', 'protection of the environment, natural resources and cultural heritage' and 'the universal right to tourism and leisure'.

The Global Code of Ethics for Tourism includes the professional and ethical norms applied in the activity of most tourism entities. They also apply to tourists and owners in rural areas. The code includes such norms as enforcing adherence to local laws, behaviours and customs; requiring a guarantee of safety for tourists, visitors and their property; directing tourism entrepreneurs to provide reliable and objective information to tourists and to demand fair prices for the tourism services they provide. It is obvious that the economic aim of a tourism enterprise operating in a free market is to make a profit. In order for the profit to be approved not only fiscally but also ethically by employees and tourists the entities of rural tourism and agritourism should consequently abide by the ethical norms and values recommended. Then, rural tourism and agritourism will strengthen the ethical values and norms which may contribute to decreasing and limiting the risk occurring in this non-agricultural activity.

The following general types of risk can be observed in rural tourism and agritourism:

- Business risk: the precarious nature of particular conditions of the functioning of a specific agritourism farm or other tourism entity in rural areas, for example low quality of tourism services, the instability of economic, natural and political dangers affecting rural tourism.

- Financing risk: indicates that the tourism entity may encounter difficulties when attempting to acquire funds or other financial aid to fulfil the commitments related to financial instruments.
- Financial risk: refers to the possibility of loss due to reckless decisions and failed investments on agritourism farms or in other tourism entities operating in rural areas.
- Cash flow risk: indicates the lack of a sufficient amount of cash available to cover the financial commitments of a tourism entity.
- Market risk: points to the segments of the rural tourism market which cannot be diversified due to the absence of orientation, the impossibility to recognise tourists interested in rural tourism and agritourism.

There are also other detailed types of risk in rural tourism and agritourism, which are specific to this type of non-agricultural business activity:

- Economic and financial risk: points to the lack of sufficient funds to purchase the means of production, land, tools of work and agritourism farm equipment, which are necessary to provide tourism services. This particularly applies to economic and financial aspects especially the costs of tourism services, their economic effects, price and innovation policies, sources of financing and accounting analysis of the business activity.
- Accommodation and board risk: Accommodation services involve ensuring the safety of visitors staying in tourism facilities in rural areas and on agritourism farms. Risk results not only from the standard and quality of the facility but also from satisfying the demand for relaxation, care, nutrition and culture. The risk is minimised by conforming to relevant legal regulations concerning tourism services and other detailed building, sanitary and fire safety regulations.
  Accommodation services also involve catering services, providing board to visitors and they are important to tourists' health and wellbeing. Risk can be minimised by taking due care to provide high quality and fresh meals prepared and served in a clean place. It is also important to adjust board to guests' needs, according to their national tradition and culture.
- Technical and utility risk: points to the appropriate management of agritourism farms and other rural tourism facilities so that tourists and other visitors can safely relax there.
- Psychosocial safety maintenance risk: concerns the characteristics of the human capital oriented towards the tourism activity. The risk applies to the personnel of rural tourism facilities and families running agritourism farms. This capital is composed of occupational qualifications, skills, personality traits, lifestyle, job satisfaction and the ability to co-exist with others. All these factors make a favourable or unfavourable atmosphere for visitors staying and relaxing in an agritourism facility.

- Cultural conditions risk: rural tourism and agritourism are based on various elements of the cultural heritage of Polish rural areas. The multitude of elements of folk culture and its diversity favours the creation of products of rural tourism and agritourism. In this aspect risk is related not only to the diversity of culture in a particular area or its absence, but also to the fostering, protection, interpretation, delivering of information, promotion and the awareness of fostering local cultural values.
- Insurance risk: farmers running agritourism farms and owners of rural tourism facilities should be insured against accidents which are hazardous to tourists' health or safety. Insurance companies offer different options for providers of tourism services, including agritourism services. Insured farmers owning tourism facilities reduce the possibility of damage and loss caused by tourists staying on their farms.

However, regardless of the classification of risk in rural tourism and agritourism, it is significant to limit it, for example, by risk management. Each type of risk endangers both the safety of tourists (the demand-related aspect of risk) and the owners of the facilities providing tourism services in rural areas (the supply-related aspect of risk).

Risk management in rural tourism and agritourism

Rural tourism and agritourism are examples of non-agricultural enterprise in rural areas. Like each kind of enterprise, they also cause positive or negative changes in the rural community and thus, they inevitably involve risk. For this reason it is necessary to take measures to eliminate or limit risk and to assume a risk management strategy. Risk management consists of tourism entities taking actions to identify, analyse and react to risk, including risk control and risk minimisation.

The course of a risk management process mostly consists of the following elements:

- identification and analysis of the risk causing danger to the owners of rural tourism facilities and tourists who use them;
- assessment of the potential influence of risk on the activity of these tourism entities and tourists staying there;
- reaction to risk, where the owners and staff of rural tourism facilities make decisions and tourists themselves take actions to reduce or eliminate risk,
- skilful coping with the consequences of unpredicted events causing loss or damage due to the risk involved;
- controlling and monitoring the risk identified, identifying new risk and monitoring the implementation of actions to reduce the risk.

The risk management strategy should also involve the owners of rural tourism facilities and tourists taking out insurance against a possible loss or legal liability and, above all, the strategy should include the introduction of safety precautions on agritourism farms and other rural tourism facilities. It is undeniable that tourism risk in rural areas can be significantly limited by widely applied practice, which is much wider than in mass tourism and which is in agreement with the ethical values and behavioural norms of the managers, owners and employees of tourism facilities and rural inhabitants (Sikora *et al.* 2014).

Thus, risk management in rural tourism and agritourism involves not only the analysis and assessment of its occurrence but it chiefly involves the preparation of specific methods resolving risk-related problems and compensating the occurrence of risk (Roszkowski and Wiatrak 2005).

References

Beck, U. (2004). *Społeczeństwo ryzyka – w drodze do innej nowoczesności*. Publisher: Wydawnictwo Naukowe SCHOLAR, Warszawa.

Giddens, A. (2004). *Socjologia*. Publisher: Wydawnictwo Naukowe PWN, Warszawa.

Global Ethic Foundation. (2009). *The Manifesto for a Global: Economic Ethic Consequences for Global Business*. Global Ethic Foundation, Tuebingen. http://www.globaleconomicethic.org/02-manifesto-02-eng.php [Retrieved 1 January 2017]

Roszkowski, J. & Wiatrak, A.P. (2005). *Zarządzanie projektem. Istota, procedury i ich zastosowanie przy korzystaniu ze środków Unii Europejskiej*. Publisher: SGGW, Warszawa.

Sikora, J., Kaczocha, W. & Wartecka-Ważyńska, A. (2014). Etyczny wymiar turystyki wiejskiej w warunkach globalizacji. In M. Kazimierczak (Ed.). *Etyczny wymiar podróży kulturowych*. Publisher: Akademia Wychowania Fizycznego im. Eugeniusza Piaseckiego, Poznań, pp. 102–112.

Sikora, J. & Wartecka-Ważyńska, A. (2014). *Wybrane uwarunkowania turystyki wiejskiej*. Publisher: Bogucki Wydawnictwo Naukowe, Poznań.

Sznajder, M. & Przezbórska, L. (2006). *Agroturystyka*. Publisher: Polskie Wydawnictwo Ekonomiczne, Warszawa.

UN. (1999). *Global Code of Ethics for Tourism*. UN World Tourism Organisation. http://cf.cdn.unwto.org/sites/all/files/docpdf/gcetbrochureglobalcodeen.pdf [Retrieved 1 January 2017]

27 Tourism segmentation in rural tourism and agritourism in metropolitan areas

Arkadiusz Niedziółka

Introduction

Agritourism is a leisure stay in the country on agritourism farms owned by farmers. Agritourism services are provided to tourists, whom we will call 'agritourists'. More rarely these services are addressed to the people who do not stay overnight at the places managed by rural accommodation providers. These people are defined as one-day visitors or trippers, who may use one agritourism service, which is usually complementary, or they may use a package of services, but they are not consumers of accommodation services.

This section of the book presents the essence of segmentation in tourism and agritourism based on the literature. It defines segmentation, determines the segmentation criteria and presents individual segments and the corresponding groups of tourists.

This section presents the essence of segmentation in agritourism, the motivation for agritourism activity and the typology of visitors to agritourism farms, with a division into agritourists and agri-trippers, that is, one-day visitors.

Segmentation in tourism

Consumers, that is, tourists, are the most important component of development in tourism and hotel management. The development of the tourism and recreational economy depends on tourists staying at hotel facilities in tourism regions. For this reason, both tourism entities and local authorities should promote their activity with different marketing tools. Hotels, motels, guesthouses, agritourism farms and other accommodation facilities as well as travel agencies and transport companies should communicate with the market effectively.

Promotion is usually defined in the functional or instrumental aspect. In the former aspect, promotion is interpreted as any personal or impersonal action encouraging purchasers to buy a product or to behave according to the seller's will and idea (Santon 1975, p. 467). In the instrumental aspect promotion is a set of tactic and strategic means of communication by means of which an enterprise sends information to the market and thus develops a favourable opinion about itself and its products. In consequence, this is supposed to motivate potential and current purchasers to buy products from the enterprise (Panasiuk 2013, p. 151).

Promotional actions in tourism are addressed to potential consumers of tourism goods and services. The aim of these actions is to reach individual segments of the market and groups of tourists. They are supposed to encourage potential tourists to visit a tourism region, use the offer of accommodation facilities and to buy a particular package of services. The people who are interested in the offer participate in the process of tourism consumption.

Tourist consumption is a process which begins before purchasing tourism products (a tourism and recreational event) and continues after the purchase. The following four stages can be distinguished in the process (Panasiuk 2013, p. 62):

- the emergence and observation of a tourist need;
- planning the purchase and making a decision;
- purchasing;
- participation in tourism and recreation;
- impressions after the tourism and recreational event.

The concept of tourism market segmentation is a term closely related to tourist consumption, because individual elements, that is, groups of tourists, participate in the consumption of tourism goods and services. Segmentation consists in dividing the market into smaller segments, which differ between each other in terms of clients' expectations concerning products, purchasing methods and other criteria (Oleksiuk 2007, p. 146). If we generalise the phenomenon, we can state that segmentation is a process of planning in marketing and the process consists in dividing the markets so as to achieve the maximum effectiveness (Oleksiuk 2007, p. 147). Segmentation enables one to gain competitive advantage over other entities when operating in the tourism market. Effective management of the segmentation process enables identification and concentration on one homogenous group of tourists. As far as market segmentation is concerned, providers of tourism services should address their offers to different groups of tourists, for example:

- tourists who prefer passive relaxation;
- active tourists trekking in the mountains, canoeing, riding horses, sailing, etc.;
- pilgrims;
- ecologists;
- spa visitors;

As far as the market segmentation in tourism is concerned, it is important to have a marketing strategy to identify segments of the market and to use appropriate marketing for each segment (Hall *et al.* 2009, p. 45). It is also important to recognise the traits of a contemporary consumer of tourism services, including increased awareness of consumer rights and a more rational attitude to the market offer:

- tourists' openness to new cultures, searching for new places of tourist exploration;

- extension of consumers' spatial mobility;
- increased respect and searching for nature and actions taken to protect the environment;
- facilitation of striking up interpersonal relationships and integration with local communities.

A modern consumer is usually a demanding client and therefore tourism entities constantly observe and monitor consumer markets in tourism. It is important to recognise consumers' new needs and preferences and to adjust the offer so as to make products more attractive and to introduce innovativeness. As far as the traits of a new consumer of tourism services are concerned, the traits related with ecotourism are particularly important, as they involve the issues of environmental protection. Aspects related with one's openness to new cultures, visiting monuments, exploring the cultural and historical heritage and striking up interpersonal relationships with local communities are also important features of ecotourism.

In order to reach consumers it is necessary to promote tourism goods and services effectively. When planning promotional campaigns it is necessary to remember the differences between the market of consumer and the market of enterprises. The information and messages addressed to individual consumers through a distributor, such as a travel agency, must encourage purchasers to buy products (Briggs 2003, p. 91).

The criteria of agritourism market segmentation

The process of market segmentation plays a vital role in marketing activity in tourism. It consists of dividing clients or potential clients within a particular market into groups, that is, into segments, where all the clients have similar demands satisfied by a specific marketing composition (Dunbar *et al.* 2003, p. 24). Downey and Ericsson (1987) define segmentation as classification of clients into segments or categories according to appropriate features. Altkorn (1995) points to the existing diversification and splitting up of tourist demand, which requires sellers' diversified reactions. Therefore, it is necessary to divide the market into relatively homogenous groups of tourists.

Tourism typology consists in identifying and describing typical traits of consumers of tourism services and in classifying them into individual groups, which can be called 'types'. A comparison of tourism types enables analysis of the demand for tourism products. Typology is a broader issue than segmentation, which was earlier described in this chapter, because it also includes a comparative study of individual groups and their classification (Niezgoda and Zmyślony 2006, p. 165).

Each tourist can be characterised by such traits as age, sex, stage of the family life cycle, household size, occupation, income, education and nationality. These are the most popular segmentation criteria. Table 27.1 presents the criteria in a clear and distinct manner.

When analysing the table above, it is necessary to say that all of the variables included in it, both the objective and subjective ones, are very important criteria

Table 27.1 The tourist market segmentation criteria

Segmentation criteria	
Objective variables	*Subjective variables*
Demographic criteria: * age * stage of family life cycle * sex * household size * occupation * income * education * nationality Geographic criteria: * geographic area * distance between place of residence and place of stay Geodemographic criteria[1] Purpose (motive) of travelling Seeking benefits	Psychosocial criteria and lifestyle: * personality * habits, customs * susceptibility to other people's influence * lifestyle Special events in one's life Reaction to product: * purchaser's status * purchasing frequency * purchasing method * degree of loyalty * stage of purchase decision * price of product or service

Source: The author's compilation based on Niezgoda and Zmyślony 2006, p. 151.

[1] The geodemographic criterion consists of combining the data concerning the age, family size and life cycle and the amount of income with a particular type of place of residence and living conditions.

of selection of the right segment of the tourism market. Tourism entities should follow these criteria in their promotional policies. However, it is necessary to note that there are a few fundamental dilemmas which emerge during the segmentation procedure, namely (Jedlińska 1999, pp. 35–36):

- How should it be done? Should we hire a marketing research agency or let our own managerial staff do it?
- How long-lasting should the selected criteria be if we know that after some time they might not account for tourists' behaviours and expectations?
- Which of the marketing instruments should be chosen and how should they be adjusted to segment profiles?
- Should the segments be as extensive as possible (this would make handling the segments cost-effective)?
- Should the segmentation be based on purchasers' behaviours rather than traits or should there be a combination of several traits, which will result in smaller segments, but will adequately determine purchasers' behaviours?

It is also possible to consider extending the offer to other segments of the market, including foreign segments. As far as agritourism is concerned, this should involve the ability of farmers and their family members to speak foreign languages. It is often possible to find an agritourism offer addressed to foreign markets in borderland areas or in places characterised by outstanding tourism values and which have a strong position among the areas of tourism response.

Segmentation may play a very significant role in the development of rural tourism and agritourism. It may contribute to specialisation of an agritourism farm in handling one or two segments of the market. These may be agritourism facilities receiving disabled persons or organised groups, such as ecologists or nature lovers. This might also be an agritourism farm which offers sports and recreational equipment for rent, where tourists following different forms of qualified tourism stay overnight. This group may also include an agritourism offer including horse-riding lessons, hippotherapy or coach rides. The farmer offering agritourism services may also offer skiing equipment for rent if the farm is close to ski slopes and lifts.

Agritourism associations may also use market segmentation. These organisations may promote their members' agritourism services, addressing their offers to different segments of the market. In the same way as an individual rural accommodation provider, these entities may effectively communicate with different groups of consumers and offer them various forms of relaxation and recreation.

The process of tourism segmentation in agritourism in metropolitan areas

Big city dwellers are the most common consumers of tourism services in agritourism. Tourists leave metropolitan areas for the country and rest on farms in an unpolluted natural environment. The process of agritourism market segmentation in metropolitan areas takes place by using appropriate segmentation criteria corresponding to a specific situation. The starting point may be either the consumer or product. As far as the former element is concerned, the classification of purchasers is based on the following criteria (Strzembicki 2003, p. 191):

- socio-economic (e.g. income, occupation, education, place in a particular socio-occupational group);
- demographic (e.g. age, sex, family size);
- psychographic (factors referring to one's lifestyle, e.g. ways of spending free time, hobbies, participation in cultural life, holidays and entertainment, or factors referring to one's interests, e.g. family, home, surroundings, fashion).

The other group of segmentation criteria includes the criteria which are specific to a particular product. According to Kotler (1999), this group of factors encompasses the variables resulting from the type of consumers' reaction to specific characteristics of the product, consumers' behaviours in particular situations, their attitudes expressed towards products and their loyalty to the offer and enterprise.

The assumption that purchase decisions are determined by consumers' values and preferences underlies the approach to product segmentation in agritourism. Thus, we can identify tourists who prefer active leisure, for example, horse riding, walking or water sports such as canoeing and sailing. On the other hand, we can also identify tourists who prefer passive leisure and spend their free time reading books, watching television or having a barbecue.

Sznajder and Przezbórska (2006) present an interesting division of tourists according to the period of their stay on an agritourism farm. They group tourists into the segments of overnight visitors and those staying on a farm without consumption of accommodation services, as follows:

- temporary agritourists – spending up to 3 or 4 hours on a farm, for example, watching farm work;
- one-day agritourists – spending a whole day on a farm, without staying overnight, for example, having an all-day picnic;
- overnight agritourists – spending a whole day on a farm and staying overnight;
- weekend agritourists – arriving on Friday or Saturday and leaving on Sunday;
- holidaymakers – spending their holidays on a farm (1 or 2 weeks, to a month or longer).

When we look at the aforementioned segments, we can observe a certain contradiction. The first two terms, 'temporary agritourist' and 'one-day agritourist', are not compatible with the official tourism terminology concerning the term 'visitor', according to the time spent by the tourist away from their place of permanent residence. In these 2 identified names of consumers of agritourism services the person who arrives at an agritourism farm does not use its accommodation offer, but wants to use one or two recreational services, such as horse-riding lessons or hippotherapy. In 1963 at a UN conference on agritourism, such people were called 'one-day visitors' or 'trippers' (the two terms are synonymous). As far as agritourism is concerned, a person spending time on an agritourism farm, but not staying overnight, could better be called an 'agri-tripper' or 'one-day agri-visitor'. In reference to the first segment given by the authors cited above, the terms 'temporary agri-tripper' or 'one-day agri-visitor' would be more appropriate options. As far as the second segment is concerned, if we continue using the adjectives 'temporary' and 'one-day', the terms 'one-day agri-tripper' or 'one-day agri-visitor' should be used. As far as the other segments of the market are concerned, that is, the 'overnight agritourist', 'weekend agritourist' and 'holidaymaker', the terms are absolutely correct.

When we focus on the 'overnight agri-tourist', one problematic issue needs to be stressed. When a visitor or visitors want to arrive at an agritourism farm for only 1 night, this option can present the host with the problem of cost-effectiveness. The reference publications rarely mention this problem. However, it is necessary to note that many agritourism farms, especially those in crowded tourism resorts, do not receive visitors for a single night (*Agroturysta* 2010, p. 28).

The process of segmentation of agritourists in metropolitan areas is a difficult task. Usually an agritourism offer in the form of an Internet commercial or advertisement placed in an agritourism catalogue is addressed to 'everybody'. However, the concentration of a particular agritourism farm on one or two segments of the market in metropolitan areas may contribute to a greater number of arrivals of selected groups of tourists. In this case the accommodation facility will specialise in providing services to a specific segment of agritourists.

The segmentation of agritourists in urban areas should be preceded by an investigation of the tourism market and marketing research. These are difficult and time-consuming operations, but if they are properly carried out, in the future they will enable an agritourism farm to specialise in providing services to one or two groups of tourists.

Selected groups of agritourists

As was previously emphasised, the term 'agritourists' was introduced by Sznajder and Przezbórska (2006). In turn, agritourists can be divided into different segments and groups of tourists. In recent years there have been numerous reference publications discussing tourists visiting agritourism farms and there have been a lot of studies on people visiting farms to relax in the country. Tourists have been surveyed to express their opinions about the agritourism services they were using at the moment and their motives for using the agritourism offer have been investigated.

According to Kosmaczewska (2013), in order to meet the expectations of a precisely defined group of purchasers of agritourism services market segmentation in agritourism might take the following traits into account:

- social – social class, occupational class and others;
- economic – income, possessions, education;
- demographic – age, sex, marital status, education, family;
- psychographic – lifestyle, personality, interests, hobbies;
- geographic – place of residence, climate, topography.

Coming back to groups of tourists, or to be more precise, agritourists, it is necessary to say that there are different agritourism segments. Usually these segments include parents with small children, elderly people, nature lovers, social groups and foreign tourists (Kania *et al.* 2005, pp. 120–121). Sikora (1999) also adds the segments of tourists playing sports, members of various clubs and associations and disabled people. As results from different studies show, families with children are the most common visitors to agritourism farms (Czerwińska-Jaśkiewicz 2013, pp. 76–86; Niedziółka 2010, p. 349; Zawadka 2010, p. 139). Also, as results from other research findings indicate, city inhabitants are the main group of tourists taking recreation in the country and using the offer of agritourism farms (Zawadka 2013, p. 112).

In Knecht's (2009, p. 26) opinion, tourists staying at agritourism farms benefit in the following way:

- they experience a different reality and satisfy their cognitive needs;
- they improve their health, spending their leisure actively and having direct contact with nature;
- they satisfy their desire for contact with people and meeting new people;
- they have an opportunity to gain experience of and learn about new cultures and traditions;

- they have an opportunity to spend their leisure in an alternative way and use unique offers that are unavailable in the city;
- they experience rural life by direct participation in it;
- they develop their interests and have an opportunity to acquire new skills;
- they have an opportunity to consume natural and fresh food and learn about the food production process;
- they have contact with animals;
- they develop the attitude of tolerance to different views and behaviours.

The main motive for using the offer of rural tourism and agritourism is willingness to rest in a different environment than the urban one. As was previously emphasised, it is related with the fact that city dwellers, inhabitants of urban agglomerations, are the most common consumers of agritourism services. The most important motive of tourists from metropolitan areas to spend their leisure on agritourists farms is a willingness to relax in an unpolluted region, in silence and to regenerate their physical and mental strength. The following segments of agritourists can be distinguished among groups of tourists arriving from metropolitan regions:

- families with small children;
- active agritourists – this is related to the presence of special values in the areas of agritourism reception: routes for hiking, cycling and horse riding; water areas; ski trails;
- lovers of history, architecture, museums;
- passive agritourists, who relax passively during all of their stay;
- pilgrims, who participate in services at churches, mosques and other places of worship in the region;
- ecotourists, for whom the most important thing is contact with nature combined with relaxation and visiting areas of natural value, including protected areas, such as national parks, scenic parks and nature reserves.

One-day visitors in agritourism

Both cultural and natural tourism values are often admired by people who do not spend even one night away from their place of residence. For example, they go for a few hours to a place situated a few kilometres from home and visit a castle, museum, open-air museum, historic church or they hike in the mountains for a few hours or ride bicycles. In tourism such visitors are defined as trippers or one-day visitors. Trippers can also enjoy different attractions on agritourism farms: usually these are complementary attractions. In this case we can talk about agri-trippers, as was described earlier in the section about market segmentation in agritourism. Thus, an agri-tripper is a person who visits an agritourism farm for one day and spends a few hours there, for example, or uses the services provided by the owner, such as a sleigh ride in winter. An agri-tripper does not use accommodation services provided by the farm, but can use board services, such as in the evening having a barbecue together with friends, who stay overnight on the farm. The recreational services provided by agritourism farm owners are usually addressed to overnight tourists. However, as was described above, they may also be addressed to agri-trippers. Recreational services provided to agri-trippers on agritourism farms include the following forms:

- barbecuing with friends staying overnight on an agritourism farm;
- relaxation in a gazebo;
- watching, photographing and feeding farm animals;
- sightseeing tours of a mini-zoo;
- horse-riding lessons given by an instructor who is or is not a member of the family providing the agritourism services;
- hippotherapy;
- coach rides or sleigh rides in winter;
- organisation of First Holy Communion receptions, baptism receptions and other special events.

The forms of recreational services listed above are addressed to agri-trippers. However, it is necessary to stress the fact that not all agritourism farms provide services to people who do not stay overnight.

To sum up the considerations on agritourists and agri-trippers, it is necessary to agree with Strzembicki (2003), who thinks that if a farm runs an agritourism activity on a small scale, the market niche strategy, which is sometimes called concentrated marketing, is the right form of market segmentation. It consists in business specialisation and providing services to one segment of the market, for example. an agritourism farm providing services only to lovers of active tourism. Concentrated marketing can also be addressed to agri-trippers.

Summary and conclusions

The success of an agritourism activity depends on an adequate number of tourists visiting agritourism farms and using different services offered by rural accommodation providers. Tourists are diversified – they might be families with children, individual holidaymakers, active tourists, disabled people or youth groups. Each of these groups of tourists is defined as a segment of the agritourism market.

Apart from agritourists, the people who do not want to stay overnight can also stay on agritourism farms. They are called 'agri-trippers' or simply 'one-day visitors'. Similarly to tourists, they can also use some recreational services such as barbecuing, bonfires, coach and sleigh rides or hippotherapy. In view of this fact, it is important to provide the offer which would also provide services directly addressed to this segment of the market.

The concept of concentrated marketing is an undertaking which may enable the option discussed above and help a particular agritourism farm to specialise in providing services to one or a few groups of tourists. This might apply to rural accommodation providers receiving only youth groups and offering educational agritourism. The target segment might be the segment of disabled tourists or ecologists. It depends on the location of an agritourism farm, its resources, appliances, facilities and the range of services provided.

References

Altkorn, J. (1995). *Marketing w turystyce.* Publisher: Wyd. Naukowe PWN, Warszawa.

Briggs, S. (2003). *Marketing w turystyce.* Publisher: Polskie Wydawnictwo Ekonomiczne, Warszawa.

Czerwińska-Jaśkiewicz, M. (2013). *Marketing w agroturystyce. Ujęcie segmentacyjne.* Publisher: Difin SA, Warszawa.

Downey, W. D. & Ericsson, S. P. (1987). *Agribusiness Management.* Publisher: Purdue University, Purdue.

Dunbar, I. & McDonald, M. (2003). *Segmentacja rynku.* Publisher: Oficyna Ekonomiczna, Kraków.

Hall, C. M., Müller, D. K. & Saarinen, J. (2009). *Nordic Tourism: Issues and Cases.* Publisher: MPG Book, Bristol.

Jedlińska, M. (1999). Zastosowanie reguły STP (segmentacja celowanie, pozycjonowanie) w działających w Polsce przedsiębiorstwach turystycznych. In Gospodarka turystyczna. Wybrane zagadnienia jej funkcjonowania. *Prace Naukowe AE we Wrocławiu,* 839, Wrocław, pp. 35–36.

Kania, J., Leśniak, L. & Musiał, W. (Ed.). (2005). *Agroturystyka i usługi towarzyszące.* Publisher: Małopolskie Stowarzyszenie Doradztwa Rolniczego, Kraków.

Knecht, D. (2009). *Agroturystyka w agrobiznesie.* Publisher: Wydawnictwo C.H. Beck, Warszawa.

Kosmaczewska, J. (2013). *Turystyka jako czynnik rozwoju obszarów wiejskich.* Publisher: Bogucki Wydawnictwo Naukowe, Poznań.

Kotler, Ph. (1999). *Marketing, analiza, planowanie, wdrażanie i kontrola.* Publisher: Wydawnictwo Felberg, Warszawa.

Niedziółka, A. (2010). Koncepcja marketingu skoncentrowanego jako ważna determinanta rozwoju turystyki. *Zeszyty Naukowe Szkoły Głównej Gospodarstwa Wiejskiego w Warszawie. Polityki Europejskie, Finanse i Marketing,* 3(52), 349 Warszawa.

Niezgoda, A. & Zmyślony, P. (2006). *Popyt turystyczny.* Publisher: Wydawnictwo Akademii Ekonomicznej w Poznaniu, Poznań.

Oleksiuk, A. (2007). *Marketing usług turystycznych.* Publisher: Difin, Warszawa.

Opioła, W. (2010). *Agroturysta nr 2 (4) – kwiecień/maj* Publisher: Wydawnictwo Metafora, Opole, Poland.

Panasiuk, A. (Ed.) (2013). *Marketing w turystyce i rekreacji.* Publisher: Wydawnictwo Naukowe PWN, Warszawa.

Santon, W. J. (1975) *Fundamentals of Marketing.,* McGraw-Hill, New York.

Sikora, J. (1999). *Organizacja ruchu turystycznego na wsi.* Publisher: Wyd. Szkolne i Pedagogiczne S.A., Warszawa.

Strzembicki, L. (2003). Marketing usług turystycznych. In *Turystyka specjalistyczna oraz turystyka rekreacyjna.* Publisher: Biuro Ekspertyz Finansowych Marketingu i Consultingu Uniconsult s.c., Warszawa.

Sznajder, M. & Przezbórska, L. (2006). *Agroturystyka.,* Publisher: Polskie Wydawnictwo Ekonomiczne, Warszawa.

Zawadka, J. (2010). *Ekonomiczno-społeczne determinanty rozwoju agroturystyki na Lubelszczyźnie (na przykładzie wybranych gmin wiejskich).* Publisher: Wydawnictwo SGGW, Warszawa.

Zawadka, J. (2013). Tendencje zmian w zachowaniach turystycznych osób wypoczywających na wsi. In K. Krzyżanowska (Ed.). *Komunikowanie i doradztwo w turystyce wiejskiej.* Publisher: Wydawnictwo SGGW, Warszawa.

Metropolitan commuter belt tourism development directions.

Source: Fotolia.com © mrtflop: Fotolia.com.

28 Conclusion

Michał Jacenty Sznajder

The Conclusion of this book shows its particular contribution to the extension of knowledge about the state, functioning, causes and mechanisms of the development of nature based tourism in metropolitan areas named Metropolitan Commuter Belt Tourism. In fact, the problems of metropolitan commuter belt tourism were considered in combination with rural tourism, agritourism, ecotourism, forest and culinary tourism. This contribution was divided into four sections: metropolisation, natural and anthropogenic tourism resources of metropolitan areas; hypotheses about the functioning of nature-based tourism in metropolitan areas; new concepts in the development of rural tourism and agritourism.

Metropolisation

It is unquestionable that in the twentieth century there was dynamic development of cities and their importance increased all over the world. Big metropolises with populations exceeding 1 million were growing particularly fast. Therefore, it is justified to ask the question: What made cities so attractive to the world population. Metropolises offer people greater opportunities of development than rural areas. It is easier to find employment and, above all, metropolises better satisfy people's administrative, cultural, educational and medical needs. Metropolises fulfil a wide range of civilisation-related functions, which are unavailable in rural areas. They are hubs of air, rail, road or even river and sea transport. They are administrative, commercial, economic, financial, educational, scientific, forensic, cultural and religious centres with specialised medicine, sports and entertainment. On the other hand, cities are places where social pathologies are increasing and this problem is difficult to solve.

However big they are, not all agglomerations can be characterised by metropolitan functions. There are agglomerations with populations of even 2 to 3 million, but it is hard to call them cities because they have not developed urban functions yet. This particularly applies to African 'cities', called sometimes Afropolises.

Cities exert influence on near and more distant territories. The strength of their influence depends on the development of their metropolitan functions rather than on their population. Therefore, people are continuously migrating from the country to cities. As a result, the share of urban population is constantly increasing and it will probably settle at a level of 80 to 85 per cent of the world population.

Metropolises constantly attract people and this creates the need to settle migrants either in the metropolis itself or in nearby areas. It is necessary to provide new areas located away from the centre for residential development. Originally metropolises developed through territorial annexation, where satellite communes were included into the structure of the city. At present, a different trend is predominant. Communes are being urbanised, but they are not included into the proper city structure – they are independent administrative units. At present the process of metropolisation consists not only in a constant increase in the population of the central city but also in the satellite communes. Central cities and the adjacent satellite communes constitute metropolitan areas, which are constantly increasing. For example, there are only 2.2 million inhabitants within the city limits of Paris, whereas the population of its metropolitan area exceeds 11.2 million. People living outside the city proper, on the outskirts of a metropolis, commute to work every day. Commuting is one of the most important problems of metropolises. The area from which these people commute is defined as the commuter belt. The term 'commuter belt' appears in the concept of metropolitan commuter belt tourism. It is not a new type of tourism, but refers to the area surrounding a metropolis where conventional forms of nature-based tourism can be observed, such as rural tourism, agritourism, ecotourism and culinary tourism.

Natural and anthropogenic tourism resources of metropolitan areas

In spite of the fact that significant metropolitan areas are constantly planned to be used for housing, trade, service, administrative and industrial development as well as for roads, urban and transport infrastructure, they still have enormous untouched or hardly modified natural resources. Furthermore, contemporary plans of spatial development in metropolitan areas guarantee the protection of these resources, on the one hand, but on the other hand, they facilitate access to them for metropolitan inhabitants. This fact is proved by descriptions of various metropolises, such as those in this collection. There is often an attractive terrain in metropolitan areas (mountains, rocks, valleys, cliffs). There are bodies of water (seas, lakes, ponds), rivers, deserts, forests, national parks and green spaces. Apart from that, these areas are also inhabited by wild animals. As newspapers sometimes report, some big and dangerous animals appear in these metropolises, for example, tigers (Borivali National Park in Mumbai, India), monkeys, brown bears (Zakopane, Poland) and polar bears (Churchill, Canada), wild boars, deer or alligators (Florida, USA) Unfortunately, the inhabitants of metropolises are often unaware of the fact that there are wonderful natural resources in their surroundings.

Metropolitan areas are the territories of commodity farming. Although farmland resources are constantly shrinking, farming will always be present there. Statistics concerning land use and the volume of plant and animal production point to the role of farming in the economy of metropolitan areas. In former villages, which are now satellite communes of metropolises, there is not only a continuing process of the conservation of old customs and traditions but also the process of enculturation. In this case, it consists of gradual adoption of old customs and traditions by new inhabitants who have recently settled in the area.

This book provides numerous descriptions of abundant natural and anthropological resources in Polish metropolitan areas, such as Warsaw, Krakow, Łódź, Poznań, Wrocław, Szczecin, Bydgoszcz, Toruń and the resources in Slovenia, which stimulate the development of nature-based tourism in these areas.

Hypotheses about the functioning of natural based tourism in metropolitan areas

Studies on the development of metropolitan areas are conducted from numerous points of view. The implementation of the findings of these studies will enable systematic and sustainable development of metropolitan areas. Therefore, there is no reason why the development of rural tourism, agritourism, nature tourism, ecotourism and culinary tourism in these areas should be omitted. I came up with the idea to research this problem in 2008, when I was investigating the agriculture and nature in the Indian city of Mumbai. It seems incredible that in this area, which is inhabited by more than 23 million people and where the population density exceeds 26,000 people per square kilometre, there are considerable natural and agricultural resources, from Borivali National Park to Aarey Milk Colony. Mumbai is not an exception. Natural resources, which enable the development of rural tourism, agritourism, nature-based tourism, ecotourism and culinary tourism, can be found in metropolitan areas all over the world. The association of natural resources, rurality and agriculture with metropolitan areas provides the basis for 5 hypotheses about the corresponding types of tourism, which are worth scientific confirmation:

- Cities, especially big metropolises, contribute to the loosening or loss of people's contact with nature, which is their natural and basic need. Natural resources in metropolitan areas, which favour practising rural tourism, agritourism, nature based tourism, ecotourism and culinary tourism, are a perfect base to restore or strengthen this contact.
- There are abundant and unique natural and anthropological resources in metropolitan areas, which predispose them to the development of nature-based tourism covering rural tourism, agritourism, ecotourism and so on.
- The stratification in metropolitan inhabitants' assets and income has influence on the opportunities to practise tourism. It is recommended that all inhabitants should have contact with nature for health and social reasons. A considerable percentage of metropolitan inhabitants have low or very low income so cannot afford expensive tourism offers. Due to low costs of transport and developed public transport networks, tourism in metropolitan areas seems to be a big opportunity for poorer people. However, both the practice and theory contradict the hypothesis. The tourism sector in metropolitan areas usually offers a less rich supply of products and services in rural tourism, agritourism, nature tourism, ecotourism and culinary tourism than the actual demand. Because the demand, especially for the products and services of holiday tourism,

is greater than their supply in these areas, the market equilibrium is reached through high or even very high prices. Although metropolitan areas should be a natural base for budget tourists, it is not so, because the supply is lower than the demand. This does not exclude the fact that occasionally initiatives of social tourism may be realised, especially when they are supported with external financing or co-financing.

- The basket of products and services offered by rural tourism and agritourism in metropolitan areas is different than that offered by more distant areas. Rural tourism and agritourism are concentrated on short holiday and weekend tourism and on one-day visits, whereas tourism in distant areas is concentrated on holiday leisure.

- The segmentation of metropolitan commuter belt tourists has not been fully investigated. This book distinguishes four different profiles of people using the offers of nature-based tourism in the commuter belt. The first profile consists of schoolchildren, who usually visit agritourism farms during their trips to the countryside. The second sector groups busy, usually young, singles or couples for whom time is at a premium and who prefer short and active forms of leisure. The third group consists of elderly people, who need care and go to submetropolitan areas as part of the social farming programme. The last sector consists of elderly but still active people, who have a lot of time and enjoy a slow pace of life and leisure. They prefer all activities which guarantee peace and quiet near their homes.

New concepts in the development of rural tourism and agritourism

This book presents new, theoretical concepts in the development of rural tourism and agritourism that, above all, but not only, concern rural tourism in metropolitan areas. These concepts concern numerous aspects. Primarily, the book systematises and presents examples of new, more specialised forms of rural tourism and agritourism, 5 of which are particularly important in metropolitan areas: holiday tourism, educational tourism, health tourism, culinary tourism and shopping tourism. This development is caused by a wide range of circumstances. For example, as people's life expectancy is longer and many societies are ageing, the importance of care provided to elderly people is increasing. Social farming gives new perspectives of leisure and care provided to elderly people, whose population is increasing in metropolitan areas. Similarly, the educational system more and more often involves practical learning about rural life and agriculture. There is high demand for so-called 'green schools' in metropolitan areas. This enables agritourism farms to specialise in this branch. Rural tourism and agritourism are also areas of interest to pedagogy, because they are very important to people's life-long education.

It has been proved that the agritourism offer in metropolitan surroundings has spatial character and is strongly polarised. This means that the offers of products changes along with the distance of the farm from the centre of the metropolis. As results from the investigations of the basket of products and services offered by agritourism farms in metropolitan areas show, the number of these products and services ranges from 5 to 45. Neither too small not too large a number of products favour good management of agritourism farms. As was observed, farms also offer products and services which are typical of other types of tourism, and which are completely unrelated to rural tourism or agritourism. The extended offer ensures better financing of these farms. Apart from that, it was found that agritourism farms additionally adapt their offer to local natural resources in a particular metropolis.

It is not easy to carry out the segmentation of tourists using the offers of rural tourism or agritourism in metropolitan areas. This situation results not only from the absence of appropriate data but above all from the adopted segmentation criterion. This book presents a few such segmentations. This indicates that it is necessary to continue investigations in this matter.

The cooperation of the stakeholders of rural tourism and agritourism in a particular metropolitan area to promote these types of tourism may cause a synergy of outlays, resulting from diversified actions as long as they are coordinated in a normative modelling process.

It is an increasingly urgent task to explain the rules of functioning of rural tourism and agritourism with an adequate economic theory. As results from the analysis, the economic base theory best accounts for the phenomenon of functioning of these types of tourism and, in a global system, it is necessary to strengthen their sustained development. Therefore, new opportunities and paradigms of its development were indicated. Information and communication technology occupies a special position in the promotion of this development.

A submetropolitan dirt road: the Wrocław metropolitan area, Poland.

Glossary

The glossary contains more than 40 most important entries related to urban sprawl and nature-related tourism in metropolitan commuter belt areas. The definitions are based on the authors' elaborations, except the entries 'city proper', 'eco-tourism', 'food tourism' and 'natural resources', which are defined as in cited publications.

Afropolis an African metropolis; the term was originally used (Pinther *et al.* 2010) to refer to 5 African mega-metropolises: Cairo, Lagos, Nairobi, Kinshasa and Johannesburg. In this monograph it refers to any African metropolis, as they differ considerably from European and American metropolises. This book describes Conakry as an African metropolis.

Agglomeration *see* Monocentric agglomeration, Polycentric agglomeration, Urban agglomeration.

Agritourism (or 'agrotourism' in some parts of Europe) exploration of agriculture for the purpose of tourism. For tourists, agritourism is a trip to a farm, ranch, food processing plant or other agricultural premises for the purposes of recreation, education or entertainment, which includes several specific agritourism products and services. As farmers are provided with a tax relief for agritourism, all over the world there are plenty of pseudo-agritourism operators whose activity does not match agritourism at all.

Agritourism product a product from agricultural resources designed especially for tourists and offered to them while they are staying on a farm, for immediate consumption or to be taken away. Agritourism products cover raw and processed food and a wide range of souvenirs. They are not usually included in the tourism offer and are considered to be elements of direct sales. According to some classifications, agritourism services are listed as agritourism products.

Agritourism services designed from agricultural resources for tourists and offered to them while staying on a farm. Sometimes agritourism services may be offered apart from a farm stay, for example, as green schools. The list of agritourism services is very long and covers accommodation, meals, participation in an agricultural process, agri-sports, agri-tainment, agri-therapy and cultural tourism. Accommodation and meals are usually included in an agritourism offer, but other services may or may not be included.

Business tourism   small conferences, training sessions, integration events or small business meetings may take place at rural accommodation facilities adapted for these purposes.

Care farms   providing short-term and long-term care chiefly to elderly people who are increasingly aware of their health and have increasing expectations concerning their old age, which should be characterised not only by fitness but also by independence and occupational and social activity.

City proper   a locality with legally fixed boundaries and an administratively recognised urban status, usually characterised by some form of local government (UN Statistics Division).

Classic (traditional) rural areas   there is no controversy about them because they are situated even several dozen kilometres away from the core city, although classic rural spaces can also be found closer to the city. These are typical rural spaces with animal breeding, farming, beekeeping, crafts, direct sales and roadside stands. The tourist will find authentic rural sense of the place or even elements of the rural idyll there.

Commuter belt   the area surrounding a metropolis (submetropolitan area) where commuters live.

Commuter belt tourism (or 'submetropolitan tourism')   any type of tourism in the commuter belt area.

Conurbation   an area of many cities, large urban agglomerations and adjacent suburban areas.

Ecotourism   according to the UNWTO's definition, "refers to forms of tourism which have the following characteristics: All nature-based forms of tourism in which the main motivation of the tourists is the observation and appreciation of nature as well as the traditional cultures prevailing in natural areas. It contains educational and interpretation features. It is generally, but not exclusively organised by specialised tour operators for small groups. Service provider partners at the destinations tend to be small, locally owned businesses. It minimises negative impacts upon the natural and socio-cultural environment. It supports the maintenance of natural areas which are used as ecotourism attractions by: Generating economic benefits for host communities, organisations and authorities managing natural areas with conservation purposes; Providing alternative employment and income opportunities for local communities; Increasing awareness towards the conservation of natural and cultural assets, both among locals and tourists.

Educational farm   concentrates on education of schoolchildren, familiarising them with farm life, providing knowledge about the origin of food and offering contact with the natural rural environment. There are two types of educational farms: addressing their programmes to children and youth.

Educational tourism   any type of tourism whose main aim is education.

Food tourism (also 'culinary tourism', 'gastronomy tourism' or 'cuisine tourism')   the exploration of food for the purpose of tourism. Food tourism is an experiential trip to a gastronomic region, for recreational or entertainment purposes, which includes visits to primary and secondary producers of food, gastronomic festivals, food fairs, events, farmers' markets, cooking shows and demonstrations, tastings of quality food products or any tourism activity related to food (Hall and Sharples 2003). In addition, this experiential journey is related to a particular lifestyle that includes experimentation, learning from different cultures, the acquisition of knowledge and understanding of the qualities or attributes related to tourism products as well as culinary specialities produced in that region through their consumption (UNWTO 2012).

Holiday tourism   a short-term leisure stay near one's place of residence during a public holiday or weekend. There are different forms of holiday tourism, the most important of which are suburban tourism, urban tourism and rural tourism, cognitive and sightseeing tourism and culture tourism.

Human footprint   in this monograph is a mark left by people on the Earth, which is visible from space and enables estimation of the population of a particular agglomeration or another area.

Megacity   a metropolitan area of more than 10 million people.

Megalopolis   a clustered network of cities, whose population exceeds 25 million.

Metropolis   a big city, a centre which occupies a particular area. It is distinguished by high population, which usually exceeds 500,000 (LUZ), characterised by high economic, political, social and cultural potential. It combines diversified functions, especially specialised services such as banking and financial services. A metropolis influences its regional, national and international surroundings by functioning in a network with other big cities or with surrounding medium-sized towns.

Metropolisation   a social process of urban space transformation which consists of a constant increase in the population of the central city and satellite communes. The relationship between the central city and other areas is changing in the structure of space use and development. This applies to housing, production, services, tourism and recreation. There are numerous benefits of metropolisation, such as dynamic development; economic, scientific and technological potential; and labour market and sociocultural infrastructure. However, it also intensifies social pathologies: in urbanised areas one can observe weakened or even broken social relations. Metropolisation and the development of nature-based tourism in urban areas are considered to be absolutely conflicting tendencies and one is thought to develop at the expense of the other.

Metropolitan area   an area of a metropolitan city that is functionally related to the city. It is a functional unit formed by a large, consistent urban (settlement) complex. Metropolitan areas have appropriate technical and technological equipment and thus they provide favourable conditions for modern business activity.

Metropolitan commuter belt tourism   any type of usually short-term tourism practised mostly by metropolitan inhabitants within the commute belt.

Monocentric agglomeration   an urban complex with one dominant city.

Natural resources   are natural assets (raw materials) occurring in nature that can be used for economic production or consumption. The naturally occurring assets that provide use benefits through the provision of raw materials and energy used in economic activity (or that may provide such benefits one day) and that are subject primarily to quantitative depletion through human use. They are subdivided into four categories: mineral and energy resources, soil resources, water resources and biological resources (OECD).

Natural tourist values   public goods created by forces of nature; a complex of natural elements which may be objects of tourists' interest and which provide tourist satisfaction. The following elements are natural values: climate, terrain, natural resources, water, faunal and floral curiosities.

Nature-related tourism   any type of tourism where the tourist uses natural resources and human tourism resources, especially nature tourism, ecotourism, forest tourism, rural tourism and agritourism.

Normative modelling   used to plan and coordinate social actions in a particular community (territorial unit) within a particular range (bundle of goals) in order to increase the effectiveness of these actions. This method promotes the synergic effect of social actions as a result of coordination of these actions.

Pilgrimage   the oldest type of tourism; a trip motivated only or mainly by religious aspects.

Polycentric agglomeration (also Conurbation)   a complex of cities of similar sizes, without one dominant city in the whole metropolitan area. A region consisting of many cities, large urban agglomerations and adjacent suburban areas.

Recreational tourism   forms of recreation which require large natural areas or open spaces the city cannot provide. The forms of recreation which require regular visits have the greatest chance for market success, because the short distance from the city is the main reason why a particular offer is chosen. This situation takes place when one does a sport or activity such as horse-riding lessons, or when one has adopted an animal.

Religious tourism   mostly motivated by religious aspects, it also includes cognitive and recreational purposes.

Rural tourism   an activity based on the resources and assets of rural areas, with maximum respect for, and integration into, economic, social and cultural structures and traditions. This classification focuses on 'rurality' as the distinguishing criterion, as compared with other tourism activities, which may use the same rural territory but without being considered 'rural tourism'.

Social farming   (also 'green care farming', 'farming for health') encompasses actions using the potential of agriculture to support therapy, rehabilitation, social integration, lifelong learning and social services in rural areas. The idea combines the farm and professional social services. Social services include education and upbringing, health care, social assistance, re-socialisation, culture, tourism, recreation and leisure, or even social housing.

Suburban tourism   *see* metropolitan commuter belt tourism.

Sustainable development   preserves the environment and leads to a perspective of intra- and intergenerational fairness developed at least through the following aspects: economic (income adjustment), social (adaptation of the quality of life), environmental (productive conservation and sustainable use of natural resources), cultural (management of cultural diversity) and manage mental (management of sustainability).

Therapy farm   a farm providing re-educational and therapeutic activities. Therapy provided by farms can be based on activities, rehabilitation and individual support. Therapy farms also provide occupational education. The therapy is supposed to compensate for deficits, make mentally disabled people fitter and help people with mental disorders or social deficits integrate into society.

Tourism in rural space   any tourism activity situated in a rural territory that takes advantage of its resources and characteristics and which is accepted by the concept, without considering social or cultural integration as critical, defining elements of the product. This interpretation finds its limits in sustainability criteria, or when a tourism activity endangers the existence and preservation of the resources which are assets attracting the visitor.

Urban agglomeration   the city or town proper and the suburban fringe or densely settled territory lying outside of, but adjacent to, the city boundaries (UN Statistical Yearbook).

Urban sprawl (also 'counter-urbanism' or 'exurbanisation')   consists of people moving to rural areas neighbouring the city. Mainly urban inhabitants and non-urban immigrant population migrate to these areas. It causes many positive and negative consequences.

Valorisation   both a description and measurement of natural values in a particular area. It gives a picture of the natural environment and enables determination of the usefulness of environmental resources for tourism. Valorisation chiefly applies to traits such as the natural environment and anthropological values that cannot be measured.

References

Hall C.M. Sharples L. (2003). "The consumption of experiences or the experience of consumption? An introduction to the to turism of taste" in *Food tourism around the world*. Elsevier Butterworth-Heinemann, Oxford, pp. 1–24

LUZ – Larger_urban_zone http://ec.europa.eu/eurostat/statistics-explained/index.php/European_cities_-_spatial_dimension#Larger_urban_zones [Retrieved 21.12.2016]

United Nations Department of Economic and Social Affairs (2005). 2002 Demographic Yearbook United Nations, New York. p233 https://unstats.un.org/unsd/demographic/products/dyb/dyb-sets/2002%20DYB.pdf [Retrieved 18.02.2017]

UNWTO United Nations World Tourist Organization (2012). Global Report on Food Tourism, Published by UNWTO Madrid. p.6 http://cf.cdn.unwto.org/sites/all/files/pdf/global_report_on_food_tourism.pdf [Retrieved 01.12.2016]

UNWTO United Nations World Tourist Organization: Ecotourism and protected areas http://sdt.unwto.org/content/ecotourism-and-protected-areas [Retrieved 18.02.2017]

Zvomuya P., (2013). Afropolis': Cities of Africa stake a claim on the future Mail Guardian http://mg.co.za/article/2013-03-22-00-sprawling-brawling-cities-of-africa-stake-a-claim-on-the-future [Retrieved 20.12.2016]

Index